Mansell Collection

JANE AUSTEN

JANE AUSTEN

by

B. C. SOUTHAM

Edited by Ian Scott-Kilvert

PUBLISHED FOR
THE BRITISH COUNCIL
BY LONGMAN GROUP LTD

LONGMAN GROUP LTD
Longman House, Burnt Mill, Harlow, Essex

Associated companies, branches and representatives throughout the world

First published 1975
Reprinted with additions to the Bibliography 1976

Printed in England by
Bradley's, Reading and London

ISBN 0 582 01243 0

Thanks are due to Faber & Faber Ltd, and to Random House Inc., New York, for permission to quote from *Letters from Iceland* by W. H. Auden.

JANE AUSTEN

I

IT SEEMS a contradiction in terms to talk in the same breath about literary greatness and popularity. Almost by definition, a literary classic implies a minority audience, the professional attention of scholars and critics and the enforced attention of students. In this light, the case of Jane Austen is remarkable. This is a writer whose novels are among the acknowledged classics of English literature, studied in schools and universities throughout the world (at the latest count, in thirty-five languages, including Chinese, Japanese, Persian and Bengali), with an enormous bibliography of scholarship and criticism. Yet the six novels also attract an audience quite unconcerned about Jane Austen's critical reputation and status, who turn to the novels simply for enjoyment. This is the only instance in English literature where Dr Johnson's image of 'the common reader' really comes alive: the idea that the ultimate test of literary greatness is not in the formal recognition of the academics but rests with 'the common sense of readers, uncorrupted by literary prejudices'; and that this individual judgement should prevail over 'the refinements of subtlety and the dogmatism of learning'.

To stress Jane Austen's popularity is not to disparage the interest of critics and scholars. Literary historians delight in her ramified allusiveness. She is a critics' novelist *par excellence*, a writer whose subtlety and sophistication have always attracted subtle and sophisticated minds. The novels have proved to be wonderfully rewarding for interpretative critics who light on such a richness of meaning in their structure of language and the vibrations of irony. Rhetoricians of fiction have developed some of their finest discussions upon the study of her narrative methods. She is recognized as a supreme artist of the novel, a judgement that comes with special authority from other novelists as well as critics. The dramatic power of her characters led some nineteenth-century writers, including Macaulay and George Lewes, to regard her as no less than a 'prose Shakespeare'; and in our own day Brigid Brophy has described Jane Austen as 'the greatest novelist of all time'.

In these terms, Jane Austen's achievement sounds forbidding. But this is precisely what the novels are not. Whatever their dignity as works of literature, as books for reading their stance is completely unpretentious. They seem to offer themselves as no more than entertainment. Even after 160 years, they continue to provide what is for most people the prime satisfaction of reading—the chance to escape from the pressures of ordinary life into the security of a created world, where another order of reality takes over for a while. As Clerihew Bentley put it, 'The novels of Jane Austen / Are the ones to get lost in'. His doggerel captures a popular truth. Her picture of Regency England still exerts a containing and hypnotic realism. For all its selectivity and exclusions, its remoteness from us in time and culture, it is a fictional world into which the reader can move easily and within which there is a powerful illusion of completeness and truth. The distance in time is bridged by the momentum of the writing, its brilliance, stylishness and drive, by the fascination of the characters, by the skill of the story-telling and by the appeal of the author's sane and sympathetic humanity. The novels offer us the excitement of sharing the vision of a creative mind and of responding to its energies of wit and understanding. Many critics have devoted many books to the analysis of these effects. But in the end, we are left with the plain fact of Jane Austen's *readability* and within this her capacity to engage us imaginatively, emotionally and intellectually.

The publication of the six novels between 1811 and 1817 marked a turning-point in the development of English fiction. To Jane Austen's contemporary audience they revealed that the novel was capable of unsuspected power, that it was not to be dismissed as a mere pastime but was to be taken seriously as a form of literature, on a level with poetry and drama; and the early reviews by Scott and Richard Whately proved that criticism of the novel could itself rank as a serious intellectual activity. In the words of George Moore, Jane Austen turned the wash-tub into the vase. In effect, she transformed the eighteenth-century novel—which could be a clumsy and primitive performance, uncertain in its technique—into a work of art. She gave elegance and form to its shaping, style to its writing, and narrative skill to the presentation of the story. She invented her own special mode of fiction, the domestic comedy of middle-class manners, a dramatic, realistic account of the quiet backwaters of everyday life for the country families of Regency England from the late 1790s until 1815. Her account of this world is limited and highly selective. Its focus is upon the experiences of young women on the path to marriage; and there is no attempt to present a social panorama (as earlier novelists, such as Fielding and Smollett, had done), nor to describe the condition of industrial England and its appalling scenes of poverty and social unrest (a task which many Victorian novelists, from Dickens onwards, were to set themselves). The modesty of Jane Austen's fictional world is caught in her remark to a novel-writing niece that '3 or 4 Families in a Country Village is the very thing to work upon', and her famous comment to a novel-writing nephew about 'the little bit (two inches wide) of Ivory on which I work with so fine a Brush' which 'produces little effect after much labour'.

However, the claim to be a miniaturist is not to be taken at face value. There is certainly a miniaturism in the artistry of Jane Austen's language and the refinements of verbal style; and another kind of miniaturism in the tight social and geographical boundaries of the stories. But the novels themselves give an impression of size and strength; their fictional world is lucidly defined; they have dimensions of space and time and a firm logic of structure and organization. And within the limits of the 'Country Village' scene and its neighbourhood of respectable families, the novels communicate a profound sense of this moment in English history—when the old Georgian world of the eighteenth century was being carried uneasily and reluctantly into the new world of Regency England, the Augustan world into the Romantic. The detailed account of its manners and fashionable pursuits is the descriptive groundwork for a highly analytical portrait of the age, which in turn conveys an implication of the deeper processes of change in early nineteenth-century society and in the individual's understanding of himself and the world around him.

II

Historically, the novels are a challenge to the idea of society as a civilizing force and to the image of man's fulfilment as an enlightened social being. They question the driving optimism of the period—that this, in the development of English society, was triumphantly the Age of Improvement. Improvement was the leading spirit of Regency England, its self-awarded palm. Certainly it was unequalled as a period of economic improvement, in the wake of the industrial revolution. The wartime economy accelerated this new prosperity. Alongside this material improvement there was an air of self-conscious, self-congratulatory improvement in manners, in religious zeal, in morality, in the popularization of science, philosophy and the arts. It was the age of encyclopaedias, displaying the scope and categories of human knowledge in a digestible form. Books and essays paraded 'Improvement' in their titles. In an essay 'On the means of improving the people' (meaning the working people), Southey struck a common chord of complacent Englanderism, rejoicing to belong 'to the middle rank of life . . . which in this country and at this time [1818] is beyond doubt the most favourable situation wherein man has ever been placed for the cultivation of his moral and intellectual nature'.

But many of the achievements of Regency improvement were more apparent than real. This is nicely symbolized in its most conspicuous manifestation, across the countryside itself. Landscape improvement was celebrated as the latest of the fine arts, much theorized about by contemporary aestheticians and brandished as a distinctively English contribution to the sum of civilization. Country houses and their grounds were expensively and elaborately improved, as General Tilney's 'improving hand' has transformed the pre-Reformation convent of Northanger Abbey into a modern home of extravagant and faintly ludicrous luxury, and as in *Mansfield Park*, Repton, the fashionable improver of the day, is to transform Sotherton Court, a fine old Elizabethan country house, destined to be adorned in 'a modern dress'.

Throughout the novels Jane Austen plays deftly with the terminology of improvement, carrying its negative overtones of novelty, showiness and superficiality into the realm of manners, behaviour and morality. Improvement can be a façade, a veneer. Jane Austen's sceptical, testing irony is the acid solution to peel it off, exposing the ramshackle foundations of social and personal morality which improvement could flashily conceal. For Mr Rushworth, Sotherton is 'a prison—quite a dismal old prison', crying out for the hand of Repton, whose speciality was making old houses look 'cheerful'. But the improving hand that first gets to work is Henry Crawford's. The cheerfulness and freedom he brings to Sotherton's 'prison' is a sexual escapade with the owner's wife!

Socially and politically, improvement had a very bitter ring. Essentially, it was a middle-class conceit. Outside the gentry's world of property and privilege was a wholly different scene. Throughout this period, a third of the country, its labouring population, lived permanently on the verge of starvation, while the rich became even richer, their prosperity more blatant. In this fertile ground, revolutionary ideas took root; and the period from the beginning of the 1790s until the Peterloo Massacre of 1819 was the most violent and repressive time in English history since the Civil War. Habeas corpus was suspended. Freedom of speech and freedom of meeting were curtailed. Bread riots were met with force and with that blunt instrument the masses were kept down. Jane Austen gives no more than a fleeting glimpse of England's violence. In *Northanger Abbey*, the London mobs come in as a joke. We never see the grinding misery of the poor; they are simply objects of charity, to be visited with a bowl of soup. It was not that Jane Austen was unaware. Hampshire and Kent, where she spent most of her adult life, were as badly hit by agricultural poverty as any other part of England. She must have seen it for herself and read about it in the essays and pamphlets of crusading reformers; and met it poignantly in her favourite poet, Crabbe, who delivered a starkly unpastoralizing report of what he observed, 'the Village Life a Life of Pain'.

There is no answer to the charge that Jane Austen should have devoted her genius to portraying the condition of England in all its misery and horror; that indeed would have been the great heroic task for a Tolstoy, a Dickens, a Zola, a Steinbeck or a Lawrence; and she would never have succeeded. Writing out of the experiences that she knew intimately, and with the particular artistic gifts of ironic commentary and observation, she was able to do something else. The restricted social vision of the novels is a satire in itself. It presents a faithful image of the gentry's state of mind. Its limitations and exclusions are those of the prosperous, leisured middle-class consciousness—self-regarding and self-centred, with its trivial time-filling preoccupations. Its gaze was steadily averted from the unpleasant social realities of an economic system which enabled the gentry to enjoy this way of life. Their turning away from the visible truth was culpable. John Cartwright protested in 1812, 'English gentlemen are perpetually travelling. Some go to see lakes and mountains' (as Elizabeth Bennet travels north with the Gardiners on a tour of the Peak district); 'Were it not as allowable to travel for seeing the actual conditions of a starving people'.

One of Jane Austen's major achievements in the novels is to have captured the total illusion of the gentry's vision, the experience of living in privileged isolation, of being party to a privileged outlook, of belonging to a privileged community, whose distresses, such as they are, are private, mild and genteel. Each of the homes and neighbourhoods is its own 'little social commonwealth', a microcosm, the centre of a minute universe. The irony is implicit. The miniature issues of these little worlds, so realistic, so much the centre of the stage, vivid and magnified to the point of surrealism, imply another, larger world beyond: 'the flourishing grandeur of a Country, is but another term for the depression and misery of the people ... to speak of the expensive luxury and refinements of the age, is but, with cruel irony, to remind us how many myriads are destitute'. John Thelwall, in *The*

Peripatetic (1793), was presenting a line of argument which was familiar to Jane Austen's audience and which the novels artfully exploit. 'The depression and misery' of the common people was a theme she could never handle directly; her way was to treat it by silent implication.

But the silence is not total. Just once or twice there is an oblique glimpse of the macabre reality that lies outside the image of the gentry's mind. This happens, for example, when Jane Austen describes Lady Catherine de Bourgh's activities in the parish of Hunsford: 'whenever any of the cottagers were disposed to be quarrelsome, discontented or too poor, she sallied forth into the village to settle their differences, silence their complaints, and scold them into harmony and plenty'. The scolding is a black joke. Hunsford's 'poor' were people starving. Several chapters earlier in *Pride and Prejudice*, Catherine and Lydia Bennet bring home the latest military gossip: 'Much had been done, and much had been said in the regiment since the preceding Wednesday; several of the officers had dined lately with their uncle, a private had been flogged, and it had actually been hinted that Colonel Forster was going to be married'. The device here is incongruity (cf. Pope's 'Puffs, powders, patches, bibles, billets-doux'). The wit is literary but the joke is not. The 'private . . . flogged' was the recipient of lashes to the number of 750 or 1000. Such punishments were widely reported. When the book appeared in 1813, these facts were in the public mind. The British Army was then distinguished as the only European army outside Russia to retain flogging as a punishment. Its abolition was debated in Parliament in 1811 and 1812. In 1810, Cobbett had been charged with seditious libel and sentenced to two years' imprisonment for an anti-flogging article in the *Political Register*; Leigh Hunt got eighteen months for printing a similar article in *The Examiner*. Writing from prison, Cobbett continued his attack upon its hideous inhumanity and the nauseating hypocrisy of its official circumlocution, *corporal infliction*: 'Why not name the thing? *Flog is flog*'. Simply and laconically, Jane Austen did just that.

Flogging was one aspect of national repression. It was a punishment handed out to the militia, to wartime conscripts on duty in England, rather than to the regular troops serving in Europe. A similar reality of English life comes into chapter XIV of *Northanger Abbey*, where Henry Tilney makes fun of his sister for supposing that Catherine's mysterious hinting about 'something very shocking indeed' in London—'uncommonly dreadful. I shall expect murder and every thing of the kind'—refers to a calamity that has actually happened. Catherine is merely talking about the latest Gothic novel; and Tilney enjoys himself, elaborating on his sister's fearful imaginings: 'she immediately pictured to herself a mob of three thousand men assembling in St George's Fields; the Bank attacked, the Tower threatened, the streets of London flowing with blood . . .'. His tone is mocking and light-hearted. How could anyone be so silly? But historically his sister's train of thought is completely credible. The novel is set at the turn of the century and in July 1795, there was a meeting of the radical London Correspondence Society, 100,000 strong, at St George's Fields. The speeches were inflammatory, with talk of 'the holy blood of Patriotism, streaming from the severing axe . . .'. In October, George III was jeered on his way to the state opening of Parliament, his carriage was pelted and a window cracked by a stone. The next day horse-guards and troops had to clear the mobs out of his way to the theatre. So Eleanor's misunderstanding and Tilney's joke touch upon circumstances bizarrely close to the truth. In this passage, Jane Austen raises the spectre of revolutionary uprising, a fear that haunted the establishment and the middle-classes throughout this period and found a terrible nemesis in the deaths of Peterloo.

Jane Austen uses Tilney again in this historical function in chapter XXIV, when he reproves Catherine for her Gothic imaginings about his father and his dead mother, the half-formed idea that General Tilney might have murdered her:

> Dear Miss Morland, consider the dreadful nature of the suspicions you have entertained. What have you been judging from? Remember the country and the age in which we live. Remember that we are English, that we are Christians. Consult your own understanding, your own sense of the probable, your own observation of what is passing around you—Does our education

prepare us for such atrocities? Do our laws connive at them? Could they be perpetrated without being known, in a country like this, where social and literary intercourse is on such a footing; where every man is surrounded by a neighbourhood of voluntary spies, and where roads and newspapers lay every thing open? Dearest Miss Morland, what ideas have you been admitting?

After this lecture, Catherine runs off 'with tears of shame'. Tilney is laying Gothic ghosts. But for the readers of *Northanger Abbey*, in 1818, the joke is hollow; the passage rings with a disquieting truth and his reference to 'a neighbourhood of voluntary spies' is a figure of speech unpleasantly literal. 'Spies' were paid informers. At this time there was an extensive 'Spy-System' (as it was then known), maintained by the government to infiltrate working-men's organizations. Informing was promoted as a citizen's patriotic duty. In Parliamentary debates in the summer of 1817, the Prime Minister, Castlereagh, maintained that 'morality, religion, and social order, are best defended at home by spies and informers'. But the spy-system was vigorously challenged then, as it had been years before, in the early 1790s, when it was employed to counter the earliest radical groups. While there was deep fear that the horrors of the French Revolution would be enacted here, nonetheless the incursions of state repression were strongly opposed. In 1812, one critic went so far as to describe the police as 'a system of tyranny; an organized army of spies and informers, for the destruction of all public liberty, and the disturbance of all private happiness'. This was a Gothicism of Regency life, all too real, that Tilney's well-bred and enlightened reasonableness could never rob of its terrors.

It is with such momentary and glancing allusions that Jane Austen reminds the reader of the England unseen, that lies beyond the blinkered social focus of the gentry's vision. But these are pin-points of light. There was another 'depression and misery' that she knew intimately, and could command fully and creatively. This was the private, personal history of women like herself, trapped and stifled within the confines of a hot-house society, recognizing its brittleness and artificiality, but with no other world to exist in. These historical issues bear most immediately upon Jane Austen as a *woman* novelist, presenting an account of society from the woman's point of view—the woman's experience of men, of other women, of their families, the social circles to which they were confined, and, ultimately their experience of themselves and of life. For the first time in English literature, outside Shakespeare, we meet heroines who are credible, with minds, with the capacity to think for themselves, with ambition and wit, with an interior life independent of men and the will to challenge them emotionally and intellectually, with the energy to shape their relationships. The intense inner drama of the novels arises from the conflict between the individuality of the heroines, their private needs and aspirations, and the levelling, restrictive pressures of a tight social morality. Their predicament is to be born into a world which values them for their marriageability, where the culmination of womanhood is to be a wife and mother, where their lives are regulated by the artificial ideals of polite femininity. The six novels are repeated dramatizations of this theme. Each of the heroines has to learn to understand herself and her relationships with other people. She has to practise the morality of compromise and discover her own way of accepting the demands of society while preserving the integrity of her own values and beliefs. Each of the heroines travels the path of self-discovery and growth; they struggle towards self-determination and fulfilment; and Jane Austen leaves it an open question, open to us as readers to decide, how far they win through, how far they fail.

The recognition of this theme shows us how inadequate it is to label Jane Austen as a 'woman' writer or as 'the novelist of Regency England'. These labels are accurate and they draw attention to important aspects of her work. But her theme has as much to do with men as with women and it relates to any society which imposes a strict code of manners and tightly-defined roles upon the people who exist within it. Jane Austen's attitude may seem unheroic. She has no stirring message, no doctrine of personal liberation. Her view is coldly realistic. She presents the sad truth that however much people may dream of personal freedom, of escaping from the constrictions of their family or of society at large, we are nonetheless tied by blood and time and circumstance with bonds of need and dependence, to people we hate or despise or are bored by, yet cannot do without. Man's inhumanity to man can be polite, intimate and domestic. The novels confirm that life is a comedy to those who think. A thinking novelist, she casts her heroines in a thinking mould. But this single truth is not exclusive: life is also a tragedy to those who feel. And the deepest and most powerful tension arises from Jane Austen's struggle to maintain a hold over experiences that threaten the comic surface of the novels with the 'feeling' tones of tragedy.

III

Some books leave us totally incurious about their authors. In the novels of Jane Austen, however, the writer's presence is strongly marked, not just in an official role, as narrator or commentator, but as an active, pervasive 'artistic' presence—controlling, arranging, manipulating—reminding us continually that the realism of the novels is wholly artificial, wholly an effect of technique; not 'realism' created out of the vast, detailed sprawl of 'naturalism', but an economic, succinct realism formed out of the selection of detail and the synergy of its relationships. The realism is moral as well as aesthetic; it offers an interpretation and criticism of life, as well as a picture of it; and unless the reader deliberately switches off, its assertion of values leaves no room for indifference, and a great deal of room for reservation and disagreement.

Many readers respond to the novels at an extremely personal level, finding a 'Gentle Jane', a presence that is intimate and lovable. Katherine Mansfield declared that 'every true admirer of the novels cherishes the happy thought that he alone—reading between the lines—has become the secret friend of their author'. These are sentimental delusions but proudly confessed to. A. C. Bradley, the great Shakespearian critic, spoke of Elizabeth Bennet as a girl we are meant to fall in love with, as he did. Kipling wrote two poems in Jane Austen's honour, one of which ends with the stirring cry, 'Glory, love, and honour unto England's Jane'. The other, entitled 'Jane's Marriage', has her transported to Paradise. When she asks for 'Love', Captain Wentworth is called up from 'a private limbo', where he has been reading a copy of *Persuasion*, which 'told the plain / Story of love between / Him and Jane'. These two poems frame a story called 'The Janeites'. This is narrated by a soldier in the trenches in the First World War. In full, fruity cockneyese, he holds forth on his discovery that the ladies and gentlemen of the novels 'was only just like people you run across any day' and connects them incongruously with figures in his own life. He has learnt about Jane Austen from his officers, the Janeites of the title, who form their own little secret society, with its code of knowing catch-words and allusions to the novels. The fiction is answered in fact, for the Janeites still exist, enthusiasts who know the novels through and through, read and re-read them, see her characters in the world around them, and talk and write about Jane Austen with an amazing intimacy and affection. Some critics dismiss the Janeite following as cultish and sentimental. This may or may not be so. What is indisputable is the depth of the Janeite response to a quality of the author's personality that comes across with a living force.

But other readers find this personality unsympathetic, even repellent. Charlotte Brontë discovered a writer altogether out of touch with the 'Passions', 'a complete and most sensible lady, but a very incomplete, and rather insensible (*not senseless*) woman'. Mark Twain boasted that she awakened in him nothing less than an 'animal repugnance'. D. H. Lawrence admired the vivid presentation of her characters, but he abhorred the writer, 'a narrow-gutted spinster'. He enlarged upon this remark in 'A Propos of *Lady Chatterley's Lover*', where he mourned the loss of what he calls the 'blood-connexion' that linked the classes in the England of Defoe and Fielding: 'And then, in the mean Jane Austen, it is gone. Already this old maid typifies "personality" instead of character, the sharp knowing of apartness instead of knowing in togetherness, and she is, to my feeling, thoroughly unpleasant, English in the bad, snobbish sense of the word, just as Fielding is English in the good, generous sense'.

These comments have a historical force as well as a personal validity. Charlotte Brontë is voicing a mid-nineteenth-century Romantic position, objecting to Jane Austen's morality of self-discipline, good sense and rational feeling, and classifying her as a 'society' novelist, not a novelist of humanity. Lawrence invokes a twentieth-century psychological romanticism, arbitrary but illuminating. During the later eighteenth century, English society lost the last vestiges of social unity, its paternalistic 'blood connexion', the better side of feudalism. By Jane Austen's day this had given way to a divisive class-system with its elaborate snobberies of money and rank. To this extent, the 'knowing of apartness' that Lawrence identified in the novels is an authentic social experience, not solely a projection of some psychological apartness in Jane Austen's own make-up.

Jane Austen's spinsterdom is also taken up in W. H. Auden's verse-epistle, 'Letter to Lord Byron', in which he asks the poet to tell her 'How much her novels are beloved down here' and continues with a confession of his own discomfort at finding such a streak of cold realism in her nature:

> You could not shock her more than she shocks me:
> Beside her Joyce seems innocent as grass.
> It makes me most uncomfortable to see
> An English spinster of the middle class
> Describe the amorous effects of 'brass',
> Reveal so frankly and with such sobriety
> The economic basis of society.

Auden's point is that Jane Austen behaves out of character—fancy an English lady, a spinster at that, betraying the secrets of her class! Auden's 'shock' is a silent allusion to the popular myth of 'Gentle Jane'—an eternal Maiden Aunt, an inspired amateur in the best English tradition, the homely spinster who put down her stitching to pick up her pen, who wrote in odd moments snatched from her domestic round, a kind of Sunday writer, who scribbled just to please herself and entertain the family, who sat quietly in the corner, silently observing the world go by, catching a turn of phrase, the flow of conversation, sketching the characters and mannerisms of her neighbours and friends, describing their comings and goings, their contretemps, their joys and sadnesses, their follies, stupidities and mentionable vices. This notion of Jane Austen's unpretentious amateurism is a touching picture with some fragments of truth. The novels were indeed based upon direct observation; and we can see from her letters that the world of the fiction is a faithful account of the small social world in which she passed her days—with its local balls, its gossip, chatter and scandalizing, its marriageable young ladies and eligible young men.

But there the myth dissolves. The facts of Jane Austen's life tell a different story, one which confirms everything that the novels convey of their author's professionalism, her capacity for critical, creative detachment and her total artistic command over the daily experiences by which her writing was fed. The sheer readability of the novels seems so natural and effortless that we take it for granted, just as we accept the feat of realism and the vitality of the characters. As Virginia Woolf recognized, 'Of all great writers she is the most difficult to catch in the act of greatness'. How difficult, and deceptive, we can see in the remarks of Henry James, who identified the 'little touches of human truth, little glimpses of steady vision, little master-strokes of imagination', but put them down to 'the extraordinary grace of her facility . . . of her unconsciousness'. He was deceived by the art that conceals art. Seeing no evidence of effort, he supposed there was none, unaware that the achievement of the novels was the fruit of twenty years' apprenticeship, of a style and technique evolved through constant experiment, and that the story of her life is not just that of a writer, but of a writer determined to be published, determined to find an audience beyond the admiring circle of her family and friends, and determined to formulate a mode of social satire that would enable her to practise as a critic from within, delighting her audience with a portrait of themselves, flattering and entertaining in its mimetic accuracy but scathing in its judgement and in the implication of its silent exclusions. G. K. Chesterton observed that 'Jane Austen may have been protected from truth: but it was precious little of truth that was protected from her'. The novels wear a deceptive charm; as Richard Simpson explained it, 'a magnetic attractiveness which charms while it compels'; and their air of modesty is the modesty of Swift's *A Modest Proposal*, insidious and explosive.

IV

Jane Austen's life was private and uneventful; and by modern standards extraordinarily narrow and restricted. Her forty-two years, from 1775 to 1817, were passed entirely among her family and friends. She visited London from time to time but never mixed in fashionable society and avoided literary circles like the plague. 'If I am a wild beast, I cannot help it'. She never married; she never travelled abroad; she was unknown to the public. The novels were published anonymously and her authorship was revealed only after her death, through a biographical notice that came out with *Northanger Abbey* and *Persuasion* at the end of 1817. The pattern of her life was set by her dedication to writing and this in turn may help us to understand her obsessive need for privacy, her choice of spinsterdom and her role in the family as a dutiful daughter, an affectionate sister and a favourite aunt to hordes of nephews and nieces. The circumstances of her life also help us to understand certain qualities in her writing—its highly personal tone; its allusiveness; its dramatic aspect, in the prominence of dialogue and in the scene-like staging of the characters and action; and its concentration on personal and family relationships.

Her childhood was spent in the small Hampshire village of Steventon, where her father, George Austen, was the parish clergyman. It was a large and literary household. Her father was a classical scholar with a taste for fiction, including the Gothic thrillers that Jane Austen was to make fun of in *Northanger Abbey*. Her mother was well known for her impromptu poems and stories. Whilst at Oxford, her brothers Henry and James edited a literary periodical, *The Loiterer*, between 1789 and 1790. There was a tradition of reading aloud; and with two daughters and five sons, the family was able to put on plays. Friends and relatives were recruited and the rectory barn was converted into a small theatre for summer performances, while during the winter they played in the rectory itself. Among the productions were farces whose humour could be very broad and unrectorylike.

From the outset, Jane Austen enjoyed the encouragement of a close and appreciative audience. Her early writing, dating from about 1787, the so-called *Juvenilia*, has come down to us in three manuscript notebooks, which contain pieces going up to about 1793. Soon after that, she wrote her first important work, a novel-in-letters, entitled *Lady Susan*. About 1795, she began another epistolary novel, 'Elinor and Marianne', which was eventually turned into *Sense and Sensibility*. In 1796–97, she completed the earliest version of *Pride and Prejudice*, then called 'First Impressions', which her father tried unsuccessfully to get published. In the next year, *Northanger Abbey* was written.

Until this time, Steventon had provided an ideal context for her work. The family was a keen audience. There was a wide neighbourhood of visitable families, of clergymen and local gentry; and further afield, throughout Southern England, the West Country and the Midlands, there was an extensive network of Austens and Leighs (her mother's family) to be visited. But this pattern of life changed in 1801 when Mr Austen gave up his parish and retired to Bath with his wife, Jane and Cassandra. He died in 1805 and, until 1809, they had to put up with a succession of temporary lodgings, or long visits to their relatives, in Bath, London, Clifton, Stoneleigh Abbey, Warwickshire (the family-seat of the Leighs) and Southampton. During this period, Jane Austen wrote little. The moves upset her; and there were other disappointments. In 1803, the manuscript of *Northanger Abbey* had been sold to a publisher, but was never printed. In December 1804, she lost her closest friend, Anne Lefroy, and a month later her father died. These events seem to have stopped her work on *The Watsons*, a manuscript she abandoned altogether. Its social picture is one of unrelieved bleakness, its heroine distressed, and its satire sharp to the point of cruelty. It signals a failing of generosity, a loss of creative power, which may stem from the sadness of these years.

In 1809 Jane Austen came to her last home, Chawton

Cottage, two miles south of Alton on the Winchester road, and not far from Steventon. Here she spent the remaining years of her life. The return to a settled domestic existence seems to have revived her energies. She took up the manuscripts of *Sense and Sensibility* and *Pride and Prejudice* to get them ready for publication; and in 1811 a publisher agreed to produce the first of these novels with her guarantee against loss. In 1811 she also began *Mansfield Park*, which was completed in the summer of 1813 and published in 1814. Between January 1814 and March 1815 she wrote *Emma*, which appeared at the end of 1815. *Persuasion* was written between August 1815 and August 1816; and in 1816 she also revised *Northanger Abbey*.

In January 1817, she began *Sanditon*, her seventh novel, writing and revising more than 24,000 words in eight weeks. But by then she was far into her last illness and the manuscript was put aside. It is an amazing document, a fierce and energetic satire on invalidism and hypochondria, Jane Austen's wry protest at her own condition. In May she was taken to Winchester to be under the care of a surgeon. Her illness was then unidentified; we now know it to have been Addison's disease. On the morning of July 18, at 4.30 a.m., she died. Asked for her last wishes, she replied, with characteristic dignity, economy and wit, 'I want nothing but death'. Six days later she was buried in Winchester Cathedral.

The course of Jane Austen's emotional life is obscure. The earliest of her surviving letters date from 1796 when she was twenty-one. They tell us of the parties and dances she went to locally, about visits to London, Bath and to the coast. But there is virtually nothing about her relationships with men. The few comments are ironic and evasive. All we have are some tantalizing stories in the family recollections and memoirs: that there was a mild flirtation with a young Irishman in 1796; that two or three years later she may have turned down a Fellow of Emmanuel College, Cambridge, staying in the locality; that in November 1802 she agreed to marry a Hampshire man, but that she changed her mind the very next morning. There are a number of other stories connecting her with someone—a naval officer, an army officer, or a clergyman—with whom she is said to have fallen in love but who died before their friendship could develop. There is no way of enlarging upon these vague and contradictory reports, for Cassandra destroyed her sister's most intimate letters. What remains, in the novels themselves, in *Sense and Sensibility* and *Persuasion* most of all, is the unquestionable proof that their author profoundly understood the experience of love, of love broken and disappointed, and the pains of loss and loneliness. As the Victorian novelist Julia Kavanagh observed, 'If we look under the shrewdness and quiet satire of her stories, we shall find a much keener sense of disappointment than of joy fulfilled. Sometimes we find more than disappointment.'

It seems unlikely that we shall ever know why Jane Austen remained unmarried. There may be a faint clue in *Lady Susan*. The heroine is a woman with a dominant, aggressive personality, talents which lead her to the brink of social self-destruction. It is a study in frustration, of a woman's fate when society has no use for her stronger, more 'masculine' talents. How far are we entitled to read this as a self-admonitory fable? Certainly, Jane Austen at seventeen was already in command of a powerful intellect which was to be turned more and more searchingly upon the people around her. Later in life she was described as 'a poker of whom everyone is afraid'. The remark is malicious. But it conveys an element of truth. Jane Austen must have been a formidable woman to meet, even as a young woman. In Kipling's sympathetic fantasy-poem, Jane Austen is a sadly resigned Anne Elliot who missed her Wentworth. This image of the older woman needs to be balanced with an image of Jane Austen when young—an Elizabeth Bennet, brilliant, vivacious and witty, yet critical, challenging and demanding, a woman who asked something of life and who never met a Darcy who could match her.

V

The six novels fall into two distinct groups. The early novels —*Sense and Sensibility*, *Pride and Prejudice* and *Northanger*

Abbey—were begun in the 1790s, and were rewritten and revised before their eventual publication; whereas the three later novels—*Mansfield Park*, *Emma* and *Persuasion*—belong entirely to Jane Austen's years of maturity. This order helps us to trace Jane Austen's technical development in the art of narration and to follow the changes in her view of life. Qualities in the early novels seem to mark them as the work of a younger woman while the imaginative temper of the second group is different. There is also the question of historical change. Jane Austen was thinking of this when she revised *Northanger Abbey* in 1816. She provided an 'Advertisement' warning readers that the book had originally been intended for publication in 1803, 'that thirteen years have passed since it was finished, many more since it was begun, and that during that period, places, manners, books, and opinions have undergone considerable changes'. This warning was more necessary than Jane Austen could have guessed, for the publication of *Northanger Abbey* was delayed until the end of 1817, when it came out as part of a four-volume set alongside *Persuasion*. Both novels have a Bath setting. But a great deal had happened to society during these years. While the story of *Northanger Abbey* is undated, its fashions and literary jokes belong firmly to the turn of the century. In *Persuasion*, the story is precisely dated and the sequence of contemporary events is used to work the story's plot: its beginning in 'the summer of 1814' is a prelude to Wentworth's return from duty at sea; in April 1814, Napoleon abdicated; and in the autumn, released from active service, Wentworth comes back on leave to Somerset. Eight years before, as a penniless Lieutenant, with a chancy life at sea, he was not considered a fit match for a Baronet's daughter. But now the situation has changed. He is a Captain, with a modest fortune in prize-money. Although the Wentworths are nobodies alongside the ancient lineage of the Elliots, he has been made socially respectable by the new heroic dignity of his profession. The nation was indebted to its navy, both for the victories at sea and the safeguarding of Britain's trading routes.

The historical distance between *Northanger Abbey* and *Persuasion* also brings out another major feature of Jane

Austen's development, the gradual shift of emphasis from literary to social satire. Her earliest creative impulse, as we can see it in the *Juvenilia*, was distinctively *critical*. The childhood pieces parody virtually every style of fiction around her in the 1790s, and the three early novels develop directly out of that tradition. Although none of the manuscripts survive, we can reconstruct the process by which they were transformed from straight parody into realistic comedy-of-manners. *Northanger Abbey* looks as if it was put together from two separate pieces: a skit on the Fanny Burney style of social novel, telling of a young woman's first experience of polite society; added to a satire on Gothic fiction. *Sense and Sensibility* began as a novel-in-letters, mocking Marianne Dashwood as a heroine of sensibility, from sentimental fiction, and exposing her correspondence to the comments of her sensible sister Elinor, who would give her sound advice on controlling her feelings, in the style of conduct fiction. 'First Impressions', the original version of *Pride and Prejudice*, takes its title directly out of the terminology of sentimental fiction, where it meant trust in one's immediate feelings, usually love at first sight.

In rewriting these early versions, it was not Jane Austen's purpose to remove the literary satire altogether, but to adjust it to a more realistic social setting. The final *Northanger Abbey* remains a Gothic satire; Marianne Dashwood still carries traces of her literary origin, and occasionally shifts back into her former role as a joke-heroine; and the 'First Impressions' theme is carried strongly into *Pride and Prejudice*. Neither did Jane Austen's interest in literary satire peter out. It was an experience that she shared with her readers and it continued, at a more subdued level throughout the later novels, until *Sanditon*, where, strangely, literary satire comes to the fore again. Today, this may seem to be a rather specialized matter. But for Jane Austen and her contemporaries, literature carried an important social and cultural significance and the novel in particular played a vital part in creating an image of middle-class identity; indeed, the novel was a product of middle-class society, catering to its interests and tastes.

Its rise, in England, came in the eighteenth century with the growth of an increasingly prosperous and leisured reading public. With the new wealth of the industrial revolution, this audience grew rapidly. By the 1770s novel-writing had become a largely commercial activity and literary hacks produced a flood of popular reading, the 'mere trash of the circulating library', as Jane Austen described it. The character of this fiction was determined largely by the character of its public, an audience of women with time and money on their hands and an appetite for easy reading. There was still an audience for the picaresque stories of Defoe, Fielding and Smollett, with their coarse vitality and the knock-about humour of low life. But the fashionable female audience ('our fair readers' to the writers and reviewers) wanted a literature flattering to them, that celebrated the arrival in English life of an improved level of society, and in which women were seen to have the good taste to cultivate their finer feelings and to develop an elaborate code of manners.

There developed a bewildering variety of fictional types and sub-types. But one principle runs throughout the 'society' literature of this period—the cult of feeling. This is one aspect of the eighteenth-century shift from the Age of Reason to Romanticism; and its significance as a symptom of deeper cultural change should not be ignored. But in fiction it had a very degraded 'social' manifestation for readers who practised a snobbery of feeling to differentiate themselves from previous generations. Sensibility became the class badge of polite society; and the central figure of its literature was the so-called sentimental heroine of feeling. Her heroism is measured by the strength of her passions and the delicacy with which her sensibility trembles. Heroines prove their ladylikeness in displays of feeling, in blushes, tears, hysterics, swoonings and madness. Lovers fall in love at sight; they are wracked by passion and the pangs of separation; and are elevated by the portrayable ecstasies of union. The plots were designed to throw them into a succession of dangers, both moral and physical, from which they could be rescued by heroes of exemplary courage and virtue. In Gothic versions, they would be swept away, in distant times, to the remote medieval gloom of crumbling fortresses ruled over by Germanic or Italianate Barons.

The cult of sensibility runs throughout the fiction of this period, in historical romances (where there was often a quieter responsiveness to the charms of the past or to an evocative, melancholic landscape), even in the novels of Fanny Burney, the only writer at this time to make a genuine attempt to portray the realities of life for a young woman entering polite society. Jane Austen was not the only one to react critically. Moralists attacked the cult as a dangerous, deceptive poisoner of impressionable young minds, while satirists made fun of it.

Northanger Abbey itself stands in a flourishing tradition of the mock-Gothic. However, Jane Austen was alone in understanding the potentialities of fiction as a form of literature, a belief that she doesn't force upon her readers, but which she tried to realize in her own writing, and to which she alluded jokingly in chapter V, where she reports a typical 1790s conversation:

> 'I am no novel reader—I seldom look into novels—Do not imagine that I often read novels—It is really very well for a novel.' —Such is the common cant.—'And what are you reading, Miss-?' 'Oh! it is only a novel' replies the young lady; while she lays down her book with affected indifference, or momentary shame.—'It is only Cecilia, or Camilla, or Belinda;' or, in short, only some work in which the greatest powers of the mind are displayed, in which the most thorough knowledge of human nature, the happiest delineation of its varieties, the liveliest effusions of wit and humour are conveyed to the world in the best chosen language.

The rhetorical claim of the last five lines is an irony in itself. This is exactly what the contemporary novel was *not*, not even the works of Fanny Burney named here; and Jane Austen is able to say this because she knew so clearly what had once been achieved half a century before in the hands of Fielding and Richardson, and what could be achieved again, through her own work.

In Catherine Morland, Jane Austen presents a stock figure of current satire, the young woman so captivated by the exotic thrills of the Gothic that she is ready to see the world through the lens of her latest reading, in this case the most popular of all such novels, *The Mysteries of Udolpho* (1794) by Mrs Radcliffe. Employing this common satirical device, Jane Austen's special twist was to show that the heroine doesn't have to look for excitement in books since there is a Gothicism of ordinary life, which can be experienced in the clear light of day.

This is the literary beginning to an issue raised again and again for the heroines of the six novels—the need to distinguish between illusion and reality, to be aware that the imagination has the power to enforce its own slanted vision upon the world. It is part of the struggle that the heroines have with the forces of pride and prejudice and with sense and sensibility, and which Emma Woodhouse faces in romantically casting Harriet Smith in the role of a distressed heroine and herself as a confidante-saviour. The educative process of the novels is to take the heroines along the path of disillusionment towards a clearer, unimpeded knowledge of themselves and their relationships, and the literary delusion is one of the blocks that they have to overcome.

Jane Austen's anti-romanticism was identified by Sir Walter Scott in 1816 in his review of *Emma*. He remarked that the story has 'cross purposes enough (were the novel of a more romantic cast) for cutting half the men's throats and breaking half the women's hearts'. No throats are cut; no hearts are broken. The novel plays with the devices and situations of romantic fiction, adjusting them to a story whose dramas and distresses are personal and domestic. Scott was looking at *Sense and Sensibility* and *Pride and Prejudice* as well; and he used this review as an occasion for placing Jane Austen's achievement in a new realist tradition of contemporary life. Whereas the sentimental romance purported to be an imitation of *la belle nature*, a higher and a nobler reality, to be aspired to, Jane Austen provided its antithesis, an imitation of the tempo and character of ordinary existence, to be faced, as Elizabeth Elliot in *Persuasion* faces 'the sameness and the elegance, the prosperity and the nothingness of her scene of life . . . a long uneventful residence in one country circle'. In the works of Jane Austen, Scott declares, we have the accuracy and realism of 'the modern novel'.

We can extend this historical placing by a glance sideways

to the situation in poetry at this time. Jane Austen's critical response to fiction is almost exactly matched in Wordsworth's critical reaction to the state of verse. Like her, he found himself surrounded by a tired, imitative school of writing, highly conventionalized and remote from the language and lives of ordinary people. His creative counter-statement was the poetry of the *Lyrical Ballads* (1798); and his formal protest was the 'Advertisement' to that volume and the 'Preface' to the second edition (1800), where he complained, in words that Jane Austen could very well have used herself, of the public appetite for melodrama and extravagance, 'this degrading thirst after outrageous stimulation' and the 'frantic novels' which were currently so popular. He drew attention to his choice of 'incidents and situations from common life', presented, as far as possible, in 'a selection of language really used by men', a formula which applies, with only a modification upwards into middle-class life, to Jane Austen's procedure in the novels. Just as the *Lyrical Ballads* set a standard in poetry, so her writing provided an implicit commentary on the state of English fiction as she found it in the 1790s. Her work was in effect a liberation of the novel from its servile function as a class-entertainment and as an instrument of cultural self-flattery. She showed instead that fiction could present an artistic image, delightful for its accuracy and realism, yet disturbing too, for within this accuracy and realism lay the incisive, anatomizing, analytical truth of its commentary upon middle-class life and manners.

VI

Jane Austen's contemporary readers paid her the highest possible tribute to an artist in the realist tradition—they confused her fiction with reality. She was plagued by people who went round finding originals for the characters. In June 1814, a month after the publication of *Mansfield Park*, she met a fantasticating Miss Dusautoy, who had 'a great idea of being Fanny Price—she and her youngest sister together, who is named Fanny'. Then there was the deluded Miss

Isabella Herries who having read *Emma* was 'convinced that I had meant Mrs & Miss Bates for some acquaintance of theirs—People whom I never heard of before'. We can smile at their *naïveté* and share Jane Austen's annoyance that strangers should foist such silly identifications upon her (including the suggestion that the Dashwood sisters in *Sense and Sensibility* were portraits of herself and her sister Cassandra). But, in all their simplicity, these comments testify to the convincing dramatic life of her characters. This quality was more deeply experienced by a Mrs Cage who came away from *Emma*, her imagination bemused: 'I am at Highbury all day', she reported, 'and I can't help feeling I have just got into a new set of acquaintances'. A cooler, more analytical note is struck by Lady Harriet Gordon, who read *Mansfield Park* when it first appeared and whose comments Jane Austen considered important enough to place in a collection of 'Opinions':

In most novels you are amused for the time with a set of Ideal People whom you never think of afterwards or whom you the least expect to meet in common life, whereas in Miss Austen's works, and especially in Mansfield Park you actually *live* with them, you fancy yourself one of the family; and the scenes are so exactly descriptive, so perfectly natural, that there is scarcely an incident or conversation, or a person that you are not inclined to imagine you have at one time or other in your Life been a witness to, born a part in, and been acquainted with.

The same point was developed more systematically by contemporary reviewers. An anonymous contributor to the *British Critic* for March 1818 remarked that 'we instantly recognize among some of our acquaintances, the sort of persons she intends to signify, as accurately as if we had heard their voices'; 'she seems to be describing such people as meet together every night in every respectable house in London; and to relate such incidents as have probably happened one time or other, to half the families in the United Kingdom'. One of the characters picked out is Isabella Thorpe from *Northanger Abbey*, 'a fine handsome girl, thinking of nothing but finery and flirting, and an exact representation of that large class of young women in the form they assume among the gayer part of the middling ranks of society'. Like other reviewers, he was struck by the accuracy as well as the lifelikeness of Jane Austen's social portraiture; her characters are seen to be representative types; and in these comments we can gauge the immediate success of the novels in the comedy of manners tradition.

In English fiction, we are familiar with the comedy of manners through the works of Thackeray, Trollope, George Eliot, E. M. Forster, and in more recent novelists, including Evelyn Waugh and Antony Powell. But in Jane Austen's day, it was essentially a dramatic tradition; beginning in the Restoration theatre and revived in the later eighteenth century by Garrick and Sheridan. It was a tradition in which Jane Austen was well-grounded. The Steventon productions had included plays by Sheridan and Garrick, as well as by a number of minor dramatists of the time; and as a girl she had experimented with scenes of burlesque drama. This theatrical tradition was a potent force in shaping Jane Austen's method in the novels, where so much of the action is realized dramatically in dialogue and where the positions, movements and relationships of the characters—whether they are alone or in a room with other people or out walking or travelling—are so graphically drawn, and convey such a full awareness of other people, their gestures, their expressions and moods. In many scenes, we are led to visualize the figures; they stand before us like actors on a plain and shallow stage, in a clear, defining light.

But this is not theatre *manqué*, as anyone will know who has tried to dramatize the novels. Dialogue which seems perfect to the eye and sounds perfectly on the internal ear, loses something in the speaking; and professional script-writers have foundered on this problem. What we have in Jane Austen is the true *fictional* comedy of manners, which creates the effect of mental theatre, of an imaginative visualization. It is the reader himself who contributes the backcloth of reality to the furniture of Jane Austen's spare, essential detail. The scenes are enriched, as no performance can be, by the author's frame of commentary and the angle of vision, as, for example, the wholly dramatic dialogue between Mr and Mrs Bennet, in the first chapter of *Pride and*

Prejudice, is sharply framed by the opening lines, the aphoristic pearl of worldly wisdom, 'It is a truth universally acknowledged, that a single man in possession of a good fortune must be in want of a wife'. Then follows an immediate shift, descending from the realms of universal bathos to the banality of a grubby neighbourhood view:

However little known the feelings or views of such a man may be on first entering a neighbourhood, this truth is so well fixed in the minds of the surrounding families, that he is considered as the rightful property of some one or other of their daughters.

The effect is of a camera panning in from outer space, to fasten on a single spot, telescopically enlarged, as chapter I places 'this truth' so solidly and comically before us in the person of Mrs Bennet, fired by the arrival of Mr Bingley, 'a single man of large fortune', within calling-distance of her household of marriageable daughters. Her husband is tired, has heard it all before, plays dumb, draws her on, mocks her. The comedy of repartee is hard and precise. It turns on the twin forces of money and marriage, upon the weary, sardonic, baiting sarcasm of Mr Bennet and the stupid single-mindedness of his wife, 'a woman of mean understanding', whose 'business' in life 'was to get her daughters married'.

The comedy of manners thrives best in a climate of social uneasiness and change, when people are preoccupied with the cultivation of manners, the pursuit of fashion and the show of respectability. Regency England provided just that situation, with its small and compact layer of middle-class gentry (estimated at about 25,000 families). Although the country was at war almost continuously from 1793 until 1814, middle-class life went on virtually unaffected. But structurally it was not a static society. The crucial distinction of gentlemanly birth was disappearing. The lower middle classes were becoming prosperous. Successful farmers, merchants, manufacturers, tradesmen and lawyers were ambitious to share the social standing of the gentry, as far as that could be achieved—by money, by mixing with them, by imitating their manners and their ways of speech. They could be 'gentlemanlike', could behave with 'civility', could start to drink tea in their summer-houses and have parlours, as the Martins dare to do in *Emma*, can dare, like Mrs Elton, the daughter of a Bristol merchant, to act 'the Lady Patroness' of the neighbourhood, usurping the place of Emma Woodhouse, the daughter of the neighbourhood's first gentleman. For young women, fashionable respectability meant being able to play the piano, to sing snatches of French and Italian, to know the gems of English verse, to be knowledgeable about the picturesque, to reel off the titles of the latest novels. These are the fashionable 'accomplishments' that Jane Austen exposes and itemizes. Music, literature and art were reduced to being the trappings of a culture specifically social, components in a shallow display, put on for the sake of polite gentility and ornamental wifeliness.

The snobberies of rank became even sharper during the time that Jane Austen was writing, one of the things she may have had in mind when she added the 'Advertisement' to *Northanger Abbey*. Bath of the 1790s had been a social mixing-pot. Everyone jostled together in the Public Rooms of the Spa. This is how such a nonentity as a Catherine Morland, the unremarkable daughter of an obscure country clergyman, could meet a Henry Tilney, the son of a great landowner; and how both of them could meet the Thorpes, the children of a rising lawyer. In the post-war Bath of *Persuasion*, their paths would never have crossed. By that time, the gentry had left the Public Rooms and entertained in private. A Tilney would have passed his time with one social set, a Morland in another.

Writing for a contemporary audience, Jane Austen's social notation is swift and economical. Money and rank place people on the social map as precisely as a grid reference. It is enough for Jane Austen to tell the reader that Mr Bingley's fortune is £100,000, his sisters' dowries £20,000 each, and that this money is inherited from a father in 'trade' in the north. This signals a family on the way up. The sisters have very superior airs. They patronize the Bennets, disapprove of Elizabeth's 'most country town indifference to decorum' in walking three miles through the mud to visit her sick sister, to arrive with her cheeks a 'blowsy' and unladylike red from the wind. Their 'darling wish' is to see their brother further respectabilize the family by the purchase of a landed estate, which he does.

Jane Austen pairs Bingley with Darcy. He too comes from the north. But there the resemblance ends. His name alone announces an aristocratic Anglo-Norman lineage, a far cry from the plebeian Yorkshire thud of 'Bingley'. He belongs to one of the ancient families of England. His income of £10,000 a year from family estates establishes him as one of a select group of only four hundred such landowners in the whole country. Although he has no title and is technically not a member of the aristocracy, his blood and wealth would make him *persona grata* at the highest levels. So Jane Austen's readers would savour the full comedy of his presence in the dingy small-town atmosphere of Meryton, with its *petite bourgeoisie* of tradesmen, merchants and working lawyers.

Jane Austen had no illusions about the society she lived in. She could see its shallownesses and superficialities and she let them speak for themselves. That Bingley was a northerner with a northern name, a *nouveau riche* of lowly origin, meant nothing to her. She records the data. He is part of the social scene and this is the way in which society would assess him. He has a function in the story and in the pattern of relationships. His extrovert warmth and friendliness, his ease in company, and his other social virtues, provide a foil to Darcy's introvert coldness and unsociability. But Jane Austen passes judgement on Bingley's human worth, not on his social pleasantry, on the fact, for example, that his 'manners' have 'something better than politeness; there was good humour and kindness'.

The novels provide us with a historically accurate picture of a society under stress, its values and its groups in a state of change. The picture is dynamic, analytical and evaluative, as well as descriptive. The pejorative meaning of 'vulgar' and 'vulgarity' is a gentlemanly coinage, to identify and put down the lowness of the lower middle classes and their manners. Jane Austen takes these words and breaks them open. Technically, Mrs Jennings is vulgar. She is a cockney, the widow of a man who traded in an unfashionable part of London. She tramples on every protocol, transgresses every rule of polite behaviour. She is emotionally vulgar, coarsely insensitive, a burden to the Dashwood sisters with her sly hints and loud whispers of suitors, lovers and marriage. She is comically vulgar in her imbecilic fancy that as a glass of Constantia wine cured her husband's 'old cholicky gout', so will it mend Marianne's broken heart. But her 'blunt sincerity' and warm-hearted innocent kindliness towards Marianne redeem everything. Jane Austen does not ask us to forget her vulgarity—it happened and it hurt people; nor does she ask us to discount this vulgarity against Mrs Jennings's motherliness. What she does do is to present us with a woman in whom these qualities and defects stand together in a critical relationship. 'Vulgarity' takes on a new meaning once we have read *Sense and Sensibility*. And a further meaning still when we encounter the brand of vulgarity displayed by Isabella Thorpe, an energetic social climber, who behaves to Catherine Morland as a treacherous and spiteful bitch.

There is also the vulgarity of the gentry. Isabella's transparent deceit is trivial alongside the hollowness of General Tilney's urbane and charming courtesies; and nothing that she does to Catherine Morland can match his callousness in sending the girl home in disgrace from Northanger Abbey. Lady Catherine de Bourgh is aristocratic in name and nature, but an arch-snob, she is supremely vulgar towards her social inferiors. Emma Woodhouse suffers from snobbish, vulgarizing fantasies. Without knowing Robert Martin, she caricatures him as a straw-chewing yokel, 'clownish', 'gross', uncouth and ill-mannered. This is her notion of yeoman farmers. But when she meets him, she discovers a man who is quiet, neat, sensible and well-mannered. He writes a good letter. He even reads the same books as she does! Darcy's 'prejudice' produces the same vulgarizing slant. Until he gets to know them, Elizabeth's uncle and aunt, the Gardiners, belong to the unvisitable, unknowable world of her 'lowly connexions'. In trade, they live within sight of their warehouse in a part of London that a Darcy wouldn't be seen in. But in the flesh he finds them pleasant and likeable; and although the Gardiners are unimportant as characters, Jane Austen bothers to underline his discovery in the last sentences of *Pride and Prejudice*: 'With the Gardiners, they were always on the most intimate terms. Darcy, as well as Elizabeth, really loved them....'

VII

Jane Austen's comedy of manners is a comedy of meanings. Language is behaviour; and the conventional, clichéd language of Regency society is an expression of the people themselves. Jane Austen identified both the slang of fashionable social culture and what she called the 'novel-slang' of its literature. In *Northanger Abbey*, Henry Tilney takes Catherine to task for her use of 'nice' and complains about its loss of meaning.

'Oh! it is a very nice word indeed!—it does for everything. Originally perhaps it was applied only to express neatness, propriety, delicacy, or refinement;—people were nice in their dress, in their sentiments, or their choice. But now every commendation on every subject is comprised in that one word.'

Jane Austen could have repeated this lecture many times over. The strength and discrimination of language that Johnson inherited from Swift and Pope, and before them, from Dryden, Milton and the metaphysical poets, had by this time been dissipated in the rhetoric of sentimental and moralizing fiction. Words passed from writer to writer like worn coins, a currency with an accepted face-value, but its meanings blurred and thin.

The semantic drama of *Sense and Sensibility*, *Pride and Prejudice* and *Persuasion* is signalled in their titles; and within the novels we can follow the scheme of characterization that brings the meaning of these words to life in the complexities and contradictions of human nature. Jane Austen denies the black-and-white morality of conduct fiction. 'Sense' can be as tiresome or as dangerous as 'sensibility'. 'Pride' and 'prejudice' can be strengths as well as weaknesses. 'Persuasion' can be interference. Other words are tested and searched—'principle', 'judgement', 'improvement', 'propriety'. There is a prominent cluster of social words—'civil', 'civility', 'civilities', 'civilly', 'uncivil', 'incivility'—relating to the principles of etiquette, of meeting the social obligations of politeness, an issue upon which Jane Austen builds a wide ranging conflict between compromise and integrity. These terms are not fixed and passive counters. *Pride and Prejudice* gives 'civility' a very personal meaning. It is the quality that Elizabeth and Darcy have to acquire to temper their superiority and aggressiveness. Her brilliance of mind and sharpness of tongue, his arrogant patricianism, threaten to isolate them from other people. So for them, 'civility' means adjustment, tolerance, sympathy and understanding. 'Duty' is a key-word in *Mansfield Park* and *Persuasion*. In the later eighteenth century it had come to carry the most solemn overtones of moral obligation and religious observance. Jane Austen takes nothing on trust; the word is flooded with a dispassionate irony. Its force as a moral absolute of Christianity is slyly questioned in the sententious invocations of Sir Thomas and Edmund Bertram. In *Persuasion*, an over-developed sense of filial duty brings Anne Elliot years of needless suffering. Duty is what you make it, what you want it to be. At the age of twenty-one, Maria Bertram 'was beginning to think matrimony a duty'; and as there is a young man conveniently at hand, with a grand country house and a princely income of £12,000 a year, 'it became, by the same rule of moral obligation, her evident duty to marry Mr Rushworth if she could'.

The semantic energies of Jane Austen's language are as powerful as the characters and human situations to which they are attached. They are mobilized within a total structure of meaning, a field of force capable of exerting the most delicate vibrations of feeling and tone, and of adumbrating the entire range of social and cultural usage that the language brings in from outside. The novels can be regarded as semantic organisms, analytical works of art that test and display the very language they are composed of; and the novelist herself belongs to that small group of writers for whom language is not only the medium of literature but a part of its subject.

VIII

The underlying theme of Jane Austen's social comedy is the predicament of being a woman in a man's world—a world ruled by men and run for their advantage, in which marriage looms as the central and decisive act of the woman's life, and where the prevailing view is (to quote Coleridge) that 'Marriage has . . . no *natural* relation to love. Marriage belongs to society; it is a social contract'. Other than marriage, no career or occupation was open to her. Her education was a grooming for polite society, providing her with fashionable 'accomplishments' to catch the eye of a future husband. The alternatives were unthinkable. To be a governess was to sell yourself into the slavery of superior servanthood. Jane Austen put it neatly in a letter: 'Single women have a dreadful propensity for being poor—which is one very strong argument in favour of matrimony'. The force of this idea is conjured up in Emma Woodhouse's fearful image of the elderly spinster ridiculed by the children of the village. At worst, then, marriage could be the solution to an economic and human problem, as Jane Austen presents it in *Pride and Prejudice*: 'the only honourable provision for well-educated young women of small fortune, and however uncertain of giving happiness, must be their pleasantest preservative from want'. This sardonic generalization is attached to Charlotte Lucas in her choice of Mr Collins. Elizabeth Bennet is saddened that her friend should humiliate herself with such a man, should 'have sacrificed every better feeling to worldly advantage'. But Charlotte makes this choice with her eyes open. She is twenty-seven, on the verge of becoming 'an old maid'. 'I am not romantic', she tells Elizabeth, 'I never was. I ask only a comfortable home.'

There were other pressures towards marriage, the right marriage, a marriage acceptable to the family, whose status and respectability were defined by the networks of relationship and association established through marriage. For the traditional landowning gentry, these values were vital to the framework of society and their own survival. The crushing force of this system is expounded succinctly in the opening pages of *Sense and Sensibility*, with a history of the Dashwood estate, its preservation from generation to generation through the elaborate legalities of inheritance and succession. The measured rhetoric of the exposition asserts the weight and solidity of the system and the need to maintain the respectability of a family name. It is a system that calls for individual sacrifice. One of the recent Dashwoods was unable to provide for 'those who were most dear to him' by selling any part of the estate, so tight was the knot of its legal bondage. Within this large social-historical image is embodied the ideology of property, its power and mystique, set at the opening of the novel to guide our understanding of the relationship between the individual and society dramatized in the story of Marianne Dashwood. An individualist, a rebel against convention, she has her own romantic 'systems', 'systems' which 'have all the unfortunate tendency of setting propriety at nought', declares Elinor, the censorious voice of social 'sense'. Marianne is eventually tamed and disciplined into behaving politely and dutifully as a young lady should, turning her back on visions of romantic love, and yoked in marriage to the respectable middle-aged suitor promoted by her family and friends—Coleridge's 'social contract' to the letter!

In *Sense and Sensibility*, Jane Austen shows a woman broken by these pressures; in *Pride and Prejudice* she shows how a woman can triumph over them. In this case, it is not the force of the heroine's own family but the weight of 'family' snobbery, pride of caste from the man's side, from Darcy himself and his aunt. This comes to a head in chapter LVI, in one of the great comic scenes of English literature, where Lady Catherine confronts Elizabeth in an attempt to warn her off, facing her with the weighty dynastic claims of the Darcys against the vulgar upstartism of the Bennets.

'Hear me in silence. My daughter and my nephew are formed for each other. They are descended on the maternal side, from the same noble line; and, on the father's, from respectable, honourable, and ancient, though untitled families. Their fortune on both sides is splendid. They are destined for each other by the voice of every member of their respective houses; and what is to divide them? The upstart pretensions of a young woman without family, connexions, or fortune. Is this to be endured! But it must not, shall not be. If you were sensible of your own good, you would not wish to quit the sphere, in which you have been brought up.'

This is comic melodrama, part of a wonderfully contrived scene. Lady Catherine's swelling indignation is pricked by Elizabeth's quiet contempt. Pope would have envied the artistry of Jane Austen's mock-heroics—Lady Catherine thundering with Biblical eloquence, 'Heaven and earth!—of what are you thinking? Are the shades of Pemberley to be thus polluted?'—and the skill of their deflation. But Lady Catherine's bombast is not all hot air. Its hard core is an argument whose authority comes from centuries of social theory and practice. She calls upon ancient sanctities: the dogma of order and hierarchy, whereby the harmony of the whole depends upon the human atoms keeping to their divinely ordained and fixed positions, the great to remain great in the company of their peers, the 'young woman without family, connexions, or fortune' to stay put in the 'sphere' in which she has 'been brought up'.

Elizabeth's social offence is to have her eyes on Darcy. Her offence, as a woman, is to dare to stand up and assert herself as a person, to think for herself, to hold opinions, and to expose herself as an individual with a will of her own. The woman's accepted role was to be passive and submissive. Her function was to be decorative in society, comforting at home, an appendage to the man. Henry Tilney puts the idea playfully to Catherine Morland: 'man has the advantage of choice, woman only the power of refusal . . . he is to purvey, and she is to smile'. The idea takes a more serious turn in the words of Anne Elliot to Captain Harville on the woman's experience of love:

We certainly do not forget you, so soon as you forget us. It is perhaps, our fate rather than our merit. We cannot help ourselves. We live at home, quiet, confined, and our feelings prey upon us. You are forced upon exertion. You have always a profession, pursuits, business of some sort or other, to take you back into the world immediately, and continual occupation and change soon weaken impressions.

In Anne's reference to 'our fate' there is no hint of rhetoric, no false note. Her own life has given her the right to use these words. The bitter truth of separation, loss and remembrance she knows only too well, and she touches on them here with dignity and restraint. Again, there is no hint of rhetoric when Emma Woodhouse reflects on 'the difference of woman's destiny', comparing the social eminence of the great Mrs Churchill and the nonentity of Jane Fairfax, soon to enter the 'governess-trade', 'the sale—not quite of human flesh—but of human intellect'. Jane Austen is expressing the woman's cause but in a way which is totally unpolemical, totally undoctrinaire. The urgent tones of Mary Wollstonecraft and the other crusading feminists of the time only get into the novels as a parody-echo, in the pert aggressiveness of Mrs Elton's warning to Mr Weston:

'I always take the part of my own sex. I do indeed. I give you notice—You will find me a formidable antagonist on that point. I always stand up for women—'

Jane Austen's standing up for women is not argumentative but dramatic. It is implicit in the creation of heroines whose claim to existence is human, whose reality comes from their self-awareness, their possession of minds and feelings, and not as a result of their conformity to some stereotype in either fashionable life or fashionable literature.

When Captain Wentworth asserts that naval vessels are no place for ladies, Mrs Croft corrects him sharply: 'But I hate to hear you talking so, like a fine gentleman, and as if we were all fine ladies, instead of rational creatures'. When Mr Collins refuses to credit Elizabeth's rejection, she has to reprimand him in the same terms: 'Do not consider me now as an elegant female intending to plague you, but as a rational creature speaking the truth from her heart'. Their rationality is something that these women have to argue for in the face of male attitudes which are not so much a consequence of prejudice or stupidity but of habit, a block much more difficult to shift. When the Dashwood sisters are locked in argument, the contest is real; they are not the author's ventriloquial dummies. Marianne is a romantic, passionate woman, but she is far from mindless. Jane Austen underlines Anne Elliot's 'strong mind', her 'maturity of mind', phrases we might think superfluous, since these qualities are so evident in all she does. In this emphatic labelling, we can glimpse Jane Austen's anxiety to press home to her Regency public the message that a woman could have qualities traditionally a man's and that a woman could surpass him in maturity and understanding, as Anne surpasses Wentworth and everyone else in *Persuasion*.

There was indeed a battle to be fought. In *Mansfield Park*, Sir Thomas Bertram comes down heavily on Fanny Price for refusing to accept Henry Crawford. Given the young man's interest and eligibility, the woman's consent is taken for granted. So her refusal is momentous, unnatural, arouses him to an angry diatribe against the new unfeminine 'independence of spirit, which prevails so much in modern days, even in young women, and which in young women is offensive and disgusting beyond all common offence'. Lady Catherine sees this new spirit in Elizabeth Bennet. In her, it is something deliberate and self-conscious, a part of her attraction for Darcy, which she is eager to discuss with him. In Jane Austen's new brand of intellectual romance, the lady can even invite her beloved to analyse the bonds of affection! At the end of the story, she wants him 'to account for his having ever fallen in love with her'; and she is just as keen to present her view of the affair: 'The fact is, that you were sick of civility, of deference, of officious attention. You were disgusted with the women who were always speaking and looking, and thinking for *your* approbation alone. I roused, and interested you, because I was so unlike *them*.' Lady Catherine interpreted her nephew's interest as a sexual infatuation, the sordid outcome of Elizabeth's 'arts and allurements'. Her suspicions are correct; but only half correct. What attracted Darcy was the challenge of a woman whose vitality and presence is intellectual as well as physical.

Each of the heroines presents a different face to the world and is attractive to men for different reasons. None of them can match Elizabeth's high spirits, her aggressive outspokenness and sheer argumentative brilliance. But they are all alike in their possession of an interior life, a dimension of psychological reality, which forms an area of action as important as the action outside and which is drawn with equal care and precision. Jane Austen's method is not stream-of-consciousness nor an elaborate psychoanalytical psychologizing. Her technique is essentially realistic in connecting the ebb and flow of experience to the circumstances of the story and to the heroine's immediate situation. Its credibility comes partly from the thoughtful, reflective nature of the heroines, partly from the train of events, and partly from the fact that the patterns of thought and feeling are so patently normal and recognizable.

While visiting the newly-wed Collins, Elizabeth Bennet has plenty of time to digest the contents of Darcy's second letter, as she goes on solitary walks to escape the company of Mr Collins and Lady Catherine:

> After wandering along the lane for two hours, giving way to every variety of thought; re-considering events, determining probabilities, and reconciling herself as well as she could, to a change so sudden and so important, fatigue, and a recollection of her long absence, made her at length return home; and she entered the house with the wish of appearing cheerful as usual, and the resolution of repressing such reflections as must make her unfit for conversation.

Elizabeth's mental and emotional existence is here traced as an active and conscious state of mind. Its progression is geared to the sequence of her movements; and through this technique, Jane Austen is able to convey the *processes* of thought and feeling as well as their quality and content.

There is often a precise enumeration of the levels of experience, the ways in which the same impression can be registered differently, sometimes contradictorily. When Marianne Dashwood hears the news of Lucy Steele's marriage, 'To her own heart it was a delightful affair, to her imagination it was even a ridiculous one, but to her reason, her judgement, it was completely a puzzle'. The impact of feeling can be registered in moral terms. At Portsmouth, Fanny Price was 'quite shocked' by a squabble in the family: 'Every feeling of duty, honour, and tenderness was wounded by her sister's speech and her mother's reply.' Jane Austen's drive is continually discriminative, towards a clarity of mind which is moral as well as rational, towards judgement based upon clear thinking and right feeling. Fanny receives a 'stab' when she concludes that Edmund Bertram's marriage to Mary Crawford is inevitable. She grieves to see someone she loves like a brother caught in the toils of a seductress whom she detests. She is heartbroken, dejected, but rallies herself and determines to 'endeavour to be rational, and to deserve the right of judging Miss Crawford's character and the privilege of true solicitude for him by a sound intellect and an honest heart'.

Jane Austen sets a high value on self-knowledge and each of the novels can be analysed in terms of the heroine's progress along this path. But self-knowledge on its own is not enough and Jane Austen joins to it the idea of a second kind of knowledge, knowledge of our duty in life. This concept appears in *Mansfield Park* where Edmund Bertram sends Mary Crawford off with an admonitory reference to 'the most valuable knowledge we could any of us acquire—the knowledge of ourselves and of our duty'. And his father, Sir Thomas, comes to the conclusion that the sexual misbehaviour of his daughters must be put down to the fact that in their upbringing 'active principle, had been wanting, that they had never been properly taught to govern their inclinations and tempers, by that sense of duty which can alone suffice'. At the end of *Persuasion*, Anne Elliot is able to congratulate herself on having done the right thing, eight years before, in following Lady Russell's advice by giving up any idea of marrying Wentworth. Lady Russell stood in the place of a mother and, dutifully, as a child, she obeyed. So her conscience remained clear, even if her heart was broken, and she is in a position to reflect: 'If I mistake not, a strong sense of duty is no bad part of a woman's portion'.

These concepts of duty are not presented to us uncritically. Sir Thomas and Edmund both deliver judgement; they enjoy putting other people right and fault-finding in themselves; and there is a glib and defensive rationalization in Anne Elliot's conclusion. But these qualifications are local. The idea of duty was important to Jane Austen, not just the formal duties of religion and family, but the internal duty of individual women towards themselves. To thyself be true. It is this concern which ultimately connects us with Jane Austen, which enables us to understand the heroines in their struggle for individuality and fulfilment, a theme at the heart of nineteenth- and twentieth-century literature, from the Romantic poets onwards; and at the heart, too, of the slow social revolution in England that followed the political revolutions of America and France. In *A Vindication of the Rights of Women*, published in 1792, Mary Wollstonecraft had argued radically that women should not seek 'power over men; but over themselves'; that they should fight free from the degradation of being regarded as mere sexual and social objects, not by overturning society but by valuing themselves as individuals with a right to fulfil themselves in their own way. This message sounds again at the end of *A Doll's House* in Nora's challenge to Torvald. Above the responsibilities of marriage and motherhood, she sees other duties:

Nora: My duties towards myself.
Torvald: Before all else you are a wife and a mother.
Nora: That I no longer believe. I think that before all else I am a human being, just as much as you are—or, at least, I should try to become one. I know that most people agree with you, Torvald, and that they say so in books. But henceforth I can't be satisfied with what most people say, and what is in books. I must think things out for myself and try to get clear about them.

'Let other pens dwell on guilt and misery', Jane Austen began the final chapter of *Mansfield Park*. She declares herself 'impatient to restore everybody, not greatly in fault themselves, to tolerable comfort, and to have done with all the rest'. Without exception, the novels close on a note of dismissive irony, with a rapid tying-up of loose ends. Jane Austen never follows her heroines into the reality of marriage; nor does she carry them to the bitter and tragic point that Nora reaches, where life falls apart and has to be put together again, slowly, painfully and alone. Nevertheless, the comic mask is only a mask. Her heroines' experiences and the meaning of their lives, as much as we are shown of them, are touched with an irony beyond laughter.

In the Foreword to *Women in Love*, Lawrence declared the importance of man's 'struggle for verbal consciousness'. It is

Nora's struggle, her fight to escape from the doll's house in which Torvald has locked her; before her, it is the struggle of Jane Austen's heroines; and today many modern men and women would accept it as their struggle too. Lawrence's enunciation of this process touches the very centre of Jane Austen's art and it helps us to understand the depth of our engagement with the compelling force of these 'verbal' heroines and the 'verbal' structures in which they have their life:

> Any man of real individuality tries to know and to understand what is happening, even in himself, as he goes along. This struggle for verbal consciousness should not be left out in art. It is a very great part of life. It is not superimposition of a theory. It is the passionate struggle into conscious being.

IX

Jane Austen's verbalism is most crucially exposed in the treatment of love. In this area, the logic is relentless. Coleridge's axiom—'Marriage has . . . no *natural* relation to love'—defines the premiss of Jane Austen's husband-and-wife comedy. The married couples duly exhibit the gamut of comic symptoms—from lovelessness and boredom to irritation aged into resentment. But the novels also deliver a stern counter-axiom: that marriage does have a *moral* relation to love; and by that test the quality of marriage is to be judged, with the equally decisive qualification that love is not necessarily related to passion or to the feelings conventionally regarded as romantic. For the heroines, a part of love is the recognition of their own needs—Fanny Price for an elder brother, Emma Woodhouse for a kindly, admonitory uncle, the broken Marianne Dashwood for a father-protector. The discovery of mutual affinities, sympathies and understandings is the justification for marriage on human and moral grounds, as distinct from the worldly contracts made for profit or convenience, or the 'social contract' marriages made for the sake of the family. Love is an awareness of the other person, sharpened by judgement into a learning experience. At the close of *Pride and Prejudice*, *Emma* and *Persuasion*, the heroes and heroines are brought even closer together as they talk about the ways in which they have affected one another morally and intellectually, as well as emotionally. This is the final stage in their process of mutual education. These scenes present a remarkable combination of analysis and personal contact in which the sense of emotional intimacy is deepened in the act of discussion.

But what of love as passion? When the couples come together in the full recognition of their feelings, Jane Austen is discretion itself—we are not to intrude upon such tender scenes, not to overhear lovers' talk. Edward Ferrar's declaration is made 'very prettily'. George Knightley delivers himself 'in plain, unaffected, gentlemanlike English'. The 'happiness' Fanny Price inspires in Edmund Bertram is conjectured to 'have been great enough to warrant any strength of language in which he could cloathe it to her or to himself'. Darcy 'expressed himself on the occasion as sensibly and as warmly as a man violently in love can be supposed to do'. Only in *Persuasion* is Jane Austen more forthcoming. The reconciliation of Anne and Wentworth, which leads on without interruption to their declaration of love, is drawn with a richness and intensity of feeling unequalled in the novels. Yet even here, the emphasis remains verbal, the reporting oblique. Their deepest contact is through 'words enough . . . the power of conversation . . . those retrospections and acknowledgements, and especially in those explanations of what had directly preceded the present moment, which were so poignant and so ceaseless of interest'.

Here, as so often in the novels, Jane Austen renders the experience of people discovering and exploring their love for one another, simply through being together, through awarenesses and understandings, spoken and unspoken. This is their making love. If we accept the playful irony of style, the narrator's pose of mock-discretion, Darcy's warmth and the violence of his love are not in question. They are proposed to us, verbally, as qualities to take on trust, part of a mild joke against lovers in general. But in the flesh, there is no warmth or violence of love whatsoever in Darcy. He admires a good figure, but no more than that. This absence from *Pride and Prejudice* and from the relationships in all the later novels is something we have to question if our reading of Jane Austen has begun with *Sense and Sensibility*. For Marianne Dashwood is a woman passionately in love, a woman whose attractiveness and vitality has a genuinely sensuous vibration, and in Willoughby she is matched by a man who has the power to disturb women. Elinor finds her judgement endangered by his presence and the physical aspects of his hold over her are spelt out.

Elinor's problem was also Jane Austen's. She too was disturbed by the power of sexuality, its threat to the security of reason and self-control, its melting attack upon the certainties of selfhood and identity (a point that Lawrence hints at). The tension is evident in *Sense and Sensibility*. The writer's engagement in Marianne and Willoughby is unmistakable. Their destruction—Willoughby blackened with a murky past, the thin and distant melodrama of having seduced a seventeen-year-old schoolgirl! Marianne devitalized through illness and cast off as a 'reward' to the patient Colonel Brandon—is gratuitous and forced, a betrayal of the novel's dramatic commitment, however neatly and maliciously their punishment completes the scheme in which the sickness of 'sensibility' is purged with a stiff dose of 'sense'. After this exercise in suppression, Jane Austen tried to turn her back on the problem. Her heroes are a dull and unvirile crew; her heroines are untroubled by passion. Sexuality is outlawed, reserved for the villains and villainesses and the silly little girls and the married women who should know better: for Wickham and Lydia, who were 'only brought together because their passions were stronger than their virtue'; for the Crawfords, whose dangerous, seductive charm has to be smeared with the taint of corruption (again, some readers have felt, gratuitously). Whatever the solid virtues of George Knightley, whatever the truth-to-life in his marriage to Emma Woodhouse, there is some shadowy objection to his avuncular and tutelary union to a girl of such brilliance, beauty and the 'bloom of full health'. *Persuasion* is *Sense and Sensibility* safely rewritten, with the rational 'romance' of maturity, and quieter, more tender, poetic charms substituted for the impulsive infatuation of youth.

Charlotte Brontë wondered where in Jane Austen is 'that stormy Sisterhood . . . the Passions'. It is a question that has been raised by many of Jane Austen's critics; it lurks within Lawrence's 'narrow-gutted spinster'. One answer is in *Sense and Sensibility*, which Charlotte Brontë had not read. Marianne Dashwood is a heroine whose courage and love she would have applauded and whose suffering she would have wept for; and surely Lawrence would have cheered her too, if ever he had read the book with an open mind. The other answer is that Jane Austen tried to undercut the passions with irony, to detach herself from them, and to subject them to the pressure of her own compelling need for order and control, the driving necessity of her imagination and her whole being, the force which stands behind the achievement of the novels both in their scope and their limitations.

X

As far as her fellow-countrymen are concerned, Jane Austen can properly be described as the most *beloved* of English novelists. Like Shakespeare, she has transcended literary greatness, to become part of our national heritage and something of a cult. Her anniversaries are commemorated, her homes are visited, and Chawton Cottage is preserved by the Jane Austen Society as a place of pilgrimage. Strictly speaking, these circumstances have more to do with social anthropology than literary criticism. But the fact remains that of all the great English novelists, Jane Austen is the only one to survive into the 1970s with such a devoted following. Her works are known with more intimacy than those of Shakespeare himself. If he is revered as our national poet, Jane Austen is loved as our national novelist, the most widely enjoyed and in many ways the most English of all English writers.

Generations of readers have treasured the novels nostalgically. They seem to immortalize a golden age in English society, ('the last voice of a happier age' commented V. S.

Pritchett). There are still people in this country who can identify themselves and their acquaintances, charitably and uncharitably, with Jane Austen's characters and their way of life. For them, the novels can be potently authenticating, as they were for their Regency audience. There is a special pleasure, the joy of recognition, in discovering oneself drawn so accurately and artistically. Like family portraits and domestic interiors of a Dutch fidelity, they flatter by the very perfection of the rendering. The basis of Jane Austen's social comedy has not dated, with its attention to manners and the refinements of social behaviour, its play upon vulgarity and the distinctions of class. The forms have changed, but the system remains, and for those who live within it the novels can be read as a celebration of traits that are cherished as typically and endearingly English—our insularity, our bluff and determined philistinism, our anti-intellectualism, our wariness of Mediterranean passion and French gallantry, our sense of order, decorum and self-control, our anxieties about social background and breeding, our respect for duty, propriety and tradition, and, the ultimate saving grace of the English, our thick-skinned capacity to laugh at ourselves and so draw the sting of any joke.

Nostalgic, wishful, chauvinistic and unliterary, jealous, possessive and snobbish, this view of the novels is partial, blind to their irony and to the force of their social judgement. Nonetheless, it is a view which has been held firmly and continuously in this country from Jane Austen's own time until the present day. Its voice can still be heard and occasionally breaks into print. In the summer of 1974, when a current domestic worry was the rising price of bread, this short letter appeared in the correspondence columns of one of our national papers:

Sir,

We hear a lot about the cost of bread and even the shortage of this essential commodity. There is a perfectly simple answer which is to bake one's own bread; we have done this for years and my cook produces much finer bread than you can obtain in the ordinary way. It is also much cheaper and requires no expensive equipment.

Jane Austen would have greeted the unconscious irony of this letter with a smile of recognition. Bread was expensive in her day too; and there was no shortage of advice from the gentry, just as well-meaning, suggesting how the poor could feed themselves economically.

According to Hobbes, 'laughter is a bad infirmity of human nature which every thinking man will attempt to overcome'. The novels of Jane Austen offer a different moral, that laughter comes to our rescue, is a necessary strength, a realistic response, an understanding, which enables 'thinking' people to hold out in the face of life's irrational and chaotic ironies. Jane Austen's vision would place her far along Nietzsche's scale of laughing philosophers, by which they are ordered 'according to the rank of their laughter—rising to those capable of *golden* laughter'. In the passage in *Beyond Good and Evil* where he presents this idea, Nietzsche goes on to speculate upon 'the Olympian vice', divine laughter:

> And if gods too philosophize, as many an inference has driven me to suppose—I do not doubt that while doing so they know how to laugh in a new and superhuman way—and at the expense of all serious things! Gods are fond of mockery; it seems they cannot refrain from laughter even when sacraments are in progress.

Jane Austen's laughter is directed at the secular sacraments and sacred cows of the Regency world—at its fashionable modes of feeling and thinking, at its idols of class and culture, at its categoricalisms, its rage for order, inherited from the Age of Reason, at its sentimental romanticism, at its litany of 'improvement', 'duty', 'sense', 'civility'. Her laughter is amused, intellectual and sardonic. But there the superhumanism, the Godlike mockery ends. For behind the laughter is sadness and compassion. And behind that is anger and frustration, the tensions of a satirist who uncovers the shams, shabbinesses and inhumanities of her world, its oppressions and claustrophobias, yet who nevertheless belongs to it, needs it, and cannot exist outside it. Its profoundest critic and historian, she is its victim herself.

JANE AUSTEN

A Select Bibliography

(Place of publication London, unless stated otherwise. Detailed bibliographical information will also be found in Vol. III of *The New Cambridge Bibliography of English Literature*.)

Bibliography:

JANE AUSTEN: A Bibliography, by G. L. Keynes (1929)

—the standard methodical bibliography, published in a limited edition by the Nonesuch Press. Includes a list of secondary material up to 1928.

JANE AUSTEN: A Critical Bibliography, by R. W. Chapman; Oxford (1953)

—second edition, 1955. A selective list, with good coverage of historical and biographical material.

Collected Works:

NOVELS, 5 vols (1833)

—the first collected edition, published by Richard Bentley. Reprinted 1866 and 1869. A volume called *Lady Susan &c* was added to the edition of 1878–9 containing *A Memoir of Jane Austen*, by her nephew, J. E. Austen-Leigh, first published separately in 1870.

WORKS, 6 vols (1882)

—the Steventon Edition. Vol. VI contains the *Memoirs* by her nephew, *Lady Susan*, and other fragments.

NOVELS, ed. R. B. Johnson, 10 vols (1892)

—illustrated by W. C. Cooke and ornaments by F. C. Tilney.

NOVELS, ed. R. B. Johnson, 10 vols (1898)

—illustrated by C. E. and H. M. Brock.

NOVELS, 10 vols (1898)

—The Winchester Edition.

WORKS, 10 vols (1899)

—The Temple Edition.

NOVELS, 6 vols (1902)

—the Hampshire edition. Decorated by B. MacManus.

WORKS, 6 vols (1907–31)

—with introductions by Lord David Cecil, R. W. Chapman, M. Lascelles, Michael Sadleir, and Forrest Reid. In the 'World's Classics' series.

WORKS, ed. R. B. Johnson, 10 vols (1908–9)
—illustrated by A. W. Mills. In the St Martin's Illustrated Library of Standard Authors.
NOVELS, 6 vols (1922)
—introduction by R. B. Johnson. Illustrated by C. E. Brock.
NOVELS: The Text based on Collation of the Early Editions by R. W. Chapman. With Notes, Indexes, and Illustrations from Contemporary Sources. 5 vols; Oxford (1923). Vol. VI, *Minor Works* (1954).
—reprinted (without coloured plates) 1926, (with corrections) 1933, (in two volumes) 1934. The definitive edition, outstanding for its careful scholarship.
WORKS, 7 vols (1923)
—the Adelphi Edition. Vol. VII contains *Lady Susan* and *The Watsons*.
WORKS, 5 vols (1927)
—the Georgian Edition. With an Introduction to each volume by J. C. Bailey which were reprinted in a separate volume, 1931.
THE COMPLETE NOVELS (1928)
—an 'Omnibus' edition in one volume, with an Introduction by J. C. Squire.
NOVELS, 6 vols (1948)
—the Chawton edition.
WORKS, 7 vols (1933–4)
—illustrated by M. Vox. Vol. VII contains *Sanditon*, *The Watsons*, *Lady Susan*, and other miscellanea. Introduction by R. B. Johnson.
[NOVELS], ed. M. M. Lascelles, 5 vols (1961–4)
—in the Everyman library.
[NOVELS], 6 vols (1969–72)
—Penguin English Library.
[NOVELS], 6 vols (1970)
—Oxford English Novels series.

Letters:

LETTERS. Edited with an Introduction and critical remarks, by Edward Lord Brabourne, 2 vols (1884).
JANE AUSTEN'S SAILOR BROTHERS, by J. H. and E. C. Hubback (1906)
—contains unpublished letters to her brother Francis.
JANE AUSTEN: Her Life and Letters, by W. Austen-Leigh and R. A. Austen-Leigh (1913)
—contains numerous extracts from Jane Austen's letters. See below under 'Biographical and Critical Studies'.
FIVE LETTERS FROM JANE AUSTEN TO HER NIECE FANNY KNIGHT, ed. R. W. Chapman; Oxford (1924)
—printed in facsimile.

LETTERS, selected, with an Introduction, by R. B. Johnson (1925).

JANE AUSTEN'S LETTERS TO HER SISTER CASSANDRA AND OTHERS. Collected and edited by R. W. Chapman, 2 vols; Oxford (1932)

—the only complete edition and a definitive text, with notes and indexes. Reprinted in one volume, with additions, 1952. A selection of letters appeared in the World's Classics, 1955.

Separate Works:

SENSE AND SENSIBILITY: A Novel, by a Lady, 3 vols (1811)

—second edition, corrected, 1813.

PRIDE AND PREJUDICE: A Novel, 3 vols (1813).

MANSFIELD PARK: A Novel, 3 vols (1814)

—second edition, corrected, 1816.

EMMA: A Novel, 3 vols (1816).

NORTHANGER ABBEY and PERSUASION, 4 vols (1818)

—contains a biographical notice of the author by her brother, Henry Austen. (Included in Bentley's edition of 1833.)

LADY SUSAN and THE WATSONS (1871). *Unfinished Novels*

—first printed in the second edition, 1871, of *A Memoir of Jane Austen* by her nephew J. E. Austen-Leigh. Reprinted together 1939, with an Introduction by J. Bailey. *The Watsons* was reprinted separately, 1923 (Introduction by A. B. Walkley); 1927 (reprinted from the MS, by R. W. Chapman, Oxford); 1928 (completed by E. and F. Brown, in accordance with her intentions.)

LOVE AND FREINDSHIP [*sic*] and Other Early Works. Now first printed from the original MS; with a Preface by G. K. Chesterton (1922)

—comprises the contents of MSS *Juvenilia*, in the Bodleian Library, Oxford.

[SANDITON]. Fragment of a Novel written January–March 1817. Now first printed from the manuscript. Edited, with Preface, by R. W. Chapman; Oxford (1925)

—reprinted, 1934, with *The Watsons*, *Lady Susan*, and 'Other Miscellanea', edited by R. B. Johnson.

PLAN OF A NOVEL, ACCORDING TO HINTS FROM VARIOUS QUARTERS. With opinions on *Mansfield Park* and *Emma*, collected and transcribed, and other documents (with facsimiles); Oxford (1926).

TWO CHAPTERS OF 'PERSUASION', ed. R. W. Chapman; Oxford (1926)

—the first draft of chapters X and XI in Vol. II.

VOLUME THE FIRST. Now first printed from the manuscript in the Bodleian Library. Edited with a Preface by R. W. Chapman (with facsimiles); Oxford (1933)

—comprises the contents of the first of three MS notebooks in which Jane Austen collected (*c.* 1793) her *Juvenilia*.

VOLUME THE THIRD. Now first printed from the MS (in the possession of Mr. R. A. Austen-Leigh), edited with a Preface by R. W. Chapman; Oxford (1951)
—the third of Jane Austen's MS notebooks.
VOLUME THE SECOND. [Love and Freindship], ed. B. C. Southam; Oxford (1963).

Some Critical and Biographical Studies:

(*Note: Writers and their Work* does not normally include periodical articles in its Select Bibliographies, but in view of their chronological significance, some articles are given below in sequence. Those marked (L) may be found reprinted in D. Lodge's *Jane Austen: Emma: A Casebook*, 1968, those marked (S) in B. C. Southam's *Jane Austen: The Critical Heritage*, 1968, and those marked (W) in Ian Watt's *Jane Austen: A Collection of Critical Essays*, 1963.)

[Review of *Emma*, by Sir Walter Scott], *Quarterly Review*, XIV, 1815
—the most important contemporary statement. (S)
[Review of *Northanger Abbey* and *Persuasion*, by R. Whately], *Quarterly Review*, XXIV, 1821
—a classic essay. (S)
'The Diary and Letters of Madame D'Arblay', by T. B. Macaulay, *Edinburgh Review*, LXXVI, 1843.
'The Novels of Jane Austen', by G. H. Lewes, *Blackwood's Magazine*, July 1859.
ENGLISH WOMEN OF LETTERS, by J. Kavanagh (1862)
—ch. XVIII, 'Miss Austen's Six Novels'. (S)
A MEMOIR OF JANE AUSTEN, by J. E. Austen-Leigh (1870)
—second edition, 1871, to which were added *Lady Susan*, *The Watsons*, *Sanditon*, *Plan of a Novel*, etc.
[Review of the *Memoir of Jane Austen*, by R. Simpson], *North British Review*, LII, 1870. (S)
JANE AUSTEN AND HER WORKS, by 'S. Tytler' [H. Keddie] (1880).
JANE AUSTEN'S NOVELS, by W. G. Pellew; Boston (1883).
JANE AUSTEN, by S. F. Malden (1889)
—in the 'Eminent Women Series'.
LIFE OF JANE AUSTEN, by G. Smith (1890)
—contains a bibliography by J. P. Anderson.
THE STORY OF JANE AUSTEN'S LIFE, by O. F. Adams; Chicago (1891)
—revised ed., Boston, 1897.
ESSAYS ON THE NOVEL AS ILLUSTRATED BY SCOTT AND MISS AUSTEN, by A. Jack (1897).
JANE AUSTEN, HER CONTEMPORARIES AND HERSELF: An Essay in Criticism, by W. H. Pollock (1899).

HEROINES OF FICTION, by W. D. Howells; New York (1901).

JANE AUSTEN: Her Homes and Her Friends, by C. Hill (1901).

CHARLOTTE BRONTË, GEORGE ELIOT, JANE AUSTEN: Studies in Their Works, by H. H. Bonnell; New York (1902).

JANE AUSTEN AND HER TIMES, by G. E. Mitton (1905).

JANE AUSTEN'S SAILOR BROTHERS, by J. H. and E. C. Hubback (1906).

INTRODUCTION TO JANE AUSTEN'S NOVELS, by W. L. Phelps (1906).

JANE AUSTEN AND HER COUNTRY-HOUSE COMEDY, by W. H. Helm (1909).

JANE AUSTEN: A Lecture, by A. C. Bradley; Oxford (1911)
—in the English Association's *Essays and Studies*, Vol. II. Reprinted in the author's *A Miscellany*, 1929.

JANE AUSTEN: A Criticism and an Appreciation, by P. H. Fitzgerald (1912).

JANE AUSTEN, by M. Sackville (1912).

JANE AUSTEN: Her Life and Letters, A Family Record, by W. Austen-Leigh and R. A. Austen-Leigh (1913)
—the authoritative biography. An indispensable record, based on family papers.

JANE AUSTEN, by F. W. Cornish (1913)
—in the 'English Men of Letters' series.

JANE AUSTEN, by K. and P. Rague; Paris (1914)
—in 'Les Grands Écrivains Étrangers' series.

JANE AUSTEN, Sa Vie et Son Oeuvre, 1775–1817, by L. Villard; Lyons (1915)
—translated in part by V. Lucas, as *Jane Austen: A French Appreciation*, with a new study of Jane Austen interpreted through *Love and Freindship* [*sic*] by R. B. Johnson, 1924.

'Jane Austen', by R. Farrer, *Quarterly Review*, CCXXVIII, 1917. (extracts in L)

JANE AUSTEN CENTENARY MEMORIAL: A record of the Ceremony of its Unveiling at Chawton, Hampshire, by Sir F. Pollock (1917).

PERSONAL ASPECTS OF JANE AUSTEN, by M. A. Austen-Leigh (1920).

JANE AUSTEN, by O. W. Firkins; New York (1920).

THE COMMON READER, by V. Woolf (1925)
—contains an appreciation of Jane Austen. (W)

JANE AUSTEN, by R. B. Johnson (1925).

THE NORTHANGER NOVELS: A Footnote to Jane Austen, by M. Sadleir; Oxford (1927)
—English Association Pamphlet No. 68.

THE ART OF JANE AUSTEN, by S. Alexander; Manchester (1928).

'Jane Austen: A depreciation', by H. W. Garrod, *Transactions of the Royal Society of Literature*, n.s. VIII, 1928.

JANE AUSTEN: A Survey, by C. L. Thomson (1929).

JANE AUSTEN: Her Life, Her Work, Her Family and Her Critics, by R. B. Johnson (1930).
INTRODUCTIONS TO JANE AUSTEN, by J. C. Bailey (1931).
A JANE AUSTEN DICTIONARY, by G. L. Apperson (1932).
JANE AUSTEN: Her Life and Art, by D. Rhydderch (1932).
JANE AUSTEN, by G. Rawlence (1934).
JANE AUSTEN, by Lord David Cecil; Cambridge (1935)
—the Leslie Stephen Lecture, 1935.
JANE AUSTEN, by E. Bowen (1936)
—in the 'English Novelists' series.
JANE AUSTEN: Study for a Portrait, by B. K. Seymour (1937).
JANE AUSTEN AND STEVENTON, by E. Austen-Leigh (1937).
JANE AUSTEN AND SOME CONTEMPORARIES, by M. Wilson (1938).
JANE AUSTEN: A Biography, by E. Jenkins (1938).
JANE AUSTEN IN BATH, by M. Ragg (1938).
JANE AUSTEN AND BATH, by E. Austen-Leigh (1939).
JANE AUSTEN AND HER ART, by M. M. Lascelles (1939).
—the first systematic study of Jane Austen's achievement. An indispensable introductory essay.
JANE AUSTEN AND LYME REGIS, by E. Austen-Leigh (1940).
'Regulated Hatred: An Aspect of the Work of Jane Austen', by D. W. Harding, *Scrutiny*, VIII, 1940. (W)
TALKING OF JANE AUSTEN, by S. Kaye-Smith and G. B. Stern (1943).
'The Controlling Hand: Jane Austen and *Pride and Prejudice*', by R. Brower, *Scrutiny*, XIII, 1945
—an outstanding essay. Reprinted in his *Fields of Light*, New York, 1951. (W)
JANE AUSTEN AND LYME REGIS, by R. A. Austen-Leigh (1946).
'Jane Austen's *Pride and Prejudice* in the eighteenth-century mode', by S. Kliger, *University of Toronto Quarterly*, XVI, 1947.
JANE AUSTEN: Facts and Problems, by R. W. Chapman; Oxford (1948)
—the Clark Lectures, Trinity College, Cambridge, 1948.
'Jane Austen, Karl Marx and the aristocratic dance', by D. Daiches, *American Scholar*, XVII, 1948.
'Technique as Discovery', by M. Schorer, *Hudson Review*, I, 1948.
JANE AUSTEN AND SOUTHAMPTON, by E. Austen-Leigh (1949).
PARSON AUSTEN'S DAUGHTER, by H. Ashton (1949).
'Fiction and the "matrix of analogy" ', by M. Schorer, *Kenyon Review*, XI, 1949.
JANE AUSTEN AND JANE AUSTEN'S HOUSE, by various writers; Winchester (1949).
JANE AUSTEN AND SOUTHAMPTON, by R. A. Austen-Leigh (1949).
MORE TALK OF JANE AUSTEN, by S. Kaye-Smith and G. B. Stern (1950).

JANE AUSTEN, by M. Kennedy (1950).
'*Emma*: A Dissenting opinion', by E. N. Hayes, *Nineteenth-Century Fiction*, IV, 1950. (L)
JANE AUSTEN, by Sylvia Townsend Warner (1951)
—a British Council pamphlet; revised eds., 1957, 1964.
MY AUNT JANE AUSTEN: A Memoir, by Caroline Austen, ed. R. W. Chapman; Alton, Hants (1952)
—from a MS dated March 1867.
JANE AUSTEN: Irony as Defense and Discovery, by M. Mudrick; Princeton (1952).
PRESENTING MISS JANE AUSTEN, by M. L. Becker (1953).
JANE AUSTEN'S NOVELS: A Study in Structure, by A. H. Wright (1953)
—second ed., 1972.
THE ENGLISH NOVEL: Form and Function, by D. Van Ghent; New York (1953)
—includes a chapter 'On *Pride and Prejudice*'.
AN INTRODUCTION TO THE ENGLISH NOVEL, by A. Kettle (1953)
—Vol. I includes an essay, 'Jane Austen: *Emma*'. (W, L)
'A Note on Jane Austen', by C. S. Lewis, *Essays in Criticism*, IV, 1954. (W)
'*Emma*: Character and Construction', by E. F. Shannon, *Publications of the Modern Language Association of America*, LXXI, 1956. (L)
'Pride unprejudiced', by M. Schorer, *Kenyon Review*, XVIII, 1956.
THE RISE OF THE NOVEL: Studies in Defoe, Richardson and Fielding, by Ian Watt (1957)
—the best account of Jane Austen's relationship to the eighteenth-century novel.
THE PELICAN GUIDE TO ENGLISH LITERATURE, Harmondsworth (1957)
—Vol. V: *From Blake to Byron*, Part II includes 'Jane Austen and Moral Judgement', by D. W. Harding.
LITERARY STUDIES, by Lord David Cecil (1957)
—contains notes on *Sense and Sensibility* and Jane Austen's scenery.
[Introduction to] Jane Austen's EMMA, by L. Trilling; New York (1957)
—in the Riverside edition. Essay entitled 'Emma and the Legend of Jane Austen'; reprinted in his *Beyond Culture*, 1965. (L)
'The Context of *Sense and Sensibility*', by A. D. McKillop, *Rice Institute Pamphlets*, XLIV, 1958.
FROM JANE AUSTEN TO JOSEPH CONRAD, ed. R. C. Rathburn and M. Steinmann; Minneapolis (1958)
—includes 'The Background of *Mansfield Park*', by C. Murrah, and 'Critical Realism in *Northanger Abbey*', by A. D. McKillop.
THE WATSONS: Jane Austen's Fragment Continued and Completed, by J. Coates (1958).

'Sense and Sensibility: An assessment', by C. Gillie, *Essays in Criticism*, IX, 1959.

'The Humiliation of Emma Woodhouse', by M. Schorer, *Literary Review*, II, 1959.

THE PARENTS IN JANE AUSTEN'S NOVELS, by J. Hubback; privately printed (1960).

JANE AUSTEN IN LONDON, by W. Watson (1960).

THE RHETORIC OF FICTION, by W. C. Booth (1961)
—includes an essay, 'Control of Distance in Jane Austen's *Emma*'. (L)

JANE AUSTEN: *Emma*, by F. W. Bradbrook (1961).

DISCUSSIONS OF JANE AUSTEN, by W. W. Heath; Boston (1961).

JANE AUSTEN'S NOVELS: The Fabric of Dialogue, by H. S. Babb; Columbus, Ohio (1962).

'The Education of Emma Woodhouse', by R. E. Hughes, *Nineteenth-Century Fiction*, XVI, 1962. (L)

'Jane Austen's *Emma*', by M. Bradbury, *Critical Quarterly*, IV, 1962. (L)

JANE AUSTEN, by S. Ebiike; Tokyo (1962).

THE NOVELS OF JANE AUSTEN, by R. Liddell (1963).

JANE AUSTEN: A Collection of Critical Essays, ed. I. Watt; Englewood Cliffs, N.J. (1963).

JANE AUSTEN'S LITERARY MANUSCRIPTS: A Study of the novelist's development through the surviving papers, by B. C. Southam (1964).

JANE AUSTEN: A Study in Fictional Conventions, by H. Ten Harmsel; The Hague (1964).

THE DREAM AND THE TASK, by G. Hough (1964)
—includes an essay, '*Emma* and "moral" criticism'. (L)

JANE AUSTEN: The Six Novels, by W. A. Craik (1965).

JANE AUSTEN: A Study of her Artistic Development, by A. W. Litz (1965).

JANE AUSTEN AND HER PREDECESSORS, by F. Bradbrook (1966).

JANE AUSTEN AND HER WORLD, by Ivor Brown (1966).

'Jane Austen and the Moralists', by G. Ryle, *Oxford Review*, I, 1966.

JANE AUSTEN, by N. Sherry (1966).

FICTION WITH A PURPOSE, by R. A. Colby (1967)
—ch. III, '*Mansfield Park*: Fanny Price and the Christian Heroine'.

A READING OF 'MANSFIELD PARK': An Essay in critical synthesis, by A. Fleishman; Baltimore (1967)
—the most detailed historical study.

'The Plot of *Emma*', by W. J. Harvey, *Essays in Criticism*, XVII, 1967. (L)

THE TRUTHTELLERS: Jane Austen, George Eliot, D. H. Lawrence, by L. Lerner (1967).

THE ERRAND OF FORM: An assay of Jane Austen's art, by Joseph Wiesenfarth (1967).

JANE AUSTEN: *Emma*: A Casebook, ed. D. Lodge (1968).
JANE AUSTEN'S ART OF ALLUSION, by K. L. Moler; Lincoln, Nebraska (1968).
CRITICAL ESSAYS ON JANE AUSTEN, ed. B. C. Southam (1968).
JANE AUSTEN: The Critical Heritage, ed. B. C. Southam (1968).
JANE AUSTEN AND HER WORLD, by M. Laski (1969).
JANE AUSTEN IN HER TIME, by W. A. Craik (1969).
[Introductions to] Jane Austen's SENSE AND SENSIBILITY and MANSFIELD PARK, by Tony Tanner (1969, 1970)
—in the Penguin English Library edition.
JANE AUSTEN, by Y. Gooneratne; Cambridge (1970).
'Narrative and Dialogue in Jane Austen', by G. Hough, *Critical Quarterly*, Autumn 1970.
CRITICS ON JANE AUSTEN, ed. J. O'Neill (1970).
JANE AUSTEN'S ENGLISH, by Kenneth C. Phillipps (1970).
THE ENGLISH NOVEL FROM DICKENS TO LAWRENCE, by Raymond Williams (1970)
—the Introduction discusses Jane Austen.
THE IMPROVEMENT OF THE ESTATE: a Study of Jane Austen's novels, by A. M. Duckworth; Baltimore (1971).
STYLES IN FICTIONAL STRUCTURE: The Art of Jane Austen, Charlotte Brontë, George Eliot, by Karl Kroeber; Princeton (1971).
'General Tilney's Hot-houses: Some recent Jane Austen studies and texts', by B. C. Southam, *Ariel*, October 1971.
THE DOUBLE LIFE OF JANE AUSTEN, by J. A. Hodge (1972).
THE LANGUAGE OF JANE AUSTEN, by Norman Page; Oxford (1972).
THE OSPREY GUIDE TO JANE AUSTEN, by J. M. D. Hardwick; Reading (1973).
THE NOVELS OF JANE AUSTEN: An Interpretation, by D. Mansell (1973).
A JANE AUSTEN COMPANION: A Critical survey and reference book, by F. B. Pinion (1973).
SOME WORDS OF JANE AUSTEN, by S. M. Tave; Chicago (1973).
WHO'S WHO IN JANE AUSTEN AND THE BRONTËS, by Glenda Leeming (1974).
A PREFACE TO JANE AUSTEN, by C. Gillie (1974).
JANE AUSTEN, by Douglas Bush (1975).
JANE AUSTEN AND THE WAR OF IDEAS, by Marilyn Butler; Oxford (1975).
JANE AUSTEN AND EDUCATION, by D. D. Devlin (1975).
JANE AUSTEN: Bicentenary Essays, ed. John Halperin; Cambridge (1975).
A READING OF JANE AUSTEN, by Barbara Hardy (1975).
JANE AUSTEN: Woman and Writer, by Joan Rees (1976).

WRITERS AND THEIR WORK

General Surveys:

THE DETECTIVE STORY IN BRITAIN: Julian Symons
THE ENGLISH BIBLE: Donald Coggan
ENGLISH VERSE EPIGRAM: G. Rostrevor Hamilton
ENGLISH HYMNS: Arthur Pollard
ENGLISH MARITIME WRITING: Hakluyt to Cook: Oliver Warner
THE ENGLISH SHORT STORY I: & II: T. O. Beachcroft
THE ENGLISH SONNET: P. Cruttwell
ENGLISH SERMONS: Arthur Pollard
ENGLISH TRANSLATORS AND TRANSLATIONS: J. M. Cohen
ENGLISH TRAVELLERS IN THE NEAR EAST: Robin Fedden
THREE WOMEN DIARISTS: M. Willy

Sixteenth Century and Earlier:

FRANCIS BACON: J. Max Patrick
BEAUMONT & FLETCHER: Ian Fletcher
CHAUCER: Nevill Coghill
GOWER & LYDGATE: Derek Pearsall
RICHARD HOOKER: Arthur Pollard
THOMAS KYD: Philip Edwards
LANGLAND: Nevill Coghill
LYLY & PEELE: G. K. Hunter
MALORY: M. C. Bradbrook
MARLOWE: Philip Henderson
SIR THOMAS MORE: E. E. Reynolds
RALEGH: Agnes Latham
SIDNEY: Kenneth Muir
SKELTON: Peter Green
SPENSER: Rosemary Freeman
THREE 14TH-CENTURY ENGLISH MYSTICS: Phyllis Hodgson
TWO SCOTS CHAUCERIANS: H. Harvey Wood
WYATT: Sergio Baldi

Seventeenth Century:

SIR THOMAS BROWNE: Peter Green
BUNYAN: Henri Talon
CAVALIER POETS: Robin Skelton
CONGREVE: Bonamy Dobrée
DONNE: F. Kermode
DRYDEN: Bonamy Dobrée
ENGLISH DIARISTS: Evelyn and Pepys: M. Will
FARQUHAR: A. J. Farmer
JOHN FORD: Clifford Leech
GEORGE HERBERT: T. S. Eliot
HERRICK: John Press
HOBBES: T. E. Jessop
BEN JONSON: J. B. Bamborough
LOCKE: Maurice Cranston
ANDREW MARVELL: John Press
MILTON: E. M. W. Tillyard
RESTORATION COURT POETS: V. de S. Pint
SHAKESPEARE: C. J. Sisson
CHRONICLES: Clifford Leech
EARLY COMEDIES: Derek Traver
LATER COMEDIES: G. K. Hunter
FINAL PLAYS: F. Kermode
HISTORIES: L. C. Knights
POEMS: F. T. Prince
PROBLEM PLAYS: Peter Ure
ROMAN PLAYS: T. J. B. Spencer
GREAT TRAGEDIES: Kenneth Mu
THREE METAPHYSICAL POETS: Margaret Wil
WEBSTER: Ian Scott-Kilvert
WYCHERLEY: P. F. Vernon

Eighteenth Century:

BERKELEY: T. E. Jessop
BLAKE: Kathleen Raine
BOSWELL: P. A. W. Collins
BURKE: T. E. Utley
BURNS: David Daiches
WM COLLINS: Oswald Doughty
COWPER: N. Nicholson
CRABBE: R. L. Brett
DEFOE: J. R. Sutherland
FIELDING: John Butt
GAY: Oliver Warner
GIBBON: C. V. Wedgwood
GOLDSMITH: A. Norman Jeffares
GRAY: R. W. Ketton-Cremer

HUME: Montgomery Belgion
SAMUEL JOHNSON: S. C. Roberts
POPE: Ian Jack
RICHARDSON: R. F. Brissenden
SHERIDAN: W. A. Darlington
CHRISTOPHER SMART: G. Grigson
SMOLLETT: Laurence Brander
STEELE, ADDISON: A. R. Humphreys
STERNE: D. W. Jefferson
SWIFT: J. Middleton Murry
SIR JOHN VANBRUGH: Bernard Harris
HORACE WALPOLE: Hugh Honour

Nineteenth Century:

MATTHEW ARNOLD: Kenneth Allott
JANE AUSTEN: S. Townsend Warner
BAGEHOT: N. St John-Stevas
THE BRONTËS: I & II: Winifred Gérin
BROWNING: John Bryson
E. B. BROWNING: Alethea Hayter
SAMUEL BUTLER: G. D. H. Cole
BYRON: I, II & III: Bernard Blackstone
CARLYLE: David Gascoyne
LEWIS CARROLL: Derek Hudson
COLERIDGE: Kathleen Raine
CREEVEY & GREVILLE: J. Richardson
DE QUINCEY: Hugh Sykes Davies
DICKENS: K. J. Fielding
EARLY NOVELS: T. Blount
LATER NOVELS: B. Hardy
DISRAELI: Paul Bloomfield
GEORGE ELIOT: Lettice Cooper
FERRIER & GALT: W. M. Parker
FITZGERALD: Joanna Richardson
ELIZABETH GASKELL: Miriam Allott
GISSING: A. C. Ward
THOMAS HARDY: R. A. Scott-James and C. Day Lewis
HAZLITT: J. B. Priestley
HOOD: Laurence Brander
G. M. HOPKINS: Geoffrey Grigson
T. H. HUXLEY: William Irvine
KEATS: Edmund Blunden
LAMB: Edmund Blunden
LANDOR: G. Rostrevor Hamilton
EDWARD LEAR: Joanna Richardson
MACAULAY: G. R. Potter
MEREDITH: Phyllis Bartlett
JOHN STUART MILL: M. Cranston
WILLIAM MORRIS: P. Henderson
NEWMAN: J. M. Cameron
PATER: Ian Fletcher
PEACOCK: J. I. M. Stewart
ROSSETTI: Oswald Doughty
CHRISTINA ROSSETTI: G. Battiscombe
RUSKIN: Peter Quennell
SIR WALTER SCOTT: Ian Jack
SHELLEY: G. M. Matthews
SOUTHEY: Geoffrey Carnall
LESLIE STEPHEN: Phyllis Grosskurth
R. L. STEVENSON: G. B. Stern
SWINBURNE: Ian Fletcher
TENNYSON: B. C. Southam
THACKERAY: Laurence Brander
FRANCIS THOMPSON: P. Butter
TROLLOPE: Hugh Sykes Davies
OSCAR WILDE: James Laver
WORDSWORTH: Helen Darbishire

Twentieth Century:

CHINUA ACHEBE: A. Ravenscroft
JOHN ARDEN: Glenda Leeming
W. H. AUDEN: Richard Hoggart
SAMUEL BECKETT: J-J. Mayoux
HILAIRE BELLOC: Renée Haynes
ARNOLD BENNETT: Kenneth Young
JOHN BETJEMAN: John Press
EDMUND BLUNDEN: Alec M. Hardie
ROBERT BRIDGES: J. Sparrow
ANTHONY BURGESS: Carol M. Dix
ROY CAMPBELL: David Wright
JOYCE CARY: Walter Allen
G. K. CHESTERTON: C. Hollis
WINSTON CHURCHILL: John Connell
R. G. COLLINGWOOD: E. W. F. Tomlin
I. COMPTON-BURNETT: R. Glynn Grylls
JOSEPH CONRAD: Oliver Warner
WALTER DE LA MARE: K. Hopkins
NORMAN DOUGLAS: Ian Greenlees
LAWRENCE DURRELL: G. S. Fraser
T. S. ELIOT: M. C. Bradbrook
T. S. ELIOT: The Making of 'The Waste Land': M. C. Bradbrook

FORD MADOX FORD: Kenneth Young
E. M. FORSTER: Rex Warner
CHRISTOPHER FRY: Derek Stanford
JOHN GALSWORTHY: R. H. Mottram
WILLIAM GOLDING: Stephen Medcalf
ROBERT GRAVES: M. Seymour-Smith
GRAHAM GREENE: Francis Wyndham
L. P. HARTLEY: Paul Bloomfield
A. E. HOUSMAN: Ian Scott-Kilvert
TED HUGHES: Keith Sagar
ALDOUS HUXLEY: Jocelyn Brooke
HENRY JAMES: Michael Swan
PAMELA HANSFORD JOHNSON: Isabel Quigly
JAMES JOYCE: J. I. M. Stewart
RUDYARD KIPLING: Bonamy Dobrée
PHILIP LARKIN: Alan Brownjohn
D. H. LAWRENCE: Kenneth Young
DORIS LESSING: Michael Thorpe
C. DAY LEWIS: Clifford Dyment
WYNDHAM LEWIS: E. W. F. Tomlin
COMPTON MACKENZIE: K. Young
LOUIS MACNEICE: John Press
KATHERINE MANSFIELD: Ian Gordon
JOHN MASEFIELD: L. A. G. Strong
SOMERSET MAUGHAM: J. Brophy
GEORGE MOORE: A. Norman Jeffares
J. MIDDLETON MURRY: Philip Mairet
R. K. NARAYAN: William Walsh
SEAN O'CASEY: W. A. Armstrong
GEORGE ORWELL: Tom Hopkinson
JOHN OSBORNE: Simon Trussler
WILFRED OWEN: Dominic Hibberd
HAROLD PINTER: John Russell Taylor
POETS OF 1939-45 WAR: R. N. Currey
ANTHONY POWELL: Bernard Bergonzi
POWYS BROTHERS: R. C. Churchill
J. B. PRIESTLEY: Ivor Brown
PROSE WRITERS OF WORLD WAR I: M. S. Greicus
HERBERT READ: Francis Berry
PETER SHAFFER: John Russell Taylor
BERNARD SHAW: A. C. Ward
EDITH SITWELL: John Lehmann
KENNETH SLESSOR: C. Semmler
C. P. SNOW: William Cooper
MURIEL SPARK: Patricia Stubbs
DAVID STOREY: John Russell Taylor
SYNGE & LADY GREGORY: E. Coxhead
DYLAN THOMAS: G. S. Fraser
G. M. TREVELYAN: J. H. Plumb
WAR POETS: 1914-18: E. Blunden
EVELYN WAUGH: Christopher Hollis
H. G. WELLS: Kenneth Young
ARNOLD WESKER: Glenda Leeming
PATRICK WHITE: R. F. Brissenden
ANGUS WILSON: K. W. Gransden
VIRGINIA WOOLF: B. Blackstone
W. B. YEATS: G. S. Fraser

EDWARD BOND: Simon Trussler
CHRISTOPHER ISHERWOOD: Francis King
IRIS MURDOCH: A. S. Byatt
V. S. NAIPAUL: Michael Thorpe
P. H. NEWBY: G. S. Fraser
TOM STOPPARD: C. W. E. Bigsby
SWIFT: A. Norman Jeffares

Sir Walter Scott

Scott began his literary career as an editor of the traditional songs and ballads of Scotland and as a writer of romances in verse. In 1814 he published *Waverley*, the first of the series of books which established him as one of the most celebrated writers in Europe. Dr Jack examines Scott's merits as a novelist and his carelessness about the technique of his art; he emphasizes the degree to which Scott's imagination was visual; he traces Scott's part in revolutionizing the status of the novel, and in making mankind more aware than ever before of historical perspectives.

Dr Jack was born in Edinburgh, where his father was a Writer to the Signet and his great-grandfather had been one of Scott's successors as a Clerk of the Court of Session. A Fellow of Pembroke College, Cambridge, and University Lecturer in English, he is the author of *Augustan Satire*, of *English Literature 1815–1832* (the volume of the *Oxford History of English Literature* dealing with the period of Byron, Shelley and Keats), and of *Keats and the Mirror of Art*. He wrote the booklet on Pope which is No. 48 in this Series.

38pp. frontis. bibliog. 140 x 215mm paperback.

The Brontës

In this study in two volumes of the Series subtitled *The Formative Years* and *The Creative Work*, Winifred Gérin shows how in their first period the Brontës produced a collective juvenilia of astounding precocity in which, not only for reasons of age, Charlotte and Branwell were the leading spirits and prolific penmen. This was followed by a lyric period, corresponding to adolescence, of joint poetic output, in which Emily alone excelled, but in which Anne revealed genuine elegiac qualities, and Charlotte emerged as a writer of romantic novelettes already notable for their penetration into motive and character. Finally, after all of them had gained some experience of life, came the great period of novel-writing. . . .

Winifred Gérin is a Fellow and Council Member of the Royal Society of Literature, and has written full-length biographies on each of the four Brontës.

2 vols, plates, bibliog. 140 x 215mm paperback.

PRAISE FOR THE NOVELS OF

BARBARA DAVIS

"Powerful, emotional, and illuminating."

—Diane Chamberlain, *USA Today* bestselling author of *Pretending to Dance*

"A beautifully crafted page-turner. . . . Part contemporary women's fiction, part historical novel, the plot moves seamlessly back and forth in time to unlock family secrets that bind four generations of women. . . . This novel has it all."

—Barbara Claypole White, award-winning author of *The Perfect Son*

"Everything I love in a novel . . . elegant and haunting."

—Erika Marks, author of *The Last Treasure*

"A book about love and loss and finding your way forward. I could not read it fast enough!" —Anita Hughes, author of *Island in the Sea*

"One of the best stories out there, and Davis is genuinely proving herself to be one of the strongest new voices of epic romance."

—*RT Book Reviews* (4½ stars)

"Davis has a gift for developing flawed characters and their emotionally wrenching dilemmas . . . a very satisfying tale."

—Historical Novel Society

OTHER BOOKS BY BARBARA DAVIS

The Secrets She Carried
The Wishing Tide
Summer at Hideaway Key

Love, Alice

BARBARA DAVIS

BERKLEY
NEW YORK

BERKLEY
An imprint of Penguin Random House LLC
375 Hudson Street, New York, New York 10014

Library of Congress Cataloging-in-Publication Data

Names: Davis, Barbara, 1961– author.
Title: Love, Alice/Barbara Davis.
Description: First edition. | New York: Berkley Books, 2016.
Identifiers: LCCN 2016019600 (print) | LCCN 2016024004 (ebook) | ISBN 9780451474810 (paperback) | ISBN 9780698191990 (ebook)
Subjects: | BISAC: FICTION/Contemporary Women. | FICTION/Family Life. | FICTION/Historical.
Classification: LCC PS3604.A95554 L68 2016 (print) | LCC PS3604.A95554 (ebook) | DDC 813/.6—dc23
LC record available at https://lccn.loc.gov/2016019600

First Edition: December 2016

Printed in the United States of America
1 3 5 7 9 10 8 6 4 2

Cover art: flowers © Ola-la/Shutterstock Images; envelope © Photosiber/Shutterstock Images
Cover design by Daniela Medina
Book design by Kristin del Rosario

This book is dedicated to Philomenas everywhere,
the faceless, voiceless young women
of the Magdalene laundries
and similar institutions who were branded, shamed,
and made to suffer the unthinkable,
and who continue the fight to be seen and heard.

Acknowledgments

I'm sure I'm not alone in saying that each of my books is a labor of love, but I promise you it's absolutely true. Like children, each novel I write is unique and extraordinarily personal, as is the process of bringing them into the world. And that's why there's always a long list of people to thank at the end of each "book pregnancy"—because no book is ever truly written alone.

And so I'll start by thanking the wonderful folks at Penguin, from my editor, Jennifer Fisher, who nudged me to get just a little more from my characters, and in doing so helped make *Love, Alice* the book I wanted it to be, to the design team and art department, who continue to astound me with their stunning covers. You guys just keep outdoing yourselves.

I also think it's safe to say that none of this would be possible without my amazing agent, Nalini Akolekar of Spencerhill Literary Agency, who is never too busy to field a question, share her wisdom, or go to bat for her writers. I'm both lucky and proud to be a member of your fan club.

To the love of my life, and my soon to be hubby, Tom Kelley, who kept us fed and clothed during deadlines and assorted freak-outs, what can I say? Without you I'd be in weeds, *mon petite fromage*. (It's code—don't worry; he gets it.)

To friend and fellow writer Barbara Claypole White, who continues to be both an inspiration and a sounding board on this crazy journey called writing—at the risk of sounding corny, thank heavens I had you to light the way.

To Diane Chamberlain, Kim Boykin, Karen White, Cynthia Lott, Erika Marks, Susan Crandall, Normandie Ward Fisher, and Anita Hughes, thank you for your support and your wonderfully inspiring work. Your kindness and generosity have meant more than you know.

To my original critique partners, Matt King, Lisa Cameron, and Doug Simpson, who were with me in the beginning and continue to be the voices in my head no matter how many miles separate us. I miss you guys something terrible, and can't wait for the day we can get the band back together.

And, of course, I have to thank independently owned bookstores everywhere who support emerging authors with events, publicity, and precious, precious shelf space. I'd also like to give a special shout-out to Flyleaf Books in Chapel Hill, North Carolina, who gave me my first "home" as a debut author; Page After Page in Elizabeth City, North Carolina, who make me feel like family; FoxTale Book Shoppe in Woodstock, Georgia, who always welcome me with open arms; and finally to Water Street Bookstore in Exeter, New Hampshire, who gave me a home when I moved to New England last year. To put it mildly, you guys rock!

And, last but not least, I'd be remiss if I didn't offer heartfelt thanks to the victims and survivors of Magdalene laundries and similar institutions around the world, who over the years have bravely shared their stories, and continue their fight to be seen and heard. Your courage and strength are what inspired me to tell Alice Tandy's story.

Love, Alice

PROLOGUE

BLACKHURST ASYLUM FOR UNWED MOTHERS
CORNWALL, ENGLAND
JANUARY 6, 1962

The place smells of sickness and damp—of tears and misery and shame.

Alice places a hand on her belly as the familiar flutter comes again, soft beatings like an angel's wings against her insides. Her baby. Her angel. The wave of sickness comes next, as it always does after the flutterings, a clammy surge of heat and nausea that threatens to buckle her knees. She swallows it down, scrubs the sudden moistness from her palms, and turns one last time to glance over her shoulder, praying Mam has changed her mind about leaving her in this terrible place, with its cold walls and colder faces.

She hasn't.

"This way, girl," comes a disembodied voice from the nameless black-clad nun in front of her. "There's more here than just you to tend, so be quick."

Tears threaten again, scorching lids already raw with days of crying, of begging, of pleading. Alice blinks them away, then drags a hand over her eyes for good measure. She has found no mercy at home, and she'll find none here, so what good are her tears? She won't cry again. Not for Mam, or for Sennen Cove, either, with its sweeping coast and Cornish blue sea, or even for Johnny, who is long past tears now, lost somewhere at the bottom of the sea he loved so well. And tears aren't good for the baby. Besides, her heart is too torn to think of Johnny just now, too hollowed out by the terrible words her mother has flung at her. Words meant to judge and shame. Words Alice can never forget—never forgive.

The nameless sister is moving away now. Alice has no choice but to scurry after her. The nun's feet are invisible beneath the folds of her black habit, strangely silent on the uneven stone floor. Finally, they halt before a heavy gray door with a small pane of glass near the top.

The door is pushed open and the nun stands aside, waiting, chilly and stiff jawed, for Alice to enter. Alice steps forward, eyeing the long room, with its tall drafty windows and bare iron cots. And then there's a hand on her back and a rough shove that nearly sends her toppling.

"This is where they've put you, and we'll have no trouble. There's uniforms in the trunk there at the foot of the cot. Change out of your clothes and leave them on the bed to be collected. You'll get them back after."

After.

Alice bristles at the word, left to dangle in the air with all its ominous meanings. After she has done her penance for her swollen belly. After she has been delivered of her *mistake*, as the Sisters of Mercy call the babies born at Blackhurst. After her child has been taken from her and handed over to strangers.

There is a ceaseless drumming at the windows, a dull gray rain blowing in off the sea, lashing at the loose panes. Alice registers the cold then, slicing through her as she moves deeper into the room, the kind that finds its way through every patched place and seam, clinging to skin and curling damply into bone, taking root in a place—or in a soul. Instinctively, her arms curl around the small bulge of her belly, quiet now, as if the child, too, is holding its breath.

There are a handful of girls in the room, sad-eyed creatures of every age and color with bellies of every shape and size, all dressed in identical brown pinnies and white cotton blouses. They are as plain as little field sparrows, stripped of the vanity that has led them to their downfall, and to Blackhurst. None look up at her as she enters.

"You'll be given new uniforms as need arises," comes the gruff voice again, jolting Alice from her staring. The nun's gaze slides with pointed disdain to Alice's belly. "You've a while yet, by the look of things. You're up at dawn for prayers, then breakfast, then work. Tomorrow you'll learn where they've put you—the laundry, maybe, or the kitchens, depending on what they need. And you'll do as you're told. No exceptions and no nonsense, or you'll be sternly dealt with. You're not here to make friends, but to repent of your sins and earn your keep while doing so. Do you understand me, girl?"

Alice doesn't answer. She wants to say that she's committed no sin, except to love a boy who loved her in return, a boy who wanted to marry her when he had saved up a few pounds. But she can't form the words. Instead, her eyes are fastened to the ponderous ring of keys at the nun's waist. So many keys. So many doors. Surely one of them—

The nun's eyes narrow, a merciless gray stare that seems to cut straight to Alice's backbone. "Don't go getting any ideas, you hear? We're careful with the doors at night, though there's been more than one girl who's ended up smashed to pieces after slipping out and losing her way in the dark. It's a straight drop off those cliffs, with nothing but rock and sea below, so you'd best take care."

Alice makes no reply as the nun turns away, slipping back out into the corridor with her silent feet and jangling keys. For a while there is only the sound of the rain and the sudden awareness that she is alone in this terrible place. The sparrows don't count. They're alone, too. All the girls at Blackhurst are alone. Finally, she lets herself think of Johnny as she cradles the little mound of her belly with both hands. A boy—she's almost certain—with brown curls and eyes the color of the sea. And they were going to take him. How would she ever bear it?

Without any awareness of her legs carrying her, she is at one of the windows, her breath fogging the rain-spattered glass. She took little notice of the landscape as Mam's old Hemsby coughed its way up the wooded drive, then passed through Blackhurst's heavy iron gates, but she takes notice now and sees it's rocky and spare where the woods peter out, desolate. And in the distance, the cliffs the nun talked about—or at least the place where they fall away—and she can't help wondering if maybe a few of the girls who'd smashed themselves to bits had known exactly where they were going when they slipped out at night.

ONE

MAGNOLIA GROVE CEMETERY
CHARLESTON, SOUTH CAROLINA
SEPTEMBER 27, 2005

Saturday's roses were already beginning to fade.

She'd known better when she bought them—too delicate for the Carolina sun, even in late September—but she'd wanted something special. They would have been celebrating their one-year anniversary today if William hadn't chosen to end his life just two weeks before they were set to walk down the aisle.

His father's bourbon and his mother's sleeping pills—that's how he'd done it. Nice and neat. No note of explanation, no clue of any kind as to why he'd chosen death over the life they'd planned together. Just . . . gone. And now, fifty-two withered bouquets later, Dovie Larkin still had no idea what had happened. Or why.

She stared at William's headstone, nestled among the other Prescott dead, carefully tended by Magnolia Grove's crew of expert groundskeepers. He would have detested the cold granite slab his parents had selected, declaring it altogether lacking in originality—an affront to his artistic tastes. But then, he hadn't bothered to leave instructions about his final arrangements. He hadn't left anything—except her.

With concerted effort, Dovie shifted her attention to her surroundings, canopy oaks and shade-dappled lawns stretching as far as the eye could see, burbling fountains, granite benches, and the curved mulch path that bordered it all. But for the neat rows of headstones, one could almost mistake Magnolia Grove for a park.

Almost.

Fishing a chicken salad sandwich and a small bag of grapes from her tote, she proceeded to spread her little picnic out on the bench beside her, pretending not to notice the scandalized double take of a woman strolling past with a fistful of cellophane-wrapped daisies.

She should be used to it by now, the scowls and pinched expressions of strangers silently scolding her for being disrespectful. She'd heard the whispers, too—words like *morbid* and *obsession*—from family and coworkers who couldn't understand why she had taken to eating her lunch every day on a cemetery bench, or why her only friend of late seemed to be Josiah Ramsey, Magnolia Grove's eighty-year-old groundskeeper.

She didn't blame them for not understanding. How could they? Only someone who'd gotten the call she had could know what it was like to lie awake, night after night, replaying a thousand conversations in your head, looking for the thing, the one thing, you'd somehow missed—the thing that might have kept your world from crashing down around your ears.

Grief was a messy thing. It was inconvenient and intrusive, not quite contagious but the next thing to it. It made people uncomfortable, and thoughtless in ways they never intended. They didn't know what to say, and so they invariably said the wrong thing. She didn't blame them. Only someone who'd suffered such a loss could understand that there are simply no words, no platitudes or pep talks, to heal the broken place left when someone you love is suddenly and explicably gone.

Which was probably why she spent her life dodging awkward but well-meaning questions. Was she *really* okay? Should she maybe think about talking to someone? A grief counselor, a priest? It had been a year, after all. She shuddered to think about what they'd say if they knew her wedding dress—the one she'd never worn—was still hanging in her closet.

Perhaps that was why she preferred her own company. She had simply reached the point where she could no longer bear the pitying looks and clumsy platitudes. Not that she saw much of the pearls-and-twin-set crowd of late. They were all married now, starting families and doing good works, holding bake sales, or rummage sales, or dinner parties to impress their husbands' bosses. Even now the thought made Dovie squirm. And from somewhere deep down in places she didn't care to examine came the guilty whisper that she had somehow dodged a bullet.

At the edge of the path, a flicker of movement caught her eye. She turned, happy to see Josiah heading in her direction. His limp was more pronounced today. His hip must be acting up. He talked about retiring, but Dovie knew better. He'd been working at Magnolia Grove since he was old enough to hold a job, back before a black man could safely walk down King Street after dark. It was all he knew. And all he cared about since losing his wife.

"Afternoon, Little Miss," he said, tipping the brim of his straw Panama.

Little Miss. It was hardly a proper nickname for a thirty-six-year-old woman, and certainly not for one who stood five-ten in her bare feet. But the truth was she had grown rather fond of it. Patting the bench beside her, she invited him to sit. They'd been eating lunch together for months now, and he still wouldn't sit until invited.

"Chicken salad today," she told him before he could ask. "No salt, like the doctor said. And grapes for dessert. Healthy."

Josiah pulled a face but took the proffered half sandwich.

"Making chess pie this weekend," he grumbled around the first bite. "Essie's recipe."

Dovie cocked a disapproving eye. "And what would your doctor say about that?"

Josiah looked sullen as he scrubbed his knuckles along his jaw. "Don't much care, really. Way I see it, an eighty-year-old man's earned the right to eat what he pleases."

Dovie hid her smile as she tucked into her sandwich. He had a point. "So, do I get to taste this pie, or did you tell me that just to tease me?"

"I'll bring you a piece Monday. And no lectures, hear? You just eat it."

She grunted but made no promises as she passed Josiah the bag of grapes. It was part of their patter, their routine. She nagged. He grumbled.

"You all right?" he asked gruffly.

"Why wouldn't I be?"

"Thought you might be having a little trouble, what with the date and all."

Dovie looked away, pretending to watch a pair of mockingbirds squabble over the crust of bread she had tossed their way. Of course he remembered. Eighty or not, there wasn't much Josiah Ramsey forgot when it came to his charges—the Prescotts, Tates, Lowrys, and Gosnells—all etched into his memory as sure as their dates were etched into their headstones.

"I'm all right," she said, finally. "Not fine, but all right. It's sweet of you to ask, though." She reached for a handful of grapes, popping one into her mouth. "Can I ask you a question?"

He nodded.

"Why is it, in all the time you've known me, from the first time you saw me sitting here with my lunch, you've never once given me one of those looks?"

"Which look is that?"

He was being kind now, feigning ignorance, but they both knew what she was talking about. "You know the look I mean. The one that says there must be something wrong with a woman who hangs out in a cemetery every day, waiting for some bolt from the blue to come along and explain why her fiancé committed suicide."

Josiah dragged a faded red bandanna from his back pocket and took his time mopping his brow. When he finally spoke, his voice had taken on the husky tenor he used when he was about to impart one of his patented bits of wisdom.

"Little Miss, I've seen a whole lot of grieving in my time. Yes, sir, a whole lot of grieving. And in all that time it never occurred to me to make it my business how folks choose to go about it. Folks hurt, and they gonna hurt for as long as they need to. And that's just the way that goes."

Dovie blinked against the hot sting of tears, always too near these days, and gave Josiah's free hand a squeeze. He wasn't comfortable with touching, she knew, but it was that or start to cry, and she still had half a day of work ahead of her. She never had been any good at patching up drippy eye makeup.

"Thank you for that."

Josiah extricated his hand, giving hers a quick pat before returning to the safety of his grapes. "You'll be ready one day, you'll see. Until then, I guess I'll just have to eat your sandwiches and put up with your fussing."

Dovie tried to look severe. "What makes you think I'm ever going to stop fussing at you?"

Groaning, he rolled his eyes heavenward. "Lord, give me strength. It's like having my Essie back. Nothin' sacred, not even my chess pie.

Don't you have somewhere to be, some kind of important new job to get back to, instead of sitting here pestering a broke-down old man?"

It was true. She did have somewhere to be. She glanced at her watch, then shot to her feet. *Damn it. Not again.* If she caught all the lights she might make it back before anyone noticed.

Get it together, Dovie.

Dovie's hopes for a stealthy reentry were dashed when she hit the front walk of the Charleston Museum of Cultural Arts and saw Jack Livingston lounging against one of pillars, puffing on a Marlboro Light. He flicked the cigarette into the azaleas, glanced at his watch.

"I'm sorry, Jack. I lost track of time. I . . ." She let the rest dangle. He'd heard it before. Twice this week, as a matter of fact.

He said nothing, but his lips thinned as he reached for the door and waited for her to walk through ahead of him. Dovie held her breath as they stepped into the cool, quiet lobby, expecting to be summoned into his office, or at the very least, followed to hers. Instead, he rounded on her, his cheeks an even deeper shade of pink than usual.

"I should think today of all days, you could have managed to get back on time."

Today of all days?

Dovie combed through a series of possible excuses but came up blank. Hardly a surprise, since she had yet to ascertain what she was apologizing for.

"Dovie." He sighed the word, like a parent weary of repeating himself. "Please tell me you haven't forgotten you had a one o'clock. The Tates have just forked over two million dollars to the museum. I'm sure they'd like to think their generosity buys them the consideration of at least your being punctual."

Dovie's cheeks flamed. Gemma Tate—one o'clock. She remembered penciling the appointment into her planner last week, but had forgotten it was today. Maybe because she hadn't bothered opening her planner this morning to check her appointments. "Oh God . . . I thought that was tomorrow."

"No. It's today," Jack said tightly. "And the reason I know that is there's someone sitting in your office right now—waiting. So you might want to pull yourself together and try looking like the professional I know is in there somewhere."

Dovie smoothed her hair and squared her shoulders, but inside she felt sick. She hated the look on Jack's face, disappointment mingled with the growing suspicion that he'd made a mistake in going to bat for her when the curator position opened up last year.

Get it together, Dovie. If not for your sake, for Jack's.

She was about to scurry to her office to salvage what she could of her meeting with Gemma Tate when Jack laid a hand on her arm. The look of exasperation was gone, replaced with a paternal concern that brought a grinding lump to her throat. *Don't,* she wanted to say. *Please don't say something kind. If you do, I'll fall apart.* She steeled herself for whatever was coming.

"Dovie, now isn't the time to talk about this, but it does have to be said. You've had a lot on your plate, losing your father, and then that awful business with William. I know you've been trying, but I wonder if stepping back might not be a bad idea, just until you get your bearings again. There will always be a place for you here, but right now you seem to be flailing a bit. Why don't you give it some thought?"

Dovie gave him a stiff nod. There would always be a place for her at the museum, just not the one she had broken her neck for three years to get. That's what he was saying. "Are you firing me?"

Jack looked away. "Of course not. But I'd be lying if I said I wasn't worried about you."

"Worried about me? Or about my performance?"

"Both, actually. I fought for you because I believed you were the right person for the job, but that was before William's accident. Today is just one more—"

"It wasn't an accident," Dovie blurted before she could stop herself. Why did people insist on calling it something it wasn't? William hadn't *accidentally* killed himself. In fact, he'd been very deliberate about it, going to great lengths to make sure he wouldn't be found until it was too late.

Jack was staring at her. "I beg your pardon?"

"William's suicide. You called it an accident. It wasn't."

"Does it matter what I call it? My point is, you're not past it, and I need someone who can handle this project—and the Tates. Right now I'm not sure that person is you."

Dovie let the words sink in, wondering just how long he'd been holding them back. "You said you're not firing me. Are you demoting me?"

"I'm not doing either. I'm just saying I need you dialed in. I'm on your side, and always have been. You know that. But the board is breathing down my neck about this new wing, and I need your head on straight. If it isn't, I need you to tell me—before you go into that meeting."

"My head is fine, Jack. Really. I'll go smooth things over with Mrs. Tate, and we'll start making plans for the fund-raiser. It's going to be great. You'll see."

Jack nodded, a single but firm bob of the head. "Go."

Relieved to have at least calmed him down, Dovie headed down the hall. She was halfway to her office, still trying to salvage the remnants of this morning's ponytail, when she heard Jack hiss something at her from the other end of the hall. She turned, motioning that she hadn't heard. He seemed to vacillate a moment, as if weighing whether to bother again. Finally, he checked his watch and, with a shake of his head, waved her on. Whatever it was must not have been important.

Squaring her shoulders, she pasted on what she hoped was her best groveling smile and opened the door to her office, prepared to meet the woman who, with a stroke of her pen, had made the museum's new art education wing possible.

"Mrs. Tate," she said, both breathless and contrite as she closed the door behind her. "Please accept my sincerest apology—"

The words dangled as Dovie registered her mistake. The person waiting for her wasn't Gemma Tate, but her son, Austin, newly crowned head of Tate Development, and keeper of the family purse strings since his father's death six months ago.

Damn.

Dovie struggled to get her bearings, not sure whether to be relieved or piqued that her visitor had yet to acknowledge her. Instead, he stood with his back to her, studying the sculpture displayed on a smoked glass pedestal behind her desk—a bust William had done of her just after they met. Even now, looking at it left her feeling exposed, the come-hither tilt of the head, the long, sinuous line of neck and collarbone, the barest suggestion of breasts and the shadowed valley between.

She'd been blown away the first time she saw it, by its beauty and subtle sensuality, but also by the realization that William saw her that way. She had teased him at first, insisting he must have modeled it after some woman from his past. He had laughed at that, vowing that before Dovie there had been no other women. It was nonsense, of course. Men like William—blond, blue eyed, and boyishly charming, not to mention well pedigreed—would always have women lined up.

"I'd say he's captured you perfectly."

Dovie dragged her eyes from the sculpture, forcing herself to focus on the man in front of her. He was tall, six-three or six-four, and even better-looking than he appeared in the social pages of the *Post and Courier*: dark hair combed back from a face that was all suntan, square jaw, and high cheekbones. And was he kidding with that Cary Grant cleft in his chin?

"It was a *he*, wasn't it?"

Dovie blinked at him, trying to wrap her brain around the question. "I'm sorry. Yes, it was. My fiancé, actually."

"That explains it," he said, his smile bordering on seductive as he trailed a finger along the slender clay neck, lingering finally, maddeningly, at the deeply hollowed throat. "A man would have to know his way around that neck pretty well to do it this kind of justice."

Dovie's hand went to her throat—to the place he had touched, but not. A clever bit of sleight of hand, a caress that involved no touching at all, and yet the warmth of that nontouch felt very real—as he had no doubt intended. It would seem Austin Tate was every bit the ladies' man rumor made him out to be. Not that she had ever doubted it. He was known for the company he kept, blondes mostly, with a closet full of skinny heels and plastic surgeons on speed dial. So why was he wasting his time trying to get under her skin?

"He's talented," Austin said, holding her gaze. "And lucky."

"He died last year."

She had said it for shock value, to shame him out of whatever game he was playing. It must have worked. His smile faltered, and for an instant his face softened. "I'm sorry. I didn't . . . I'm sorry, really."

"Thank you," Dovie said, once again off balance.

Had she only imagined the change that seemed to come over him? The fleeting sense that for a moment someone else had been looking at her through those mossy green eyes? Whatever it was—if it had been there at all—was gone now, hidden behind a facade clearly designed to give nothing away.

"I'm Dovie Larkin," she said, extending a hand. She needed to get control of this meeting, to get things back on a professional footing and keep them there. "I'm the museum's curator. I was expecting your mother, I believe?"

Austin took her hand. Cool, dry, brief—a man in charge of his surroundings, even if those surroundings belonged to her. As if to thrust the point home, he eased himself into the nearest chair, which happened to be the one behind her desk.

"My mother hasn't been well since my father's death. She asked me to take the meeting in her place, but I'm a little pressed for time. I'd like to get started if that's all right with you."

Dovie stared at him. This wasn't going to work. She had a fund-raiser to plan, and her job to save, apparently. And here she stood, on the wrong side of her desk, engaged in some testosterone-fueled mind game with a man she'd be willing to bet didn't give a damn about art.

"Mr. Tate, why don't we—"

"Austin, please."

"Austin . . . why don't we just reschedule when your mother's feeling better? I'm sure you're much too busy, and not at all interested in planning a gala."

He shot her a crooked smile. "I'm never too busy for a party."

So I've heard.

Dovie took a deep breath and managed to swallow the retort. "I'm not sure we're talking about the same kind of party, Mr. . . . Austin. This is a black-tie fund-raiser, which entails very careful planning. The kind your mother is probably better suited to handle."

Austin leaned forward, steepling his fingers beneath his chin. "You thought I was talking about a kegger?"

"No, of course not. It's just that there's an enormous amount of work involved in these things—the venue to choose, a menu to plan, entertainment to arrange—all of which require a hefty time commitment. I assume you'll be too busy with business to spare that kind of time. I'm sorry, by the way—about your father passing, I mean. I should have said so earlier."

He sat back in his chair, his expression darkening into something Dovie couldn't label but didn't like the look of. "Thank you. But the business runs itself. My father made sure of that."

Dovie looked down at her shoes, not sure how to respond. She'd hit a nerve of some kind. Or maybe she had only imagined the sudden edge in his voice. Who could say with this man? After a moment he seemed to shake off whatever it was, ready to return to the business at hand.

"I'll tell you what, Miss . . . Larkin, is it? Why don't you just go over whatever it was you'd planned to discuss with my mother, and let me decide if I'm in over my head, hmm?"

Dovie nodded coolly. If he was going to pretend to be interested in his mother's pet charities, he deserved the full show. "I'll need to get to my files."

"Fine."

"They're in my desk."

Dovie waited for the words to sink in, then realized they already had, just without the desired effect. She had hoped he'd take the hint and vacate her chair. Instead, he wheeled back a few feet, making room for her to step around and retrieve the necessary paperwork.

He can't be serious.

She tried to ignore his proximity, the mingled scents of soap and cologne that lingered about him as she opened and closed drawers, gathering a stack of legal pads and neatly labeled folders. She could feel his eyes, studying her so intensely that she was tempted to turn and ask if there was something she could help him with. Or better yet, tell him to get his entitled ass out of her chair, although she was pretty sure Jack would tell her two million dollars entitled him to sit where he damn well pleased.

With the requisite materials rounded up, Dovie settled for one of the conference chairs, relieved to at least have the desk between them again.

"The first thing we'll need to settle on is a date, which will depend on our choice of venue. There are three possibilities, at this point." She paused, laying out several brochures for him to look at. "Unless, of course, there are other options you'd like us to consider? We'll need facilities for about two hundred, I should think. CPAC—Charleston Performing Arts Center—is my personal pick. There's plenty of parking, and the Silver Room has great acoustics, not to mention that beautiful ceiling."

She sat very still, waiting for some sort of response. Instead, she saw that his attention had wandered back to William's sculpture.

Fabulous. Not only passive-aggressive, but the attention span of a gnat.

Exasperated, she sat back, folded her hands, and waited for him to notice she'd stopped talking. Eventually, he did.

"I'm sorry. You said two hundred?"

Dovie bit her lip, keeping her face bland. "I did. I also said I thought the Performing Arts Center would work well for our needs. Unless you or Mrs. Tate has other venues you'd like me to check out?"

"No. I'm sure that will be fine. My mother—"

He broke off when his cell jangled. Mouthing an apology, he fished the thing from his shirt pocket and took the call. Dovie was still trying to decide if she should remain where she was or give him some privacy when he held up a hand, motioning her to stay put.

"Fine. Where are you now?" he asked whoever was on the other end. "All right. Stay there. I'll meet you at the clubhouse in half an hour."

He was on his feet the minute he ended the call. "I'm sorry, but something's come up and I'm going to have to cut this short and reschedule. Or, if you'd like, we can do it over dinner. Cypress has a great menu, and the wine list is incredible. Or McCrady's is good."

Dovie stared at him, astonished. He had just dumped out of a meeting for an *emergency* at his *club*. Now he was asking her to dinner?

"Thank you, no," she said, getting to her feet. "I can't . . . I mean, I don't . . . I have very strict rules about keeping my business and personal interests separate."

Something about her response must have amused him, because

the smirk was back. "Who said anything about getting personal? You can bring your brochures if that makes you feel safer. I just thought a meal might make the business more pleasant, but suit yourself. I'll have someone call to reschedule."

Dovie drifted toward the door, ready for the meeting to be over. "It was nice to meet you," she managed as she ushered him out into the hall. "I'll wait to hear from you."

When he was gone, she sagged into her chair, eyes straying to the sculpture in the corner, to the slight hollow where Austin Tate's fingers had lingered moments before. With any luck, his mother would soon be on the mend and today's meeting would be her first and last encounter with the head of Tate Development.

two

Austin yanked his tie loose as he headed for the parking lot. *I have very strict rules about keeping my business and personal interests separate.* Yeah, well, so did he. All he'd said was dinner—a business dinner. How in God's name had she made the leap to a date?

But he already knew the answer to that. She made the leap because he'd wanted her to, because he'd goaded her into it. He wasn't proud of it, but he knew himself well enough to know it was true. From the moment she walked into her office, fifteen minutes late and clearly flustered, he hadn't been able to help himself. He had gone out of his way to rattle her. And it was clear that he had. Perhaps more than even he had intended.

She'd looked so damn vulnerable, all harried and flushed in her crisp black suit and wilted blouse, sprigs of blond hair springing from her samurai-tight ponytail. She had been trying so hard to keep it together, though he'd be willing to bet his life she was two steps from unraveling. He knew that look. Knew it well, in fact.

Austin shook off the uncomfortable thoughts as he slid behind the wheel. He was still bristling as he jabbed the key into the ignition and gave it a savage crank. Where the hell was all this coming from anyway? The woman was buttoned up tighter than a missionary's wife, nothing like the women he usually dated—if you could call what he did dating. The women he saw socially weren't looking for complications; they just wanted to have a little fun, champagne and dinner at the club, followed by the inevitable drive back to his place. And that was how he liked it. There was less chance of wrecking someone's life if you limited your dates to women even more superficial than yourself. They were safe, but more to the point, they were the kind of women he deserved.

Dovie Larkin was another animal altogether. She'd been anything but happy to find him waiting in her office. Perhaps she hadn't heard what an important guy he was now that his father was gone. Head of Tate Development and overseer of the family fortune, portfolio, and real estate holdings. Yes, sir, he was a big freaking deal. Only those things didn't impress someone like Ms. Larkin, or him, either, for that matter. They did at least have that in common. God knows, she wasn't his type, in her tailored black suit and discreet diamond studs. No flash, just substance.

Except for the shoes.

Four inches at least, hiding beneath those neatly tailored slacks. A glimpse of patent leather, a shiny silver buckle—and hot pink polish peeking out at the toes. Unexpected to be sure, but then, they weren't for him—or any man. Of that much, he was certain. She wore them for herself, a guilty pleasure kept carefully out of sight, like a box of truffles secreted away in a bottom desk drawer.

Perhaps Dovie Larkin wasn't as buttoned up as she pretended to be. Part of him thought it might be fun to find out. And he could do with a change. Candice was starting to wear out her welcome, getting a bit too comfortable on his arm. Yes, Ms. Larkin might be just the kind of change he'd been looking for. She'd be a challenge, though; she didn't like him much. Not that he held that against her. He didn't like himself much, either.

Goosing the BMW out of the lot, he turned up South Street, forcing himself to focus on the call he'd just received from Ted Atkinson. He and Ted had started the Outlook Club two years ago to provide a place for kids who were struggling with home and family issues. It was by far the most rewarding thing he'd ever done, but there were moments when he seriously wondered what he'd been thinking—like now. Tyler Burns had run again, and his father was burning up the phone lines looking for his son. But Austin already knew where they'd find Tyler: the marina. The kid had fallen in love with sailing from the first time Austin took him out, something his father would know if he wasn't so busy trotting his new trophy wife all over Charleston.

Finding Tyler wasn't the problem. It was what to say when he *did.* He knew all too well what it was like to have a father who forgot you were there most of the time. How was he supposed to look a thirteen-year-old kid in the eye and tell him everything was going to work out?

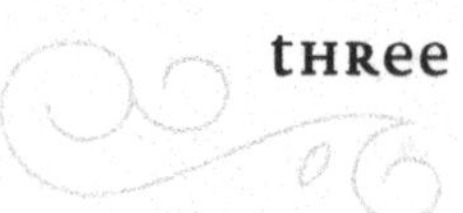

three

As always, Rowena Larkin was flawless, her silver-blond hair swept into a tasteful chignon, her deep coral suit carefully chosen for the Society of Southern Sisters annual charity luncheon. Dovie watched as her mother sipped her third vodka gimlet, then set her glass back down with exaggerated deliberateness.

She was drinking more and more these days, starting earlier in the day, conveniently unaware of how many she'd put away, since she just kept topping off the glass she started with. In her mind that counted as one, but Dovie counted differently, and she was starting to worry that since her father's death her mother had grown much too dependent on cocktails for company.

A cloisonné cockatiel in shades of blue and green glinted brightly from her coral shoulder; one of her signature bird brooches. Birds were her passion. So much so that when her daughters came along she had named them after two of her favorites—the robin and the dove. Dovie's sister once teased that the only reason Rowena had agreed to marry their father was so she could change her name to Larkin, which had a distinctly avian air. Now, as Dovie sipped her sweaty glass of sweet tea and stared at the oversize pin on her mother's shoulder, she couldn't help thinking that she looked like a cross between a wealthy widow and a tipsy pirate. Still beautiful, though, at sixty-two, despite her well-powdered, well-coiffed grief.

The room was abuzz with gossip and the clink of busy silverware, the air awash with scents of coffee and overcooked vegetables. Robin sat beside her; pretty, plump, and seven months gone with her third child. She was picking at a bit of fish in some sort of white sauce, pretending not to notice their mother slowly numbing herself across the table. She looked bloated and tired beneath the heavy layers of concealer she wore these days, but then with two toddlers and a husband to look after, that was to be expected. Not to mention the playdates, mommy groups, bake sales, and afternoon teas she dutifully orchestrated and attended.

While Dovie had spent most of her adult years shunning the idea of a marriage, Robin had done it up right, managing, with her sorority-girl smile, to marry into an old Georgia family, with even older Georgia money. She had then produced a pair of grandchildren in rapid succession to seal the bargain and was raising them in a sprawling home in one of Charleston's most desirable zip codes. Dovie, to her mother's everlasting disappointment, had opted for a career and small house overlooking the marshes of Mount Pleasant, purchased with the money from her father's life insurance settlement.

A server in a pale pink uniform appeared with a pitcher of iced tea, topping off glasses as she made the rounds. Dovie placed a hand over her glass, and the girl moved on. She was already floating and wanted only to be away from the solicitous glances of her mother's well-meaning friends. But even as the thought formed, Gladys Houser was making a beeline for her, under full sail in a dress of lemony ruffles and wearing an air of determination that made Dovie long to bolt.

Too late.

Pasting on a smile, she braved a cloud of White Shoulders and accepted the hand of the woman who had sponsored her mother's membership in the club. "Mrs. Houser, what a divine dress," Dovie gushed in her best Scarlett O'Hara, hoping to deflect the questions that were almost certainly coming.

Gladys waved off the compliment. "Nonsense. The thing's older than Moses. But tell me, honey, how are you these days? Your poor mama has been worrying herself to a frazzle since William's accident. Why, just look at her, worn to nothing. She was so happy for you, so glad you were finally making a life for yourself. Such a wonderful match, and then . . ." She paused with a doleful shake of the head. "Such a terrible waste. Still, one must move on, mustn't one?"

Dovie nodded, steeling herself for what always came next. *So, are you seeing anyone? It's been a year, after all, and you're not getting any younger. Ticktock. Ticktock.*

Mercifully, Robin came to her rescue. "Mrs. Houser, how is Michael these days? He should be about through with his residency, shouldn't he?"

Mrs. Houser was only too happy to pivot to her son, the brilliant and altogether selfless reconstructive surgeon. "He'll be finished in June. Then he'll be at Children's Hospital in Atlanta. A heart of gold, that boy has, I swear. Anna will be glad to have him home, I think, with the twins on the way."

Dovie shot Robin a profound look of gratitude. Mrs. Grant-Adkins was at the podium, calling for the attention of the assembled ladies, ready at last to start the auction. With any luck, she'd be able to cut out in about an hour.

The first article up for auction was one of her mother's paintings, a small, unframed oil of a goldfinch perched atop a full-blown thistle. Dovie recognized it. It was the one she had finished just before Gerald Larkin left her for his twenty-nine-year-old receptionist. Her mother hadn't painted a stroke since. She claimed it was because she had lost her muse, but Dovie suspected it was because she'd decided to devote every second to her husband when he finally returned, hat in hand, after being thrown over for a corporate attorney named Chet.

The decision still galled Dovie. Not that her mother had quit on her art, but that she had quit on herself, abandoning what could have been a promising career in favor of a husband whose midlife crises had been the topic of conversation at every dinner table in Charleston. She had taken him back, and that was that. For her, at least. And even for Robin, who didn't seem to understand that their father hadn't just cheated on his wife but on his daughters as well. But Dovie had never forgotten—or forgiven.

Watching her mother's life grow smaller and smaller had at least taught her something. She learned that marriage meant sacrifice and broken promises, and that it was a short and slippery slope from *I do* to losing yourself entirely. Perhaps that was why she had always steered clear of the cataclysmic brand of romance her friends were forever tumbling in and out of, opting instead for relationships based on shared interests and mutual respect. Admittedly, there had been few.

And then William had come along. Funny, easy, undemanding William, with his passion for art and his irreverent sense of humor. They had met at the Southern Sisters' annual spring supper. She hadn't been able to take her eyes off him, and eventually he'd caught her staring. Moments later, he appeared with the obligatory glass of punch. He was fresh out of school with an MBA from Cornell, while she had still been working on her master's at Charleston Southern, which explained why they'd never run into each other.

He was a wonderful conversationalist and laughed easily. He also had an uncanny knack for mimicry, and had most of the women in her mother's retinue down pat. She had laughed until she cried, and then they had gone for pizza. They were inseparable after that, spending every free moment of that first summer together, haunting museums, swimming and playing tennis, cooking together, which they both enjoyed, gathering with friends for good food, good wine, and good conversation. There had been no fireworks, no soaring violins, no moment of impassioned declarations. Instead, the relationship had snuck up on them, not a torrid romance, but an easy bond forged between two people who saw the world the same way and didn't want what everyone else did. It had been so easy, so comfortable and uncomplicated. In fact, if it hadn't been for the insistence of William's mother, they might never have gotten around to setting a date. On their part, at least, there had simply been no urgency.

A smattering of polite applause startled Dovie back to the present. Across the table, her mother was beaming. Apparently, her goldfinch had fetched a tidy sum for the Charleston County ASPCA.

The rest of the auction was a blur: tickets to some concert, a weekend spa retreat, a gourmet meal prepared by some celebrity chef, three months with a personal fitness trainer. Mercifully, it all went rather quickly. Dovie tried not to look bored as she waited for the final gavel to sound.

The minute it did she grabbed her tote, scanning the room for a clear path to the door. She had no wish to run the gantlet of her mother's matchmaking friends. She turned to Robin to say good-bye, then gave her belly bump a pat, a girl to be named Grace Elizabeth. "Take care of my niece. And slow down a little, will you? You look tired."

Robin cracked a grin. "I'll be sure to give that a try. Not hanging around to mingle, I take it?"

Dovie rolled her eyes. "Not for all the sweet tea in Charleston. I've got some errands to run before the game starts."

Robin's eyes went wide. "Are we playing today?"

"It's October, and it's Saturday. What do you think?"

Robin was still searching for a sharp retort when Dovie spotted their mother, sidling around the table in their direction. She swallowed a groan, eyeing the door, but it was too late. Robin, however, had managed a clean getaway, leaving Dovie alone in the crosshairs. She'd be sure to thank her later.

"Dovie, honey, you're not going already?" Her mother's voice shrilled over the buzz of feminine chatter. "I want you to meet Katherine Darden. She's a new member and has a son about your age. I thought you might know him."

"I'm sorry, Mama. I need to run. You know I have things to do. It's Saturday. And Saturday is—"

"Flower day. Yes, I know. How well I know."

Dovie scanned the room anxiously. "Please don't start in, Mama. I've had a lousy week, and I just want to be by myself."

"No, Dovie. You want to be with dead people. In fact, they're the only people you *ever* want to be with these days, and folks are beginning to talk."

"They're not *beginning* to talk, Mama. They've been talking. And it's none of their business how I choose to spend my time."

"Perhaps not, but it's awkward. I never know what to say."

"Then don't say anything."

"I can't do that, Dovie. They're my friends, and they mean well."

Dovie sighed. "No Mama, they don't. They mean to be nosy. Now, I have to go." She leaned in, dropping a kiss on her mother's powdered cheek, then whispered close to her ear, "Please don't have any more to drink."

She didn't wait for her mother's response. She didn't need to. She'd seen it often enough: the petulant huff, the scowl meant to remind her that mothers lectured daughters, not the other way around. And maybe she had a point. She was the last person on earth who should be giving advice on how to handle grief.

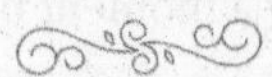

Saturday was flower day at Magnolia Grove, the day most families came to replace wilting bouquets with new ones, to visit their dead, and to pay their respects. Dovie had come to do the same. Clutching a fistful of sunflowers, she headed down the freshly mulched path. She waved to Josiah, bent on one knee several plots away, pulling weeds by hand. Groundskeepers didn't work on weekends, but there he was, dutifully tending his charges. Because he had nowhere else to be. Neither did she, it seemed.

She slowed as she approached the Prescott family plot, picking her way past the grave of Patty Sue Prescott, killed four years ago by a drunk driver while on her way home from a football game. William hadn't been the first of the Prescott children to predecease his parents, just the most shocking.

Why, William?

The question was with her always, when she rose, showered, ate, worked, even when she slept. The *why* never left. That was what her mother didn't understand, what none of them understood—that the grief might fade, but the *why* would last forever. Because there was no way to know what was going through William's mind that night, no way to understand such a cruel and final choice. She'd never been much for New Age mumbo jumbo, but she was beginning to understand why people plunked down good money to see psychics. The need to know, to finally find some kind of closure, could be crippling—*was* crippling.

In the distance, a growl of thunder sounded. Dovie turned her eyes skyward, wishing she had thought to bring an umbrella. She'd need to hurry if she didn't want to get soaked.

Last week's flowers had already been removed, she saw as she approached William's grave: Josiah's doing. He knew she'd be bringing fresh ones today. She bent down, placing the sunflowers in the slender bronze vase, fussing a moment before stepping back to assess her work.

She was just bending down to rearrange a few blooms when she spotted the woman. She moved haltingly, a slow shambling gait that conveyed an unmistakable sense of determination, as if each step cost her dearly. But it was her clothing that truly captured Dovie's interest, as if she'd just stepped out of an old black-and-white film. Her jacket and skirt were decades out of date, and she wore a hat, a crumpled cloche of drab gray wool, with a sorry little feather tucked into the band. Even her black patent leather handbag looked as if it had come from a vintage shop.

Dovie watched as she drew near, thin and stooped. She had expected her to move past. Instead, the woman halted a few yards away, pulled off her wire-rimmed glasses, and stood staring at the life-size angel standing sentinel over a nearby grave.

It wasn't unusual for visitors to stop and stare. *Alice's Angel*, as the statue had come to be known, was something of a local landmark. With her graceful wings, tearstained face, and woeful upturned eyes, she wasn't only a thing of beauty; she was part of local lore. Or maybe *gossip* was a more appropriate word. Thirty-two years ago, she had been erected to mark the grave of Alice Tandy, the young maid who had, to the bewilderment of locals, been buried in the family plot of one of Charleston's richest families, fanning talk that Harley Tate had kept a mistress right under his wife's nose.

It had always made Dovie a little sad. People came from all over, taking pictures and rehashing the gossip, but there were never any flowers that she had seen, no visitors who came because they had known and loved her.

Until now.

Something about the old woman, the unyielding posture, the profound aura of misery hovering about those stooped shoulders, told Dovie this was no amateur taphophile, here to make a rubbing and cross another monument off her bucket list. No, she hadn't come to see the angel. She had come to see Alice, to grieve for Alice, and Dovie's heart ached for her.

The old woman was shaking her head now, her anguish palpable as she shuffled away from the grave, a hand pressed to her lips. She wobbled a bit, then sagged onto a nearby bench, as if with Alice's passing, some hope or dream had slipped through her fingers. And it had, of course. Death was always about the loss of hope. And about regret.

What was it the old woman regretted? Words spoken in anger? A promise not kept? Or perhaps, like Dovie, her regret was a shadowy thing, the dull certainty that somewhere along the way, without realizing it, you'd let things go terribly wrong, that one step—taken or not—had been someone's undoing. Yes, it was there in the old woman's face, too—the *why?* It was written in the lines around her mouth, the shadows in her eyes, grief etched deep. This old woman felt guilt, Dovie realized with a bone-deep jolt of recognition—the kind that bent you over and broke you if you let it.

It was all Dovie could do not to go to her, to offer some hollow word of comfort. But an intrusion, even one kindly meant, might not be welcome. Grief was a private thing. And so she took a seat on her own bench and watched, an uneasy voyeur with a head full of questions.

Thirty years was a long time to grieve. Or maybe it wasn't. She wasn't sure anymore. Was there an acceptable length of time to put one's life on hold? A *normal* length? People certainly seemed to think so. But what of the woman on the bench beside hers? Surely her life would run its course long before her grief did. It was a daunting thought, perhaps because Dovie had the uneasy feeling that she was being given a glimpse of the future—her future. Would she still be sitting on this bench in thirty years, waiting for answers that never came?

Another rumble sounded overhead, closer than the last, and more ominous, but the woman seemed not to hear. Instead, she pushed to her feet, weaving as she crossed back over the path and came to an abrupt halt before Alice's grave. For a moment, she stood very still, as if she'd forgotten why she left her bench, and then she reached down and opened her handbag. Dovie was expecting a tissue or handkerchief, but she sat up a little straighter when the woman produced what appeared to be a letter. She stood staring at it for a moment, then pressed it to her lips and with heaving shoulders laid it at the angel's feet—a penitent's offering.

Dovie watched her turn and shuffle away. A letter. Of course. It was simplicity itself. But what did one write in a letter to the dead, when there was no hope of an answer? Or maybe it wasn't about answers. Maybe it was about emptying yourself of anger and guilt and grief, letting it bleed out onto the page until you were finally free of it, a catharsis of pen and ink. Once again, she found herself wondering about the old woman's regrets, about the kind of anguish that survived decades. What became of it after so many years? Did it fade, or merely harden?

Another rumble of thunder sounded. Dovie eyed the sky, then the pale envelope lying at the angel's feet. It would be ruined. A ridiculous thought, since no one would ever read it. And yet the idea of leaving it there, until its pages were soaked through, its words blurred and lost, sent an irrational wave of panic through her.

She didn't realize she'd made a decision until she got to her feet. She wouldn't read it. She'd just take it home for safekeeping, then return it tomorrow. Surely there was no harm in that. Still, she hesitated when she reached Alice's grave. It wasn't easy to find yourself eye-to-eye with an angel, even one made of stone, and not feel as if you'd just been caught in some heinous act, particularly when you were about to commit one. She stood there a moment, waiting for a bolt of lightning to split the sky, a crack of thunder to warn her away. But as she stared up into those cool stone eyes, she found no censure, no disapproval or warning of any kind. And so she plucked up the letter and dropped it into her tote.

She was preparing to slip away when she saw the old woman's glasses lying on the bench, forgotten in the emotion of the moment.

She had no idea what to do with them, but again, leaving them to the coming storm felt wrong. She scanned the grounds, looking for Josiah, but didn't see him anywhere. She'd ask on Monday. Scooping up the glasses, she dropped them into her tote and kept walking, anxious to be gone before she was confronted, and what—arrested? It was a letter, not a kilo of cocaine, or the launch codes to a Soviet missile silo. Still, her conscience niggled. Never in her life had she taken something that didn't belong to her—and now this. Perhaps her mother was right. Perhaps it *was* time to talk to someone.

four

Dovie dropped into her favorite rocker and propped her legs up on the deck railing. The tide was going out, the narrow estuaries that snaked through the salt marshes beginning to empty, leaving behind pungent mudflats teeming with microscopic life. It was the smell of her childhood, of summer days spent with her mother as she painted on the banks. She filled her lungs, then let the breath out, watching a pair of herons wading in the shallows. Taking a long sip of merlot, she savored the velvety warmth as it went down. She hadn't drunk much since William's death, a promise she'd made to herself not to become one of those women who lived on red wine and melodrama. She hated those women. But tonight she needed something to dull the voice of her conscience—or to prop it up. She wasn't sure which.

The letter weighed almost nothing as she lifted it from her lap. No more than a page, surely. She turned it over, and then over again. There was no writing on the envelope, no clue on either front or back as to the identity of the woman who had written it or what her relationship to Alice Tandy might have been. Not that it mattered. It didn't belong to her, though she couldn't say with any certainty who it *did* belong to. Alice was certainly past reading it. And hadn't the author relinquished her claim when she left it in the cemetery and walked away? Perhaps it belonged to no one. Or, perhaps, by some inexplicable twist of fate, it had been left for her to find, a message from a kindred soul, a woman whose grief, while nowhere near as fresh as her own, was clearly just as raw—a woman who understood.

She closed her eyes, blotting the envelope from view, if not her thoughts. The right thing—the decent and respectful thing—would be to put it back where she found it. Unread. And yet the need to know what it contained continued to gnaw. What harm could there be in appeasing her curiosity, in seeking some thread of insight in the words of a fellow sufferer? The girl was dead, after all, the old woman a stranger she wasn't likely to see ever again.

Flipping the envelope over, she ran a finger over the flap. Such an easy thing—a mere flick and it would be open. And then, with almost no effort, it was done. Inside was a single sheet of paper, the same creamy hue as the envelope, carefully folded. A brief pang of remorse reared its head as she teased the page free, then spread it open on her lap. There was still time to do the right thing, to close it up and put it away. Instead, she began to read.

My dearest girl—for so you still are,

You have been gone from me so long that I scarcely know how to begin. And yet I must. I have crossed an ocean in the hope that your heart might have softened toward the woman who did you such a terrible wrong. If you're reading this you have refused to see me. But please, for the sake of the mother who always loved you, and loves you still, read on. What I have to say has been on my heart too long to think of taking it to my grave unsaid. You must know, my girl, that all I did—my God, can it really be forty years now?—I did with love. You were so young, so unschooled in the ways of the world. You hadn't learned yet how cruel life can be. But you did learn, and you have me to thank for that lesson. In my anger, I spoke of sin. Now I know the sin was mine. To turn my back, close my heart against my own flesh and blood, was unpardonable. No words can undo the horrors you were made to suffer, or restore what was taken from you. If there were, I would say them now. You said when you left that you would never be back, that you were through with me, and with Sennen Cove, and you've kept your word. I know nothing of your life. You've taken pains to make sure of that, which is a fitting punishment, I suppose. When my letters came back unopened, it broke my heart, but I understood. You didn't want me in your life. And so I left you alone. But time passes, and a mother's heart still hopes. I'm old and unwell, and my time is short. I don't pretend this means anything to you, but it grieves me to think of leaving this world without seeing you once more, without knowing you're well and have found some measure of happiness. Or without begging one last time for your forgiveness, my beloved daughter, for a mother who meant no harm, but did great harm just the same. I have taken a room at the Palmetto Moon, should you change your mind and want to see me. I pray you do. If not, I understand.

With more regret than you can possibly know—
Mam

Her mother, then, Dovie thought bleakly as she refolded the letter. A mother who hadn't known her daughter was dead until she'd crossed an ocean, from—where? Dovie let the single sheet of stationery flutter to her lap, wishing to God she'd never read it. No insight, no comfort. Just pain and more questions. She polished off the last of her merlot, then closed her eyes, trying to imagine coming halfway around the world in search of forgiveness, only to find you'd come too late.

five

Sundays were busy at Magnolia Grove, the one day a week Dovie usually skipped. But she had come today, determined to return the letter and separate herself from the questions that had plagued her dreams, questions that lingered even now—about shadowy sins and a mother's plea for forgiveness, about mistakes, and grudges, and broken hearts. What was the woman's story to her anyway? Before William's death she would never have done such a thing, would never have let her emotions run away with her, never been tempted to cross such a line. But she had crossed it, because somehow in her jumbled head and heart, the letter had become about William, about the need to comprehend the incomprehensible, to wind back the clock and right some unnamable wrong. Except none of that could ever be. And so she waited. For the flowers to be left, and the prayers to be said, and the endless parade of families to leave, so she could undo yesterday's terrible mistake.

There was no sign of the old woman. Dovie couldn't decide if she was relieved or disappointed. She was, however, dismayed when Josiah broke from a nearby stand of oaks. He changed course the minute he spotted her, sweeping off his Panama as he approached. "Didn't expect to see you today. Thought you took Sundays off."

Dovie cocked an eye up at him. "I thought you did, too."

He studied her a moment, then frowned. "Something up? You're lookin' kinda pasty, like you seen a ghost or something."

Dovie forced a smile but let the remark pass. She didn't believe in ghosts—not the real sort anyway. "I had some time on my hands, and it was such a beautiful day. I thought I'd get out in the sunshine."

Josiah's eyes narrowed as he settled his hat back on his head. "I might be wrong, but I hear they've got places for folks to enjoy the sunshine. Call 'em parks, I think. Hear they're pretty popular, too."

Dovie fixed him with her best scowl. "I see we had a big bowl of clown for breakfast."

Josiah smirked, showing off one gold incisor. "Nope. Chess pie."

"Did you save any for me?"

"I told you I'd bring you a piece on Monday, didn't I?"

"Humph. A bribe, to keep me off your back, but I'll take it." She paused a moment, weighing what she was about to say. "Josiah, what do you know about Alice Tandy?"

The question clearly caught him off guard. He pushed back his hat, eyeing Dovie cannily. "What you askin' about that poor girl for? All this time she's been right there near your William, and you ain't never once wondered about her."

"I know, but yesterday there was a woman—an old woman—who came to visit Alice's grave. She was so sad, so . . . I don't know . . . broken. I just wondered if you knew who she was, or what her story might be."

Josiah shrugged. "No idea about the old woman, but I remember the day they planted that girl in there with all them Tates—like poking a dandelion right in the middle of a rose garden. Raised a lot of eyebrows. As far as anybody knew she wasn't no relation to any Tate, living or dead. But then, rich folks do as they like, and who's gonna tell 'em no?"

"You don't know who she was, or where she came from?"

"The girl?" He shook his head. "No. She and me wouldn't have run in the same circles back then. Worked for Mrs. Tate as a maid or something, though talk around town was she did more for Mr. Tate than for his wife, if you catch my meaning. Folks like to talk like that, even when they don't know what's what, so no telling if there's any truth in it. I just know there was a stir for a while, and no one in town could shut up about the Tates. Some say it's her—the face on that angel—but I doubt there's any truth to that. Could be, I guess. When you've got enough money you can do just about anything. And the Tates surely have their share."

Yes, Dovie thought, they certainly did, and they'd just given a sizable chunk of it to the museum. And she was in charge of spending it, or at least recommending to the board how it should be spent. It was a rather unsettling coincidence that she now found herself knee deep in a family spat involving Mrs. Tate's dead maid.

"It's odd, though, don't you think?" she said, staring up at the angel's tearstained stone face. "Burying a maid in the family plot, then placing such a fancy marker on her grave?"

Josiah's shoulders heaved again. "Like I said, rich folks do as they like. Why you so curious all of a sudden anyhow?"

"I have her glasses," Dovie told him, rummaging in her purse for proof. "The woman I told you about—she left them on the bench. I was hoping you'd know who she was so I could return them."

"Can't help you there. Never saw her. Just leave 'em at lost and found. If she comes for them, that's where she'll go."

Dovie blinked up at him. "The cemetery has a lost and found?"

"Sure do. Over to the office. You look surprised."

"I am, a little. I never thought of a cemetery having a lost and found. It seems, I don't know, weird somehow."

"Why? Folks leave all sort of things behind."

Dovie perked up. "What kinds of things?"

Josiah scrubbed at the grizzled stubble along his jaw. "Hats and umbrellas, mostly. Gloves. Glasses. The usual things. But there's other stuff, too—stuff you wouldn't expect."

Dovie's curiosity ratcheted up another notch. "Like what?"

"Crazy stuff that don't make no sense but must've meant something to somebody. A few years back I found an old cast-iron frying pan leaned up against a stone. Then there was the big old globe I found on Edna Barstow's grave. Had some fun with that one. We used to try to outdo each other, making up stories about what the things meant. Came up with some doozies, too."

Dovie gnawed her lower lip, hesitating. "Have you . . . has anyone ever found letters?"

Josiah scrubbed at his chin again. "Not me, but I wouldn't be a bit surprised if they had. Can't think of much we ain't found over the years." His gaze sharpened. "Why you ask?"

"No reason. I just wondered."

Josiah's old eyes settled on her, shrewd and all-seeing. "It's a funny thing to just wonder about. Kinda . . . specific. You wouldn't be holding somethin' back, would you? Somethin' you might ought to be tellin'?"

For a moment she considered lying, then decided there wasn't much point. He always saw right through her. Pulling the letter from her purse, she slid it from its envelope and placed it in his hands. "I found this yesterday."

He ran an eye over it, then shot her a sideways glance. "Found?"

"The old woman I told you about—she left it."

"On the bench?"

Dovie shook her head. "On Alice's grave."

"You took it?"

"Yes."

Josiah gaped at her. "What in hell's fury is wrong with you?" He lowered his voice as a mother with a pair of twin girls walked past. "That letter wasn't none of your damn business, to just go and snatch it like that."

"I know, Josiah. That's why I came today, to put it back."

"To put it back? You mean like you never read it? Never stuck your nose where you didn't have no business sticking it?"

"Yes. No!" Dovie's cheeks were beginning to burn. She needed him to understand. "I wish I could unread it, but I can't. It's so sad. I just want to put it back and not think about it anymore."

"You think that'll make it right? You of *all* people? How'd you like it if someone peeked in on your grief when you weren't looking? Made entertainment out of your pain?"

"Please, Josiah. It wasn't like that. And I know it was wrong. All I want is to make it right. But there are so many people around. I can't just . . ." She paused, scanning the grounds as an idea began to take shape. "If I gave it to you, you could put it back for me—later, when no one's around."

His lower lip jutted. "Why you think I want to do your dirty work?"

"Please don't look at me like that. She was just so sad and so miserable, she reminded me of me. Then I saw the letter, and I thought maybe she'd found a way to deal with her grief, to write it down and finally let it all go. I thought if I read what she wrote, it might help. Only, it didn't. Oh, Josiah—" Dovie's voice crackled. "She came halfway around the world to make amends for something that happened forty years ago, only to discover her daughter was dead."

"And what's that got to do with you?"

Dovie swallowed the sudden lump in her throat. "Nothing, exactly. Except now there's no way for her to ever make things right, which means she'll live with her guilt for the rest of her life. She'll never be free of it."

She was surprised when Josiah's calloused hand closed over hers.

"And you think that means you, too, but it don't. Time will heal you up, Little Miss, when you're good and ready. Meantime, you need to stop trying to fix the whole world's problems and take care of yourself. Leave the letter to me. I'll look after it. You go take the lady's glasses to lost and found, and be sure to tell Loraine where you found 'em so she can note it down."

Dovie watched him go, grateful for his comforting words as she turned toward the office. A pall of white dust and the steady banging of hammers greeted her as she stepped through the door marked VISITOR SERVICES. She tiptoed across the blue plastic tarp, navigating her way around handsaws, sledgehammers, and caulking guns until she finally reached the counter. A woman with a head of suspect red curls looked up at her with an apologetic smile.

"Morning. You'll have to excuse the racket. We're remodeling. Otherwise, I promise you, I wouldn't be here on a Sunday. What can I help you with?"

Dovie rooted in her purse for the wire-rimmed spectacles and set them on the counter. "I found these yesterday and wanted to turn them in. Am I in the right place?"

The redhead—presumably Loraine—nodded. "Sure are, even if everything is all turned upside down. We're tearing out a few walls to make space. About time, too. It's like a rabbit warren back there, and so much junk there's no way to find anything. Been at it almost a week now, and they tell me it's going be at least two more. I swear, I hear those hammers in my sleep. Anyway, enough griping. Let me take those from you."

She gave the glasses a quick once-over, then set them aside while she rummaged through a nearby drawer, eventually producing a small plastic bag and a form of some kind. She scribbled the date at the top, jotted down a brief description in the space provided, then looked back up at Dovie. "Can you tell me where you found them? What part of the cemetery, I mean? We try to box items by section."

"They were on one of the benches near the Prescott family plot. Actually, I guess it was the Tate plot. I'm pretty sure they belong to an old woman I saw yesterday."

Loraine pulled a pen from behind her ear and began scribbling and checking off various boxes on the form. Dovie waited for her to finish, feeling a twinge of claustrophobia as she surveyed the clutter. Storage boxes three and four deep, bulging with an untidy assortment of umbrellas, hats, raincoats, and gloves, not to mention enough stuffed animals to populate a small zoo. It was mind-boggling that anyone ever found anything.

Finally, Loraine affixed her initials to the bottom, dropped the glasses into a plastic bag along with the form, and sealed it with a quick zip. "There we go. All set. If she comes looking, we'll have them for her."

"Thanks so much. I have to say I was surprised to learn the cemetery even had a lost and found. I never thought about people leaving things behind, but I guess they do."

"Heavens, yes. All sorts of things. Some are left on purpose. Some not. We can't ever say for sure which is which, so we treat it all as lost."

Dovie eyed the untidy boxes again, several of which had already split their seams. "What happens to it? The unclaimed stuff, I mean?"

"We donate most of it. We try to do it quarterly—that gives folks enough time to claim what they mean to—but sometimes it gets away from us, like now. I can't tell you how much junk we've unearthed since we started remodeling. I mean really old stuff from who knows how far back, and none of it labeled. But then, I'll bet there hasn't been any work done on this place since the fifties, maybe earlier. At this point, I'm counting the days until I can toss it all, and finally get organized. Anyway, thanks again, for bringing these by."

Dovie thanked Loraine, then picked her way back toward the door. As she stepped out into the bright Sunday sunshine, she found herself thinking about the globe Josiah had discovered on Edna Barstow's grave, and the guessing game Magnolia Grove employees used to play. In the end, she decided the globe had been a grieving husband's way of giving his wife the world, something he had promised once but had never managed to do while she was alive.

Dovie felt a huge pang of relief when Josiah appeared along the path. It had been three days since she last saw him. Three days of solitary lunches, of no chess pie, of not knowing what had happened to the letter. Had he put it back? Thrown it away? Now, finally, she would have an answer.

He didn't smile as he came to a halt in front of her. "Little Miss."

"Josiah, it's been three days. Where have you been? I thought you were mad at me."

His lower lip jutted. "Might be. Ain't made up my mind yet. But that's not why you ain't seen me. I been staying over to the office, nights. Construction fellas been working straight through, so someone had to stay. I go home and sleep some in the mornings. That's why I ain't been around. Not 'cause I was mad, which I probably ain't, even though I should be."

Dovie fought a smile, more relieved than she could say. It would sadden her to lose his friendship. She held out half her tuna sandwich, but he waved the offer away, taking the space beside her without invitation. "I need to tell you something."

Something in his manner made Dovie anxious. "Did you put the letter back?"

Josiah turned to peer over one shoulder. "Not exactly, no. Like I said, I been over to the office." Reaching into his back pocket, he retrieved something and pressed it into her hands. "Found these in the office last night, under all that mess."

They were letters. On top was the letter from Alice's mother, the one she had given him to put back. But there were five more with it now, plain envelopes of cheap yellowed paper. Dovie glanced at them, and then at Josiah.

He nodded toward the letters. "Probably wouldn't have noticed them if you hadn't been talking about letters the other day, but there they were, lying right there on the floor. They were open when I found them," he added. "Or I wouldn't have read them. I was only trying to figure out where they come from, and, well, I think you ought to take a look."

Dovie fanned the envelopes in her lap like a hand of cards. They were identical, yellowed at the edges, and curiously blank, devoid of address, stamp, or postmark. She shot Josiah a sideways look. "I don't understand. Why are you giving me these?"

"You asked if anyone ever found any letters. Looks like they must've done."

"But the other day you were furious. Now you're just . . . giving them to me?"

"Here's how I figure it. Whoever wrote 'em is long gone, so reading them isn't going to hurt no one. And they might just help you."

Dovie still didn't understand. "Help me how?"

"By making you see that sometimes when people take a thing with them to the grave they mean for it to stay there, 'cause maybe it wasn't so pretty. You're all the time dying to know *why* when the truth is, that *why* might be better left alone. Now I see you got it in your craw over this old woman. My Essie was like you, over her no-account brother getting shot out back of some juke joint in Ravenel. She had to know why. Well, she dug and she dug until she found out. Truth damn near broke the woman's heart. So maybe you'll read those letters and realize some secrets are best left in the ground. I sure hope so. Be a damn shame to get my arthritic ass fired over a handful of old letters."

Dovie picked an envelope at random, holding her breath as she teased out the single sheet and spread it out against her knees. The handwriting was meticulous, the letters round and precise, like a page from a schoolgirl's diary. She had to squint to decipher the faded ink strokes, but finally the import of what she was holding hit her full force.

Her head snapped up. "Josiah, these were written by Alice Tandy."

"Go on, and take 'em," he told her gruffly. "Damage is done. We both goin' to hell now."

SIX

Blackhurst Asylum for Unwed Mothers,
Cornwall, England
February 4, 1962

Little one,

You will never read this letter. And yet I find I must write it, to pour out the rage that has been choking me. Rage for my fate and yours, for the other girls here, and for the other babies. But I suppose I must begin at the beginning if I truly mean to tell it all.

You don't know me, and never will if the Sisters of Mercy have their way. And they will have their way. My name is Alice—Alice Tandy—though here I am called Laurel. No one is to know I'm here, you see, shut up in this place of sadness and secrets, because I've brought shame on my family. Except I have no family. Only the mother who sent me here, who is as good as dead to me now.

She says I have no shame, and I confess that is the truth. I'm not ashamed of you, or of the love your father and I shared. That's what makes me a sinner, I suppose, my lack of shame—and now I'm being made to pay for those sins—and so are you.

My "mistake." That's what they call you here.

But you weren't a mistake. How can something—someone—created from love, ever be a mistake? And you were created from love, my little one. Your father's name was Johnny. Johnny Barnes. He was a beautiful boy with brown curls and eyes the colour of the sea. It was the sea that took him from me—from us—and that's why I've been sent to this terrible place.

This isn't my first letter to you. I was made to write another just now—the same one they make all the girls write—as penance for our sins. One of the sisters stands over us and tells us what to write, that we aren't fit to bring up our babies, that we're fallen women, sinful and corrupt, unfit to rear good moral children.

It will be left to your new parents—your good and moral parents—to decide if you'll ever read the words they made me write. I pray you do not. I can't bear the thought of you growing up thinking of me as a sinner, or believing for one moment that I didn't want you. I'd prefer you not think of me at all.

For months now, I have carried you beneath my heart, but soon—far too soon—we will be parted. You're my flesh and blood, a part of me forever, and I will never willingly give you up. But, my darling, they will take you. I've seen them do it, have heard the girls weeping and screaming, pleading for their babies. But the sisters are all deaf here, and the die has been cast. The same fate awaits me as all the other girls.

I'll never hold you, or know the colour of your eyes, never know if you're a boy or a girl, if you look like your father or like me. I'll give you life but won't be allowed to give you a name. All these things they'll take from me. But they will never take you from my heart, little one. Never from my heart. And so I'm writing this, with a mother's love, and the foolish hope that somehow the truth will find its way to you.

All my love,
Mam

Blackhurst Asylum for Unwed Mothers,
Cornwall, England
March 14, 1962

Dearest little one,

We are allowed one letter a month, but I have no one to write to, and so I will write to you. Silly, I suppose, since neither you nor anyone else will ever see it, but it helps to pass the time and is the only way I have of pouring out the poison in my heart, the anger I feel toward Mam, the nuns, the world that judges girls like me. That I should find myself in such a place, cast out and alone, is like a nightmare from which I can't seem to wake. And so I write when I can.

The days have become unbearable, spooling out with no one to talk to, hours on end filled with sadness, silence, and grueling work. We're up before the sun, jerked awake by the hollow clang of the morning bell. We have ten minutes to wash and dress, or we get no breakfast. Not that any of us cares for the tasteless mush and watery tea that passes for our morning meal. Then it's off to the laundry, hour upon hour with our bellies bent over enormous pots of steaming sheets, towels, and prison uniforms—scrubbing, rinsing, wringing—as if all that scrubbing will somehow cleanse the stain from our souls.

It's whispered that there's money being made from our sweat. Restaurants, hospitals, even prisons, paying the good sisters for the work we do. There's money from the government, too, paid for every swollen belly that passes through Blackhurst's iron gates. We, of course, receive no wages for our labor, only aching backs and sore red hands.

It would be easier, I think, if I had someone to talk to, but friendship isn't allowed here. Girls who make friends are soon separated, while repeat offenders are punished with isolation, beatings, or worse. Last week, two girls were caught whispering during prayers. The next morning they were made to stand at the head of the mess, heads shaved and stripped to their skins, while the rest of us ate our breakfasts. No one uttered a word for the rest of the day—or the day after.

Shame is a weapon here, used to break the spirits of poor girls who've been given no say in what's to happen to them or their babies. Like birds in a cage—and I am one of them now. Some are here voluntarily, because they're alone in the world, without friends, or family, or other means of support. But most are here against their will. Some will never leave—will actually die here—shut away at the edge of the world like the inconveniences they've become, some as young as thirteen with terrible stories in their haunted eyes. There are whispers of rape and incest, of good families where unspeakable things happen, where the offenses of uncles and stepfathers are swept under the carpet, while their victims are made to pay, stripped of dignity and branded as sinners.

Those stories are squashed, of course, their victims threatened into silence. But there are ways to spot those cases, to see past the forced silence to the eerie quiet beneath, the almost uncanny stillness of a girl who has given up and is simply biding her time. And then one morning there's an empty bed when the bell clangs, and a vacant place at breakfast.

Another sparrow smashed on the rocks.

My story is different. Your father didn't shunt me off when he found out about you, though I've ended here just the same. Nor are the looks I get from the good sisters any different from those reserved for any of the other girls here with sad stories and swollen bellies. Perhaps they don't believe what I told them about your father, that we were in love, that as soon as he saved up a few pounds he meant to marry me. They've heard it before, I'm sure, from girls who wanted badly to believe it.

Perhaps they don't believe Johnny's dead. I didn't want to believe it myself when I heard he'd that been thrown into the sea during a squall and drowned. Perhaps they think he abandoned me, and I'm just too proud to say so. It's a common enough tale here. But I know the truth. I loved your father, and he loved me. It would have been hard at first. We wouldn't have had much, but we would have had each other—and you, little one—and that would have been enough. He had such a big heart, your father. Big enough to love us both, no matter what anyone else thought or said.

I kept you a secret for as long as I could, not because I was ashamed, but because with Johnny gone my heart was too broken to think about what came next. But soon the time came when I couldn't hide you anymore, and it was time to tell Mam how things stood, though by then I think she had guessed. More than once, I'd felt her gaze lingering, a question in those shrewd grey eyes of hers. She'd be angry, I knew, and disappointed that after all her lecturing I'd gone and gotten myself in trouble, but I never expected the things she said to me that day, or knew she could be so cruel.

We were washing up after supper when I finally found the nerve to utter the words I'd been rehearsing all week. I saw her stiffen, hands braced on the edge of the sink, then watched her round in my direction. I didn't see the slap coming until my head snapped back, and there were tiny lights dancing behind my eyes.

She stood there a moment, staring at the tiny bulge beneath Johnny's oversize jumper, as if she could see straight through to my backbone. "It was that boy, I suppose. That fisherman's son."

I nodded, still dizzy from her slap. "Johnny," I whispered. "You know his name is Johnny."

"Well, fancy that!" Her eyes were wild as she fixed them on me, her knuckles wet and white as bone as she fisted them on her hips. "After all my talk, all my warnings about what boys want and what they do once they get it, what has my stupid girl done but got herself pregnant—and by a boy who's gotten himself dead!"

The words were worse than any slap she could have dealt me, like a knife twisted in a fresh wound. And her eyes—I'll never forget the look in them—like all of a sudden I was something to be stepped over in the gutter. I felt my mouth working, but no sound would come. And what was the point? There were no words to make this right, nothing I could say that would undo the fact of it. I was going to have a baby, Johnny's baby, and no amount of railing, or shaming, or pleading, would change it.

And I didn't want to change it.

There was never any talk of . . . getting rid of you. It was too late for that sort of remedy, at any rate. But I knew the moment the words were out of my mouth that Mam was never going to let me keep you. I tried. God knows I did. But when I finally found my tongue she wouldn't listen to a word I said.

"How could you?" she hurled at me as she prowled our tiny kitchen. "How could you be so foolish, so thoughtless? After all I've done, all I've sacrificed, to make sure you didn't end up like me, buried here in Sennen Cove and dying just a little every day. I worked like a slave to afford the best schools, two jobs, sometimes three, pinching pennies so you could go to university one day, and all on my bloody own! Why? So you'd make something of yourself, not wind up a fisherman's wife with a houseful of brats! And this is what I get for my trouble, a silly girl who throws her life away on a boy too stupid to keep himself alive!"

I hated her at that moment.

That she could say such a thing to me, when she knew my heart was still so raw, was unforgivable. It didn't matter to her that I never wanted to leave Sennen Cove, or that I wanted to be a fisherman's wife—to be Johnny's wife. That I wanted to keep and raise our child. Nothing I said, no amount of tears or pleading would sway her. And just like that, the decision was made, as if she'd had a plan tucked away in her apron pocket all along. And maybe she had. Maybe that's what she'd been thinking about all those times I felt her eyes on me.

I would go to Blackhurst when the time came, have the child and give it up, then return home and finish school like I was meant to. We'd tell people I'd spent the winter in Truro, nursing a sick aunt, which no one would believe, but everyone would pretend to. It was an old story, after all, but then so was mine. If I defied Mam she would wash her hands of me, sling me out, and leave me to fend for myself.

And so here I am, shut away from the world in this terrible place, counting the days until they take you from me. Please understand, little one, and try to forgive. I had no money and no place to go, no way to keep myself, or you. It isn't the way I wanted things to be. I wanted you with me always. Please believe that, and know that no matter where you end up in the world, you will always, always, belong to me.

All my love,
Mam

Blackhurst Asylum for Unwed Mothers
Cornwall, England
May 9, 1962

My dear little one,

I vowed when I passed through the gates of Blackhurst that for as long as I was here I would not shed another tear, but I find I cannot keep my promise. There was another empty place at breakfast this morning, a girl called Kathleen who'd been here less than a week, a poor sad girl who spoke to no one and kept her eyes on the floor. I've been crying all day, for her, and for the child who died with her.

No one had to say what happened. We all knew. She wasn't the first, nor will she be the last. Still, it was hard not to let my eyes slide to that empty place, to think that it could have been any of us. We're all just one hard day away from stealing out onto those cliffs, from flinging ourselves and our mistakes out into the nothingness. A sin, the sisters remind us, lest we be tempted to follow Kathleen's example. And maybe it is, but to hear them tell it we're all doomed here anyway, so where's the harm? And then I think of you, my angel, and know I could never venture out onto those cliffs. It's not my place to speak for the others, or to judge what's in their hearts. We each have our crosses to bear in this world, and must all make our own choices. I only know I could never do myself harm if it meant hurting you.

And so I do what I can to take care of myself—for your sake. Still, there's a new weariness I can't seem to shake, and a racking cough that has settled in my chest. I can't say I'm surprised. We're none of us fed enough, and the damp here is terrible, the walls and floors forever clammy, our bedsheets never quite dry. At least they've moved me out of the laundry. They've put me onto sewing now, which at least keeps me off my feet. They say it's because my belly is getting too large to bend over the vats, but I'm not sure that's it.

There are girls here who work in the laundry right up until their time. I think the real reason is my cough—in case it's catching. It wouldn't do for all the girls to get sick at once. There'd be no one left to wash the clothes then, and no way for the sisters to collect their money. Only now it seems there are others who have been culled from the herd, given a needle to wield instead of the heavy wooden paddles in the laundry.

The word "tuberculosis" is whispered down the supper tables when Sister Mary Agnes isn't around to silence us, as if not saying the word aloud will keep the thing from being true. I don't worry for myself, but for you, my angel. They give us medicine twice a day now—great big pills the colour of cow dung—but I don't swallow mine. I've heard what those pills can do, babies born with stunted limbs or other deformities. There are stories about what happens to those children—the damaged ones no one comes for. They're shut away, it's said, forgotten, or worse, their fates unknown beyond the iron gates of Blackhurst. There's talk, terrible talk, of newborn souls wrapped in plain cloth shrouds, thrown into large pits, their tiny bones forgotten as they sink into the cold dark soil—lost. Not you, little one. I won't let that happen to you, no matter what they do to me.

Our time together grows short. Only three weeks now if I've counted properly, maybe four, and then you'll be gone. And I'll be back in Sennen Cove. I can't fathom the emptiness of it, of knowing that somewhere in the world your tiny heart will go on beating without mine—that you'll be the apple of some other mother's eye. I tell myself all I want is to know that you're happy and loved, but it isn't true. I want so much more than that. I want to be a part of your life, and for you to be a part of mine. I want to see your father's eyes shining back at me when I hold you in my arms. I want to press my cheek to yours, to hear you laugh. But that can't ever be, as I am reminded daily by the vacant eyes and empty arms of the girls whose babies have already come.

I must close now and hide this. The dinner bell will ring soon and Sister Mary Agnes will be cross if my sewing basket isn't empty when she comes. Please know that you are always in my heart, and that my every thought is for you.

All my love,
Mam

seven

MAGNOLIA GROVE CEMETERY
CHARLESTON, SOUTH CAROLINA
OCTOBER 4, 2005

Dovie experienced an uneasy pang of déjà vu as she folded up the letters and slipped them back into her tote. It was the third day in a row she'd spent her lunch hour rereading Alice's letters, and the third day in a row she sat staring at an enormous stone angel because it made her feel more connected to the woman who'd written them. And yet it felt right, somehow, as if she'd been drawn here.

Or maybe she was just trading one obsession for another.

God knew, it was starting to have all the earmarks of an obsession. For starters, she was spending far too much time grappling with images she'd just as soon forget. But once you knew a thing, you knew it. It stayed with you, taking up space in your head. And now Blackhurst was in her head. Young mothers shut up, never to be heard from again. Dead babies tossed into pits. Girls throwing themselves from cliffs. How had she never heard of such atrocities? And more important, how had they been allowed to happen?

She supposed it might all be exaggeration, the invention of a young woman abandoned and distraught, but that didn't seem likely. Alice had been writing to her unborn child, letters written in secret that no one was ever meant to read. What would she have gained by lying?

Dovie sighed as she stared up at the woeful stone angel. For days now, she'd been scouring the letters, hoping for some sign that things might still end well. So far, she hadn't found any, and wasn't sure she was ready to know what the rest of the letters contained. It was all just too terrible. And yet Alice had managed to make it all the way to Charleston. Was it possible that, against all odds, she had actually managed to reunite with her child?

Dovie closed her eyes, rolling her neck from side to side, tired of her head swimming with the same questions over and over again. She needed to let it go. She had enough grief. She didn't need to borrow someone else's. At any rate, it was none of her business, and certainly nothing that could be remedied with poor Alice in the ground. But there was a part of her that longed to know the rest of the story, a part that hungered for understanding, and closure. The hardest goodbyes were the ones that were never said—William's suicide taught her that. It seemed Alice's mother had learned it, too.

Sighing, she reached for her tote. It was time to get back. She had a two o'clock budget meeting, and the proposal she promised to have ready was still sitting on her desk, waiting for final figures. Jack was already watching her like a hawk; the last thing she needed to do was show up for the meeting empty-handed.

She was just preparing to stand when a bit of movement caught her eye. She had to squint against the sun, but the old black lace-ups and patent leather bag were all she needed to see. Her stomach did a little flip as the woman came into view, like a ghost conjured by her thoughts.

She was wearing the same skirt and jacket as last time, even the same hat, but somehow the clothes fit her differently, as if she had withered substantially in only a few days. Her approach was plodding and labored, though whether her trouble had to do with weakness or pain, Dovie couldn't say. Finally, she halted before her daughter's grave, her grizzled head bowed. There was the sound of muffled weeping, and then a choked sob as the woman stumbled forward.

Dovie was on her feet in an instant, scurrying across the path to place a steadying hand beneath the woman's elbow. "Can I help you? You seem . . . unwell."

The woman's head came up with a look of blank surprise, her eyes the color of the sky on a cloudy day. "I was only . . ." Her voice trailed away as she glanced about, trying to get her bearings. "No, thank you. I'm . . . I'm quite well."

She had delivered the words with something like dismissal, but Dovie wasn't convinced. She was far too pale, and her lips had a slightly bluish cast. "Is there someone I can call? You really don't look well."

"I'm only a bit knackered from the walk," she answered testily. "I'll be quite right in a moment." Her voice was thready and gruff, thick with the West Country vowels Dovie recognized from the summer she'd spent in the U.K. studying neoclassical art.

"I'm Dovie. I saw you here the other day."

The woman nodded, dabbing her eyes with the crumpled remains of a tissue. "I'm Dora Tandy." She raised a hand, pointing to the stone angel. "My girl's there. Her name was Alice."

"Yes, I know." The words were out before Dovie could stop them. "What I meant is that everyone knows that statue. People come from all over to see it."

Dora's gray eyes lit with something like astonishment. "They come to see my Alice?"

"Her monument, yes."

"Whatever for?"

Dovie glanced up at the statue, at its sorrowful, tearstained beauty, and knew she needed to tread lightly. No need to bring the Tates into it. Or the speculation about her daughter's inexplicable presence in the burial plot of one of the richest families in town. "I suppose it's because she's so beautiful. It's the tears, I think, that make her so compelling. Does it . . . look like her? The angel, I mean. Does she look like your daughter?"

Dora studied the stone face for a moment, then turned away, wandering to the nearby bench. "No," she said wearily. "It isn't her. The tears, though—the tears look like her." Her voice broke, and she reached for her handbag, fumbling a moment until she produced a wallet-sized photograph. "That's her. It was taken on her birthday, not long before she left. I'm ashamed to say I've lost track of how old she'd be now. For me, she's still the girl who left home all those years ago."

Dovie felt a queer, almost inexplicable connection as she studied the photo—not recognition, exactly, but something close to it, like a stranger you'd almost swear you've met but know you haven't. This, she thought with an anguished pang, this was what Alice Tandy looked like the day she entered Blackhurst—young and pretty, with a head of thick blond hair and large soft eyes like a doe's. There was a boy in the photo, a handsome boy with dark curls and mischief in his eye. He had an arm hooked around Alice's shoulder. It was Johnny, of course, lost at sea before he could marry Alice and give their child his name.

"It's my fault she's here," Dora said dully. "I drove her away. Because I cared more about what folks might think than I did for my own girl, and this"—she paused, nodding toward the angel—"this is what happened."

Dovie had no idea how to respond. It wasn't her place to judge, especially without knowing all the facts, but it was hard to deny Dora's culpability in Alice's misfortunes. And yet there was no way to know the extent of those misfortunes, or to know for certain that Alice's life after Blackhurst, brief though it was, hadn't at least been modestly happy.

"Dovie—is that English?"

Dovie was both relieved and surprised by the abrupt change of subject. "I don't think it's anything. My mother likes birds. She paints them—used to paint them."

"She's gone?"

"No. She's alive. She just doesn't paint anymore."

Dora fell silent for a time, eyes fixed on her hands, studying the ropy map of dark blue veins there. "Have you little ones, Dovie?"

Dovie shifted uneasily, sensing that they were heading back toward prickly ground. "No, I'm not married. I was almost married once, but . . ." She let the words trail, wondering why she'd said them at all.

"That's why you're here, then? Because of your young man?"

Dovie nodded, not quite meeting Dora's eyes.

"How long now?"

"A little more than a year."

Dora's head came up, as if Dovie's answer had surprised her. "And you still come?"

"Every day. He . . . killed himself just before our wedding, and I can't seem to get past it."

"Because you blame yourself?"

"I don't know. Maybe. There was no note, nothing to explain why he did what he did. He just swallowed a handful of pills and that was it." Dovie pressed a hand to her lips, embarrassed to be rambling about William when the woman had her own grief to tend. "I'm sorry. I don't know why I blurted all that out."

It wasn't true, though. She knew exactly why she'd brought William into the conversation. It was her way of evening the score. Dovie knew things about Dora's loss, things she'd learned in a less than forthright manner. It only seemed fair that she share something about her own grief. Tit for tat.

Dora drew a long shuddering breath, then released it slowly, her rounded shoulders drooping like a deflated balloon. "It's the not knowing," she said quietly. "The reason we can't get past it. And so we just keep bleeding, because we don't know, and we'll never know. If we could have one more chance, have that last moment back, maybe we'd do it differently. But we'll never have that chance."

There were tears in her eyes. She closed them, letting the tears spill over. "My daughter left home almost forty years ago. I drove her away. There was a boy, you see, and there was going to be a baby. And then the boy went and got himself killed before they could get married. All I could think of was what folk would say, how they'd look at my girl like she was some bit of trash—the way they looked at me when I was pregnant with her—and I couldn't bear it. I'd worked so hard to give her a better life than I had. She didn't understand, of course. No way she could have. But I had my reasons. She deserved better—so much better. She was smart, good with words and a pen. A gift, her teachers said, enough of one to make something of herself. But not with a baby to raise on her own. And so I . . ." Her voice broke. She pressed a hand to her lips, shook her head. "I sent her away."

Dovie laid a hand on Dora's arm. She could feel the tremors running through the woman's fragile body. Or maybe it was she who was trembling. It was torture sitting there, listening to Dora tell her story, knowing, perhaps better than she, what came next. And yet there was nothing to do but listen as the rest came pouring out.

"We grappled for days, she and I. She was set on keeping that baby, husband or no. She didn't understand what it would mean, how people would look at her, how it would ruin her. I was at the end of my tether. I . . . threatened to call the constable. They'd arrest you in those days for that kind of thing—not the boys, mind you, just the girls. I don't know how I ever could have said such a thing. I'd bite off my tongue before saying it now, but I did say it. I was that desperate to keep the tongue-waggers from finding out. I told her . . " Dora's head fell again, another stifled sob escaping her. "I told her if she didn't go to the unwed mothers' home I would turn her out, disown her. That's the moment I lost her, when I said that awful thing."

Heart aching, Dovie covered the old woman's hands with her own, surprised to find them ice-cold. Even knowing what had come of Dora's dreadful edict—the hardships and horrors her daughter had been forced to endure—a small part of her understood. Dora Tandy had acted out of desperation and a need to protect her child at all costs, to spare her the treatment she herself had endured as an unwed mother.

"Please don't torture yourself." Dovie knew the words were useless, but there was nothing else to say, no words of comfort to be found. In the end, Dora *was* to blame.

"I've been torturing myself all these years. I'm afraid I don't know how to stop. And it's what I deserve, isn't it? She came home, after, but not to stay. She was there just long enough to pack her things and make off with the money I'd been saving for her to go to university. Then she disappeared. A year later, there was a letter from Charleston saying she'd found a job, and promising never to come back to Sennen Cove. And she didn't. I never saw her again—or my grandchild. I think of the babe sometimes, even after all these years, and wonder what became of it, if it was boy or a girl, if it's still alive somewhere in the world. It's why I came. I had to see Alice one last time before I . . . I had to see her one last time, to beg her forgiveness. I didn't know she was gone until I went to the address on the envelope and asked after her. The maid who answered the door looked at me funny and said I must be from out of town. She said everyone in Charleston knew where to find Alice Tandy."

Dora's sobs came in earnest then, breaking in great heaving shudders. Dovie tightened her grip on the woman's arm but remained silent. There were no words to comfort a mother whose daughter had died despising her.

Finally, her tears ran out. She fumbled a moment to open the old black handbag and extricate another rumpled tissue. "Poor girl," she said, blotting her eyes. "I'm sorry to go all cakey, prattling on like an old fool, and to a perfect stranger. I'll go now, and leave you to your young man."

Dovie watched as Dora fumbled with her handbag, breathless and clumsy. She didn't look well, certainly not well enough to drive herself back to wherever she'd come from. "Did you drive here today, Dora?"

"Taxi." Her voice was thready again, her breath coming in short, thin bursts, and the bluish tint had reappeared around her mouth.

"Is there anyone I can call? Anyone who could pick you up and maybe look after you?"

"No one. I just need a taxi, and I'll . . . be on my way."

Dovie checked her watch, thought of the budget folder sitting on her desk, and made a decision. "No. I'll drive you back. Just give me a minute to make a call."

Stepping away, she punched Jack's cell number into her phone, half hoping as she waited for him to pick up that the call would go straight to voice mail. It didn't.

"Hello, Dovie. What's up?"

Had she only imagined the gruff impatience in his tone? She didn't think so. "Hey, Jack. I just wanted to let you know that something's come up, and I'm going to be late getting back. It's a . . . a friend of mine. She's sick and I need to drive her home. I was wondering if there was any way we could push the two o'clock meeting to three?"

There was a pause, the kind that meant the person on the other end was weighing his words before speaking. "Dovie, you know how important this fund-raiser is, right?"

"Yes, of course I do."

"And that we can't afford to look like we don't know what we're doing with Gemma Tate's endowment and this new wing?"

Dovie closed her eyes, gnawing her lower lip. "Yes."

"Good. I just wanted to make sure. Take care of what you need to take care of, and we'll reschedule in the morning. I'm booked today, from three on."

There was no time to say thank you before the line went dead.

Dora protested the whole way down the path, arguing that she was quite capable of taking a taxi, but finally divulged the name of her motel—the Palmetto Moon. Dovie recognized the name as soon as it was out of Dora's mouth. She had mentioned it in her letter to Alice. She knew the place, an old flat-roofed mom-and-pop out on Highway 17, popular for its budget rates and no-frills efficiencies.

They drove in silence. Dovie resisted the urge to ask questions. The less she spoke, the less chance there was of blurting out details she had no *legitimate* way of knowing. Her thoughts crept to the letters in her purse. Maybe she should just come clean and hand them over. They didn't belong to her. But was there anything to be gained by giving Dora the letters? Perhaps, in the old woman's case, as Josiah said, the not knowing was a blessing. At least that's what she told herself as she pulled into the Palmetto Moon's rutted parking lot.

"I'm there on the end," Dora told her, pointing to the end unit near a kidney-shaped swimming pool. "You can just drop me at the door."

The lot was small and crowded with cars that had seen more than their fair share of miles. Dovie pulled into the space in front of unit 12 and cut the engine, scouting her surroundings while Dora fumbled in her purse. Finally, she produced a large plastic key fob stamped with the number 12. Dovie reached for it, and got out of the car. "I want to make sure you get in okay."

Actually, she wanted to make sure the place wasn't infested with roaches—or worse, was some kind of firetrap. A whiff of musty air greeted them as they pushed inside—dampness mixed with Pine-Sol and less-than-clean carpeting. It was everything Dovie had expected, cramped and shabby, though minus the roaches, thank heavens. There was a bed with a faded floral spread, a small table and a pair of chairs, a vintage television and battered dresser, and in one corner, a tiny kitchenette equipped with a minifridge, a two-burner stove, and a sink barely large enough to accommodate a dinner plate. Depressing, but habitable.

"Not much of a place, is it?" Dora said, as if reading her mind. "But it's what I could afford. I booked for a full month, but now . . ."

Now Alice was dead, and there was no reason to stay. That was what she'd been about to say. "You'll be going back to Cornwall, I suppose?"

Dora looked up from the handbag she'd been placing on the dresser. "I don't recall saying I was from Cornwall. Did I?"

Dovie could have kicked herself. She'd always been clumsy when it came to secrets. "No," she said, recovering quickly. "You didn't tell me. But I recognized your accent. I spent some time in the U.K. when I was in college."

If Dora found the explanation suspect she gave no sign. Instead, she shook her head. "Bought one of those cheap, nonrefundable tickets, so I'm here awhile yet, like it or not. I thought there'd be time, you see. I thought we'd talk things out, that maybe I could make amends. But I was too late."

Dovie pressed her lips together, reminding herself that none of this was her business. And yet she'd made it her business, hadn't she, the minute she picked up the letter from Alice's grave? She was convinced that she was right about Alice's letters. Keeping them from Dora was an act of kindness, a way of shielding her from the horrors her daughter had suffered during her stay at Blackhurst. But did that mean Dora shouldn't at least try to discover what had befallen Alice after leaving Cornwall?

Surely the Tates would be able to provide some information. How she died. What sort of life she had lived. If she'd ever found her child. Not that she was in any position to presume on her connection with the Tates—if you could even call it a connection. And there were risks on that front. What if, while attempting to trace her daughter's footsteps, she was to get wind of the rumors surrounding Alice and Harley Tate? For an instant, the voice in her head was back, warning her to steer clear of things that didn't concern her. Then she looked at Dora, at her weary posture and desolate expression, and pushed the voice aside. "Have you thought about trying to learn what happened to your grandchild?"

A parade of emotions passed over Dora's face as she sagged down onto the edge of bed. "I tried once, back home, but there aren't any records. Blackhurst—that's the place I sent Alice—is closed now, and no one seems able to help me. They don't like folk nosing around about those places, not even family—or maybe especially family. All I know is most of the babies born there wound up in America or Canada."

"It's a start, at least," Dovie said. "And a lot of old records are online now, which would make it easier. You'd be surprised what people turn up."

"It's been so long. I wouldn't know where to begin—or how."

Dovie stared at the poor woman, at the despair etched into her withered face, the hope laid bare in her gray eyes, and felt herself wavering. Would it be so wrong, so unthinkable, to contact Gemma Tate and ask a few questions on behalf of a grieving mother? To risk offense in the name of compassion? She already knew what Jack would say if he ever got wind of her intentions. It would begin with *What the hell were you thinking?* and end with her on the unemployment line. And yet she couldn't help herself. The words were out before she could weigh them further. "I think I might be able to help."

The next morning, Jack was waiting in her office when she arrived, seated in one of the conference chairs in front of her desk. He glanced at his watch as she stepped through the door, prompting her to glance at her own. Right on time, thank God, though she could see that he was still miffed about their meeting yesterday.

"Morning, Jack," she said, trying to sound nonchalant as she slid behind her desk. "About yesterday—"

"I know. You had to drive a sick friend home."

Dovie bristled at the unspoken implication that she had made up the story. "I did, as a matter of fact. Her name is Dora, and she's . . . she's . . ." Dovie let the words dangle. What was she?

Jack stood, his pink face grim as he crossed to the door and closed it. "You were at the cemetery again, I take it, when you called me?"

"I was at lunch when I called you," Dovie shot back.

"Dovie, I don't pretend to understand your need to go and sit with a bunch of dead people, but if that does it for you, great. My concern isn't where you eat your lunch. It's that you sometimes forget to come back. And then, when you do finally get back to your desk, you seem to have left your mind behind. You can't deny it."

He was right; she couldn't.

The silence stretched, thick and uncomfortable. Finally, Jack let out a breath, resignation or disgust; Dovie wasn't sure which. "The proposal you were supposed to have ready for yesterday's meeting—do you have it?"

Dovie's gaze slid to the folder sitting on the corner of her desk. She'd meant to bring it home last night, to check her figures and give it one last polish, but she forgot to slip it into her tote when she left the office, and hadn't remembered until after midnight. "I'll definitely have it for you by the time we meet."

Jack leveled a hard gaze at her across the desk. "We're meeting now, Dovie. This *is* the meeting."

Dovie's mouth went dry as she once again groped for words. "It just needs a few finishing touches, Jack. I can have it ready in—"

"It was supposed to be ready yesterday, Dovie. Not today. Not later. Yesterday."

Dovie could only nod. His tone stung, perturbed, and more than a little weary, as if she'd just told him the dog had eaten her homework. "I'm sorry, Jack."

"Dovie, we've talked about this. In fact, we seem to *keep* talking about it. I've cut you plenty of slack—you can't say I haven't—but we're coming to a place where I'm going to have to make a decision. Sooner or later the board is going to notice things are falling through the cracks—things under your purview. And then it's going to be my ass on the line, since I'm the one who put you in that chair. It's not that I minded covering for you. I was happy to do it—in the beginning. But I can't keep pretending you're up to this when it's becoming more and more obvious that you're not."

Dovie remained mute. How could she defend herself when he was right? Her mind *was* somewhere else most of the time, and the *whys* and *wheres* didn't matter. "You're right, Jack," she said, struggling past the sudden sting in her throat. "About all of it. I have been . . . distracted. All I can say is I'm sorry, and I promise to get myself together."

"Sooner would be better than later," he said, then softened his tone. "This new wing, and everything to do with it, starting with the fund-raiser, has got to go down without a hitch. No gaffes. No overruns. No oversights."

"Yes."

"I mean it, Dovie. I won't be able to help you if you blow this."

Dovie folded her hands on her desk blotter and met his gaze squarely. "You won't have to, Jack. And I won't make you fire me. If there's a problem, any kind of problem, I'll resign."

eight

MAGNOLIA GROVE CEMETERY
CHARLESTON, SOUTH CAROLINA
OCTOBER 6, 2005

Austin's stomach clenched as he rounded the curve and saw the angel come into view. He didn't like cemeteries, this one least of all, but he'd promised. And so here he was, while his mother lay in a dark room with a cold compress over her eyes, fighting another of the debilitating migraines that had escalated in both frequency and intensity since his father's death. Stress, the doctors said, which was the *only* reason he'd decided to stop shirking his duty and assume the reins of the largest real estate development firm in the southeastern United States.

But there had been a few bonuses. Like imagining Harley Tate rolling in his grave when he began changing the way the family firm conducted business, starting with the immediate cessation of all dealings with his father's old business cronies—men so crooked they'd have to be screwed into the ground when they died. *King Tate.* That was how he'd always thought of his father, because that was how he treated people: contemptuous of his subjects, dismissive of his wife, and disgusted with the prince and heir who had never lived up to his expectations.

Well, it was his turn to wear the crown now. And if he was going to be chained to a desk, he was damn sure going to make it worth his while, starting with a big fat endowment to Charleston Museum of Cultural Arts in his mother's name. God knew, after thirty years of marriage the woman deserved some kind of reward, if not a medal. Next was his BuildGreen initiative, something he'd tried for years to get his father to consider, not just because it played to Charleston's shifting demographics, but because it was the right thing to do. His father would have despised both ideas, but he didn't care. Tate Development had been greasing palms and cutting corners for years, getting rich off the backs of Charleston and its residents. Now it was time to give back. To hell with the old man.

It was hardly an appropriate thought to have while standing in front of his father's grave, he knew, but what else did he have? There were no *good* memories. No Saturdays spent fishing. No playing catch in the backyard. No camping trips to the mountains. None of the father-son stuff most guys had to look back on when their fathers passed away. He'd been left with nothing to mourn. He'd worn the appropriate expression of grief at the funeral, said all the proper and respectful things. He'd gotten good at that—at the show. Wearing the right face, feigning things he didn't feel, maybe because life had given him so many opportunities to practice.

His mother, though, was a different story. Her grief was all too real, as fresh and raw as the day her husband had died. It baffled him, that kind of love—the kind that kept right on loving, despite the costs. But Gemma Tate was made of strong stuff, built to bend but never break. And she'd been tested over the years. Survival instinct, some would say. Perhaps that was where he'd learned it. And yet he'd never understand how she could mourn Harley Tate—a man who had treated her like part of his portfolio, just another asset to be leveraged.

Enough, Austin told himself. He wasn't here to confront his father's ghost. He glanced at the bouquet of pink peonies he had just picked up from Morton's—Alice's favorite. For as long as he could remember, his mother had had a standing order for a bouquet of pink peonies every sixth of October, in honor of her dear friend's birthday. Only this year, she wasn't able to bring them herself.

He let his gaze wander to the tearstained angel a few yards away, no less beautiful now than the day he had first laid eyes on her, and then down to the tarnished nameplate at her feet.

ALICE TANDY
Beloved friend
October 6, 1946–January 4, 1969

It should have said so much more.

He swore softly and looked away. He had promised himself he wouldn't go there, that this time he wouldn't let himself to be dragged down memory lane, and yet here he was, dredging up memories of the past.

The idea had been tabled at breakfast the morning of his fifth birthday. His father had coolly announced that if he was ever going to be a real Tate, it was time he went away to school. The announcement had been received by his mother with stunned silence. Alice, on the other hand, had committed the unpardonable sin of standing up to his father, listing all the reasons it was wrong to send a five-year-old boy away to school. By then he'd been sobbing so hard he'd been sent to his room without his breakfast. Later, Alice brought him a tray with a slice of birthday cake and a single candle to make a wish on. She became his champion that day—and a perpetual thorn in Harley Tate's side.

The barest of breezes brushed the back of Austin's neck, like cool fingers against his skin, reminding him where he was and what he'd come to do. He bent down, placing the peonies at the angel's feet, then straightened, brushing bits of dried grass from his knees. That's when he saw Dovie Larkin perched on a nearby bench—watching him.

He squinted to make sure he wasn't seeing things, but no, it was her. She hadn't been there when he came down the path, and he was pretty sure she hadn't walked past him, but somehow she was there. Then he remembered—the sculptor fiancé. Perhaps he was buried here somewhere. God knew, half of Charleston was.

Was she holding . . . a sandwich?

Sandwich forgotten, Dovie watched as Austin Tate went down on one knee to place a bouquet of pink flowers at the foot of Alice's grave. He was the last person she had expected to see when she came strolling down the path. In fact, she almost kept on walking when she first spotted him. She wasn't in the mood for conversation, least of all with Austin Tate, which was why she had purposely left a message with his office that there was no need for them to meet again, and that she would just leave the folder of brochures at the front desk to be picked up at his convenience. And yet here she was, on her usual bench—playing the voyeur.

He was standing now, brushing at the knees of his khakis, and turned to lock eyes with her. There was a moment of recognition, followed by another of embarrassment. Dovie lowered her sandwich, wondering what he must think of a woman who ate her lunch in a cemetery. The same thing everyone else thought, probably.

Don't come over. Don't come over. Do. Not. Come. Over.

But she needn't have worried. With the curtest of nods, Austin turned away, stalked down the north path, and disappeared.

Long after he vanished, Dovie continued to stare at the empty path, trying to digest what she'd just witnessed. At first glance, she assumed he had come to pay his respects to his father. But the flowers told a different story. For some reason, it never occurred to her that he might have known Alice, but after a quick calculation it was almost certain he had. He looked to be in his late thirties, which meant he'd been born in the early '60s. According to the plaque, Alice died in '69, presumably while still working for the Tates, which meant there had to have been at least some overlap. But Dovie didn't really need the math. His body language as he placed the flowers on Alice's grave was enough to prove he'd known her—and had been fond of her.

NINE

Dovie sipped her third cup of coffee as she waited for Theda Okona, head of the museum's native cultures department, to look over the proposal she had labored on all weekend. Jack had given her an extra two days to polish it up, a generosity she hadn't expected, given their last conversation. It was a good thing, too, since she had discovered three glaring errors on her final pass, hence the need for Theda's eagle eyes this morning. She needed to be certain every *i* had been dotted, every *t* crossed.

Staying focused had been a challenge. So had sleeping. She couldn't help thinking about Dora sitting all alone in room 12, waiting to hear from her, knowing that every day without answers must be fresh agony. She had been by the Palmetto Moon twice since that first day. The first time, to check on Dora's state of health and leave her contact numbers at the front desk, in case Dora seemed unwell or needed anything. The second visit had been to deliver several bags of groceries from Harris Teeter, including canned soup, fresh fruit, copious amounts of Earl Grey tea, and three packages of chocolate digestives, which Dovie had never heard of until Dora requested them, but now couldn't seem to leave alone.

Her stomach rumbled as she thought of the package of digestives stashed in her bottom desk drawer, a reminder that she'd skipped breakfast. She reached for them now, fishing out one of the chocolaty biscuits and beginning to nibble. It was hardly a proper breakfast, but she needed something in her stomach before her ten thirty with Jack.

"Give," Theda said, holding out a hand. "Thanks, by the way, for hooking me on these things. Like my backside isn't already big enough."

Dovie smiled as she handed her a cookie. There was nothing wrong with Theda's backside—or any other part of her, for that matter. Like most Gullah woman she knew, Theda was beautiful inside and out, a voluptuous warrior-goddess with a sharp wit and wisdom to match. But then, when you remembered what the Gullah people had been through—generations of slavery, oppression, and marginalization, followed by the daily fight to maintain their lands and their culture—it wasn't hard to imagine where that mental toughness came from.

"This looks fine," Theda pronounced, handing back the report. "But since when do you have me check your homework? It's usually me coming to you."

Dovie made a face behind her coffee mug. "Since Jack and I had a little talk the other day. He pretty much let me know I'm on borrowed time."

"Because this report was late?"

"Because of everything. He was pretty bent about me not coming back from lunch the other day, and missing our meeting. The report was just the last straw. And it's not like he's wrong. I'm not dialed in. I know that. It's been a year, and I still can't seem to get it together—which is why I told Jack I'd resign if the fund-raiser didn't go off without a hitch."

Theda's face went blank. "You what?"

"I said I'd resign. I can't put Jack in a position to have to fire me. Not after he went to bat for me with the board."

"Have you lost your mind?"

Dovie shrugged. "Maybe."

"I thought you were getting better, that things were, you know, stabilizing."

Dovie sighed and reached for her mug. Theda didn't understand—no one did, except maybe Dora—but she did mean well. "I'm trying, Theda. Every day, I'm trying. It's just . . . hard."

Theda's lips thinned as she weighed her next words. "I know you hate the idea, Dovie, but maybe it's time to talk to someone. I don't mean a shrink, necessarily, but maybe you could find a support group or something, other people who've been through what you have."

"Let me think. Do they have support groups for people whose fiancés opt for suicide rather than marriage? I'll just check the Yellow Pages."

Theda's chin lifted a notch. "That's not fair, Dovie. You know I'm just trying to help. You're not yourself, and I'm worried."

Dovie felt a pang of shame. "I'm sorry. I didn't mean to go all passive-aggressive. I don't know what's wrong with me these days."

"Well, I do. You need to get out, instead of holing up on your back porch. It's time to rejoin the living, girl."

"It isn't that easy, Theda."

"It is. It's as easy as going with me to the Rooftop after work tonight. As easy as sitting with a friend and having a drink."

"Theda, I'm not really in the mood for—"

"Say yes."

Dovie had to admit it *was* tempting. The Rooftop had always been their favorite after-work hangout, back when Dovie still had a social life—good food, cold drinks, and a view few Charleston bars could rival. But there was Dora, waiting alone in room number 12. "I wish I could, but there's something I need to—"

"Say yes," Theda insisted, cutting her off again. "And do whatever it is later. You need this, Dovie. You'll see. It'll do you good to get out with people—living people."

It was becoming obvious that Theda wasn't going to quit until she got her way. "All right, a drink at the Rooftop. And then I really do have something I need to do."

"Great! I'll meet you out front at—"

Theda's eyes suddenly shifted to the open door. Dovie followed her gaze, praying Jack hadn't been standing there for the last five minutes, listening to them talk about shrinks and support groups.

If possible, it was worse.

"Mr. Tate . . . ," she blurted, tongue-tied at suddenly finding him in her doorway. Their awkward encounter at the cemetery was still fresh in her mind, and she had no wish to revisit it now—or ever really. "Was there something you needed? I did tell your secretary I'd leave the folder at the front desk. Everything your mother needs should be there. All we need her to do is look through the information and give us her preferences. If she has any questions—"

Austin ducked his head, looking almost sheepish. "Yeah, that's the thing. I just stopped by the front desk and they had no idea what I was talking about, so they sent me back here."

No. No, no, no, no, no, no, no. She couldn't have . . .

Dovie felt the tips of her ears go hot as she recalled placing the folder on her kitchen counter last night beside the coffeemaker—where it would be impossible to miss this morning. It would have been a brilliant strategy, too, had she taken the time to actually make coffee before dashing out the door to work.

Theda must have read the panic in her eyes, and took her cue to leave, swiping the package of digestives off the desk on her way out.

Traitor.

Dovie's face flamed as she turned her attention back to Austin. "I'm so sorry, Mr. Tate. I was working on the folder at home last night, and I must have left it on the kitchen counter. I'll definitely have it for you tomorrow. I can run it by your office, if that's convenient."

If Austin was peeved he gave no sign. "Tomorrow's fine, and I can pick it up here. I'll be by around lunchtime."

Dovie breathed a sigh of relief as she watched him go. It could have been worse. It could be Jack she had to explain herself to. As it was, she'd have the folder in Austin's hands by noon tomorrow, with no one the wiser. And this would be her absolute last blunder concerning the Tates.

"Ms. Larkin?"

Dovie started, nearly knocking over her coffee. She hadn't heard Austin step back into the doorway. "Please, call me Dovie," she managed with a pasted-on smile. "Was there something else you needed?"

"Actually, yes. There's something I've been wondering about."

Of course there was. You ran into people you knew at the grocery store, the post office, the movies—but the cemetery? "What's that?"

"The other day at the cemetery, I could have sworn I saw you holding a sandwich."

Dovie lifted her chin, a tiny show of defiance. "Smoked turkey on whole wheat."

"Do you make a habit of eating lunch at the cemetery?"

"Every day, as a matter of fact. Why, is that odd?"

The unexpected quip brought a smile to his lips. "I was thinking more along the lines of eccentric."

"Well, that's a nicer word than most people use."

"Your fiancé—" he said, the smile gone. "You told me the first time we met that he died. Is that why you go? Because he's there?"

Dovie let her eyes drift to the sculpture in the corner, recalling Austin's first visit to her office. "You might say I've developed a bit of an obsession. Or at least my family would. I go every day to sit near his grave and wait."

She was hoping to creep him out, to send him scurrying from her office. Instead, he seemed to settle in, propping a shoulder against the doorframe. "What is it you're waiting for?"

Dovie shrugged. "Answers, I guess. He killed himself two weeks before we were supposed to get married. No note. No warning. Nothing. So I guess I'm waiting for answers."

"Have you gotten any?"

"No, and I won't. But it's kind of a habit now."

"And that's why your friend thinks you need to get out more?"

Dovie flashed him a look of annoyance. "Didn't anyone ever tell you it's impolite to eavesdrop?"

"I wasn't eavesdropping. I was coming down the hall and happened to overhear. And yes, I was told that. More than once, in fact. I'm not nosy, but I am curious. So?"

Dovie looked at him, not sure why she was participating in this conversation, or why she even cared what he thought. "Her name is Theda," she said finally. "And she worries about me. She thinks I need to rejoin the living."

"And what do you think?"

Dovie sighed, then shrugged. She was tired of the question, but even more tired of not having a good answer. "I'm not sure I know how—or if I even want to. How's that for eccentric?"

"Sounds about right, given the circumstances."

Something in his voice, a softness Dovie hadn't expected, left her feeling off balance. She needed to change the subject, fast. "What about you? Why were you at Magnolia Grove?"

"I was bringing flowers to a friend of my mother's on her birthday. She normally goes herself, but she hasn't been feeling well, so I offered."

Dovie fought to conceal her surprise. She needed to tread very lightly. "Alice and your mother were friends?"

Austin's face remained stony, but something like wariness had kindled in his eyes. "She came to work for my family when I was a kid, and she and my mother became close. Why are you so interested in Alice Tandy?"

Nice going, Dovie. So much for treading lightly. "No reason. I'm just curious, like everyone else in Charleston." There was no use pretending she hadn't heard the rumors. Everyone had. And Harley Tate's death had only refueled them.

"It isn't true," he said flatly. "What they say about my father and Alice—it never happened."

"So you remember her?"

"She was my nanny."

Dovie blinked at him as she digested this snippet of information. Dora's daughter had been Austin Tate's nanny. She hadn't seen that coming, though she supposed it shouldn't come as a shock that one of the richest families in Charleston would have an English nanny. "How old were you when she died?"

Austin eyed her with open suspicion now. "Seven. Eight. Why?"

"I was just thinking that it must have been hard on you. Were you close?"

Austin shoved his hands into his pockets, offering a halfhearted shrug. "She taught me to tie my shoes and made me eat my vegetables."

The halfhearted answer didn't jibe with the emotions she had witnessed at Magnolia Grove. "Do you remember how she died?"

"No."

Again, Dovie was less than convinced. His answer had been too quick—and too harsh—as if he had suddenly drawn the shutters down over his emotions. Or maybe little boys didn't get attached to their nannies. If she could just get him to open up, she might actually have something to tell Dora when she visited later on.

She was still trying to formulate a fresh approach when Theda appeared behind him in the doorway, pointing frantically at her watch. *Oh God.* Her meeting with Jack. She had exactly three minutes to get her notes together and get to the other side of the building.

"I'm sorry to rush off," she said, standing abruptly, "but I'm about to be late for a very important meeting. I'll be sure to have that folder out front for you tomorrow before noon."

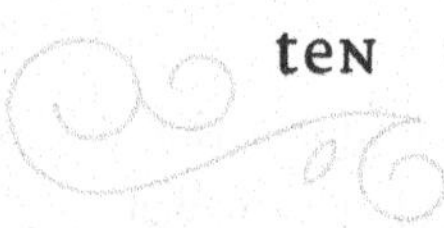

ten

Dovie adjusted her sunglasses as she gazed out over Charleston Harbor. She hadn't been to the Rooftop in over a year, but the view was just as spectacular as she remembered, all sun and sky and dark sparkling sea. And the breeze off the water was perfect, soft and balmy against her bare arms.

The bartender wasted no time making his way to the end of the bar. He was handsome almost to the point of pretty, and clearly knew it. "What's your pleasure, ladies?"

Theda ordered her usual: margarita, no salt. Dovie opted for a Tanqueray and tonic.

Theda shot her a look. "Going for the hard stuff, I see."

"If there was ever a day when I needed the hard stuff, it's today."

"Jack still giving you a hard time? I thought the proposal looked great."

"No, the meeting was fine, and Jack was happy with the proposal, though not so much with having to wait for it. It's just been a muddle of a day, that's all. First, I leave the folder of stuff I've been working on for Gemma Tate sitting on my kitchen counter, and don't remember it until her son is standing in my office. Then Austin and I end up in this very weird conversation about the dead people in our lives, during which I'm pretty sure I managed to piss him off by asking too many questions. And finally, to top it all off, I left him standing in my office because I forgot I had a meeting with Jack. Thanks, by the way, for saving my tail."

"You talked about dead people with Austin Tate?"

"Yes, but he started it."

"What are you, five? What do you mean, he started it?"

"I mean, he was the one who started asking questions—about me, and why I eat lunch in the cemetery."

"How would he even know that?"

"Because he saw me. I was at Magnolia Grove a few days ago, and who should come strolling down the path with a handful of flowers?"

"He brought you flowers?"

"No, he brought Alice flowers."

Theda just stared. "Who in the world is Alice?"

"The girl. The maid. You know—the one in the Tate plot that everyone whispers about."

"Oh, the girl with the angel."

"Yes. Her name was Alice Tandy, and it turns out she was the Tates' nanny."

Theda's brown eyes went large. "How do you know that?"

"I asked him."

"You just walked up and asked him?"

"Not then. But I saw him leave the flowers. So I asked him about it today and he told me she used to be his nanny."

"So what's weird about that?"

Dovie held her answer until Chad finished delivering their drinks. "It wasn't weird at all," she said, lifting her glass for a first sip. "It was kind of sweet, actually, seeing him bend down and leave the flowers. But today, when I asked, he acted like he barely remembered her."

Theda set down her glass, fixing her with a hard stare. "Okay, the first thing I have to ask is why do you care? Is this about William, somehow?"

Dovie fiddled with her lime. She had opened a can of worms, and knew Theda too well to think she'd be let off the hook without spilling the whole story. But first, she'd need to go back to the beginning.

To Theda's credit, she said nothing as the story tumbled out: the moment she first saw Dora Tandy grieving in the cemetery, her reckless decision to take and read the letter, the handful of letters Josiah had come across in lost and found, the horror Alice had endured at Blackhurst, and finally, Dovie's promise to help Dora learn what had happened to her daughter and grandchild.

When she was finished, she sat with her hands folded, waiting for some kind of reaction. After a long stretch of silence, Theda pushed back her empty glass, signaled Chad for another, and turned sharp eyes on Dovie. "On second thought, I think you *do* need a therapist. Are you insane?"

"I know. I know. Bad idea. Lots of them, in fact."

"Do you have any idea what Jack would say if he knew you were thinking about snooping around in Gemma Tate's private business? You won't have time to resign, honey. You'll be out on the sidewalk before you have time to clean out your desk."

"I know. I just couldn't help myself. Dora's so sad, so . . . desolate."

"This *is* about William, isn't it? Somehow this has to do with his suicide."

"Maybe, but not the way you think. I know what it's like to grieve like that, Theda, to never know if what happened was your fault. If I can help Dora Tandy to not feel like that anymore . . ."

"You still won't know," Theda finished for her. "Helping this woman isn't going to change anything. You get that, right? That you'll probably never know why William did what he did?"

Dovie nodded, relieved to see Chad approach with fresh drinks. "Yes,

I get it. I've always gotten it. But Dora's situation is different. There's someone who knows what happened to Alice, someone I can talk to."

Theda laid a hand on her arm. "Dovie, I'm serious. This has got to stop. It's one thing to bail on your friends and your social life, but this is your career we're talking about, and from the sound of things the ice is already pretty thin. Why would you go playing with fire? I mean it, Dovie. Walk away now and forget this."

Dovie traced a finger around the rim of her fresh gin and tonic. "I'm not sure I can, Theda, or that I want to. I'm not asking you to understand. No one can, except maybe Dora."

Theda sighed. "You know I'm here for you. For anything. But I don't like where this is headed. You know the rumors about that girl and Harley Tate. People *still* talk about it. And here you go, wanting to rub his wife's nose in it, six months after they put him in the ground."

"I wouldn't be rubbing her nose in anything. I have no intention of bringing that up. I just want to know how Alice died, and if she can tell me anything about the baby she gave up. So, you see, it won't even be about the Tates. It'll just be about Alice."

Theda shook her head. "Okay. But I want to go on the record as saying this is a bad idea."

"Fine. You're on the record. Now, can we change the subject? I've had quite enough of the Tates for one day."

Chad reappeared with a pair of menus, in case they had changed their minds about ordering food.

"He's nice," Theda purred as she watched him walk away. "Nice eyes."

Dovie cleared her throat. "Those aren't his eyes you're staring at, Theda."

"It doesn't hurt to look, honey. And speaking of looking, don't you think it's time you started?"

Dovie's eyes went wide. "After everything we just talked about, that's the advice you have for me. Start looking?"

"No, honey. My first advice was for you to forget the silliness with the old woman, but you're not going to listen to that. So I moved on. Maybe if you had someone in your life—if you had a life *period*—you wouldn't have time to get yourself into this kind of trouble."

"New subject," Dovie said drily.

"Okay, how's your sister?"

"Robin? She's perfect, as always. Already fat as a butterball, though she's not due until December. They're going to name her Gracie, after my grandmother. Grace Elizabeth."

"Nice. I'm glad the old names are coming back. We've had enough Kaleys and Kirstens for a while. But somehow I doubt a daughter of mine would thank me for naming her after my mother."

"Anyika is a beautiful name."

"Maybe, but it's not exactly playground friendly, is it? And my grandmother's name is even worse."

"How is Mama Hettie these days? Still going strong, I take it?"

Mama Hettie was Theda's grandmother, or her *granmammy* in the Gullah dialect. Thirty years ago, Hettie opened a restaurant called the Porch out on Highway 17, which had quickly become renowned for its shrimp and grits.

"Old thing's still in the kitchen every day," Theda said, grinning. "I swear she's getting younger. It's all those spices and roots she cooks with. Gullah women think you can cure just about anything with food, and I'm half convinced it's true. She's been asking about you, by the way. She wants to know when you're coming back. She thinks you're mad because she wouldn't give up her shrimp and grits recipe."

"I know," Dovie said with a wisp of a smile. "It has been a long time. I just haven't been in a going-out mood lately."

"There doesn't have to be a guy, you know. Your friends miss you. Hell, I miss you."

"We see each other every day, Theda."

"Yeah, but that's work. I miss us going out and doing stuff. I miss this." She held up her glass, waiting for Dovie to follow suit. "To rejoining the living."

Dovie raised her glass briefly before setting it back on the bar without sipping, hoping it had escaped Theda's notice that she had neatly sidestepped the toast. It wasn't that Theda was wrong about her need to rejoin the living. It was that at the moment, she had more pressing things on her mind, like reading the last of Alice's letters before she went to see Dora tonight.

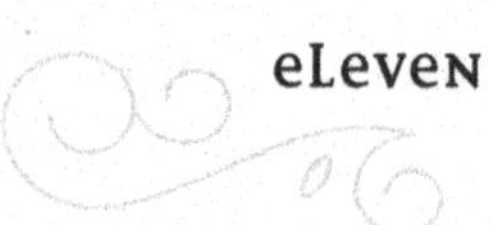

eLeveN

Blackhurst Asylum for Unwed Mothers
Cornwall, England
June 3, 1962

Little one,

My cough has grown worse. There's more blood now, and last week I slumped over in the supper line when I couldn't get my breath. That's how I ended up in the infirmary. It's a terrible place filled with weeping and coughing and terrible smells, but it's the rumors that keep me awake at night, gruesome whispers about girls who came here and never left, about sloppy procedures and hushed-up deaths, about tiny bodies dumped like dead puppies into the old cistern behind the kitchen, where no one is allowed to go. Maybe it's all just rumors, but maybe it's not. I only know I don't want to be one of those girls who doesn't live long enough to bring her child into the world, and is never heard from again.

The sisters prod my belly with their cold, hard hands and tell me you'll be arriving any day, words that should fill a mother's heart with joy. But there is no joy for me. Only dread. As long as you're in my belly they can't take you from me. Until then, you belong to me.

There's a girl I've just met, a young novice named Marianne, who has just been assigned to the infirmary, and will talk to me now and then, when there's no one to overhear. She's a kind girl, but sad, too, like so many of us here. One day I told her my story, about the day your sweet father was lost at sea, and Mam threatening to disown me if I didn't agree to give you up. There were tears in her eyes as she listened and remembered another young man, another child, both lost to her now.

She'll take her vows soon, as girls here do from time to time—girls without hope, or support, or means of steady work. She became all of those things when her family turned her out and told her never to come back. I have never asked, but I sometimes wonder if she regrets the choice to give her life over to these so-called Sisters of Mercy, whose idea of Christian service is robbing young women of their children and then selling those children to strangers. After what they took from her—what they'll eventually take from us all—I simply can't fathom it.

She told me how things work with the babies born here at Blackhurst; how they're taken away and sent—sold, in truth—to rich American couples; how easily passports can be arranged when enough money is put into the right hands; how church coffers are padded while authorities turn a blind eye. All in the name of Christian charity.

America.

The mere word fills me with despair. It can't be right, whatever my sins, to send you so far away, where there's never any hope of glimpsing your face at a park or in some small crowd, a frozen moment when our eyes meet and hold for the tiniest fraction of a second—and you know me. Yes, I've held to that secret hope, silly as it is. But now I know it can never be, and must find a way to keep you in my heart. Always, always in my heart.

All my love,
Mam

Blackhurst Asylum for Unwed Mothers
Cornwall, England
June 16, 1962

My dearest little one,

They have taken you. My water broke just after breakfast, but you took hours to come, as if you, too, wished to put off our parting. The pain was like nothing I've ever felt—a white-hot knife slicing up through the middle of me, splitting me in two. The wages of my sin, I heard one of the good sisters say through the haze of pain and exhaustion. There are drugs now that they can give for the pain, but nothing like that was offered during all those long hours. No kind word, or comfort given, only cold eyes and prodding hands, eager to be done with their distasteful task. I was to remember this—the pain and the shame—they told me, the next time I thought about bringing disgrace to my family.

I'll never forget the moment you finally slid free, the rush of relief mingled with despair, the terrible sense of emptiness, of endings. And then, almost before I realized it, you were gone, hurried away to some other room, where the babies are kept and mothers aren't allowed. I could hear your tiny squall as they carried you away, growing fainter and fainter. I fought to sit up, to see your little face when they pulled you free, to glimpse you just once before I lost you forever, but the sisters had me pinned to the mattress, and there wasn't enough breath left in me to fight them.

I wept for you then, sobbing and writhing like a wild thing. I begged them to bring you to me—my baby, my angel—but they wouldn't. They just turned away, slipping from the room in their silent shoes, the distasteful business of bringing another mistake into the world finished at last. Next came the papers, shoved into my hands before I had even stopped bleeding. When I refused to sign them, Sister Mary Agnes was called in to explain how things went for girls who were determined to be troublesome. They would send me away, she told me without batting an eye, to a place Mam couldn't pay my way out of, even if she could have afforded it. I asked if I could at least see you, to hold you just once before I signed my name, but they said no. They wouldn't even tell me where you were. They said you weren't my concern anymore.

They call themselves the Sisters of Mercy, these women with their withered hearts and scathing eyes, but where was all their mercy then, when they ripped you from me, and my heart was breaking?

Lately, I find my mind drifting to the cliffs. You're gone now, and there's only me to think of. It would be over quick enough, a moment or two suspended in the empty air, a brief spattering of blood and bone, and then . . . nothing. No sadness. No emptiness. Just . . . nothing.

Another sparrow smashed on the rocks.

Only Marianne has shown anything like pity, but her kind words and downcast eyes only fan my anger. She's one of them now, a bystander in the theft of my child, and doubly guilty since she was once made to endure the same crushing loss. I pleaded with her, to tell me if you were a boy or a girl, if you were fair like me or dark like your father. She just shook her head and said knowing would make it harder.

She offered to pray with me then, but I told her to save her breath. I didn't want her prayers, or anything to do with a person who could be part of such a barbaric business. I called her a traitor and a fool, and asked her if she'd forgotten what it was like to carry her own child all those months, to love it as her own flesh and then have it torn away. She hasn't forgotten, of course. I could see the anguish of it in her eyes as I flung the words at her. She'll never forget, and in that moment I knew I wouldn't, either—if I let them separate me from my child.

And so, little one, I have decided I will not let them separate us—at least not for long. It sounds preposterous, I know, but I've made up my mind to do whatever must be done. I won't be at Blackhurst forever. I'm growing stronger every day, and my cough is much better, hardly any blood at all now. Soon I'll leave this place, and then nothing will keep me from getting you back. I don't know how yet, my little one, but someday our eyes will meet and you will know that you belong to me, now and forever.

All my love,
Mam

twelve

Dovie checked her watch as she pulled into the empty spot in front of room number 12. It was a quarter to eight, but there was no light visible in the motel room window, no sign that Dora was inside. Perhaps she'd gone for a walk, or gone to sleep early. She knocked, waited, then knocked again. A few seconds later, a slice of watery light appeared in the chink between the curtains and she could hear the chain sliding.

"You came," Dora said, pulling back the door.

"I'm sorry I'm late. I had something I needed to do after work."

Dovie surveyed the room as she stepped inside, the rumpled bedspread and dented pillow, the half-eaten frozen dinner beside the bed, the milky cup of tea gone cold. "I'm sorry. Were you sleeping?"

Dora flapped a blue-white hand. "I'm an old woman. I spend half my life sleeping and the other half trying not to drop off. Would you like some tea?"

"Yes, please, but let me get it. I'll make us both a cup. Have you got any digestives left?"

Dora pointed toward the tiny cupboard above the sink. After a few minutes, Dovie located the unopened package, then set about making the tea while Dora turned on a second lamp and began tidying the bed. When the tea was finished brewing they settled at the tiny kitchen table, sipping in silence until Dovie finally spoke up.

"I have some news."

Dora lifted her eyes over her thick white mug. "About my girl?"

"Yes, about Alice. It isn't much, but it's more than we knew before."

Dora set down her tea, waiting.

"She worked as a nanny for a family here in town. A very wealthy family."

"A nanny," Dora repeated, as if tasting the word. "For rich people."

"Yes. Their name was . . . is . . . Tate. I don't know anything more than that, but at least now there's someone we can talk to, and maybe leads we'll be able to follow up on. She's buried in the Tate's family plot, so it's fair to assume she was still working for them when she died, which means they can at least tell us what happened to her."

Dora's eyes shimmered with unshed tears, but behind the shimmer was hope. "And the baby? Maybe they know what happened to the baby?"

Extricating another biscuit from the package, Dovie stalled for time, breaking off a small piece and popping it into her mouth. While it seemed likely that Gemma Tate would know how Alice died, she had doubts about her knowing about Alice's time at Blackhurst. An illegitimate child wasn't the kind of thing a young girl shared with a prospective employer. Still, there was a chance that Alice had shared her story, as well as her dream of reuniting with her child, which meant there was a chance, albeit a slim one, that Gemma might be able to provide information about the fate of the child. It was the asking that was going to be tricky.

Dovie washed down her biscuit with another sip of tea, aware of Dora's eyes on her, luminous with newfound hope. It was good to see, but she needed to understand that there was no certainty that Mrs. Tate would be willing, or even able, to help them. One thing the poor woman did *not* need to know was why Mrs. Tate might be reluctant to talk about her son's nanny. Dovie didn't know if the rumors about Alice and Harley Tate were true, or even if Gemma knew for certain, but the last thing she wanted was for Dora to get wind of them.

"Dora," Dovie said gently. "Have you ever thought that you might learn things you don't want to know?"

Dora's gaze drifted away. "Anything is better than letting your mind fill in the blanks. You of all people should understand that. You're right; hearing how my little girl died will break my heart, but no worse than thirty years of not knowing has done."

Dovie bit her lip, wishing now that she had waited until she was sure Gemma would or could help. The thought of having to come back to Dora empty-handed, of extinguishing the hope she had kindled in those tired eyes, was heartrending. Still, she needed to be honest. Better to tamp down expectations now than to crush the poor woman later.

"Dora, there's something I should have told you about Mrs. Tate. Something that could make talking to her a little tricky."

"Tricky?"

"The Tate family is highly respected here in Charleston, not to mention very wealthy. So wealthy, in fact, that they just donated two million dollars to the museum I work for. The problem is, she's been ill since her husband's death a few months ago, which might make it difficult to actually meet with her. Her son has been acting as a go-between. His name is Austin. I spoke with him this afternoon."

"This Austin—he was the boy my Alice looked after?"

Dovie looked at Dora's face, lit once again with hope. "He was very young when she died, but yes."

"He remembers her?"

"She taught him to tie his shoes and made him eat his vegetables," Dovie said, repeating Austin's words verbatim. "Beyond that, he wasn't much help. As a matter of fact, he didn't seem to want to discuss it. And since I'm not in a position to step on any toes at work just now—especially Tate toes—I couldn't really push it."

"Why?"

"Let's just say we got off to a rocky start, and I'm in a bit of a spot with my boss."

"You're in trouble at work—because of me?"

Dovie sighed, then shook her head. "No, Dora. It's got nothing to do with you. I was promoted last year. It was a really big promotion, one I'd been working toward for years, and then William . . . took the pills." She shrugged as she picked up her mug, staring down into the dregs of her rapidly cooling tea. "Everyone was great about it—at first. Until I started doing things that freaked people out. I sort of checked out of my life, stopped seeing my friends, started hanging out at the cemetery. I even made friends with one of the groundskeepers—an eighty-year-old man named Josiah. And then—"

Dora reached for her hand, giving it a pat. "And then I showed up and dragged you into my problems."

"You didn't drag me into your problems, Dora. I involved myself. All I'm saying is I need to be very careful in how I go about asking one of the museum's biggest donors about her son's nanny."

"You can't do it," Dora said with a firm shake of the head. "I won't have you getting sacked for a silly old woman and her sins. I've mucked up quite enough without adding your job to the list."

"But Alice . . ."

"I haven't the right to ask you to do this, no right to get you in a fix, no right to bother anyone—not after what I did. I meant well, but I was wrong. I didn't want folks looking at my girl like she was rubbish. They looked at me that way once, when her father left me flat with a full belly and nowhere to go. I couldn't bear for my little girl to go through that."

"Alice's father refused to marry you?"

She sighed, a heavy woeful sound. "He was gone almost before I finished telling him how things stood. I never saw him again, and my family washed their hands of me. It was terrible back then. No decent man would have you after that, and so I raised her on my own. *All* on my own. I worked three jobs and put away every cent I could so that she could go to school when it was time and have the kind of life she deserved."

She was crying now, her tears creating shiny rivulets along the creases on either side of her mouth. Dovie took her hands and let her talk out her grief.

"By the time she came to me I had already guessed, and poor Johnny was dead, drowned in a storm. My girl was alone, just like I'd been, and I couldn't bear it for her—the memories and the shame, the life she was about to throw away. And so I sent her to Blackhurst. I did it because I loved her. So she could get on with the life I had planned for her. I thought I knew best, but I was wrong. So wrong. I just thought if I could talk to her one last time, explain why I did what I did—so she wouldn't end up like me—she might forgive me."

"She never knew about her father?"

Dora shook her head. "I told her he died before she was born—a lorry accident. I was too ashamed for her to know the truth—that I'd been a fool. But I would tell her now if I could, no matter what she thought of me. Anything to make her understand that I only wanted her to have a better life than I had. Even when she was threatening to leave I wouldn't tell her. Because I was too proud. I didn't think she'd really go." She paused, taking another swipe at her cheeks. "I've always been proud, much, much too proud—and it's cost me everything."

Dovie felt her heart squeeze, aching for this woman whose life had gone so terribly wrong. "I can't promise anything, Dora, except that I'm going to do everything I can to find out what happened to Alice. Gemma Tate was Alice's friend. She's also a mother. She'll want to help."

"I can't let you risk your job, Dovie. Not for me."

"I won't be doing it for you," Dovie said. "At least, not just for you." She paused, groping for a way to explain without explaining. "I know what it's like to live with questions, to agonize over things you should or shouldn't have done, and wonder if there was some way it could have turned out differently. I'll never know what William's last hours were like, or why he did what he did, but if I can help you find your answers—and maybe help you find some peace—then I have to at least try."

Dora looked away. "There might not be time."

She wasn't talking about her return flight to Cornwall, and they both knew it. There was no denying Dora's precipitous decline since their first meeting. She was already more fragile, little more than a scarecrow, and growing thinner by the day. But far more alarming were the bouts of wheezy coughing that left her blue around the lips.

"You're sick," Dovie said.

Dora did her best to look stoic, an expression Dovie suspected she had perfected over the years. "A chest complaint, the doctors say. One that's not likely to improve." She heaved her shoulders, and the mask fell away, her sorrow stripped bare. "I don't mind, really, only I'd hoped to set things right before I . . . what is it you Americans say . . . kick the bucket? But that can't ever be."

Dovie felt tears scorching up into her throat. How had she lived with it all these years, with the unbearable weight of it always pressing on her soul? She'd made a mistake—a terrible, terrible mistake—but she had made it with her heart, and with a mother's love. Because she hadn't been able to see beyond her own scars, beyond the shame and isolation she had endured in bringing a fatherless child into the world. If only she had dropped her pride and told Alice the truth, things might have been different. There might have been no Blackhurst letters, no lost child, no broken hearts. But it was too late now. Those things existed. Dora Tandy had been living with them every day for thirty years, and for better or worse Dovie was living with them now, too.

thirteen

Anyone who had lived in Charleston any length of time could point out the Tate home. The house at the end of East Battery was impossible to miss, with its sweeping brick steps and white-pillared porch.

Dovie took her foot off the accelerator as she approached the long brick drive, still questioning the wisdom of what she was about to do. At the moment, she was inclined to agree with Theda; she was definitely insane. And yet the wrought-iron gates stood open, beckoning. Before she could change her mind, she turned up the drive, cut the engine, and climbed out of the car, grabbing the manila folder from the passenger seat.

She had phoned Jack earlier to let him know she'd be a few minutes late. Her excuse? She was dropping off some paperwork in order to save Austin a trip to the museum. Which was true. He had seemed pleased that she was taking the initiative, going out of her way to coddle the Tates and their two-million-dollar donation. Probably because she'd left out the part where her good deed included a surprise visit to Mrs. Tate's home, and a handful of embarrassing questions.

It was hard not to be awed as she stepped onto the neat slate path that led up to the front steps. The place seemed even larger than it had from the street, and more breathtaking, if that was possible, like something right off the back lot at MGM. Even the door knocker was over-the-top, a massive brass shield emblazoned with a stately lion's head. She rapped it tentatively and held her breath.

Crap on a cracker! What am I doing?

Theda was right. If Jack knew the real reason she was here, he'd fire her on the spot. For one panicked moment she thought about tearing back down the steps and beating a hasty retreat to her car. And then the door was opening and there was nothing to do but stand there with a plastered-on smile.

She was startled when Gemma Tate appeared in the doorway. She'd been expecting an employee of some kind, a maid or butler. *Do people even have butlers anymore?*

It took a moment, but she managed to find her voice. "Mrs. Tate, I'm Dovie Larkin, from the museum. I just stopped by to drop off the folder I've been working on for the gala. If you've got a few moments I'd love to go over some of the venue choices, and maybe discuss the guest list."

Gemma Tate gave a vague shake of the head, as if trying to rattle some loose thought back into place. Her hand was still on the doorknob, giving Dovie the impression that she was using it to steady herself. "I'm sorry. Did we have an appointment this morning?"

"Well, no. I just thought I'd save your son a trip and drop the information off on my way in this morning."

"Well, then, come in. I was just having coffee."

Dovie felt vaguely disoriented as she stepped into the large octagonal foyer, keenly aware of the hollow tap-tap of her heels on the green marble floor, and the spicy floral scent wafting from the profusion of lilies blooming from the surface of an inlaid mahogany table. No doubt delivered fresh every week, and no doubt costing a fortune.

A fresh wave of misgiving threatened as she contemplated the questions she'd come to ask. What right did she have to come into this woman's home and dredge up old memories—possibly painful ones? And just months after she'd buried her husband? This wasn't her business. Alice, Dora, Gemma—none of it had anything to do with her. It wasn't too late to back out. She'd just do what she said she was here to do, discuss the venues and the guest list, and then be on her way.

"If you'll follow me back to my study, I'll have Kimberly bring another cup. Or perhaps you'd rather have tea?"

"Coffee will be fine," Dovie answered as she turned to follow her hostess.

It was hard not to gape as she trailed Mrs. Tate through a front parlor filled with gleaming antiques and lush Turkish carpets. She'd never seen so many beautiful things in one room, but there was a sense of gloom hanging over everything, too, a mausoleum-like quality that reminded her of the old *Addams Family* TV show. The drapes, deep green brocade trimmed with a heavy fringe and a braided satin cord, were still drawn, shutting out all traces of the morning sun. Was it a mourning thing, she wondered, like covering the mirrors? Or was it always like this?

Whatever it was, it carried over into the study, where the curtains were also closed, the room cool and dim. There was a large writing desk in the center of the room, French and feminine in design. Gemma moved to it and clicked on a lamp, then picked up the phone to request a fresh pot of coffee and a cup for her guest. Dovie used the moment to scan the room, hoping to get a sense of the woman from her work space. Contemporary furnishings, cool, pale fabrics, good art on the walls.

"You're a fan of Ivey Clark's, I see," Dovie said, studying the painting nearest to her, an impressionist depiction of King Street awash in rain. "We have several of his pieces up at the museum. I love the way his work captures the feel of Charleston, the way he paints the light at different times of day, how it plays over the streets and buildings, muting everything."

"Do you paint, Miss . . . ?"

"Larkin," Dovie supplied. "No, I don't. My mother used to paint, but the gene skipped me. All I can do is appreciate it."

"It's apparently served you well at the museum. My son tells me you've just been promoted."

Dovie nodded, surprised that Austin would know that, or bring her up at all. "Yes, that's right, although it's been about a year now."

"Please have a seat," Gemma offered, settling at one end of a buttery leather sofa. The door swung open as Dovie took a seat at the opposite end. A young woman appeared in the doorway, carrying a tray laden with china cups and a silver coffee service. "Thank you, Kimberly. You can set it here on the table. And take the other away, if you would."

Kimberly nodded and did as instructed, then left the room without making a sound. Dovie studied her hostess as she set out two cups and reached for the pot. Her hand shook as she poured. They had never met in person, had never even spoken on the phone, but Gemma Tate was hardly a stranger. Her picture was always in the paper, smiling graciously beside her husband at some dinner or other, always heading up some local cause. On occasion, she even made the national news. But the sparkling woman from the social section was nowhere to be seen today.

She was beautiful despite her sixty-odd years, flawlessly turned out in a navy blue suit and smart two-tone pumps. But there was a fragile quality, too, beneath the carefully maintained sheen, like a fine bit of porcelain marred with invisible cracks, damaged but still lovely. For a moment, Dovie was reminded of her mother—a smile of iron and a backbone to match beneath all the finishing-school charm. Mustn't let them see you flinch. It was a strange thought to have; they were nothing alike, and yet the comparison felt right somehow.

Gemma spooned an almost invisible amount of sugar into her cup, stirring with dainty circular strokes. "Please, Ms. Larkin. Help yourself."

"Thank you, and please call me Dovie."

"Dovie it is. Now, you said you had a folder for me?"

Dovie breathed a mental sigh of relief to be getting down to business. And that was all today was going to be about—business. There would be no interrogation, subtle or otherwise, no questions that might swamp this lovely and gracious woman in fresh waves of grief. Maybe at some point down the road, when the gala was over, and she was on better footing at work, she could try again, but not today.

Dovie laid the folder open on the sofa between them, feeling lighter now that she had decided to abandon her quest. Austin wouldn't like her being here one little bit. Of that she was certain. At least now she could tell him with some measure of honesty that her visit had been strictly gala related.

"Mr. Livingston said you'd like to be involved in the planning stages, so I put together some information on the venues I think might work best, places we've used in the past that do a good job with large events. I've also included some sample invitations. You don't need to decide right now, but we are a little crunched for time if we're going to schedule before the holiday events book up. Take a day or two to look everything over, and please feel free to call me with any questions. My card is there, inside the folder."

Gemma nodded as she thumbed through the selection of brochures. "You've done a very thorough job. Thank you for all the information. I should be able to get back to you by Wednesday at the latest."

"Great," Dovie said, beaming. "As soon as I hear back, I'll get everything booked. That just leaves the guest list. We have a master list of patrons that we'll be inviting, of course, but I'm sure you'll want to add some of your own acquaintances to that."

Gemma nodded as she reached for the coffeepot to top off her cup. "As a matter of fact there are a few. I've been working on a list. If you could just grab my planner off the desk there, I can give it to you now."

Dovie stood and moved to the desk, spotting the red leather planner lying open on the blotter. She folded it closed as she picked it up and was about to return to the sofa when she noticed a cluster of small silver frames scattered around the base of the desk lamp. Her eyes locked on one in particular, a young boy in school clothes—penny loafers, preppy plaid shorts, a dark blazer with a crested pocket.

Even with the tussled hair and missing front tooth, it was impossible not to recognize Austin Tate, his boyish face already hinting at the rakish good looks he would eventually grow into. He was grinning in the photo, as if he'd just been told a secret, and Dovie found herself wondering when he had last smiled like that. He was gripping a lunch box with one hand, grasping the hand of a young woman with the other. Dovie stared at the woman's features—dark doe eyes and honey blond hair—and felt a little flutter behind her navel.

Alice.

"My son," Gemma said with the wisp of a smile. "He was six there. It was the first day of school."

Dovie managed a nod but couldn't take her eyes off Alice. She was older here than in the photo Dora had shown her, and much thinner, the girlish fullness that had softened her face replaced by something sharper and harder.

"Who's the girl in the photo with him?" Dovie ventured, trying to sound offhand.

Gemma's spoon went quiet. "Her name was Alice. She was Austin's nanny. Caused quite a stir, too. Perhaps you've heard?"

Dovie kept her face blank, aware that she was being tested. "I'm sorry. I haven't. But then, it was probably years ago."

"It was. Back in the sixties, when it was the fashion to have a black woman raising your children. You can imagine the scandal when word got out that I'd gone and hired a white girl, and an English girl at that."

Dovie felt certain she had detected a hint of amusement in

Gemma's voice, perhaps even the trace of a smile. "Is that why you hired her?"

"No," Gemma said wistfully. "That isn't why, though it certainly was a bonus. I hired her because she had nowhere else to go, and I didn't have the heart to send her away."

"That was generous of you, taking a complete stranger into your home. Not everyone would have been as kind."

Gemma's cup and saucer clattered as she set them on the tray and came to her feet. "I'm sorry, Miss . . . Dovie, but I'm going to have to cut our meeting short. I've been fighting a terrible headache all morning, and I'm afraid it's suddenly grown much worse." She was already moving to the door, calling for Kimberly, who appeared almost instantly.

Dovie stood and gathered her tote, bewildered by the change that had suddenly come over her hostess. She'd gone white as chalk and was trembling now, as if a ghost only she could see had appeared somewhere in the room.

"Please show Miss Larkin out, Kimberly. I need to go upstairs."

"Yes, ma'am. Would you like me to bring a compress and your pills?"

"No. I just need to lie down for a while. I'll be fine. Dovie, thank you for the information. I'll look it over and be in touch in a few days."

And then she was gone, leaving Dovie to follow Kimberly back through the gloomy parlor, to the floral-perfumed foyer and the waiting front door. Perhaps it *was* only a headache. It would explain the pulled drapes and darkened rooms, but as she stepped out onto the Tates' front porch, she couldn't help feeling there was more to it.

fourteen

Dovie was still wrestling with her emotions as she pulled into the museum lot and cut the engine. In terms of learning anything new about Alice, the morning hadn't exactly been fruitful, but she couldn't shake the memory of Gemma's face when Alice's name came up, which could have been a coincidence, but felt like something else.

At least she'd done something right as far as Jack was concerned. She'd gone the extra mile and had established a rapport with Gemma Tate, something even he hadn't managed to do. So why did she feel as though there was something she was forgetting, that somewhere there was another shoe waiting to drop? She was probably just being paranoid, but she reached for her planner, just to be on the safe side.

"Looks like I almost missed you."

It took a moment to register the words, another to realize they were meant for her, and still one more to notice Austin standing at the top of the steps. "Mr. Tate," she said as she began to climb. "To what do I . . . ?"

Her words trailed off as she realized with a prickle of horror that there was in fact something she'd forgotten to do—call Austin's office and let someone know he wouldn't need to pick up the folder as planned. At least she'd managed to catch him before he went inside and found out for himself, and potentially made a scene, which, after two wasted trips across town, he would certainly be within his rights to do. She supposed there was nothing to do but paste on a smile. "I'm glad I caught you. You're here for the folder, aren't you?"

"Please don't tell me it's still in your kitchen."

"No, it isn't in my kitchen, but it isn't here, either."

"Let me guess," he said, folding his arms across his chest. "The dog ate it?"

"Actually, your mother has it," she said more bluntly than she'd intended. "I dropped it off on my way in this morning, and meant to call your office."

"You dropped it off at my mother's house?"

Something in his tone made Dovie want to take a step back. "I thought I'd save you a trip and just run it by on my way in."

"But you haven't saved me a trip, have you? As you can see, I'm standing right here."

"I really did mean to call your office, but the morning got away from me. I'm so sorry."

"You seem to be saying that a lot lately."

There was nothing to say to that. It was true. She had dealt with him on three different occasions, and out of those three, she had been late to a meeting, and had failed to deliver the same folder not once, but twice. Not exactly a stellar record.

"Again, I apologize. The meeting with your mother ran longer than I expected, and then when I—"

"You had a meeting with my mother?"

"Well, not a meeting, exactly. I really didn't expect to see her at all. I thought I'd just leave the folder with whoever answered the door, but then *she* answered the door and invited me in. She seemed very pleased with what I'd put together and promised to look things over when she was feeling better."

"She was sick?"

Dovie didn't like the way his mouth had thinned, or the deep furrow that had appeared between his brows. "It was just a headache, but it came on all of a sudden. She said she just needed to lie down."

Austin closed his eyes and drew a deep breath, as if counting to ten. "They're not *just* headaches. They're migraines, the kind that send her to bed for days. But then I think I explained that at our first meeting. I believe I also made it clear that all arrangements for the fund-raiser were to go through me. I did, didn't I?"

Dovie's cheeks went hot. "Yes, but I thought I could—"

"Through me," he snapped, cutting her off. "Are we clear?"

"I was trying to be helpful. And we actually had a nice chat. We talked about your first day of school—and about Alice." She was on dangerous ground, she knew, deliberately goading him, but his snarky tone had gotten under her skin, and she couldn't seem to help herself. If she was hoping for a reaction, she certainly got one.

He took an abrupt step forward, then seemed to check himself. "Ms. Larkin, my mother has had quite enough of people meddling in things that are none of their business. In the future, please try to remember that your connection with my family has to do with the museum, and nothing more."

Dovie managed a cool nod, but inside she was fuming. Who did he think he was, telling her where she could go, and who she could talk to? But even as the question tripped through her head, she knew the answer. He was the man who held the purse strings on the museum's new education wing. He was also a man used to getting his way.

"Fine," she said, just short of snapping. "You can pick up the folder from your mother's. I'll need your preferences for a venue and the menu by Wednesday. Oh, and your choice of invitation as well."

"Someone in my office will be in touch."

Dovie was still glaring at him, trying to think of something cutting to say, when she saw Jack standing in the shade of a large oak, puffing on one of his infernal cigarettes. He was watching her—watching them—and if her guess was correct, *had been* for quite a while. He met her gaze, then flicked his cigarette away, shaking his head as he turned and headed for the side door.

Austin followed her gaze. "Someone you know?"

Dovie sighed. "Only my boss."

With a perfunctory nod, Austin turned and walked away. Dovie watched him go, fighting the urge to stick her tongue out behind his back. It had already been a disaster of a day and it wasn't even half over.

Rounding the curve of Magnolia's north path, Dovie did her best to shake off this morning's debacle and enjoy what had turned out to be a gorgeous afternoon. The air had a new feel to it, fresher and lighter now that the cloying humidity of Charleston's scorching summer months had finally lifted. The sky was different, too, no longer a stretch of hazy blue-white, but a crisp azure canvas dotted with puffs of clean white cloud. Here and there, hints of color appeared among the trees, the hickories and sweet gums beginning their subtle turn toward fall. Even the flowers on the graves had changed, the pulsing pinks and reds of summer gone now, replaced with splashes of orange, yellow, and gold.

Fall wasn't coming. It was here.

Where had the year gone? What had she been doing with her time that months—whole seasons, in fact—had slipped away without her noticing?

Taking up her normal spot near William's grave—and Alice's—Dovie fished around in her tote, eventually producing a battered ham and Swiss on rye. On cue, Josiah appeared on the path, raising a gnarled hand as he approached. Smiling, she patted the empty spot on the bench beside her, then waited while he reached for the red rag he always kept in his back pocket and carefully wiped his hands.

When he had stuffed the rag back into his pocket and settled down beside her, she handed him half the sandwich, then watched as he painstakingly plucked the caraway seeds from the bread and tossed them into the grass.

"Seeds get up under my plate."

"Sorry. No rye. I'll remember next time."

"Been thinking about you," Josiah said, tucking in to his sandwich. "Don't see you as much since I've been helping out nights over in the office. How you been doing?"

Dovie looked down at her lap, fiddling with a bit of bread crust. "I'm fine."

Josiah's sandwich halted midway to his mouth. "No one says *fine* unless they ain't. Let's have it."

Dovie dipped her head in resignation. She should have known better than to try to hide anything from Josiah. "Okay. I'm not fine. I'm not even close to fine. I'm screwing things up all over the place, and I can't seem to stop. All my life, I've been this annoyingly together person, dotting all the *i*'s and crossing all the *t*'s. Now all of a sudden I'm this train wreck."

"What kind of things you screwing up?"

"Everything. I forget meetings, leave work at home. I can't even get to the office on time anymore. And to top it off, there's this guy . . ."

Josiah shot her a sideways look. "'Bout time, too."

"Not that kind of guy. It's a work thing."

"Course not. God forbid."

Dovie let the dig pass. "Anyway . . . he's the son of one of our donors. I don't know what it is, but every time we meet we end up bumping heads. I can't seem to stop pissing him off—like I did this morning. And this time my boss was watching. Needless to say, he's not very happy with me. In fact, I'm pretty sure I'm about to get called to the principal's office. And the last thing he's going to want to hear is that all this friction isn't my fault."

"Is it your fault?"

"Maybe. A little." She paused, tossing the last of her sandwich crust to a nearby sparrow. "Okay, more than a little. But he's always got this attitude, like he has a million better things to do than talking to me about this fund-raiser. It just gets under my skin, and I end up saying the wrong thing."

"This work guy—he's big money for the museum?"

"It's Austin Tate."

Josiah whistled, long and low. "Yup. That's big money all right."

"Yes, it is. Very big money." Diving back into her tote, she fished out a pair of oranges and handed one to Josiah. "And this time I crossed the line. The worst part is, I knew I was crossing it when I did it. There's a good chance I'm going to end up getting myself fired."

"You been stealing pens or something?"

Dovie grinned in spite of herself. He was trying to lighten the moment, and she loved him for it. "No, I haven't been stealing. I went to see Gemma Tate this morning—after being told not to bother her. I pretended it was to do with the fund-raiser, but it wasn't. It was about Alice, and a promise I made to her mother."

Josiah had been peeling his orange, prying away the bright skin with his thumb. He paused and turned to look at her. "You need to back up some, Little Miss, 'cause I got no idea what you're talking about."

"The woman—Alice's mother."

"Lordy," Josiah sighed with a shake of his grizzled head. "You still stuck on that?"

"Her name is Dora," Dovie said, ignoring his peevish tone. "She came back and sat right there on that bench. We talked."

"You tell her you took her letter and read it?"

"No. But she told me why she was here. She's sick, Josiah, the kind of sick you don't get over, and she wanted to see her daughter before she dies, to beg forgiveness for what she did. The poor woman didn't even know her daughter was dead."

"And what's that got to do with you?"

"Nothing. It's just that I know what she's going through, and I'd like to help her if I can."

Josiah hung his head. "Wish I'd never give you them letters now. You pass 'em along to the old woman?"

"Dora. Her name is Dora. And no, I didn't."

"You still holding 'em?"

"Yes, and please stop looking at me like that. You read those letters. You know what they say. I couldn't stand the thought of her reading them, knowing what happened in that place. She came here to find peace, Josiah, not more guilt. And that's why I promised to help her find out what happened to Alice and the baby—and why I went to see Gemma Tate."

Josiah stared at her, his mouth gaping. "Have you gone clean outta your mind? You're telling me you went and jeopardized your job—that job you paid hell getting—because you made a promise to some old woman you don't know, about a dead girl you ain't never met?"

Dovie dropped her eyes to her lap, rolling the unpeeled orange between her palms. "I know, I know. It sounds crazy."

"Only 'cause it is."

"You wouldn't think that if you knew her, if you saw her face when she talks about her daughter. She's been torturing herself for years. I can't *not* help her."

"This ain't about Dora Tandy. You know that, don't you?"

"Yes, it is. Maybe it didn't start out that way, but it is about her, Josiah. Maybe it's a little bit about me, too—and William—but mostly, it's about Dora. Which is why I'm going to keep my promise, if I can. I know it sounds weird, but it doesn't feel like an accident that we met. I mean, think about it. She sits on the bench right next to mine, and her daughter just happens to be connected to the Tates, who just happen to be connected to the museum. It feels, I don't know . . . like fate."

"Feels like trouble, if you ask me."

"I know it does. Nothing I do these days make sense, not even to me. They say time heals all wounds, but I don't know. I was just sitting here, wondering where this year went. I don't even remember most of it, as if nothing at all happened."

Josiah popped the last segment of his orange into his mouth, licking juice from his lower lip. "That right there oughtta tell you something."

Dovie gave him a patient smile. "I feel one of your patented bits of wisdom coming on."

"A few minutes ago, you went out of your way to make sure I knew this Austin fellow had to do with work, and nothing else. Like you having someone in your life would be wrong because of what happened last time. But that don't make no sense. William's gone and you're still here, with a whole lot of life left in you. Sometimes you just have to get on with things. All kind of things."

Dovie nodded as Josiah stood and gathered his orange peels into the empty sandwich bag. "You think about that," he said gravely as he zipped the bag closed and wadded it into his back pocket. "I may be an old coot, but a man don't get to be my age without knowing a little something."

fifteen

It was nearly five o'clock when Dovie wrapped up the last of the day's meetings and finally made it back to her office. Her head had begun to throb somewhere around two, and she was more than ready to be home, to pour a glass of wine and put the day behind her, but first she needed to clear her desk and jot a few things down before they flew out of her head. The fund-raiser might be front and center these days, but the daily ins and outs of running the museum still needed her attention.

Jack hadn't mentioned her little scene with Austin the other day, though whether that was because he hadn't heard enough of their conversation, or because he was simply biding his time, she couldn't say. All she knew was she wasn't giving him any more ammunition if she could help it. If she managed to survive the fund-raiser, and find a way to keep her promise to Dora, maybe she'd be able to get her mind back on her job—and her life.

Josiah's words drifted back as she settled behind her desk and opened her planner. *Sometimes you just have to get on with things.* He was right, of course. Everyone was. Theda. Her mother. Robin. All of them. But how? A girl could get pretty banged up trying to jump back on a merry-go-round that had been spinning without her for a year, and she already had enough bruises, thank you very much. Besides, she didn't have time for a life right now, especially one she had to build from scratch. Just the thought made her tired. She gave the elastic holding her ponytail a tug, shaking out her hair with a relieved groan, then turned her attention back to her planner and tomorrow's growing to-do list.

"You should wear it like that more often."

The voice from the doorway nearly startled her out of her chair. She turned to find Austin lounging in the doorway, assessing her with cool green eyes.

"What are you doing here?" It was hardly a polite response, but then, neither was sneaking up on a person and scaring her to death.

"I'm sorry. I didn't mean to startle you. I came to bring you this."

Dovie stood, taking the thick manila folder he was holding out to her. "Thank you."

"You said by Wednesday."

"I did, yes. And here you are, right on time."

"Actually, I'm not on time. I'm a day early." He paused, offering her a toothpaste commercial smile. "Do I get extra points?"

Dovie stared at him, trying to wrap her head around that smile. Was he actually . . . flirting with her? After his lecture on the steps the other day? If so, he was wasting his time.

"I'll be sure to make a note in my planner," she told him coolly, hoping to signal the end of their conversation.

"What if I want to redeem them now?"

"What?"

"I came to strike a truce, to make friends."

"Why?"

"Because I'm afraid I might have gotten you in some hot water the other day with your boss, and that wasn't my intention. So"—he held out a hand—"friends?"

Dovie ignored his outstretched hand. "We don't have to be friends to work together."

"What if I *want* to be friends?"

Okay, he was definitely flirting. But why? When he could have his pick of any southern belle in Charleston? Flustered, she dropped back into her chair and opened the folder, scanning its contents. "I see you went with my recommendation on the Performing Arts Center. I'll give them a call first thing in the morning and get the ball rolling."

"You didn't answer my question."

"What question was that?"

"What if I *want* to be friends?"

"I have a standing rule never to mix business with pleasure, so please don't take it personally if I decline."

Austin stood staring at her, as if the idea of anyone declining his friendship was unthinkable. "Are you always so serious?"

"This is business, Austin. The fund-raiser, the new wing, it's my business. If I don't take it seriously I won't have a job."

"So I did get you in trouble."

"No, I got myself in trouble, as you were quick to point out the other day."

"Let me make it up to you. Have dinner with me tonight."

"No."

"Why?"

"I just told you why."

Austin folded his arms, a crooked grin turning up one corner of his mouth, an attempt at boyish charm that turned out to be alarmingly effective. "That wasn't a reason, Dovie, it was an excuse."

Dovie's eyes widened. "Needing to keep my job is an excuse?"

"I meant the mixing-business-with-pleasure bit."

"It wasn't an excuse. And what's wrong with taking things seriously?"

"Nothing. I just think you're taking things seriously enough for the both of us, and that maybe if you took your nose out of that planner for one minute and came out with me, you might just remember how to have a little fun."

"That's funny coming from the guy who stood on the steps the other day and scolded me like I was a child. And it seems to me you're having enough fun for the both of us."

Dovie bit her lip, realizing she was about to burn her last bridge. Instead, she closed the folder and set it aside. "Why are you flirting with me?"

"Why do you think?"

"I have no idea, since you clearly dislike everything about me."

He looked her up and down, a long, slow sweep that seemed to miss nothing. "Not everything."

Dovie sighed as she pushed to her feet. She wasn't sure what kind of game he was playing, but whatever it was, she'd had enough. "I can see you're having a wonderful time, but I don't find this amusing. You treat everything like it's a joke—including me. Well, I've got a news flash for you. Life isn't a joke. It's serious, and it's hard. And some of us are just trying to do our jobs, and hold the rest together."

Her words seemed to hover a moment in the charged air, like angry birds looking for a place to land. She hadn't meant to be so blunt, or to sound quite so desperate. She also hadn't realized Jack was still in the building until he stuck his head in at the door.

"I thought I heard voices back here," he boomed, leveling a warning glance at Dovie as he offered his hand to Austin. "Good to see you again, sir. What brings you by? Nothing wrong, I hope?"

"Not at all. Ms. Larkin was kind enough to drop off a folder for my mother to look over, and I was just running the information back to her."

"No hitches, then? Everything to her liking so far?"

It was all Dovie could do not to roll her eyes. He looked as nervous as a girl on prom night, his smile too wide, his tone too eager. In another minute he'd be bending down to kiss the signet ring Austin wore on his right hand.

Austin flashed another toothpaste smile. "Not a hitch in sight. Ms. Larkin and my mother are in lockstep on the details. Apparently, they've become quite chummy."

Chummy?

Dovie would have choked if she hadn't been so busy holding her breath. Had he just used the word *chummy* to describe her relationship with his mother?

"Well, now," Jack said, his laugh dangerously close to a snort of surprise. "That's good to hear. Good to hear. Please pass my respects along to your mother, and be sure she knows I'm available for her anytime."

Dovie was still trying to think of something to say when Jack's head swiveled in her direction. "Lock up for me, would you? If I miss dinner one more night this week I'm going to be sleeping in my car. We'll talk in the morning."

She nodded, too numb to muster a smile. She watched as he stepped out into the hall, already fumbling for his pack of Marlboro Lights. When he was out of sight, she sank back into her desk chair. "Do you do it on purpose?"

"Do what on purpose?"

"Wait until you know my boss is going to be somewhere nearby, and then show up and pick a fight with me? Because I have to say, you're awfully good at it."

"I wasn't the one picking the fight, remember? I was the one suggesting a truce. And I did try to fix it. I told him you and my mother were chummy. You're welcome, by the way."

Dovie closed her eyes, biting back the first response that had popped into her head. "I'd really like this day to be over. But I'll settle for your leaving."

"I don't do it on purpose," Austin said quietly. "I think you'll see that if you think about it. And I really did come by to suggest a truce."

"Please. Just go."

"Fine. You've got your folder. Call me when you need something else." He was almost out the door when he turned back around. "Not my mother—me."

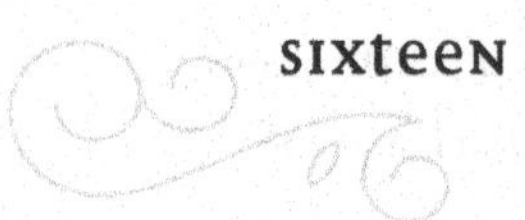

sixteen

Austin kicked off his shoes at the door, grabbed a tall glass of sweet tea, and headed straight for the deck. A rush of salty air slapped his cheeks as he pulled back the sliders and stepped outside. He stood a moment at the railing, savoring the view he never grew tired of, the dunes with their soft sand and waving grasses, the stretch of blue-green sea blurring into the distance. Closing his eyes, he drank in the sea's timeless song, rhythmic, earthy, calming.

After a few minutes, he moved to one of the deck chairs, propping his legs up on the railing. He took a long sip of tea, almost wishing he still drank. It had been that kind of day—the kind that started out shaky and got progressively worse, ending with the rather awkward scene in Dovie Larkin's office.

He really had gone to the museum with good intentions, determined to smooth over his harsh remarks from earlier in the week. If they were going to be working together they might as well be friends. At least that was what he told himself when he got in his car. Instead, he'd acted like a snarky frat boy, trying to impress the homecoming queen. What was it about the woman that made him so crazy?

But he already knew the answer; she was everything he wasn't.

Serious, committed, and probably damn responsible when her head was on straight, which it clearly wasn't just now. Her opinion of him hardly helped matters. He knew what she saw when she looked at him, an entitled playboy who had skated through life on his inheritance and his name. And why would she think any different when that pretty much summed it up?

She was still in his head when he went inside to refill his glass. She was in trouble at work, she'd as much as admitted that, but there was something else going on, something he couldn't quite put his finger on—as if she were walking some invisible tightrope. He knew that feeling all too well, had been staring it in the face every day for longer than he cared to admit. And now he saw it in Dovie, the kind of resignation that comes from knowing your life has come apart at the seams.

He was reaching for the tea pitcher when his cell went off, jolting him back to the stainless and granite reality of his kitchen. He frowned at the screen. *Candice.* Damn. He'd forgotten they were supposed to be meeting at McCrady's tonight—an oversight that might have proven awkward had Dovie actually taken him up on his dinner invitation. Biting the bullet, he answered the call.

"Candice. I was just about to call you. I'm afraid I'm going to have to bail on dinner. I hate to do it on such short notice, but something important came up." He wasn't crazy about lying, but he wasn't in the mood for company, not even the kind Candice offered.

"More important than me?"

It was all he could do not to laugh at the ridiculousness of the question. They'd met two weeks ago at a party, and been out exactly twice. "It's work," he said instead. "We've got a big bid due in two days, and I need to go over it tonight."

"Aren't you a little old for homework?"

"I run the largest real estate development firm in the Southeast, Candice. That means I have responsibilities."

"Since when is a bunch of stuffy old paperwork more important than having fun?"

It wasn't hard to understand her confusion. Until a few weeks ago, nothing had gotten in the way of fun and female companionship, but now, for reasons he couldn't begin to explain, the idea of spending time with a woman he didn't particularly like—even a gorgeous one—held little appeal.

"Look, I'll call you when things smooth out," he told her, knowing he'd do no such thing. It was a clumsy brush-off, and they both knew it. And yet he felt no guilt when Candice hung up in a huff. He was getting good at pissing off the women in his life.

Not that Dovie Larkin was *in* his life, although she was certainly in his thoughts an awful lot these days. And she wasn't even his type. He was only pursuing her because he knew it annoyed her, and because flirting was his default position any time an attractive woman entered the picture. But Dovie was more than an attractive woman. She was a puzzle—one he was becoming more and more interested in solving. And when he had solved the puzzle—what then? Jesus, what was he even thinking?

Right now he was going to make a little dinner, then get to work on the bid he'd been putting off for over a week. It wasn't how he'd hoped to spend the evening, but he'd consider it his penance for lying to Candice. On his way to the kitchen he flipped on the stereo. "Walking in My Shoes" filled the living room with its deep melancholy beat. The song always reminded him of Monica. His wife had hated Depeche Mode, probably because Martin Gore's sometimes dark but always brilliant lyrics hit just a little too close for comfort, conjuring the demons she had ruthlessly tried to numb with a steady diet of pills and booze.

They had married young, sneaking off to Palm Beach one weekend to tie the knot without a prenup. It was the final straw for his father, who saw Monica as an opportunistic little gold digger, which was precisely what she'd turned out to be—one with a growing substance abuse problem. She'd done a good job of hiding it while they were dating, and after they married he had done an even better job of pretending not to notice, though near the end he was pretty sure they hadn't been fooling anyone. It had lasted almost two years. Two years of screaming matches and icy silences, of pill-induced stupors and terrifying near misses. Two years of hell. And then one night, it was over.

It had begun the way most of their blowups did, with one of her booze-fueled rants about him refusing to give her money to get high. When she finally ran out of venom she had packed a bag, informing him on her way out the door that he'd be hearing from her attorney. He had never been so relieved in his life. He was still trying to figure out how to avoid his father's *I told you so* when he got the call that she had wrapped her car around a telephone pole out on Highway 17.

It was the only time he was ever glad his father had friends in high places. He had used his influence to keep the drugs and booze out of the papers. As far as anyone knew, Monica Tate had died trying to avoid a deer. He never mentioned the argument to anyone, not even his mother. To this day, not a soul knew his wife was planning to leave him the night she died—had, in fact, already left him.

Her ashes had been flown back to Indiana, and a private memorial was held. He had played the grieving widower flawlessly, mostly for his mother's sake. He had never really cared what anyone else thought. No one spoke of it. It wasn't what the Tates did. But he'd always suspected—and still did—that his mother knew there was more to the story, and had chosen not to press him. It was a kind of unspoken pact they had—to honor one another's secrets, and keep their wounds to themselves.

Now, a dozen years later, when he was alone and Monica's ghost seemed to hover, the questions still haunted him. Could he have prevented her death? If he hadn't been such a codependent ass? Hadn't turned a blind eye to her growing addiction and the train wreck her life was becoming? Hadn't been so goddamn relieved to see her pack her bags? He'd never know—and would never stop asking.

Was it any wonder he steered clear of anything that could be mistaken for interest in the blissful state of matrimony, and chose instead to entertain himself with a revolving door of recreational blondes—the Monicas and Trishes and Candices of his world? Yes, they were vapid and cloying and exhausting, cookie-cutter socialites with a passion for champagne and shiny things. But they were safe. And these days, he was all about safe. He couldn't—wouldn't—be responsible for another person. Not when he'd already failed so spectacularly.

Lord God, how had he wandered into such grim territory? Moments ago, he'd been thinking about dinner. And somehow from there he'd moved on to his dead wife. But before that he'd been thinking of Dovie.

Monica and Dovie. For a moment their faces merged in his mind's eye, superimposing like a pair of ghosts. Could there be two more different women? One so out of control she'd managed to get herself killed before her twenty-first birthday, the other zipped up so tight he doubted she knew what losing control even meant.

The CD player startled him from his thoughts, whirring softly as it switched discs, and then the opening notes of "The Sweetest Condition" filled the room, languid and elastic. It had always been his favorite track from the *Exciter* album, and right now the slow, oozy lyrics suited his mood. He stood there, clutching his sweaty glass of tea as Dave Gahan let the lyrics bleed out, obsessive and raw with need, blotting out all thoughts of Monica, leaving only Dovie Larkin's wide-set blue eyes floating in his head.

Subtle thunder, indeed.

seventeen

Make nice.

Those had been Jack's words of advice this morning, delivered in a way that made it clear he wasn't just offering a suggestion. Apparently, he'd heard enough coming down the hall last night to question Austin's assertion that everything was fine, which was why she had been ordered to smooth things out ASAP, and why she had just dialed Austin's office to invite him to meet for coffee tomorrow afternoon.

"Hi," she blurted, caught off guard when the receptionist put her straight through.

"Hi, yourself. I wasn't expecting to hear from you so soon. What's up?"

"I was wondering if you'd be interested in grabbing coffee tomorrow afternoon. We could . . . talk."

"Talk?"

"You said you came by to offer a truce. I'm calling to take you up on it."

"Why?"

"Because it's the sensible thing to do. We'll be working together on this wing for quite a while. It doesn't make sense for us to be at war."

"No, for real—why?"

Dovie sighed. "Because my boss said I needed to make nice. There. Does that make you feel better?"

He chuckled but offered no answer.

"Well, are you in?"

"Not for coffee, no. Make it dinner."

"I already explained—"

"I thought Livingston said to be nice. What do you think he'd say if he knew you shot me down right out of the gate?"

Dovie was flabbergasted. "You'd blackmail me into dinner?"

"Technically, it would be extortion, not blackmail, and I was kidding. I'm not going to strong-arm you into dinner. I'm just going to ask—nicely, this time. And I'm free tonight, if you happen to have some time open in that little black book of yours."

Dovie closed her eyes and counted to ten. "Lunch," she said. "Tomorrow."

"I can't. I have plans. Dinner. McCrady's. Eight o'clock. Should I pick you up?"

"No," Dovie blurted, determined to regain control of the conversation. "I'll meet you. And this is business."

"Right. Business. But no suit. I've got a reputation to live up to, and women in business suits don't quite fit my profile."

Dovie fumed as she doodled a passable likeness of Satan on her desk blotter. "I could ask to borrow my sister's cheerleading uniform. Would that work for you?"

"I don't care, as long as you leave the suit at home. Think of it as therapy."

"Therapy for what?"

"For whatever it is that keeps you all buttoned up. I promise, you'll be quite safe. No need to don your armor. See you at eight."

There was a click, and he was gone.

McCrady's was crowded for a weeknight, the bar overflowing with smiling, chatty patrons sipping wine or pastel-hued martinis while they waited to be called to their tables. Dovie was glad she had arrived early, and that there was no sign of Austin yet. She needed a minute to get her bearings.

Making a beeline for the bar, she slid onto the last empty stool, the one at the end, near the server's station, and ordered a glass of Sonoma-Cutrer. She felt conspicuous as she scanned the crowd, painfully aware of her solitary state in a room where no one else seemed to be alone. She couldn't remember the last time she'd been in a crowded restaurant, surrounded by people who were laughing and sharing conversation, simply enjoying themselves.

It was a jarring realization. How had she become so isolated, so detached from the world that seemed to be carrying on without her? Was there a precise moment when she had severed the cord, some specific fraction of a second when she had decided to withdraw from the human race? If there was, she couldn't recall it, though it was hard to deny that at some point she had begun a slow but steady separation from the living—including her own family. Her life was about work now, and her list of friends consisted of exactly three people: Theda, who was beginning to have serious doubts about her sanity, an eighty-year-old cemetery worker, and a dying woman seeking forgiveness from her dead daughter.

God, she was a mess.

The reflection in the bar mirror did little to bolster her spirits. After several aborted wardrobe changes, she had settled on a sleeveless black dress and jacket. Not a suit, she told herself as she fiddled with the collar. Not exactly. She'd never done casual flirty, nor was she interested in that kind of night—with Austin, or anyone else.

Business, she reminded herself as she eyed the planner tucked into her tote. Tonight was about business, and nothing else.

Thankfully, the bartender was quick with her wine. Between sips she studied the bar's soaring brick archways and tried not to look as though she was checking her watch. She was wondering when this had started to feel like a bad blind date when she spotted Austin, smiling and waving as he made his way toward the bar. She watched, fascinated, as the crowd gave way, like the waters parting for Moses. He wore gray slacks and a navy blazer over a crisp white oxford, and looked better than any man should for a business dinner. He smelled good, too, as he came to stand in front of her, a blend of spice and soap she hadn't realized she associated with him until now.

"I'm sorry you had to wait," he said over the din. "I believe our table is ready. Or I can have them hold it, and we can hang out here for a while. Your meeting. Your call."

Dovie grabbed her glass and slid off the barstool. "The table, I think," she said feeling vaguely disoriented as she looked up at him. Had he always been this tall, or was the wine doing things to her spatial abilities?

The blonde at the hostess stand greeted Austin by name. Her eyes lingered a moment on Dovie, a brief but unmistakable inventory, before grabbing a pair of heavy black menus and turning to take them to the dining room.

Fresh eyes followed them as they were led to a cozy brick alcove. The hostess removed the RESERVED sign from the table, giving Austin a polite nod. "Enjoy your dinner, Mr. Tate. Troy will be taking care of you, as usual. I'll be sure to let him know you've been seated."

Troy arrived momentarily, all nods and smiles and swarthy good looks, as he delivered a chilled bottle of Pellegrino to the table.

"More wine for the lady?" he asked with an accent that might have been Italian or Spanish, or merely put on.

"Yes," Austin replied before Dovie could open her mouth.

"And the lady is drinking?"

Dovie blinked up at Troy a moment, then realized he was talking to her. "Sonoma-Cutrer chardonnay."

"Very good." Another bow, and he was gone.

Dovie had just located the dinner section of the menu when Troy reappeared with a bottle of Sonoma-Cutrer and a chilled silver bucket. When he had filled her glass, he returned the bottle to the bucket, whisked Austin's empty glass away, and promised to return after they'd had some time to look over the menu.

"Aren't you having any?" Dovie asked as Troy disappeared.

Austin shook his head. "I don't drink."

His answer took her by surprise. She just assumed he'd be the hard-drinking sort. "Did you think I was going to drink an entire bottle of wine by myself?"

"I didn't think about it one way or the other, really. Troy just always brings a bottle."

"I would never have pegged you as teetotaler."

"I wasn't always. Far from it, in fact."

"Why did you stop?"

"Things change."

Had she only imagined the shadow that seemed to pass over his face? She didn't think so, but decided to let it go, returning to the menu instead.

"You seem surprised."

"I guess I am, a little."

"It's not that I have anything against it. I've just chosen not to. I guess you could say I had a wake-up call. I figured I'd already given the papers enough to chew on. I didn't need to give them that, too. So one day I just swore off."

"How long ago was that?"

"Ten years or so."

Dovie shifted her attention back to the menu, resisting the urge to ask about his wake-up call. They were here to forge a truce and improve their working relationship. They didn't need to know the intimate details of each other's lives for that—even if she *was* curious.

Troy reappeared to take their order. Dovie went with the scallops and lobster risotto, while Austin ordered *the usual.* Whatever it was, Troy knew precisely how he liked it, medium rare, without bleu cheese crumbles. He nodded crisply and, after topping off Dovie's wineglass, backed away.

"So," Austin said, startling her a little when he propped his elbows on the table and fixed her with a deep green stare. "Is this all for show, or did you mean what you said on the phone yesterday about calling a truce?"

Dovie sipped her wine, wondering if there was a trap in the question. "Did you?"

"Yes, I think so. Maybe not at first, but I do now."

"Why now?"

"Because we got off on the wrong foot, and that was mostly my fault. And because I feel like a heel about your boss being pissed at you. You seem to love what you do, and to be pretty good at it, too, when you're not distracted."

Distracted.

Dovie felt herself flush. It was such a polite word for what she was these days. Still, she didn't want him thinking she was a complete train wreck, or that she needed saving. "Jack's fine. He's just really invested in this new wing. I think he's terrified that your mother will pull her two million dollars, and then the rest of our funding will disappear. And speaking of your mother, when did she and I get to be chums?"

"Apparently, the day you popped by her house. You made quite an impression. She liked that you recognized the paintings in her study. She also liked that you took the initiative to bring the paperwork by. I didn't like it—and still don't—but she did. In my book, that makes you chummy."

"I see."

"She also said you were lovely. Actually used the word *lovely.* And for the record, there's something I'd like to get straight. It wasn't my mother who shelled out that two million. It was me. Not that it matters. She'd been begging my father to do it for years, but he hated all her causes. Never very big on giving, my father. Anyhow, I just wanted that on the record."

"I didn't know. Thank you." She tipped her glass in salute, peering at him over the rim. "You seem rather . . . protective of your mother."

Austin traced a finger along the blade of his knife, his expression thoughtful. "I've had to be," he said finally. "It's been hard since my father died. He was a lousy husband, but people knew better than to mess with my mother when he was alive. Now that he's gone, she's an easy target. Everyone wants the dirt on the old bastard, not that it would be hard to find. There are all sorts of rumors. I'm sure you've heard them. Everyone has."

Dovie gave a halfhearted shrug, curious, but wise enough to remain silent.

"Not all of it's true, of course. But some of it is, and the last thing my mother needs is to have her nose rubbed in it again. That's why I jumped down your throat the other day. It's a knee-jerk reaction I have to anyone pestering her. God knows after forty years with my father, she deserves a little peace."

Dovie was relieved when dinner arrived. She sat back while Troy delivered their plates, then wielded an enormous pepper mill with the same flair he used to pour her wine.

"Is there anything else you require, Mr. Tate?"

"No, thank you, Troy. We're fine."

Austin looked at her expectantly as Troy stepped away, clearly waiting for her to take her first bite before cutting into his steak. Instead, she surprised him by asking the question she'd been pondering almost from the moment they sat down. "I'm getting the sense that you and your father had a pretty strained relationship."

If Austin was offended, he hid it well. "We didn't have *any* relationship."

"I don't understand. You were his son, the heir apparent. You were groomed to take over his company."

Austin snorted. "I was *groomed* to do anything but. Oh, I did the architect thing, and the MBA thing, but that was for my mother, because she wanted it *for* me and I didn't have anything better to do with my time. Besides, a young man with money's got to do something with his life, or he starts to look a little spoiled, don't you think?"

Dovie forked up a mouthful of risotto to avoid answering.

"Meanwhile, Mom kept sending the quarterly reports and the minutes from the board meetings. I went over them, watched the stock, kept up with industry news, but we both knew the old man was too much of a control freak to ever hand over the reins—least of all to me."

"I thought you were an only child."

"I am."

"So, if he didn't mean for you to take over when he died, he must have had some other plan for the company."

"I'm pretty sure his plan was not to die, probably thought he'd pull it off, too. Which is why he died intestate."

Dovie looked at him, eyes wide. "Your father didn't have a will?"

"No need for a will if you're going to live forever. I'll bet no one was more surprised than my father when he keeled over in the sauna at his club."

"So . . . ?"

Austin shrugged. "Everything ended up going to my mother, which I can assure you is the only reason I'm calling the shots now. If I'm sure of anything, it's that the old man is spinning in his grave at the thought of me sitting behind his desk. Funny how things work out."

"Yes, I suppose," Dovie said, fiddling with the napkin in her lap. "Things don't always work out the way we plan."

"Well, that's my tragic little story," Austin announced as he speared a mushroom with his fork and popped it into his mouth. "Or at least one of them. My father never loved me. Now you."

Dovie blinked at him across the table. "Me?"

"Isn't this what friends do? Share their life stories? I just told you mine. Now it's your turn. So, tell me, what makes Dovie Larkin tick?"

What made her . . . tick?

Did she even have an answer to that? These days, she seemed to be ticking like a defective watch, no sense of time, except to know that it was passing much too quickly—and without her.

"Oh, you don't want to hear about me," she said, hiding behind her wineglass. "There's not much to tell, really. I go to work, and then I go home."

"The day we met you told me your fiancé had died."

The abruptness of the question startled her. She put down her glass, dabbed her mouth with her napkin. "A year ago, yes."

"An accident?"

"No. On purpose."

"Oh."

"Yes . . . oh."

"I'm sorry. I didn't know. I didn't mean to—"

"He swallowed a handful of pills two weeks before we were supposed to get married."

"Did you . . ."

"Have any idea he was thinking about killing himself? No. No one did. And there wasn't a note, so we'll never know why."

"I'm sorry. Truly."

Dovie eyed him across the table. She wasn't sure what to make of this new Austin. Sensitive. Genuine. And wholly unexpected.

"It must have been rough."

"It was," she said. "It is."

"That's why you go to the cemetery every day. Because you need to understand what happened. And why."

Dovie's head came up. How could he know that?

"You think if you keep asking the same questions over and over again, one day you'll get it."

"Something like that."

"What was his name?"

"William. He was an artist—a sculptor. But you know that."

"And what else?"

She stared at him, confused by the question. "What else?"

"Sometimes it helps to talk. You don't have to, but I've been told I'm a pretty good listener. What was he like?"

Dovie pushed a bite of scallop around on her plate, wondering where to begin, or if she wanted to begin at all. "He was funny," she said finally. "And kind, and sweet, and talented. We met at a club social. He wasn't much on that kind of thing, and neither was I, so we snuck away from the party and spent the rest of the afternoon talking. After that, we were never apart. Except when he traveled for work. He was always flying to New York for some show or gallery opening."

"You didn't go with him?"

"I couldn't. I was finishing up my MBA. I'd been begging for a promotion for over a year, and rumor had it the curator position was going to be opening up. I wasn't about to take time off and risk getting passed over."

"Were you living together when it happened?"

"No. He had his own place, a little studio on Church Street where he worked. I used to call it his garret. I've only been there a handful of times."

"Seriously?"

Dovie shrugged. "He became very reclusive when he was working on something big, almost protective. I respected that, so I just steered clear. That's where his brother found him—on the floor in the bathroom."

"Jesus. His family must have been stunned."

"We all were."

"Are you still in touch with them? Were you close?"

"I thought we were, but since William's death things are different. It's like they're ashamed of what he did, and I remind them of it. I think maybe they blame me, or at least think I should have seen it coming."

"Do you blame yourself?"

"Honestly, I don't know. It's a question I've been asking myself for a year. Should I have seen it coming? Maybe. There were times when I felt like he was holding something back, like there was this part of him he didn't let anyone see—not even me—but I wrote it off as a moody artist thing. Maybe if I'd paid more attention, asked more questions . . ."

"You can't do that to yourself, Dovie. Take it from me. You can drive yourself mad with those kinds of questions, and still never get the answers you're looking for. There *are* no answers. And no do-overs."

"I've been hearing that a lot lately. I guess it's what people do. They try to fix you. Because it's uncomfortable being with someone else's pain, thinking for even one minute that you might find yourself in those same shoes one day."

Austin set down his knife and fork and sat back in his chair. "I wasn't trying to fix you. I just see that you're not in a good place right now. William sounds like a great guy, but maybe you weren't as close as you think. Maybe there were things you didn't know—or chose not to know—and that's why you keep beating yourself up."

Dovie set down her fork with a clatter. "What is that supposed to mean? We weren't as close as I thought we were? We were two weeks away from being married."

"People keep secrets, Dovie. Some are very good at it. Especially when we help them by looking the other way."

She was trembling all over now, her face flushed, her hands clammy against the white tablecloth. She didn't want to talk to him about William. In fact, she didn't want to talk to him at all. "I think I'd better be going."

"I'm sorry. I shouldn't have said any of that. I was just—"

Dovie pushed back from the table and stood, ignoring the curious stares aimed in her direction. "I think it would be best if in the future we limited our contact as much as possible. I'll designate a contact person to keep you up-to-date on the fund-raiser, and you can do the same."

"Dovie, please sit down. We don't have to—"

She didn't wait for him to finish. Before he could get the rest out she had picked up her purse and was heading for the lobby. She'd be willing to bet it was the first time in Austin Tate's life that a woman had left him sitting alone in a restaurant.

So much for their truce.

eighteen

"People keep secrets, Dovie."

William's headstone shimmered pearly gray in the afternoon sunlight, moving in and out of focus as Dovie replayed last night's conversation with Austin. What kinds of secrets had he been talking about? Another woman? A dark past? Code-word clearance with the NSA?

And what did he know about it anyway? Her relationship with William was none of his business, though he seemed to think otherwise. It was nervy enough to suggest William had been harboring some deep dark secret, but he had crossed the line when he insinuated that she had somehow been complicit in that secret, that somewhere along the way she had made a conscious decision to not look too closely at the man she was preparing to marry—for fear of what, exactly? It was ridiculous.

William's suicide had come as a complete surprise, like a bolt of lightning on a perfectly sunny day. How could anyone expect a thing like that when there hadn't been so much as a cloud on the horizon? And there hadn't been—had there?

If the looks on the faces of William's parents the day of his funeral were any indication, they hadn't seen it coming, either. His brother, however, was a different story. He'd looked more resigned than stunned, as if finding his brother cold and unresponsive on the bathroom floor had somehow been inevitable. She hadn't mentioned it at the time. Now she wished she had.

"You're late today."

Dovie looked up to find Josiah approaching, a trowel and bucket in his gloved hands. She shook off her dark thoughts and reached for a smile. "Hey, Josiah."

"Looked for you around lunchtime. Thought maybe you were sick or something."

"No, I just had some work to get through, so I ate at my desk."

He nodded, slow, thoughtful. "You still got a job, then. That's good."

"For now, yes."

"That old lady still around?"

"Dora? Yes, she's still around. Why?"

"'Cause I got something the two of you just might be interested in."

Dovie sat up a little straighter, shielding her eyes with one hand to get a better look at his face. "What is it?"

"Just what you think it is. Two more letters. Same writing, so I expect it's the girl who wrote 'em." He eased down beside her, slipping the letters from his pocket. "One looks like it's been gnawed a little bit at the corner. We had mice there for a while. Might have got hold to 'em."

Dovie stared at the envelopes, trying not to think of some small-eyed rodent making a meal of Alice's words. "Where did you find them?"

"Office. Same as the others. Picked up an old schoolbook someone left behind, and there they was. Like they was just waiting to be found."

Dovie wanted to hug him but knew it would make him uncomfortable. "Did you read them?" she asked instead.

"Nope. Way I see it, one of us snooping around in a dead girl's business is enough."

"Then why bring them to me at all?"

Josiah lifted his hat, rubbing a palm over his grizzled head. "Not sure, exactly. Maybe I'm hoping there's enough in 'em to keep you from sticking your nose somewhere that's gonna get you fired."

Dovie ducked her head. "You mean I shouldn't bother Mrs. Tate again."

"I mean you shouldn't bother any of them. Just steer clear of the whole family. Nothing good's gonna come from you poking around in rich folks' business. You know that, don't you?"

Dovie let her gaze slide from his. "I had dinner with Austin Tate last night."

Josiah's eyes shot wide. "Now you're pestering the son?"

"I'm not pestering him. It was a business dinner. Sort of." Perhaps it was best not to share the fact that they hadn't discussed anything remotely businesslike, or that she'd ended up walking out, leaving him sitting alone in one of Charleston's trendiest restaurants.

Josiah was shaking his head now, mumbling something about playing with fire.

"You don't have to worry, Josiah. I'm all through with Austin Tate. We left things . . . Well, let's just say I'll be steering clear of him from now on."

"You make him mad?"

"No, I didn't make him mad. He made *me* mad. That's allowed, right? I'm allowed to get mad when the rich playboy crosses the line?"

Josiah stiffened. "He get fresh with you?"

Dovie blinked at him. "Fresh? No. No, he just asked a lot of questions about things that were none of his business."

"Like what?"

"Things about William, about our relationship. He asked if I thought he'd had any secrets—like he knew something I didn't."

"He know your William?"

"No. He was just being nosy."

"And how is that different from what you've been doing? Dropping in on his mama, asking her about that girl? How is that your business?"

"It's not. It's Dora's business. I'm doing it for her."

"You say that, but you haven't shown her the letters. How is that helping *her*?"

"Josiah, we've had this conversation. I know what I'm doing—and why."

"Maybe. But I wonder if you don't have this woman's grief all mixed up with yours, and if you think helping her answer her questions will somehow help you answer yours."

"That doesn't even make sense, Josiah."

Josiah nodded, then dropped his hat back on his head. "Long as you know that."

Dora seemed surprised when Dovie knocked on her door at a little after six. She slid the chain and pulled back the door, her expression one of faint alarm. "I didn't expect to see you this evening. Is anything the matter?"

Dovie just stood there, trying to figure out how to answer. "We need to talk, Dora. About Alice."

"Have you found something, then?"

"Yes, actually. But I need to explain how I found it, before I tell you anything more. Why don't I fix us both some tea before we sit down?"

Ten minutes later, they were seated at the tiny table in the little kitchenette, sipping Earl Grey while Dovie fumbled for where to begin. In the end, she decided there was only one place *to* begin. "I have something I need to tell you, something I need to . . . confess."

Dora sat very still, preparing herself for whatever was coming.

"The day you left the letter on Alice's grave, I was there. I watched you leave it. And then, after you were gone, I . . . took it."

Rather than being angry, Dora seemed confused. "Why?"

"I wanted to know what someone wrote in a letter to a dead person. It was wrong, I know, but when I saw you, so sad and . . . so much like me, I felt a kind of attachment to you. My friend Theda thinks I'm losing my mind, and she might be right, because I've never done anything like this before."

"Why are you telling me now?"

"Because of something another friend said to me today, about me mixing up my grief with yours. I think he might be right. That's why I needed to tell you, and to give you this." Reaching into her tote, she extracted Dora's letter and slid it across the table. "I'm so sorry, Dora. Truly sorry."

Dora laid a hand on the letter, eyes closed, as if remembering the words contained in its pages. "I didn't know she was dead when I wrote it. I only wanted forgiveness."

"I know. Dora, there's more I need to tell you."

Dora's fingers tightened around her mug as she waited.

"I have a friend who works at Magnolia Grove, and after I read your letter I asked him if anyone else had ever left letters at the cemetery. I'm pretty sure he thought I was crazy for asking, but a few days later he brought me several that had turned up in the office. Today he brought me two more."

Dora's face went blank.

Dovie tried again. "They were written by Alice, Dora. And somehow they ended up in the cemetery's lost and found."

"Letters? From my Alice?"

"Yes, from Alice."

Dora's gray eyes kindled with hope. "Were they . . . to me?"

"They were to her child—the one she gave up at Blackhurst. She started writing them almost as soon as she arrived, and apparently kept on writing them after she left."

"She wrote . . . to the baby?" Her voice broke and she began to cry.

"Yes, she did." Dovie reached for her hand, giving it a squeeze. "I didn't know how to tell you, or if I even should."

"Why?"

"Because they're . . . terrible. They're about Blackhurst, and the things that happened there, and I just didn't want you to blame yourself any more than you already do."

Dora lifted her head, her expression one of astonishment. "Who else is there to blame? I sent her there, didn't I? Why should I be spared the truth?"

"I have them with me," Dovie said, already dreading what would come next. Reaching into her tote, she pulled out the stack of faded envelopes and placed them on the table beside Dora's mug.

Dora stared at them for what felt like a very long time. Finally, she lifted her gaze to Dovie's. "Will you read them to me? I seem to have misplaced my glasses."

NINETEEN

Blackhurst Asylum for Unwed Mothers
Cornwall, England
August 20, 1962

My dearest little one,

This will be my last letter from Blackhurst. Sister Mary Agnes informed me this morning that I am to be returned to my family, like a parcel that has gone astray and is to be returned to its sender, a bit battered after its travels, but returned nonetheless. I could see in her dour old face that she thought I should be glad—or at least grateful. I am neither. Home is an empty word now. There can be no home for me without you.

How I miss you, my little one, and pray for you morning and night. I pray that you are well, wherever you are, and that the woman in whose care you have been placed will endeavour to love you as I do, with a mother's true heart. It's hard to imagine a stranger being able to love you properly, when your flesh and hers have always been separate, when the blood in her veins and the blood in yours have never mingled. How I wish they had let me hold you just once so I could look into your tiny face. I could close my eyes and imagine you then, as the years stretched out, growing tall and strong somewhere in the world. Instead, I'm left with a blank where your face should be, and a terrible hole in my heart. Forgive me, little one. I have grown morose, which was not my intent when I began to write.

I am mostly well now. Only a small cough and the occasional shortness of breath remain of my chest infection, as the sisters still insist on calling the devastation that has swept through Blackhurst over the last several months. In all, seven girls died, along with their unborn babes, but the word "tuberculosis" is still not uttered here—at least not by the nuns—though everyone knows that's what it was. Denial and death, it seems, are preferable to the truth, if that truth means someone might get wind of what life is really like for the girls sent to Blackhurst. The last thing the good sisters want is a lot of godless do-gooders poking their noses into church business and upsetting their profitable little apple cart, though I very much doubt anyone cares what girls like us are made to suffer.

The innocents, though, in the cistern behind the kitchen, might raise a brow or two. Or perhaps not. Sins of the father, and all that. Or in this case, sins of the mother might excuse turning a blind eye. I don't know. I only know I put no faith in kindness or mercy, qualities grudgingly bestowed at Blackhurst, and in the world in general, I suppose. I've become hardened during my time here, as one must in a place of such ugly truths.

How long, I wonder, will I carry the memories of this place—the dull faces and crushed spirits, the harsh words and grueling days, the empty, brokenhearted nights? But I already know the answer. I'll carry them as long as I carry my memories of you, dear one, which will be for all my life.

I'm set to leave the morning after next. Mam was going to come and fetch me, but I rang her and told her not to come. I'll walk to the train instead. The day can't come soon enough. And yet I dread it, too. I suppose I should be happy to be leaving at all. Many of the girls here never leave. They have nowhere to go, you see, no one willing to take in a disgraced girl of low character. Girls like Marianne, who have lived so long inside these merciless walls that they've forgotten what it's like to love and be loved, who replace the missing parts of themselves with platitudes and prayers.

Mam is eager to have me back home, though, now that my belly is flat and no one is the wiser. But I am not eager. There's nothing left for me in Sennen Cove. No future, and no forgetting, either, when everything I see will remind me of how much I've lost. Besides, there's you, my little one, somewhere out there, waiting for me to keep my promise. And I will keep it.

I went to Marianne when I learned I was leaving. We hadn't spoken in weeks—since I had called her a traitor—which must be why she seemed surprised when I sought her out in the chapel. She looked up and gave me one of her beatific smiles, ready to forgive, but I pulled away. I needed her to know how deeply she hurt me when she refused to help me find you, and to know there was only one way I would ever forgive her. I waited impatiently, knees aching, while the chapel slowly emptied, all the little brown birds filing out of their pews and off to their day's work. Marianne continued to finger her beads, lips moving soundlessly. It took a moment to realize she wanted me to pretend I was praying, in case anyone had remained behind. I laced my fingers together and bowed my head.

"I'm going home tomorrow."

Marianne's eyes remained closed, but her fingers went quiet on her beads. "Yes, they told me. I'm glad for you."

I drew a deep breath, tamping down my impatience. It wasn't her gladness I wanted. "I need your help, Marianne. I need to know where they've sent my baby. I need to get my child back."

"I can't," she hissed, her fingers moving once again, beads clicking. "You know I can't. And even if I could, there's nothing to be done now."

"There is. There has to be!"

Marianne's eyes opened a fraction, flashing me a sidelong warning.

I lowered my voice, but the intensity was still there. "Tell me where. Please. I'll go. I'll find him—or her. No matter what I have to do, where I have to go. Just tell me."

Marianne's eyes opened but remained fixed on her rosary. I could see that she knew, that she could help me if she wanted to. I could also see that she wasn't going to.

"Alice . . ." She sighed the name, like someone reaching for words of comfort. "You brought the child into this world, gave it blood and bone and breath. That was your work. And now it is another woman's work to raise it, to love it, and care for it—to tend its soul for God. What's happened has happened for the best. You have to try to find peace in that."

Marianne's words seem to hang in the candle-scented air. I waited a moment for them to land, and then to sink in, like a blow that needed to be absorbed. How could I find peace when I knew you were without your mother—not the stranger who had paid the necessary fees and signed the proper papers, but the woman who carried you in her body, who bled and cried and railed when they took you from her?

"Have you forgotten what this feels like?" I demanded, fighting to keep the reins on my tongue. "Have you? To have the child you wanted with all your heart torn away and given to strangers?"

"You know I haven't."

There were tears in her eyes now, threatening to spill down her cheeks, but I didn't care. I needed her to break, to tell me what I needed to know. "Do you ever think about it, wonder whether it was a boy or girl, if it looks like its father?"

Her chin began to quiver and she turned away. "Every hour of every day."

"Then how can you sit there and tell me to find peace? Have you?"

"I'm trying," she said, gulping down a sob. "Every day, I'm trying."

"How?" The word exploded against the silence, echoing off the chapel's stone walls. I didn't care that Jesus was looking down from behind the altar, glowering at me with his tortured face and bloody brow. I had to make her understand. "How can you even think of finding peace when every day must be a reminder of what they took from you? And then to become one of them, to become a part of it—how can you?"

She turned to face me, her eyes moist, but queerly empty now. "Because God has a plan for us, Alice. For you and me, and our children. We, each of us, have our work to do. That's what I mean by finding peace. Accepting our place, and doing God's work."

I was unnerved by her stillness, and by the eerie flatness of her words, delivered by rote, like a child's catechism. "Please tell me you don't believe that, Marianne. Please tell me you don't believe the things that happen here are part of God's grand plan."

Her face crumpled then, breaking into a thousand miserable shards. "I have to, Alice. I have to believe it, or I'll never be able to forgive myself."

I left her then, sitting in the pew with her tears and her beads. I had done what I set out to do. I had broken her. And come away with nothing to show for my cruelty. She has made her choice, chosen her way, and I have chosen mine. I have no idea where to begin looking for you, my little one, or how I'll ever manage it. I only know I have to try.

All my love,
Mam

Blackhurst Asylum for Unwed Mothers
Cornwall, England
August 29, 1962

Dearest little one,

I'm home again, in Sennen Cove, though it scarcely feels like home now. It's hard to believe I was happy here once, that I had friends and a life I never once thought about leaving. Now all I think about is leaving.

I walked the six miles from the station, too weary to pay any mind to the steady drizzle, or the muddy puddles that soaked my shoes and stockings through. I could have called Mam to pick me up, but I didn't. I was in no hurry to see her. I said terrible things the day she drove me to Blackhurst, hateful, unforgivable things—and I knew I had plenty more to say. I'd been storing them up, you see, rehearsing them in my head every day while bent over my washtub or my sewing, and then again at night, while I lay in the dark, rolling them over in my head until they were as hard and polished as stones, waiting to be flung.

It wasn't that she didn't deserve to hear them. She did. It was only that just then I knew I was too exhausted to make a proper job of it. I needed her to know, to understand in the marrow of her bones, that there would never, ever be forgiveness, that what she had done to me, and to you, my little one, was a sin she would carry for the rest of her life. And so I walked all the muddy way to town—and kept polishing my stones.

There was no warm welcome waiting for me when I reached town, only hushed whispers and long sideways stares. Mam had fooled no one with her flimsy story. I knew it the moment I passed by the chemist's and bumped into Ellie Gleason as she came out with a yellow umbrella and an armload of parcels. Her eyes went wide, then slid toward my belly.

"Well, well. It's good to see you home again, Alice. I take it your . . . aunt . . . has recovered?"

"Yes, thank you." I tried to smile but couldn't. I hated the way she was looking at me, her eyes sharp and glittering.

"Nothing catching, I hope?" she inquired, hitching one iron grey brow. "I only ask because you look as if you might have suffered a bout of something yourself. You're so thin and pale, poor thing."

Her voice was like treacle, as sticky-sweet as her pointy little smile, and I wondered who the pantomime was for, since we both knew perfectly well I had no aunt, sick or otherwise. I couldn't blame her for staring. I'm sure I looked like something straight out of a cornfield, pale and reed thin, my mud-spattered dress hanging like a rag from my shoulders. All I wanted at that moment was to be away from her, and yet I couldn't walk away and leave that simpering smile on her face.

"It's very kind of you to be concerned, Mrs Gleason," I said, my voice low and grave. "As a matter of fact, I have been ill. A nasty lung infection I just can't shake." I paused, pressing the heel of one hand to my chest, and summoned a deep, rattling cough. "Quite contagious, I'm afraid. They say I'll always have it, and that it might even worsen with time."

Mrs Gleason's smile froze, then vanished, her umbrella faltering as she ducked behind the shield of her parcels. She took a step back, and then another. "Sorry to hear it. My goodness, will you look at the time? Give my best to Dora, won't you?"

And then she was gone, retreating at a near run down High Street. It was the first time I could remember smiling since the day I arrived at Blackhurst. My glee was short-lived, though, fading the moment I turned down Trimble Lane and saw the dark red roof of our cottage come into view.

I stood outside in the drizzle for half an hour before mustering the will to go in. The mingled scents of apple, onion, and brown sugar greeted me, childhood smells that meant comfort and home. I followed them to the kitchen, where I found Mam at the counter, rolling out a round of pastry dough. She was making squab pie—no doubt in honor of my homecoming.

She must have sensed me in the doorway, because she turned. Her eyes filled with tears when she saw me, her mouth working, gasping at the air like the fish Johnny used to catch and then toss on the bottom of his boat. I never could stand the sight of those fish, gasping and writhing. I always looked away. But I didn't look away from Mam. Instead, I stood there, letting her survey the damage, my hollow eyes and gaunt face, the outline of shoulders and ribs beneath my soaking-wet dress.

It hurt her to look at me. I wanted it to hurt, not just then, but always. But when her sobs began in earnest I did look away, pretending to fumble with the laces of my muddy shoes.

"Here," Mam whispered, her voice choked and hoarse. "Hand them to me. I'll set them in the oven to dry for a bit."

I straightened, then turned, staring at her outstretched hand, reddened from the laundry she took in to help pay for my schooling. Her words stunned me, as if I'd just returned from a trip to the market. And yet I nearly did as she asked. I was wet clear through, and so very tired, my chest aching from the exertion and damp. At that moment, all I wanted in the world was to fall into her arms and hear her tell me that everything was going to be all right. It wouldn't be, though. It would never be. Not between us. And so I picked up my shoes and moved past her, tossing them into the bin on my way to the stairs.

Upstairs, I peeled out of my dress, slip, and stockings, letting them fall to the floor, and stood gazing around the room I had grown up in. After the crowded wards at Blackhurst, it felt both empty and claustrophobic. One bed instead of a dozen narrow cots. One small window overlooking a stony shoreline, instead of six peering out over chalk-coloured cliffs. I shivered, recalling the sad-eyed girl—Kathleen—who had hurled herself out into the deep blue nothingness beyond those cliffs rather than live another day at Blackhurst.

But I'm not Kathleen. I have survived Blackhurst and all its miseries, not unscathed, perhaps, but I soldiered through it, paid my penance. And now I have a promise to keep—the promise I made to you, little one—though just now I don't know how I'll do it. I have no money, and no idea where to begin.

I thought again of Marianne, of her face as I left her in the chapel that day, desolate and shiny with tears. She had wanted so badly for me to understand her choice, and I wanted her to understand mine, but we were simply too far apart, our hearts too much at odds to ever mend our fences. I was surprised to see her waiting by the gate as I was leaving, her eyes full of pleading. She said nothing as she threw her arms around me, her damp cheek pressed tight to mine. I just stood there, arms at my sides, unwilling to forgive. After a moment I pulled away, pretending not to notice the folded note she slipped into my pocket. I already knew what it said. She was sorry. It was for the best. God had a plan.

Perhaps he does, but so do I. And all Marianne's tearful apologies won't help me see it through. And yet, as I stood there in my room, staring down at my discarded clothes and the weeping stain they were making on the bedroom carpet, I found myself thinking about that note, wondering if it was still in my pocket, or if it had dissolved during my lengthy trek in the rain.

Crossing to the closet, I pulled out the first skirt and blouse I laid my hands on and dragged them on. They swam on me, as if they belonged to someone else, but I didn't care. I only wanted to be warm. Then I crouched down, retrieved my sodden dress from the floor, and fished the damp note from the pocket. It was wet but intact, the writing only a little smeared. I smoothed it flat against the grey wool of my skirt, my hand trembling at my mouth as I read the single line scribbled there:

Sacred Heart Children's Society. Charleston, S.C.

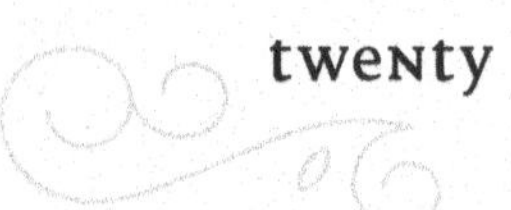

twenty

PALMETTO MOON MOTEL
CHARLESTON, SOUTH CAROLINA
OCTOBER 14, 2005

It was near midnight when Dovie folded the fifth letter and laid it on the stack with the others. Across the table, Dora sat as pale and still as stone, her silver lashes starred with tears.

Dovie looked away, her throat thick. She didn't want to imagine what it must be like to hear your own daughter say such terrible things—bitter things no mother could ever forget—or to acknowledge that she was the reason Dora had just heard them. She had tried several times to stop reading, but each time Dora had pressed her to continue, absorbing each page like the lash of a whip, a necessary penance. Now, despite Dora's urging, Dovie found herself unable to go on. The rest of the letters would have to wait.

Josiah told her once that people had their reasons for taking their secrets to the grave, and that sometimes it was better that they did. Perhaps he was right. Dora was certainly no better off for having heard her daughter's words. She was weeping into a handkerchief now, shoulders hunched and shuddering.

"I'm sorry, Dora. I never should have told you about them. I should have realized—"

Dora choked back a sob as her head came up. "I wanted to know the truth, didn't I? Those letters are the truth."

"But some of the things she wrote were—"

"Deserved," Dora said, mopping at her eyes. "I did a terrible thing, Dovie. She had every right to hate me. I just wish I'd had the chance to tell her I was wrong. I tried when she came home, but she wouldn't listen. She just shut me out. And then one day I woke up and she was gone."

"There was no note? Nothing saying where she was going?"

"No. But I knew. She made no secret of the fact that she meant to look for the child, or that when she left she would never be back. I didn't believe her, of course. I thought she was only saying it to punish me. Other than Blackhurst, she'd never been out of Sennen Cove. I couldn't see how she'd ever manage it, but she did, clever girl." She sighed, mopping her eyes again. "There was a tin I used to keep under the kitchen sink. I used to put my laundry money there every week, savings for when it was time to send her to university. She took it, can and all. And the gold watch and chain my own mam left me. The thing hadn't run in ages, but I guess she thought she could get something for it."

Dora closed her eyes, letting her handkerchief flutter to the floor. "What kind of mother does what I did, Dovie?"

"The kind who wants what's best for her daughter," Dovie said, reaching for the fallen handkerchief and pressing it back into Dora's hands. "Even if she's wrong about what that might be. What you did, you did out of love."

"That's what I told myself, too. But the truth is, I did it for me—because I was ashamed. There was no end to the talk when I arrived in Sennen Cove with a baby on my hip and no ring on my finger. I told everyone my husband had died, but they knew. Somehow they knew. Maybe my face gave me away, I don't know. Or maybe I just tried too hard to look respectable. Nothing I did mattered. The talk spread like wildfire. I was stared at, whispered about, even by the church ladies—especially by the church ladies."

She paused, squaring her shoulders, as if she could still feel their eyes between her shoulder blades. "It took a long time for them to let me in, and some never did. I didn't want that for Alice. I knew what the whispers would sound like. *The apple doesn't fall far from the tree. Like mother, like daughter.* I couldn't bear it. So I kept my secret—and became as cruel as the people I wanted to protect her from."

Out of words, and near tears herself, Dovie stood, picking up Dora's mug of cold tea and carrying it to the kitchen. The facts were the facts, and a fresh cup of tea wasn't going to change them, but it was all she knew to do. Her mother always made her tea with honey when she was down with a cold. But Dora wasn't suffering from a cold. She was heartsick, broken deep down in places tea couldn't reach.

Dovie tidied up a bit and inventoried the cupboards while she waited for the Earl Grey to steep, then carried the mug to the bedside table. "Time for your medicine and sleep, I think. We can talk more tomorrow, but right now you need some rest."

Dora rose stiffly and lumbered toward the bed. "Tell me again why you're being so kind to a dotty old woman."

"I wouldn't say I've been particularly kind to you tonight. All I've done is dragged up a lot of bad memories and given you more to beat yourself up about. Which makes me all the more determined to help you find out the rest of Alice's story."

Dora stared into her darkening tea. "I've resigned myself to never knowing."

"And you might not," Dovie told her. "But there are still things to try. I'm going to get online and see what I can find. Maybe I can find something about Blackhurst, and the babies who were born there. It might wind up being a total dead end, but it's at least a place to start. But if I should happen to find something else, something unpleasant . . ."

Dora's mug came down on the nightstand with a bang. "You'll tell me. Whatever it is, Dovie, I want to know. Promise me you won't ever try to spare me anything."

Dovie nodded, though it was against her better judgment. "All right, I promise."

"Good. Go on now. You look tired, and I need to sit with all this for a day or two."

"Good night, Dora."

Dovie laid a hand on Dora's shoulder, a gesture that was as much about guilt as it was comfort. Maybe Josiah was right. Maybe she had been fooling herself, blurring the lines between Dora's need for closure and her own. She'd begun it as a kind of mission, hoping to soothe the grief of a fellow sufferer. But she had never stopped to consider the very real possibility that she would uncover things that might prove more damaging than healing. Now, if there was a way, she needed to put the lid back on Pandora's box.

twenty-one

It was different being at Magnolia Grove on a Sunday. There was a different feel to the grounds. More people milling about. Church clothes instead of work clothes. Adults with children. Adults with aging parents. A sense of ritual, of family, and tradition. A collective grief that was more distant, mellowed by years of weekly visits.

Dovie pulled in a lungful of air, savoring the crisp, leafy scents of fall, or what passed for fall in the Carolina Lowcountry. Josiah had already been by, she saw, to tidy the headstones and remove last week's wilted blooms. He did it for the families, he said, so they'd know their loved ones were being looked after. It was this kindness that had drawn her to him in the first place, along with his crusty brand of wisdom.

She could do with a little of that wisdom now. On the off chance that he was still roaming the grounds, she settled on her usual bench and turned up the collar of her jacket. She was surveying the bouquet of chrysanthemums and roses she had just placed on William's grave when she spotted a man coming down the path. She knew at first glance that it wasn't Josiah. He was too tall, for starters, and his stride was all wrong, long and rangy, and distinctive somehow as he moved in her direction.

He slowed as he drew near but seemed not to see her, his attention focused on the neat rows of stones to his right. When he came to a halt in front of William's grave, she sat up a little straighter. He wore a slate-colored duster over black slacks and a matching turtleneck, and gave off a faintly European vibe. Dovie racked her memory, trying to place him. There was something about his posture, about the set of his shoulders, the way his arms hung down at his sides, that seemed familiar, and yet she'd swear she'd never laid eyes on him.

And then she realized what it was that seemed so familiar. It had nothing to do with his height or the color of his hair; he was in mourning. She knew the signs all too well, the bowed head and brittle shoulders, the hollow-eyed stare of someone whose life had caved in. But who was this stranger to William? A friend? A relative?

Dovie couldn't say if it was curiosity or an inexplicable pang of possessiveness, but suddenly she was on her feet, approaching almost stealthily, until she had come to stand just behind his left shoulder. He seemed not to notice her at first, his eyes fixed on the neat block letters etched into William's headstone. Finally, he turned, blinking at her as if he'd been shaken from a dream. His face was all angles, sharp bones and dusky hollows, the kind of face that might have been chiseled from some exotic species of stone, smooth and pale and cool to the touch.

"You're her," he said, startling her with a dismissive flick of cold blue eyes. "Dovie."

Something in his voice, the faint hint of distaste when he said her name, set Dovie's teeth on edge. "And you are?"

"Kristopher Bloom."

Dovie studied him another moment. He wasn't unkempt, exactly, but there was something faintly scruffy about his appearance, something that didn't quite fit his clothes. His hair was raked back from his forehead, dark and longish, just grazing his collar in back, and his jaw was shadowed with stubble—not the kind sported by movie stars and *GQ* models, the kind that hinted at abandoned habits.

"You're William's agent from New York."

"I was William's agent, yes."

He had a slight accent, his vowels long, his *S*'s soft. Not British, but definitely European. She held out her hand. He took it, squeezing a little more firmly than was necessary. "You're prettier in your pictures."

Dovie's eyes widened, stunned by both his grip and the bluntness of the remark. So stunned, in fact, that she could think of no reply. For one thing, it was probably true. She hadn't bothered much with her appearance since William's death—not that it was his place to point that out. Especially when he looked so untidy himself.

"Yes. I'm *her*," Dovie said when she had finally recovered. "I don't recall speaking to you at the funeral. In fact, I don't recall seeing you there."

"Because I wasn't."

"Oh." It was all she could think to say, though she found it odd that as William's agent he hadn't bothered to attend.

"I came later," he added, as if reading her thoughts. "After everyone was gone."

Dovie nodded, wishing she'd had that choice. "I think half of Charleston was here that day. William's parents know everyone from here to Savannah."

"Yes, well, I wasn't sure I'd be welcome. I decided to err on the safe side."

"Not welcome? Why?"

Bloom smiled, a fleeting curl that was gone almost as soon as it appeared. "Come on. Let's not play games. Billy's parents hated that he chose art over a real career. I was the one who told him he was the real deal. And he listened. As far as they're concerned I wrecked his life."

Dovie said nothing. It was true. William had always credited Kristopher with encouraging him to follow his passion for sculpture. And he was spot-on about the Prescotts. When it came to William's art, they had never been supportive, treating it like a phase he would eventually grow out of. In fact, she was pretty sure that was why his mother had been in such a rush to see them married. She was hoping that once her son took a wife he would see the folly of pursuing art as a career and would follow his father into the world of finance.

"He was, you know," Kristopher said. "The real deal."

"Yes. He was. And you're right about his parents. They just knew he'd come to his senses one day and want a normal life."

"Ah yes, a pension plan and two-point-two children."

Dovie studied him through lowered lashes, the hardened line of his mouth, the sharp flare of nostrils, as if he'd just caught a whiff of something rancid. Everything about him was bristling with hostility, though she hadn't the slightest idea why. She'd never met the man.

"So, you're down from New York," she said, hoping to prod him into opening up.

"I'm in town for a few weeks, visiting my sister. I thought I'd pay my respects. Nice flowers," he said, pointing to the fresh bouquet. "You?"

"Yes."

"I was also hoping to talk to you."

This came as something of a surprise to Dovie, since his initial reaction to finding her there seemed to imply quite the opposite. "You dropped by the cemetery on the off chance that I'd be here?"

"No. I really did come to pay my respects. I would have called, but I didn't have your number, and you're not in the book. I knew you worked at a museum, but Charleston has about a hundred of those, so I figured I was out of luck. And then here you are."

"Why talk to me now that William's dead? We never talked when he was alive."

"I'm hoping you'll be able to help me with something. I wanted to wait until things . . . died down before I came around, but I thought it was finally time. There's a piece in William's collection I'd like to have—as a keepsake. It's the one he was working on when he died."

Dovie bit her lip, ashamed to admit she didn't know what he'd been working on. "I'm sorry. With the wedding plans and all, I'm afraid I lost track. Besides, he was always rather secretive about it. I thought it might be a wedding present, so I didn't ask questions."

"It wasn't a wedding present. It was something he was doing for me. And I'd very much like to have it."

Dovie thought of the studio key lying in a bowl on her dresser. She could take him there if she wanted to, let him in, but she really had no right. The studio, and everything in it, belonged to William's parents now. "You'll need to speak to William's parents about that. It all belongs to them now."

"I've been trying to do just that since I got into town, but I haven't had any luck getting them to return my calls. Not that I'm surprised."

Dovie *was* surprised. The Prescotts could be snobbish at times but she'd never known them to shirk the proper social forms. "Why should they refuse to return your calls?"

Kristopher stared down at his shoes. "That's rather a long story—and a private one, if you don't mind."

"As a matter of fact, I do mind. William and I were engaged. Anything to do with him has to do with me. We didn't have secrets."

"Well, he had at least one, if the sleeping pills are any indication."

The words hit Dovie like a dash of icy water. "I think I get why the Prescotts won't take your calls."

"Touché," Kristopher said, with a frosty nod. "I'm sorry. That was cruel, and I'm not usually cruel. I'm just . . . Jesus, this thing with the Prescotts is making me crazy. I've come all this way. I can't—I won't—go back without what I came for. But I'm not very optimistic about my chances. Which is why I was hoping you might put in a good word."

Dovie gaped at him. Until ten minutes ago she'd never laid eyes on the man. And in that ten minutes he'd managed to not only insult her looks, but question her relationship with her fiancé. Now he was trying to enlist her help in something that was none of her business. "What makes you think anything I say to the Prescotts will make a difference?"

"You were about to marry their son, give them grandchildren, make all their dreams come true. They must love you, while I'm just the enemy."

Dovie scowled at him. He was probably overstating it, but she got what he was saying. What he didn't know, what almost no one knew, was that William's parents had grown rather distant since the funeral, their phone calls to check on her growing more and more infrequent—and more and more strained.

"Don't take it personally," she told him. "They've shut out a lot of William's friends since the funeral. It's like they'd rather pretend they never had a son than deal with questions about his death. Suicide isn't supposed to happen in good families, I guess. Anyway, you're going in with two strikes against you—the friend thing *and* the agent thing."

"Not if you set up the meeting . . . and then went with me."

"Go *with* you?"

"You could help smooth things over, break the ice."

"When did this become my problem?"

"Billy said his parents were crazy about you. Especially his mother. According to them you were his perfect match in every way."

Dovie narrowed her eyes, perplexed by the almost tangible resentment in his voice. Was it possible Bloom saw her as a threat to his interests? Had he been worried that William might, in fact, do as his parents hoped and seek a more traditional means of supporting his wife? It would certainly explain his hostility. "Look, I appreciate what you're up against, Mr. Bloom, but I'm really not the one . . ." The words died away. "You called him Billy?"

A shadow darkened Kristopher's face but was quickly gone. "It was a joke between us. It stuck." He reached into the pocket of his coat and pulled out a card, handing it to her. "Look, give me a call if you change your mind. This is important to me, and I could really use your help. If it counts for anything, Billy would want you to do this."

Dovie said nothing as he turned to go, just stuffed his card into the pocket of her jacket and watched him walk away.

Billy?

Dovie stifled a yawn, then gave her shoulders a roll, attempting to ease the knot that had taken up residence between her shoulder blades. She'd been trying all evening to shake this afternoon's encounter with the prickly Mr. Bloom, a feat that had proven more challenging than she'd expected, despite spending the past four hours researching Magdalene laundries, as institutions like Blackhurst had been called in their day.

It had been slow going at first, but eventually articles began popping up—each worse than the last—and it soon become evident that Blackhurst had been far from the only one of its kind. While the majority of Magdalene asylums existed in Ireland, similar facilities had operated in England, Scotland, Australia, and the United States.

It seemed the matter had come to the public's attention in 1993, when a mass grave containing one hundred and thirty-three unidentified bodies was discovered on the grounds of one of the convents in Dublin. Once the media got hold of the story, the floodgates had opened, and women began stepping forward with vivid accounts of life in the laundries.

The stories were all too familiar. Women locked up with no say in the matter, hostage to both church and state, to the tune of thirty thousand in Ireland alone. But perhaps most astonishing was the fact that the last Magdalene asylum hadn't closed its doors until 1996. It was hard to believe such abuses had prevailed so late into the twentieth century, and even harder to believe that after all the publicity, the Church still refused to acknowledge the cruelties or apologize to the women who had suffered at the hands of such institutions.

Penitents.

That was what they called the inmates, some as young as eleven and twelve. Even now the word made Dovie furious. It should have been hard to believe such ghastly tales, to imagine being shut up in a place where every moment of every day was dictated by someone else, where even your name was taken from you, where you were force-fed a steady diet of guilt and shame, where the workday was twelve back-breaking hours long, and meals consisted of stale bread and watered-down soup, where you were forgotten by friends and forsaken by family. Voiceless. Friendless. Hopeless.

It should have been hard, but it wasn't.

It wrenched Dovie's soul to think of the lives that had been hijacked in the name of piety, most beyond any hope of reclamation. Without a family member to vouch for them, or money to pay their way out, many of the women had remained in the asylums for the rest of their lives, often taking religious vows. She thought of Marianne, the young novice who had befriended Alice in the infirmary, her only option to take the veil and remain at Blackhurst with the women who had taken her child—a different kind of victim perhaps, but a victim just the same.

There had been little mention of Blackhurst in the articles she had managed to find, other than a few brief details of its fate. It had become a pensioner's home for a while, and then a hospital for the mentally ill, before being torn down in 1993 after a fire ravaged at least half the dormitories. There was a certain savage satisfaction in the thought of Blackhurst burning to the ground, the stone walls that had imprisoned Alice and countless other girls pulled down to rubble. And yet the damage remained. Hundreds, perhaps thousands, of women still living, bearing scars they would never be rid of and wondering what had become of the babies they'd been made to give up.

Unfortunately, her actual mission, finding some clue as to where Alice's child might have ended up, had resulted in disappointment. When it came to records, either their existence or their whereabouts, she had also come up empty. She had even researched the Sacred Heart Children's Society, only to find the agency had disbanded sometime in the late '70s, its records reportedly lost when the roof of the warehouse where they were being stored collapsed and the building subsequently flooded. And so she was back where she started, exhausted but no wiser.

It felt good to stand and stretch, and even better to leave the laptop behind, to shake off the melancholy that had stolen over her while scanning dozens of sad-eyed sepia images. It was chilly on the back porch, but soothing, too, as she stepped out into the darkness, listening with closed eyes to the muffled chorus of night things. She loved the sound of the marsh at night, the steady chirp of unseen wings, the croak of soft green throats. It was quieter now that summer was over, but the magic was still there, the pulse of life throbbing just beyond the porch railing, a reminder that despite disappointment, tragedy, and unspeakable loss, life went on.

twenty-two

Dovie sat bolt upright in bed, heart thumping as she threw back the tangled sheets and touched her feet to the floor. She had dreamed of William again, of the terrible hours and days after his suicide. The ringing phone that had jarred her from a sound sleep the morning after her bridal shower. The eerily calm voice on the other end. William's brother, telling her he'd just found William on the bathroom floor in his studio apartment. An empty prescription bottle belonging to his mother. A half-drained bottle of his father's Bowman Islay single-malt scotch.

And then she was at the cemetery, wearing nothing but the Gamecocks jersey she usually slept in, staring at the gaping wound they had dug in the earth for her fiancé. The reek of lilies and Celia Prescott's signature Shalimar. The sun glinting tawny and warm off William's rosewood coffin. And all around her, a sea of faces, saddened, stunned, and just a little relieved that it wasn't their loved one who'd chosen to leave family and friends in such a terrible way.

But this time there had been a new face in the crowd, one she knew, but didn't. Kristopher Bloom's blue eyes had been cold and unreadable as they locked with hers. Was it reproach she saw there?

Or a plea of some kind? She had no idea. She only knew that something wordless had passed between them in the dream. Some odd sense of knowing—but knowing what?

It took a moment to remember what she had done with his card, but she finally found it in the pocket of the jacket she had worn yesterday. She had tucked it away without looking at it, certain she'd have no use for it. She peered down at the heavy gray stock with its crisp linen finish and clean block letters.

KRISTOPHER BLOOM

FINE ART

NEW YORK · SAN FRANCISCO · LONDON

She was dialing the number before she even looked at the time, hoping Mr. Bloom hadn't planned to sleep in. The answering voice was gritty and thick, but at eight o'clock on a Sunday she supposed he had a right to that.

"Mr. Bloom?"

"Yes?"

"It's Dovie Larkin. I was wondering if you'd meet me for coffee this morning."

There was a pause, a clearing of the throat. "Yes. Where?"

"There's a place on Meeting Street, the Daily Bread. Do you know it?"

"No, but I'll find it."

"In about an hour?"

"That's fine." The line went quiet, and for a moment Dovie thought he'd hung up. After another moment, his voice came again. "Thank you, Dovie."

Dovie felt the faint niggling of guilt as she ended the call. She knew what he thought, that she had reconsidered his request to help him smooth the way with the Prescotts. She hadn't. In fact, she hadn't given it another thought. She had her own reasons for wanting to meet this morning. Maybe she was crazy. Practically everything she did these days was. But for more than a year now she'd been sitting at William's graveside, waiting for some kind of answer. Perhaps Kristopher Bloom *was* that answer, or could at least supply it. At any rate it was worth a cup of coffee and an hour on a Sunday morning.

The smell of fresh-baked bread greeted Dovie as she entered the café, reminding her of Sunday mornings growing up, her mother in the kitchen, up to her elbows in flour and dough, an apron tied about her waist. She really had tried to create a *Leave it to Beaver* life for her family. Maybe she'd stop by the house later, offer to help out in the garden, or take her downtown for brunch.

She was unbuttoning her jacket when she spotted Kristopher, hunched over a corner table, a cup of something tall and frothy cradled between his palms. She lifted her chin in greeting, feeling awkward all of a sudden, as if she were on a job interview, or a blind date. She could feel his eyes as she waited at the counter for her macchiato. On impulse, she asked the barista to throw in a pair of bear claws. A bribe of pastry couldn't hurt.

She kept her face neutral as she set down the coffee and plates, and took the chair opposite Kristopher. "I ordered you a bear claw. They do the best bear claws in town here. I figure it's the least I can do after dragging you out of bed on a Sunday morning."

Kristopher glanced up from his cup with red-rimmed eyes. He looked like hell, unshaven and gaunt, like a man who'd gone without sleep for far too many nights. Still, he was handsome in a lean, brutal sort of way, one might almost say sensual.

"I'm glad you called. And a little surprised. I was an ass yesterday. I'm sorry."

Dovie tore off a corner of her pastry and popped it in her mouth, stalling for time. She had no idea how to reply, or how to go about asking what she'd come to ask. How did one broach such a subject? *By the way, do you happen to know why my fiancé swallowed a bottle of sleeping pills right before our wedding?*

"When did you last see William?" she asked, steering the conversation toward less acrimonious ground. "I mean, how long before . . ."

"Less than a week. He was up for the show in Soho."

"That's right. I forgot about Soho. We barely saw each other that week. I was up to my ears in wedding plans, and William was locked away in his studio. I sometimes wonder—"

"Don't." The word seemed to burst out of him, ragged and angry. "Don't say you wonder if there was some way you could have stopped him. That is what you were going to say, isn't it?"

Dovie nodded. "Do you wonder, too?"

"Every day."

"Did you know he was . . . thinking about it?"

Kristopher looked both stunned and angry. "Don't you think I would have stopped him, if I had?"

"I just thought he might have talked to you, as a friend. That maybe you'd noticed a change in him, some clue that he was depressed."

"Depressed?" He repeated the word as if she'd just said something ridiculous.

"It *is* the usual state of mind for people contemplating suicide."

"I guess I just can't imagine what he could have had to be depressed about. His career was taking off. He was about to get married. The world was his oyster."

Dovie set down her cup and crossed her arms. "Why do you do that?"

"Do what?"

"Get all snarky, like I'm the enemy or something."

Kristopher picked up his fork and began flaking bits of pastry off onto his plate. "I'm just so sick of everyone thinking they knew what would and wouldn't make Billy happy. No one was ever interested in what he wanted. They were too busy planning his life for him. Now that he's dead, people suddenly care. It pisses me off, is all."

Dovie nodded. On some level, she got what he was saying, but she couldn't escape the feeling that she was part of the *everyone* Kristopher was talking about. "The Billy thing," she said, changing the subject. "How did that happen?"

Kristopher put down his fork and picked up his cup, sipping while a small smile formed. "A friend of mine, Brian, owns a club on the West Side. William and I went for drinks after one of his shows. I introduced him as William, but Brian decided then and there that his nickname was Billy Boy. And that was it. I never called him anything but Billy. None of us did, actually. He wasn't William Prescott the Third when he was with us. He was just . . . Billy."

"And he was okay with that?"

"I think he was, yes. He was suffocating down here, trying to please all the people in his life."

"People like me, you mean?"

"It was his parents, mostly. You just bought the package they were selling. Not your fault. And for the record, he never blamed you."

He was talking in riddles. "I have no idea what *package* you're referring to, but thank you for that. I think."

Dovie tore off another bit of pastry and folded it into her mouth. It was an odd conversation to be having. Asking questions she should have known the answers to. Listening to answers she could never have given herself. She wasn't sure she liked it. And yet there was a strange comfort in it, too, a fragile connection to something lost. They had cared about the same person. They missed the same person. Their pain was their bond.

"I should thank you. You were a good friend to William." She paused, surprised to find herself smiling. "I'm sorry, I just can't call him Billy. To me, he'll always be William."

"Billy. William. It doesn't matter. He was a hell of a guy. Crazy, at times, but a hell of a guy."

Dovie chuckled as a memory flickered to life. "He was crazy. He used to do these voices. That's how we met, actually. We were at this god-awful luncheon, and he started mimicking all the women there. He had me laughing so hard I nearly wet my pants."

"Talk about peeing your pants—try sitting beside him at the Starbucks drive-through when he orders a Venti triple-shot vanilla latte sounding like Donald Duck."

This was a new one for Dovie, but she could see it so clearly she threw her head back and laughed. And just like that, the tension between them seemed to evaporate, like clouds shredding after a storm.

"And then, when he got the vanilla latte, he added even more sugar to it."

Kristopher smiled. "Four sugars, to be exact. He couldn't drink anything unless it was sweet enough to curl his hair. I swear, I've seen the man add sugar to sweet tea. I seriously wonder how he had any teeth left."

It was true. William had had an insatiable sweet tooth, especially when it came to coffee or tea. And four sugars was precisely the number he added to his latte. She was surprised that Kristopher would remember that. But it made her like him better.

"He had so many pet peeves and idiosyncrasies," Dovie said wistfully. "I miss them."

"You mean you miss the way he'd go off on a tirade anytime someone used the expression *irregardless*?"

"I swear, his eyes would roll back in his head."

"Or *supposubly*?"

"That is not a word!" Dovie mimicked, doing her best William impersonation.

"Are you going to help me with Billy's parents?"

The question brought Dovie back to reality with a bump. She

picked up her mug, sipping thoughtfully. "I wasn't going to, but now I think I might."

"What changed your mind?"

"I don't know, really. Maybe your knowing how many sugars he took. Anyway, I said I *might*, not that I was going to."

"And what will it take to convince you?"

Dovie studied him over the rim of her macchiato. His voice had been silky just then, almost seductive, and yet she'd never met a less available man. Perhaps he was married. He didn't wear a ring, but that didn't prove anything one way or another. Lots of married men skipped the ring. Or maybe he was just the kind of guy who had rules about mixing business with pleasure. She understood that. He'd come to Charleston on a mission, and he was hell-bent on seeing it through. "Tell me again why you want this sculpture."

Kristopher pushed back his uneaten bear claw and folded his arms on the edge of the table. "I want it because it's the last thing he ever did, the last thing he'll ever do. And I want it because it was supposed to be mine. I asked him to do it."

"It may not even be finished."

"I don't care about that."

"I'll do it," Dovie blurted before she could change her mind. "I'll help you. Because I think William would want me to."

"Thank you."

There was such relief in his voice that she felt the need to warn him. "Please don't get your hopes up. I'm not sure the Prescotts will even know the piece you're talking about. They took no interest in his work, other than to disapprove of it, so I'm not sure they'd want any more of it out there."

"I would never sell it. I'd make sure they knew that."

"Kristopher, I'm not even sure they'll talk to *me* about this, let alone talk to you. They blame William's art for what happened. And I'm pretty sure that means they blame you, too."

"But his art made him happy. In fact, it was the *only* thing that did."

Dovie stared down into her cup. "I used to think I made him happy. Apparently, I was wrong."

"He cared for you a great deal."

"Just not enough."

"Don't do that, Dovie. Don't make this your fault. He chose. Billy . . . William chose what he did. I never imagined he would do it. He was never big on choices. He was always too busy trying to please everyone. That's what killed him. Not the pills. Not the bourbon. It was not being able to choose."

Dovie shook her head. "I don't understand what you're saying."

"It doesn't matter now. I just want the sculpture. Help me get it and I'll go away and never bother any of you again."

He was sitting up straight now, his body tight as a bowstring as he waited for her answer. "I'm just wondering," Dovie said, still studying his body language. "Are you this passionate about all your clients' work?"

"Billy was more than a client. He was a friend. A best friend."

Dovie nodded with a sad kind of knowing. "He was that for me, too."

twenty-three

Austin used his key to let himself in, depositing the pair of framed prints he'd just picked up for his mother on the entry table. It was Sunday, which meant Kimberly wasn't around to harass him about scratching the furniture. Not that anyone would be able to see a scratch if he left one. Why did his mother insist on keeping the place shut up like a tomb?

Squinting through the gloom, he ran an eye around the parlor, eerie now in its stillness, like a theater set after the players had departed the stage and the lights had been switched off. The show had closed, at last, a flop by even the kindest critic's standards. A tragedy. Or perhaps a farce. Annoyed, he shook off the thought. What the hell was wrong with him? All this bitterness and looking back was pointless, and yet he couldn't seem to help himself. It was as if a door somewhere in his memory had been wedged open a crack, and he couldn't keep from peering in.

Peeling off his jacket and draping it over the newel post—another habit sure to drive Kimberly to distraction—he called upstairs to his mother. When no answer came he poked his head into the kitchen, then ventured down the hall to her study. Both were empty. Perhaps she'd gone out, but that was unlikely. She rarely left the house these days, and never alone.

Finally, he caught the faint rattle of china and followed it out to the sunporch. He lingered in the doorway a moment, startled by the sight of his mother in this unguarded moment, without makeup and still in her robe, her hair loose about her shoulders, threaded here and there with strands of silver. For an instant, he was reminded of the days after Alice's death, when she had slowly gone to pieces. A nervous complaint, the doctors called it, brought on by grief. They had prescribed heavy doses of Valium and Seconal, but nothing seemed to work. And then, when people began to talk, she was sent to the Groves—a spa-slash-sanitarium in the Carolina mountains. And he had been sent to school.

He must have moved or made a sound, because she turned, her face suddenly brightening. "There you are. I wondered if you'd come by. I've been missing you."

"I know. I'm sorry. I'm finding the crown a bit heavier than anticipated. I did manage to pick up the prints, though. I'll hang them while I'm here if you know where you want them."

"Well, I thought I did when I bought them, but now I think I'd like to live with them for a few days first." Gemma smiled up at him, patting the settee. "Come sit, and tell me what's new in your world."

Austin pushed aside the stack of gardening magazines she'd been browsing despite the fact that she hadn't set foot in the gardens in years. He watched as she poured him a cup of tea, noting the slight tremor as she passed it to him. Coffee was what he needed, the stronger the better. He'd been on the phone with Tyler Burns half the night, talking the poor kid off yet another ledge.

His phone had gone off at quarter to twelve, midway through the third quarter of the Arizona game he'd been pretending to watch. He recognized Tyler's number the minute it appeared, but the call had dropped before he could answer. Three minutes later, it rang again, this time with Tyler sobbing on the other end, blubbering that no one would even notice if he was dead. He'd finally managed to get the kid calmed down, but it was clear that the time had come to have a talk with the boy's father, no matter how crowded the man's social schedule might be. It would mean breaking his word to Tyler—a solemn vow to never breathe a word of their conversations to his father or anyone—but that was just too bad. When a kid started talking about dying everything changed, including promises.

"You look tired," his mother said, touching a hand to his cheek. "You've got circles under your eyes."

"A boy from the youth center," he said over the rim of his teacup. "He called around midnight in a pretty bad way. I was on the phone with him most of the night."

"Then you should be home in bed, not here."

"Can't. I'm taking him out sailing this afternoon. Besides, I promised to come by and see my best girl. I couldn't very well go back on my word, now, could I?"

She smiled, patting his cheek again. "You always were a charmer."

"How are you, Mother? You're looking a little tired yourself."

Gemma rolled her eyes. "Nothing a little Estée Lauder won't fix."

"Have you been to see Dr. Randolph lately?"

"I have, as a matter of fact, and he says I'm fit as a fiddle, so you can take that look off your face. I'm not sick. I'm just starting to show a little wear and tear around the edges. I'll be seventy next month, in case you've forgotten. That's an awful lot of miles."

Austin nodded. She had a point. And Tate miles weren't easy miles. "I just want to make sure you're taking care of yourself. You are, aren't you?"

"You're sweet, even if you do look like death on a Triscuit. Have you eaten, at least?"

"Thanks, I think. And no, I haven't. When have you ever known me to want breakfast?"

"But it's nearly noon. Let me fix you some eggs and toast. You'll feel better."

Austin chuckled. "You mean, *you'll* feel better. No, thanks. This is all I need." He reached for a piece of biscotti from the tray and nibbled the end, doing his best not to make a face as he swallowed. It tasted like last week's coffee cake.

"Well, now that we've established that I'm not going to kick the bucket anytime soon, let's hear what's happening with you."

Austin set down his tea, hoping his mother wouldn't notice the uneaten biscotti concealed between cup and saucer, then nudged the stack of magazines to give himself a bit more room. Frowning, he glanced down at several sheets of stationery imprinted with the museum's distinctive logo.

"Where did this come from?" he asked, holding up the sheets.

"From the museum, just like it says at the top. Why do you look like you're about to throw a tantrum?"

"Because I told her," he shot back. "I made it clear that from now on all details for the gala were to go through me, and that you weren't to be bothered. And here she's brought you something else."

His mother regarded him with wide, somewhat surprised eyes. "I assume by her, you mean Ms. Larkin, though I don't understand why you're upset. It's just a letter confirming the venue and menu choices we discussed the day she came by. It arrived the other day, and must have gotten scooped up with my magazines. And why on earth would you forbid her to have contact with me?"

"I just didn't want her bothering you."

Gemma folded her arms, a sure sign that she was less than pleased. "Because I'm so frail, so doddering, that deciding between the chicken and the fish might give me a stroke?"

"No. Of course not. I know how you feel about the museum, and how important this new wing is. That's why I made the donation in the first place. But there's no need for you to be sucked into all the tiny details."

"Austin, this isn't about getting my name on some plaque. It's something I care very deeply about, something I want to be involved in."

"I understand that. I just didn't want her coming around and making a nuisance of herself. That's why I told her to stay away. You've got enough on your plate without her loading you up with a bunch of questions."

Gemma seemed baffled at first, and then astonished. "Enough on my plate? Austin, I have nothing on my plate. You say I look tired, and I am, but I can promise you it's not from having too much on my plate. It's from having absolutely nothing on my plate. When your father was alive there were dinners, parties, benefits, something to do every night. Now I never leave the house. There's nothing I'm supposed to do. Nowhere I'm supposed to go."

"You could start going to the club again. Have lunch with your friends, like you used to. And you used to play bridge. You could get the Wednesday group together again. Or maybe get back out in the garden."

Gemma sighed, shaking her head. "That isn't what I mean. I mean I'm not useful anymore. Not . . . needed."

Her words hit home. "I'm sorry, Mother. I didn't realize—"

"Don't be sorry, honey. It's the way things work. We get old. The torch is passed. And I'm proud that it's been passed to you. Someday some woman will stand beside you, the way I stood beside your father. At least, I hope she will. Until then, I'd appreciate it if you'd stop treating me like a piece of Waterford crystal. I'm not going to splinter into pieces if I'm asked to make a few decisions. Besides, I told you, I like that girl. She cares about what she's doing, and she's sweet. Beautiful, too, in case you hadn't noticed."

Austin saw where this was going, and decided to stop it cold. The last thing he needed at this moment was a sales pitch on Dovie Larkin. "She is. But I'm not in the market for what you're talking about. I don't want my picture taken, but if I have to, I promise you I don't need a woman standing next to me when I do."

"Yes, you do. Everyone needs someone standing next to them, honey. We're just wired that way, to belong to something besides ourselves. And you're not getting any younger. All I'm saying is maybe it's time to give up the party girls and think about settling down. I wouldn't mind a grandchild or two, you know. I'm not getting any younger, either."

"And what would you say if I told you I liked my life the way it is?"

"I'd say your father's dead, and it's time you stopped trying to punish him."

Austin felt a muscle begin to tick in his cheek. He didn't want to have this conversation now—or ever, really. "This hasn't got anything to do with him."

Gemma lifted one unpenciled brow. "Monica wasn't about your father?"

"Monica was a mistake."

She sighed as she set down her cup and took both his hands, refusing to let go when he tried to pull free. "You married Monica because you knew she was the last woman on earth your father would ever approve of. You did it to hurt him."

"And all I did was hurt everyone else." This time when he pulled away, she let him go. He stood, stalking toward the far end of the sunroom.

"It wasn't your fault, Austin. She had problems."

"And I sure didn't help, did I? And now you're suggesting I wreck someone else's life? No, thanks. I've swallowed enough guilt for one lifetime."

"It wouldn't be like that, honey. You'd be choosing a partner this time, not a weapon. And I don't mean one of those Barbie dolls you've been seeing. I'm talking about a woman you'd be proud to share your life with. Someone like . . . well, like Dovie, for instance."

He stared at her, incredulous. "That's what all this is about? Setting me up with Dovie because *you* like her?"

"Sometimes you get a feeling about someone the minute you meet them. You just know who they are, and what they're all about. I just thought—"

"She was asking about Alice," he said, cutting her off. "You asked why I told her not to bother you. That's why. She was asking about Alice."

His mother paled visibly, hands fluttering in her lap like a pair of startled birds. "What . . . what did she want to know?"

"I don't know. I stopped her before she could get very far."

"Do you think she's heard the talk—about Alice and your father, I mean? Do you suppose that's why she asked?"

"I have no idea what she knows, but I'd say it's a pretty safe bet that she has. I don't think there's anyone in Charleston who hasn't heard the talk about my nanny and that bastard."

"Austin, please. Show some respect. The man was your father, and my husband."

"He might have been your husband, but he was never any kind of father to me. As far as I'm concerned, he was just a man who lived down the hall. He sent me away the first chance he got, because he couldn't stand the sight of me. So please don't sit there and tell me to show some respect. I can't. Come to think of it, I don't recall him being much of a husband, either, so why you're always trying to make him out to be some kind of saint, I'll never know."

He regretted the words as soon as they were out, but it was too late. He watched as his mother's face drained of color, her hand to her cheek, as if his words had struck her there.

"It's always easy to throw rocks at someone else's house, isn't it?"

she said softly. "To peer between someone else's blinds and think you know what's going on inside. But it's not always that simple, Austin. There are things you can't see, things people keep to themselves. Things that would change everything if you knew them. Or have you forgotten that?"

Austin looked away, unwilling to meet her gaze. It was the closest she'd ever come to admitting she knew there were things he had neglected to share about his marriage to Monica, ugly things he had let go with her to her grave.

"No," he said, finally. "I haven't forgotten."

twenty-four

It had taken three phone calls to get the Prescotts to agree to meet with Kristopher, and then only on the condition that Dovie be present. He would have thirty minutes to make his case, and not a moment more, after which he would accept their decision as final, leave their home, and never attempt to contact them again. The terms alone had Dovie convinced that they were wasting their time.

Dovie managed a smile as she slid into the passenger seat of Kristopher's rental car. "Time to get the show on the road, I guess."

"I can't thank you enough for making this happen, Dovie."

"Nothing's happened yet," she reminded him. "I've gotten you in the door, that's all."

"How does the old saying go? It's better than a poke in the eye with a sharp stick."

Dovie cocked an eye at him. "That's an actual saying?"

"For my grandmother, it was. One of her favorites, actually. And in this case it's spot-on. Any meeting, even a hostile one, is better than no meeting at all."

"I just don't want you to get your hopes up. If Amanda Prescott's tone was any indication, they've pretty much made up their minds already. They *really* don't like you."

Kristopher's jaw tightened as he shifted the car into reverse. "The feeling's mutual."

It was an odd remark, given the fact that he'd never even met William's parents, but Dovie decided to let it pass. At the moment, she had more important things to worry about, like making sure Kristopher didn't say something that would get him tossed out on his ear. She just hoped the drive across town would give her enough time to do some coaching. For the next fifteen minutes, while Kristopher navigated the maze of Charleston's downtown streets, she ran through the list of dos and don'ts. *Keep your temper, no matter what's said. Don't let them draw you into an argument. Don't mention the word* suicide. *And above all, under no circumstances refer to their son as Billy.*

She watched him as he pulled up the circular drive and cut the engine. He was staring at the house, a furrow between his dark brows. He must have felt her eyes. He turned, hands tight on the wheel. "I meant what I said earlier, Dovie. Whatever happens in there, I want you to know how much I appreciate what you've done. I see now why Billy picked you. You'd have been good together. You've got a big heart. So did he."

The unexpected compliment made Dovie squirm, as if some battle had just been lost, some precious ground yielded. She glanced at the clock on the dash. There wasn't time to ask. "We'd better get going. You've got thirty minutes. You can't afford to waste them sitting out here."

It was Tilda who answered the door, looking as dour and starched as ever in her light blue uniform. Her smooth dark face remained impassive as she showed them into the front parlor. The Prescotts were waiting, seated side by side on the sage green sofa, their intent, no doubt, to present a united front. Neither stood as they entered the room.

Mrs. Prescott gestured toward a pair of wingbacks, then returned her hands to her lap. Dovie scanned the coffee table, bare except for a cut crystal bowl of creamy white roses. She had never known William's mother to receive guests without a tray of refreshments nearby, but there was no tray today, no pitcher of iced tea, no clever little cookies from Blanc Pain—because they weren't guests. This was business. So be it.

Mr. Prescott tipped his head in Dovie's direction, the barest of acknowledgments. Dovie recognized the gesture for what it was—an indictment. In arranging this meeting for Kristopher, she had chosen sides, though in what she still couldn't say. What she did know was that she was suddenly determined that Kristopher would leave with what he'd come for.

"Mr. and Mrs. Prescott," Dovie began when everyone was settled. "The reason Mr. Bloom asked for this meeting is quite simple. William was working on a piece for him when he died, and he'd like to have it."

"So I gathered," Harold Prescott said, raking cold eyes over Kristopher, "based on the messages he's left on my phone. What I'm not clear on is why Mr. Bloom thinks I'd be inclined to give him anything."

Dovie stared at him. She'd never seen William's father be anything but gracious. Where was all this hostility coming from? Hoping to find an ally in William's mother, she shifted her gaze, but Amanda remained mute, an air of accusation lurking just beneath her well-polished surface.

Perhaps if she approached it from a different angle. "Harold. Amanda. I know neither of you was happy when William decided to pursue his artwork as a career, but today isn't about that. At least it shouldn't be. What it's about is doing what William would have wanted. He and Kristopher weren't just business associates. They were friends. And the piece we're talking about carries a great deal of sentiment. Which is why he—why *we*—came today. Because

Kristopher would like something to remember your son by. Surely you can understand that."

The silence that settled over the room was brief, but uncomfortable. It was Amanda who finally broke it. "How dare you come into my home and lecture me about what my son wanted? You, of all people, who claimed to love him, and then let him do what he did? He wanted to throw his whole life away, to turn his back on his family and everything he was brought up to be. You were supposed to stop him. How in God's name can you stand there and claim to know what he would want now that he's dead when you obviously didn't care enough about him when he was alive?"

Dovie was too astonished to respond. Not once since William's death had Amanda Prescott ever hinted that Dovie had been in any way responsible for her son's suicide. Now, inexplicably, she had done just that, and in a way that made Dovie think she'd been holding her tongue for some time. From the corner of her eye, she saw Kristopher preparing to bolt up out of his chair. She shot him a quelling look. It was sweet of him to want to leap to her defense, but it wasn't going to help his case one tiny bit. Quite the opposite, in fact.

Knotting her hands in her lap, Dovie tried again, determined to ignore Amada's tirade and finish what she started. "Mr. and Mrs. Prescott, the sooner we decide this matter, the sooner we can all just part company. That being said—"

"Mr. Bloom," William's father said, clearly not interested in anything Dovie had to say. "What is this really about? You say you're here because you want one of my son's sculptures, but frankly, I'm not buying it. I've seen his work, and it's hardly what I'd call art. So let's get down to business, shall we?"

Kristopher looked baffled. "Business?"

"I can only assume this is some sort of shakedown. You made a meal ticket of my son, and now that he can't help you, you show up on my doorstep. So, how much are you after?"

It was Kristopher's turn to look astonished. "You think I came here for money?"

"I assume William gave you some idea of our financial situation?"

"If you mean, did he tell me you were well off, then yes, he did. Though what you think that has to do with why I'm here, I have no idea. I don't want a cent from you. All I want is what belongs to me—the sculpture your son was working on when he died."

"Come, now, Mr. Bloom, I wasn't born yesterday. You don't expect me to believe this is about a silly piece of plaster, do you?"

"Mr. Prescott, the piece we're talking about is done in clay, not plaster, which you would know if you'd ever bothered to take an interest in your son's work. And I can assure you, I'm not *after* anything that isn't rightfully mine. I asked Billy to do the sculpture last May."

Amanda peered at him over the tops of her glasses. "Who on earth is Billy?"

Dovie closed her eyes, bracing herself. Had he not been paying attention in the car on the way over?

"Your son, Mrs. Prescott. I called him Billy."

Amanda's eyes blazed. "My son's name was William, Mr. Bloom. Use it, please."

Kristopher regarded her coldly but said nothing.

Mr. Prescott, on the other hand, seemed wholly unconcerned with the use of his son's nickname, and returned to the original thread of their conversation. "Did you pay William for this work?"

"You mean, was it a commissioned piece?"

"I mean, did you give him money in exchange for the work you requested?"

"Well, no. It was supposed to be . . . a gift."

"A gift. I see. And how much do you think something like that might be worth?"

"Worth?"

"Worth," Mr. Prescott repeated sharply. "How much would the piece sell for?"

"I don't . . . I have no idea. It was never meant—"

"You're an art dealer, and you don't know how much a client's work is worth?"

Kristopher stared at him, clearly flustered. "Are you asking me to pay for the sculpture? Because I'll be happy to pay whatever you ask."

Dovie held her breath, watching as Mr. Prescott regarded Kristopher with shrewd eyes, as if sizing up an enemy before the start of battle.

"No," he said, the word like a shot in the silence, cold and final. "I don't want your money, Mr. Bloom. And I don't want you here. Not now, and not in the future. Do you understand me?"

Dovie cut her eyes at Kristopher, bracing for the inevitable outburst of righteous indignation. Instead, he looked beaten, his shoulders slumped, his face a weary blank. "Mr. Prescott," she blurted, not ready to give up. "I'm asking you to reconsider. You said yourself that you never cared for William's work, but this piece is important to Kristopher. And as he said, he'd be happy to pay whatever—"

Amanda stood before Dovie could finish, her face impassive as she smoothed the wrinkles from her blue linen skirt. "My husband has made his decision, Dovie, and I'm asking you to respect it. I'll call Tilda to show you out."

"That won't be necessary," Dovie said stiffly. "I know the way."

She and Kristopher were already heading for the foyer when Amanda Prescott spoke again. "I don't know what you hoped to accomplish by coming here today, Dovie. Or why you've taken up with the likes of Mr. Bloom. I always thought better of you. It appears I was mistaken."

Dovie turned, fixing her with a cool glare. "It appears we both were."

Neither of them said a word when Kristopher pulled into Dovie's driveway. Kristopher, because he was either too miserable or too angry to speak. Dovie, because there seemed nothing appropriate to say. It had been a peculiar sort of afternoon. William's father had been spectacularly unfair in assuming Kristopher's motives had to do with money, and his mother had stopped just short of calling him a degenerate. Though neither came right out and said it, they seemed to see their son's friendship with Kristopher as the root of all his problems, as if everything would have been fine if his talents had simply gone undiscovered.

"You okay?" Kristopher asked, still hunched over the steering wheel.

"Who, me?" Dovie reached for a smile but couldn't quite manage it. She shrugged instead. "I'm fine. You're the one who came away empty-handed."

"For what it's worth, she was out of line back there. There was no way you could have known what Billy was planning. Hell, his own parents didn't have a clue. Or like to pretend they didn't. He was good at keeping things to himself. Too good. That was part of his problem—all of his problem, actually. Promise me you won't let what she said get to you."

"It's not like she said anything I haven't said to myself at least a thousand times. But it was different somehow, hearing it from her, seeing that awful look on her face. There were so many things I wanted to say, questions I wanted ask. But it wasn't the right time. I'm not sure it ever will be."

"What kind of questions?"

Dovie stared down at her hands, at the narrow groove where her engagement ring used to sit, still visible after more than a year. "Things like, am I the only one who wonders if William chose what he did—I mean the *way* he did it—completely out of the blue? He took a bottle of his mother's sleeping pills from the house, then downed half a bottle of his father's favorite scotch. I mean, was that really just a coincidence? There was no note, but sometimes I wonder if he wasn't leaving his own kind of message—one only his parents would understand."

Kristopher reached for her hand, squeezing it so hard she nearly winced. "You're not the only one who wonders, Dovie. And I'd bet anything it wasn't a coincidence."

Dovie glanced away, pretending to look out the passenger window. "It's hard to fathom, you know, a parent squashing a child's happiness because it doesn't mesh with their idea of respectability. To be so ashamed of your own flesh and blood that you can't just let him be who he is and live the life he wants."

"You don't have to fathom it, though, do you?" Kristopher said with a terrible air of resignation. "You've seen it in action today. And you've seen what it does. They pretend it's other things, that it hasn't got anything to do with them—but they know. And it's killing them. So they take it out on you, and me. Because it's easier than pointing the finger at themselves."

"It must have been so hard on him—to be disapproved of by the two people who were supposed to love him no matter what. I'm glad he had a friend like you, someone who believed in him. They should have believed in him, too. I'm sorry, by the way, about the way they treated you. They had no right to say the things they did."

"Forget it. But thanks for trying. It means more than you know."

"You'll go back to New York now, I suppose?"

He shook his head, looking so very tired. "Time to get back to the real world."

"I won't see you again, will I?"

"Not unless you happen to be invited to my sister's wedding next month. You're not, are you?"

Dovie managed a grin. "No, I'm afraid not. But you'll be coming back?"

"Just for a few days. It seems I'm giving the bride away. Sometime at the end of October. You have my card if you want to get together for a drink. No pressure, though. Something tells me after today you're going to want to forget you ever met me."

Dovie laid her hand over his. "What's that old saying? Any friend of William's . . ." It was true, too. The thought of never seeing Kristopher again made her a little sad, as if she were losing William all over again. "Don't be surprised if I call you someday and take you up on that drink."

Kristopher tried for a smile, but it didn't take. "I'd like that. Go on, now. You look tired." He dropped a kiss on her cheek as he leaned over and reached for the door handle. "Any friend of Billy's . . ."

Dovie stood on the front porch, watching, as he backed down the drive and pulled away. Right or wrong, she was still smarting from Amanda Prescott's remarks. She had been ready for their hostility toward Kristopher, had even expected it. But nothing had prepared her for the venom William's mother had hurled at her. It was pain, she told herself, the bitter rant of a mother who had lost her only son in the worst way imaginable. But there was something else nagging at her, some nebulous thought that had yet to gel. Perhaps it was something to do with William's father, and the lack of anything like grief for his dead son. What was it about families that made it so easy to wound one another, that turned love to rage, that made it so hard to forgive?

She thought of Dora and Alice, of the wounds that had festered for generations, grudges that had survived both years and miles, and felt the pull of Alice's unread letters. It might be too late to mend the wounds in William's family, but she still had hope that she could help Dora find the answers she so desperately longed for.

twenty-five

Riddle's Boardinghouse
Charleston, South Carolina
January 4, 1963

Dearest one,

I'm here at last! I arrived two days ago, and have only just gotten settled in. I can scarcely believe I've made it all the way to the United States from tiny Sennen Cove. I would have come sooner, but I had to make travel arrangements, and it was difficult with the little bit of money I managed to scrape together. I don't feel bad about taking Mam's under-the-sink money. She said it was for me to go to school with, so I could have a better life, but the only life I want now is one with you in it. I do feel a little bit bad about taking her watch, though I suppose if I tried very hard I could justify that, too, since it would have come to me eventually. This is just sooner, and for a good cause. For the cause of you, my darling.

I wonder sometimes, when I close my eyes at night, what your gram must have felt when she came to my room that morning and found me gone, if she was sad, or angry, or worried for me. I left no note, nothing saying where I was going, or why. I didn't see why I should. I'd made it plain from the start that I intended to find you and raise you on my own, and as she wanted no part of you in the beginning, she'll have no part once you're found. And you will be found, my angel. I feel you each morning when I open my eyes, somewhere out there in this sprawling city of palm trees and church steeples, waiting for me to find you, and when I do, all the hardship will have been worth it.

It wasn't easy to keep my plans secret in a place like Sennen Cove, where everyone knows everyone's business, and some old hen would surely let slip that she'd seen me down at the docks. Thank heavens for your father's friends, who knew who I should talk to, and helped me make arrangements. Regular passage was too dear, but I managed to hire on as a laundress on a ship called the Carinthia II, which went to New York first, and then on to Charleston.

After Blackhurst the work seemed almost easy, despite being seasick most of the voyage. I even made friends with one of the other girls in the laundry, Cathy Gardiner, who was fleeing Liverpool to escape her great bully of a boyfriend, and who now shares a room with me at the boardinghouse, where Mrs. Riddle lets me clean and do laundry for half board. It's cheap and passably clean, but best of all, no one here asks questions. I have told no one about you, and say only that I have just left a convent in Cornwall and have come to find work. It's not that I'm ashamed of you, little one. I'm not, and never will be. But people here are very pious. They spend five days out of seven at church, and are forever quoting the Bible. And they have a way of looking at you—or perhaps I should say looking through you—that makes me anxious. An unmarried girl in search of her baby isn't likely to be welcome among such vigorous Christians.

At times I fear I have embarked on a fool's errand, that I've come all this way only to have my hopes dashed. It's only my promise to you that has kept me going, and soon I will make good on that promise. I have looked up the address of the Sacred Heart Children's Society, and as soon as I am strong enough I'll go to talk to someone. I know once they hear my story, about how you were taken from me against my will, and sent all the way across the ocean, they'll give you back to me. Good night, my darling. I will dream of you tonight and, God willing, be with you soon.

All my love,
Mam

Riddle's Boardinghouse
Charleston, South Carolina
January 12, 1963

Little one,

I doubt you will ever see this letter. There are things a mother should not share with her child, things that are best left unsaid. And so I suppose I am writing this particular letter for myself, because I cannot bear to keep it inside any longer.

As promised, I have been to Sacred Heart. I got there early and had to wait, huddled in the doorway until someone came to let me in. And finally someone did come, although by then I was blue with cold, my teeth chattering so badly I could barely tell them why I was there. I wore a dress I borrowed from Cathy, and Mam's gold watch and chain. I wanted to look respectable, like the kind of woman who could be trusted with a baby, but I must have fallen short. The iron-haired woman behind the counter—Mrs. Jennings—looked me up and down over her black-framed glasses like I was something that had blown in off the street.

I suppose I did look a bit dodgy after walking all that way, and I'm still so thin from being sick on the ship. I don't think my cough helped, either, or the tears that wouldn't stop. Before I could finish, Mrs. Jennings jerked a tissue from the box on the counter and handed it to me with a chilly sniff. She then removed her glasses and fixed me with what must pass for sympathy at Sacred Heart.

"Before we could begin any kind of records search, we'll need some sort of proof that the child you're seeking is actually yours. Something tangible, like a birth certificate or hospital records." She drummed her fingers on the scarred wooden counter. "Do you have those documents with you?"

I stared back at her across the counter, scrambling for a way to make her understand the way things worked at Blackhurst. "No. I don't have anything. They took my child the moment it was born and they made me sign some papers. I wasn't even told if it was a boy or a girl!"

"You signed papers relinquishing the child?"

"Yes, but I didn't want to. They said there were worse places than Blackhurst and that's where I'd end up if I didn't sign. They told us all that."

Mrs. Jennings's sympathy became annoyance. "Do you think you're the first girl to change her mind? We see one like you at least once a month. You get yourselves in trouble, then run to the church for help, only to change your mind a few months down the road."

I felt something like hysteria bubbling up in my throat as I again tried to make her understand. "I didn't run to Blackhurst. I was sent there against my will. My child was taken against my will! And I want it back!"

"Young woman, if you don't lower your voice and speak in a civil manner, I'll have to ask you to leave. Now, I've told you what is required to open a case like yours, and you're apparently unable to comply."

"Please," I begged her. "Isn't there anything you can do? There must be records of some kind, something that says where the babies come

from." And then I remembered. "There was a letter! They made us all write one and sign it. They told us it would be sent to the baby's new home. Surely that's a place to start."

Mrs. Jennings sniffed at me again as she looked down her nose. "Miss . . . Tandy, is it? Such letters, if existent, would be strictly confidential, as would any adoption paperwork you might have signed."

"How can they be confidential? I wrote that letter. It's my signature on those papers!"

"Precisely. You gave the child up voluntarily, which means you relinquished all parental rights, including the right to know the identity and whereabouts of the adoptive parents."

I felt myself coming apart at the seams. It wasn't possible that I had come all this way only to have my heart broken again. "I didn't come to learn the identity of the adoptive parents, Mrs. Jennings. I came to get my child back!"

"Under the circumstances, I'm afraid that isn't possible. You've just told me you're unmarried, which, based on this agency's criteria, or any agency, really, makes you an unsuitable candidate for raising a child."

I blinked at her, trying to understand. "How can I be unsuitable? I'm its mother. Isn't a child always better off with its mother?"

Mrs. Jennings sighed, her face a mask of rehearsed benevolence. "Children, Miss Tandy, are always better off in a stable home with a family of means, and by family I mean both a mother and a father. Only in a two-parent home can a child thrive and reach its God-given potential." She paused, pasting on a sickly smile. "And that's what we all want, isn't it—for your child to thrive? You might not realize it now, but you were doing your Christian duty when you signed those papers. In time, I'm sure you'll see that and be glad you did the right thing."

They were Marianne's words—or very nearly. But they were threadbare platitudes delivered by a woman whose heart had clearly never been robbed of a child. She no doubt repeated them daily to girls like me, a feeble attempt at comfort. But I refused to take comfort from them, any more than I had when Marianne had whispered them in the chapel at Blackhurst.

Desolate, I watched Mrs. Jennings turn away, directing her attention to a woman in a fur-trimmed coat who had just stepped up to the counter. I had been dismissed, without answers, without hope, and without you, my angel.

I barely remember moving to the door, or descending the cracked brick steps to the sidewalk, but I do remember feeling the pressure of a hand on my shoulder when I had gone a few steps. The man's face was a blur when I turned, a watery smear of greasy hair, crooked nose, and heavy dark stubble. I shook off his hand and mopped my eyes on my sleeve, then regarded him again. I dimly registered dirty boots and gray coveralls that buttoned down the front. "What do you want?"

He grinned as he dropped a half-smoked cigarette and ground it out on the sidewalk. His front tooth was chipped and a dark shade of yellow. "Name's Danny."

Something about his smile made me angry. "I didn't ask your name. I asked what you wanted."

He narrowed one eye, sizing me up. "The feisty type. And not from the good old U.S. of A., either. Doesn't matter. I saw old Jennings show you the door a minute ago." His eyes were inky dark and glinted when he spoke, like hard little stones at the bottom of a river. "She likes doing that."

"How do you know what—"

He jerked his head back toward the front of Sacred Heart. "I work in there. I'm the janitor, mostly, but I do other stuff, too. I run errands, pick up lunch, deliver papers. All kinds of papers."

He drew the last words out, thick and slow, as if there was something I should understand but didn't. I could feel the tears coming again, and turned away, too heartsick to respond. I had just taken a step when he caught me by the wrist.

"I can help you find that baby of yours."

I spun back around, my throat so tight I could barely breathe. "How?"

"Like I said . . . papers."

I shook my head, trying to make sense of the single word. "I don't understand."

"They got whole filing cabinets full of 'em in there, and there's me, all alone at night with my mop and bucket—knowing right where they keep the keys."

I felt my mouth working like a fish out of water. "What . . . how . . . what are you saying?"

After a furtive glance over one shoulder, he leaned in close and dropped his voice. "I'm saying we might be able to do a little business."

"You know where my baby is?"

"Not at the moment. But I could . . . if the price was right."

My heart sank. After paying for my passage and two weeks in advance for my room and board, Mam's under-the-sink money was already running low. "How much?"

"Well, now. Let me see. Information like that don't come cheap. I mean, I'd be putting my job on the line."

I waited while he pretended to do his calculations, though somehow I knew I wasn't the first girl he'd offered to help. Nor would I be the last.

"A hundred," he announced finally. "Not sure how much that is in pounds or whatever it is you Brits use, but over here it'll cost you a hundred bucks."

I stood there, gaping. It was an enormous sum, an impossible sum, nearly every cent I had left. But how could I say no? I came to Charleston with one purpose in mind—to find you, my darling, and get you back—and this man with his stubbled chin and grimy coveralls was offering me hope. Still, there was a pang of doubt, a sense that it was all too good to be true. "How do I know you're telling the truth?"

"You'll know when I give you what you want—a name and an address—and I'll give you that when you give me the hundred bucks."

"How would it work?"

"You tell me your name, where the kid was born, and when. Then you show up tonight after the place closes. Say seven o'clock, and we do the deal. Just that easy."

But it wasn't easy.

I left Mrs. Riddle's as soon as I cleared away the dinner dishes. We had agreed to meet in the small lot behind Sacred Heart. It was dark by the time I arrived, and there was only one car left in the lot. He got out when he saw me walk up, approaching with his hands in his pockets.

"Got the hundred?"

I swallowed, near tears. How on earth could I tell him no? I had rehearsed what I would say all the way there, but suddenly my throat went dry. "I don't have all of it. I thought I did, but when I went back and counted I realized I was short. I had to pay in advance when I moved in last week, and I haven't found a job yet. I . . . I was wondering if you'd take eighty-five."

"I said a hundred."

"Please. I'm desperate. It's every penny I have in the world."

"What else have you got?"

"Nothing. I haven't got anything else."

His eyes slid to my chest, lingering there. "The watch. Throw that in and we'll call it even."

My hand flew to Mam's watch, covering it protectively. "It isn't mine. It belongs to my mother."

"Eighty-five dollars and an old watch. A fair exchange for a baby, I'd say."

For a moment I was tempted to hand the thing over, but in the end I couldn't do it. I still don't know why. "I could pay you a little each week," I offered desperately. "Until I make up the difference."

"I'm not a bank, darlin'. Pay me, or I'm going home."

"Please. There's got to be a way. Some way."

He was silent for a moment, and I held my breath, praying with every cell in my body that this greasy man would take pity on me.

"Maybe there is," he said, his voice suddenly soft in the dark. "But only 'cause I'm bighearted."

"What?" I asked, grabbing at whatever bit of hope he was offering. "Whatever it is, I'll do it."

"I'm parked right over there," he said, jerking his thumb toward the shadowy lot. "You could come back to the car with me and . . . make up the difference that way."

"You want me to . . ." I looked away. I couldn't make myself say it.

"You ain't exactly my type, honey. I like my women with a little meat on their bones, but under the circumstances I guess I'd be willing to call it even."

I don't remember much after that, don't remember saying yes, or saying anything at all, but I must have, because all of a sudden I felt his hand between my shoulder blades, shoving me into the back of an old green Chevy that reeked of cigarette smoke and stale beer.

It was over quickly, or maybe it wasn't. I only remember the steamy, fuggy air and a brief bit of fumbling before finally counting the bills out into his sweaty palm. He grinned as he folded them in half and stuffed them into his shirt pocket, then fished out a small scrap of paper and handed it to me.

"Pleasure doing business," he drawled as he reached over and threw open the car door.

I barely registered the sound of the car starting behind me. I was too busy scurrying to the streetlight out near the curb, hands trembling as I unfolded the paper he'd given me and read the three crooked lines written there.

Mr. and Mrs. Harley Tate
9 East Battery Street
Charleston, S.C.

Even now, my heart soars to think of it. To know where you are, my angel, to know how close I am to you at this very moment, is a joy I thought I would never feel again. And as for how I came by this knowledge, I haven't the luxury of being squeamish. It was an exchange and nothing more, something for something, like buying milk or a newspaper. At least that's how I've chosen to think of it. Tomorrow, I will take the bus downtown and go to East Battery Street. I don't know what I'll say when I get there, but somehow I'll find a way to make them understand that you belong to me. And then, sweet angel, we will be together.

All my love,
Mam

twenty-six

Dovie returned the letter to its envelope, shuddering as she dropped it back into the desk drawer with the others. Just when she thought Alice's journey couldn't possibly get any worse—there was Danny. How could she ever share such a thing with Dora? And yet she had promised to do just that when she agreed to hold nothing back. It was a promise she was beginning to regret more and more every day.

In the kitchen, she rustled up some dinner—if cold chicken and asparagus eaten over the sink could be called dinner—then slipped out onto the back porch with a glass of chardonnay, hoping to shake the gloom that was suddenly threatening to engulf her.

It was a glorious evening, balmy and fragrant the way only a Lowcountry evening could be, the sun sinking into the golden grasses, shadows playing tag with the light as night slowly settled over the marsh. It was the time of day she enjoyed most, in the place she loved best, but tonight, as she closed her eyes and pulled in a lungful of dusk-scented air, she couldn't relax.

Every time she tried to thrust thoughts of Alice from her mind, the ugly events of this afternoon crowded in to fill the space, along with the nebulous disquiet that had been niggling at her from the moment she slid back into the passenger's seat of Kristopher's car—like a pebble in her shoe. She still couldn't put a name to the sense of unrest, but she was pretty sure it had to do with the look on Kristopher's face when Mr. Prescott had referred to William's sculpture as a silly piece of plaster. He'd been astonished that the man knew so little about William's work, so little he hadn't the first clue what his son had been working on when he died. And neither did she—and still wouldn't if she hadn't chanced to meet Kristopher in the cemetery that day. The realization hit her like a dash of cold water. And suddenly she knew. The pebble in her shoe was guilt. The kind that didn't go away just because you discovered it.

It was that same guilt that finally nudged Dovie into retrieving the little-used key from the bowl on her dresser and driving across town to the old brick warehouse on Church Street where William owned a studio apartment on the third floor. It was almost nine by the time she arrived, the street deserted.

Standing on the curb, she began to question her decision to come. What difference could any of it make now? William was gone, and had been for more than a year. For all she knew, his apartment had been emptied and sold to someone else, the lock changed.

There was only one way to know for sure. Digging the key from her pocket, she stepped into the dingy hallway, climbed two sets of groaning stairs, and stopped in front of apartment 306. The key slid home so easily she was almost surprised, probably because she'd never actually used it. There was never a reason for her to come by when William was away, no plants to water, no cat to feed. In fact, she'd rarely visited the studio at all. It had been William's, and William's alone, the creative hallowed ground to which he would retreat, often for days at a time, turning off the phone and living on takeout while the muse was upon him. And then, without warning, he would reappear, sheepish and freshly shaven, with a bottle of wine in one hand and a fistful of flowers in the other. And now she was here, lurking in the hallway, like a thief or a spy.

It was strange that she should find herself here now, more than a year after William's death, when she had never come before. For more than a year she'd been telling herself she wanted—that she *needed*—to know why William had committed suicide, and yet she had never been able to come to the place he held most sacred. It had been grief at first that kept her away. She wasn't sure she could stand to look at the place where he had been found. Then, later, it had simply seemed off-limits. With William gone the property belonged to his parents, the key their son had given her no longer hers to use. And yet that hadn't stopped her from coming tonight. Was it possible she had stayed away on purpose, because she was afraid she might actually find the answers she claimed to want? Answers she might not like? She shook off the thought as she turned the key, cursing Austin for her sudden pangs of self-doubt.

She was met with inky silence as she pushed inside and snapped the bolt behind her. In the darkness, her sense of smell seemed more acute, the air thick and stale, sharp with the shut-up smells of a sculptor's studio—dust, clay, metal, stone. William had loved those smells the way actors loved the smell of greasepaint and writers reveled in the smell of old books. They were part of him, not just of what he did, but of who he was, and more than a year after his death they still lingered, like the art he'd left behind.

She groped for the switch she knew was somewhere just inside the door, squinting against the sudden glare of overhead bulbs. The place was as stark as she remembered, bare brick walls, scarred oak floors, arched windows stretching from floor to ceiling. But there was a sense of barely controlled chaos in the small space now: discarded sketches and unopened mail littering the furniture and floor, crates of dusty books crouching in one corner, tattered issues of *The Brooklyn*

Rail covering the old wooden dolly that served as a coffee table. It was an unsettling sight. The place had never looked like this when she visited. Perhaps William had cleaned up before she came. Or maybe, near the end, he had just stopped caring.

It was a morbid thought, and one that stayed with her as she moved down the hall, forcing herself to pause in the doorway of the bathroom. She wasn't sure what she'd expected, but there was no sign that anyone had died there: no bloodstains, no chalk outline, just a leaky sink and rust-stained tub.

A few more steps and she was standing in the room William had used for both work and sleep. The bed was a mess, a muddle of striped gray sheets tumbling onto the floor, the way they might after a night of passion. Or of nightmares. Beside the bed was a makeshift nightstand, William's prized collection of vintage *Derrière le Miroir*, the issues dating as far back as 1946, stacked and topped with a heavy square of glass. His watch was there, and the signet ring he always wore on his little finger. She had wondered the night of the viewing why she hadn't seen it on his finger. She just assumed his mother had kept it for personal reasons, but here it was, where he had last taken it off.

From the corner, a canvas-draped object beckoned, like a ghost waiting patiently to be noticed. Dovie moved closer, circling a metal cart cluttered with supplies—wire loops and small wooden paddles, rolls of heavy-gauge wire, modeling clay wrapped in thin waxy paper—the tools of William's trade. She was reaching for one of the paddles, caked with a film of dried clay, when she remembered something William once said.

"The most precious tools a sculptor has are his fingers. It's how he brings a piece to life, by feeding his blood and soul into the clay. That's all sculpture is, really, an act of memory."

Her eyes slid back to the canvas concealing the work Kristopher had come more than seven hundred miles to claim. William's blood and soul. And she had no idea what it was. Slowly, and with great care, she dragged off the sheet, letting it slide to the floor in a dusty heap. Her breath caught as the piece came into view—a pair of entwined torsos, all muscle and sinew and raw animal need. Faceless. Limbless. And absolutely stunning.

She laid a hand against the clay, dry now after so many months, and cool to the touch. She hadn't expected coolness somehow. Perhaps because the subjects seemed so lifelike. And for good reason. Until meeting William, she never realized that budding artists studied anatomy with all the zeal of a first-year medical student, that they spent exhaustive hours learning muscles and bones, their origins and insertions, their hollows and curves. And in William's case it had clearly paid off. With eyes closed, she allowed her fingers to wander the satiny contours of belly, ribs, and buttocks. It struck her then, like a faint electric shock running the full length of her spine.

". . . when it's all said and done, sculpture is an act of memory."

She hadn't seen it at first, but now, with her fingertips, she finally grasped what she hadn't with her eyes alone: the telling sameness of the sculpted bodies, angles where there should have been curves, planes where there should have been hollows. An act of memory brought to life. Williams's memory—and Kristopher's.

For a moment the room tilted, and Dovie had to close her eyes against the words crowding into her head. *"People keep secrets, Dovie. Some are very good at it. Especially when we help them by looking the other way."*

Like a house of cards collapsing in on itself, all the signs she had ignored, the clues any fool would have seen, came tumbling down around her. Kristopher's hostile remarks the day they met. William's frequent, and often sudden, trips to New York. Mr. Prescott's inexplicable hostility toward his son's best friend. They had known, or at least suspected. Which explained Amanda's persistent lobbying for a shortened engagement. She was afraid William would back out—or worse, *come* out—before she could get him down the aisle.

The dizziness came again, worse this time, her throat so tight it seemed all the air had left the room. Squeezing her eyes shut, she waited for the world to right itself, and for the wave of giddiness to pass. She was about to open them again when she felt it—a subtle shift in the air around her, like a ripple of current moving over her skin. For a moment she wondered if she had only imagined it, but then it came again, accompanied by the groan of floorboards, and the skin-prickling certainty that she was no longer alone.

She turned to meet Kristopher's gaze. "How long?" she whispered. "How long have you loved him?"

"Longer than you." There was no hesitation in his answer, and no shame, only the dead calm that came with finally saying the thing you've longed to say. "I'm sorry," he added. "I know I should have told you, but I needed your help. I was afraid if you knew . . ."

Dovie glared at him. His words might have trailed away, but his meaning was clear enough. If she had known the truth—that he and William were lovers—she would have been less inclined to help him get what he wanted. He had a point, but it didn't stop her from wanting to give him a good hard slap. "And after? When you knew the Prescotts weren't going to give you what you came for—you couldn't have told me then?"

Kristopher shoved his hands into his pockets, like a schoolboy standing before the headmaster. "I could have, yes. But I didn't see the point. I loved Billy, and he loved me. And he loved you, too, in his way. Enough to ask you to marry him. Which gave you just as much right to your grief as I had to mine. Besides, I liked you too much by then to hurt you."

"So you just left me to figure it out on my own."

"I had no idea you'd come here, or that you'd put the pieces together. You hadn't up until now." He stepped forward, running the flat of his hand over one of the clay torsos with almost aching tenderness. "He called it *The Agonies*. Appropriate, don't you think, after the mess we made of things?"

Dovie fought the urge to soften. "Why did you come here tonight?"

"To say good-bye, I suppose."

"To the sculpture?"

"To everything."

"I locked the door behind me. You have a key?"

"Yes."

Dovie paused a moment to digest this, wondering how often Kristopher had come and gone without her knowing it. "Did you come often?"

His eyes skittered away as he nodded, as if the admission pained him. "I never stayed more than a day or two. It was too risky. It was hard being apart, but harder, I think, being together, sneaking around behind everyone's back, holed up here like a couple of criminals. It was easier in New York."

"Why?"

"Let's just say people in the South have their own ideas about what a man is and isn't. Not all of them, but enough. And certainly, the Prescotts. It isn't like that in New York, at least not in the city. We could be ourselves, go out with friends, entertain. There was no sneaking around. We were just . . . a couple."

"How long have you been . . . out?"

Kristopher smiled, a sad smile that seemed to come slowly to the surface, as if from a great depth. "I don't think I was ever really in. It never occurred to me to be anything but what I was. It was different for Billy. It never occurred to him to be anything but what his family expected. He wasn't . . . comfortable in his skin."

There was truth in that. William had often grumbled about his parents' expectations. They'd always had very clear ideas about what their son should do with his life—and with whom. He had resented them for it, but had resented his propensity to conform to those ideas even more. It was Kristopher who had given him the strength to follow his dreams—and his heart. No wonder the Prescotts hated him. And loved her—the woman who would return their wayward son to the fold of respectability. Sadly, their calculations had proven disastrous.

Dovie met Kristopher's gaze, still reeling. She needed to understand, to know it all. "You said before that William loved you. He told you that?"

"This wasn't some kind of fling, Dovie. We'd been together almost two years when you entered the picture."

"You must have hated me."

"I did. To a gay man, the other woman isn't something you typically have to worry about. But then, Billy wasn't typical. When he told me, I didn't know how to deal with it—with the idea of you and him. I didn't mind so much at first, or pretended not to, as long as I didn't have to see the two of you together. I knew you were in the picture to get his mother off his back, and it worked for a while. But things weren't moving fast enough for Mrs. Prescott. She must've gotten nervous, because she started in again, talking about honeymoons and grandchildren. I told him it was time to break it off, that what he was doing wasn't fair to you or to me, and he agreed. So you can imagine my surprise when I came across a little velvet box in his dresser drawer—an empty box. That's how I found out he'd asked you to marry him. He swore nothing would change between us, that he could. . . . love us both."

Dovie stood staring at him, trying to imagine a more surreal conversation. She couldn't. Instead, she sank down onto the edge of the bed. The tears came then, silent and stinging, until Kristopher's angular frame began to blur. He moved toward the bed, holding out a crisply starched handkerchief. She stared at it as if it were an apparition.

"A gentlemen never leaves home without a handkerchief," he said, easing down beside her. "Poor thing. You didn't deserve any of this."

She blinked up at him through damp lashes. "And you did?"

"At least I knew what was going on. You got blindsided."

"I'd say we both got blindsided."

He nodded, his eyes shiny-wet. "I called him a coward," he said finally, his voice hoarse with emotion. "I told him I wasn't sneaking around with a married man. In fact, I was tired of sneaking around, period. I meant it, too—or thought I did. I laid it on the line. I told him if he didn't give you up and come out to his family we were finished. When he said he couldn't do it I told him to leave. To this day I still don't know if I was bluffing." His gaze slid from hers, creeping toward the entwined torsos in the corner. "I wasn't going to settle for half a relationship. Look what I got instead."

Dovie closed her eyes a moment, trying to get a handle on her whirling emotions, to isolate, label, and somehow bring them to heel. But there were too many to deal with at once: shock, anger, betrayal, all warring for center stage, until they bled together into a kind of numbness. And yet through that numbness came the disconcerting awareness that she wasn't alone in her pain. Beside her, Kristopher sat very still, hands hanging over his knees, eyes hollow.

"Kristopher, you said it yourself. No one's to blame for William's death but William. He made his own choice."

"I was talking about you when I said that, Dovie. I meant *you* weren't to blame. I can't say the same for myself. I pushed him into making a choice I knew he couldn't make, and that's why he killed himself. I have to live with that now. So do you. And so do the Prescotts."

Dovie shook her head as the weight of it all began to sink in. "So many things are beginning to make sense now that didn't before, things about William's family. Like why his mother was so anxious to move the wedding up, although I'm not sure what she hoped to accomplish. A wedding ring was never going to change what William felt for you."

"No, it wasn't, but she had to try. People like the Prescotts can't let themselves believe what William and I had could ever be real. Because if it turns out that love is just love, everything they believe gets turned on its ear. It's easier to hold tight to their beliefs and just keep throwing rocks at things they don't understand."

"No matter who they hurt along the way."

"I'm afraid so. But then, I've caused my share of pain in the last week or so, wouldn't you say? I come here and dredge up all your grief, then turn it into something else, because I forgot I'm not the only one who misses him." He shook his head as he stared beyond the darkened window. "I never meant to, by the way—hurt you, I mean."

"No, you just lied to me, then used me to get what you wanted from the Prescotts."

"It didn't seem like lying in the beginning. Or maybe I just rationalized it that way. Would you rather I told you the truth that first day, standing over Billy's grave?"

She glared at him through narrowed eyes, remembering that first day, and the parade of emotions he had aroused in her—confusion, irritation, even a peculiar sense of possessiveness—and wondered if some part of her had sensed the truth even then.

"I really don't know," she said as she pushed to her feet and headed for the doorway. "I don't think I know anything anymore."

The faintest of smiles tugged at Kristopher's mouth, humor mingled with regret, and perhaps a little bitterness. "I don't suppose there's much chance of us getting together for that drink now."

Dovie did her best to return the smile. "I think we've had our fill of each other, don't you? No need to pretend we're old friends."

It was Kristopher's turn to stand. "No," he said, squaring his shoulders. "I suppose not. Still, I'm glad I met you, Dovie Larkin. And the crack about you being prettier in your pictures—don't you believe it." He bent down to plant a kiss on the top of her head. "I was just being catty."

Dovie stiffened at his touch, but managed a nod. "Be sure to lock up when you're through. Do what you want with the key."

twenty-seven

Dovie hugged her paper coffee cup with both hands, savoring the fading warmth against her fingers as she stared at William's headstone, the dark sun around which her life had seemed to orbit for the last thirteen months. She was exhausted, and chilled to the bone.

A storm had blown in sometime around three a.m., rattling the windows until she'd finally gotten up to open the blinds. She wasn't sure how long she sat there in the dark, watching the lightning flash and listening to the rain lashing the marshes, but she'd done a lot of thinking. When dawn finally came she got dressed, left a message for Jack that she wouldn't be in, and grabbed her keys.

Now, sitting on a chilly bench, huddled against an even chillier wind, she wondered why she'd come at all. Habit, she supposed, a default setting somewhere in her brain that said this was where she went, this was what she did. Only there was no reason for her to be here now, no reason to sit vigil, no reason to pay penance, and no more answers to seek. She had her answers, and they had turned out to have very little to do with her.

Without warning, a pang of anger struck her full force, like a wave slamming her from behind, driving her under. She hadn't felt one of those in a long time, perhaps because she'd trained herself to stop feeling them. After William's death, she hadn't let herself be angry. It had seemed wrong, somehow, to be mad at someone who'd been in so much pain that the only way out was a handful of pills. And so she had stuffed it down, focusing on her guilt instead. It was better that way. Anger was a selfish emotion. Guilt, on the other hand, was allowed. Guilt was pure. Guilt was selfless. Even if you didn't know what you were guilty of.

And then, suddenly, she understood why she had come. She had come to cry, to rail, to rage, to surrender to the emotions she'd been keeping in check because she didn't believe she had a right to them. Now, finally, she was giving herself permission not just to feel her anger, but to throw open the floodgates and allow it swamp her, to let it come with all its fist-clenching fury and break her wide-open.

She had no idea how long she sat there, rocking and crying in the eye of the storm, but when she finally wiped her eyes and looked around, Josiah was heading in her direction. She was still blotting her cheeks with her sleeve when his shadow fell over her.

"Don't go mopping up on my account," he said matter-of-factly. He was wearing gloves today and a heavy gray jacket. "You ain't fooling no one with that face."

Dovie sniffled and gave him a watery smile. "Hey, Josiah."

"What are you doing here first thing on a Monday morning?"

"I called out sick."

"You *called* out sick? Or you *are* sick?"

"All right, have it your way. I'm playing hooky."

Josiah hunched deeper into his jacket and squinted up at the sky. "Seems like you could've picked a better day for playing hooky. Better place, too."

Dovie nodded. "Maybe. But I needed to come."

"So what's got your nose all swollen up like that?"

"I'm just having a bit of a week, is all."

"Anything I can do?"

Dovie sighed and shook her head, not sure how much of yesterday's revelations she was willing to share. "Something happened, Josiah. Something I never saw coming, and, well . . . nothing's what I thought it was."

"You want to talk about it?"

"I don't think I can. Not yet." She paused, feeling fresh tears tugging at her throat. "But thank you."

Josiah eased down beside her and pulled off his hat. "I can see you're hurting, and I'm guessing whatever's knocked the breath out of you probably has to do with your young man, but let me ask you a question. Long as I've been knowing you, you been saying you wanted answers. Now that you've got 'em, would you rather *not* know?"

Dovie closed her eyes, sitting with the question. After a moment, she shook her head. "No, I'd rather know. Nothing's more painful than not knowing. When you don't know, you just invent things in your head, and you keep reinventing them, so there's never any closure." She paused, waiting for him to say something. When he didn't, she went on. "I did take your advice about one thing, though. The other day, you questioned my motives in helping Dora. You thought I might be mixing up my grief with hers, and it made me think. So, the other day, I told her about the letters. And then I read some of them to her."

Josiah's eyes widened. "You trying to kill her, or something?"

Dovie couldn't help grinning. "No, I'm not trying to kill her, but you had a point. The letters weren't mine, and neither was the decision about whether or not Dora knew what was in them. It wasn't pretty, but I'm glad I told her the truth. I know it sounds strange, but I think Dora's glad, too. I just hope she still feels that way after I read her the last two letters. She made me swear that if I did find something, even if it was terrible, I'd tell her. And they are pretty terrible."

Josiah mouth opened, then closed again. But Dovie wasn't letting him off the hook. "What is it? You were going to say something. What was it?"

Josiah let out a long sigh. "I got something for you. Been holding on to it since the weekend. Only now I'm not sure I ought to give it to you."

Dovie felt something skitter in her belly. "It's another letter, isn't it? From Alice?"

"Not just one letter. It's a whole bagful. The plastic kind with the zipper thingy. They were hauling stuff out to that big Dumpster on Saturday afternoon, and there they were, sitting on top of one of the piles. I didn't say nothing, just picked up the box and headed out to the Dumpster with it."

Dovie's mouth fell open. The thought of Alice's letters lying at the bottom of a Dumpster was both startling and terrible. "Josiah, you didn't!"

"No, I didn't. I stuffed the whole bag under my jacket when I got out there, then snuck it out to my car. That's where it is now, in the trunk. It's yours if you want it. If not, it's going in that Dumpster. Probably what I should have done in the first place."

"Why didn't you?"

Josiah shrugged. "Don't know, really. Been working here more years than I can remember, and I ain't never taken a thing that didn't belong to me. And I wouldn't have taken those letters, except you went and got yourself mixed up with an old lady and a dead girl, and I know sure as I'm sitting here that you ain't gonna let it rest until you've pulled every last thread loose." He paused, cocking an eye at her. "Plus, I guess I believe like you do. They ain't mine."

Dovie closed her eyes, trying to imagine an entire bag of letters, and what those letters might contain. News that might help Dora find peace, or more anguish and guilt? She opened her eyes to find Josiah watching her.

"So, what you think? You want 'em? Feeling like you do right now, after learning whatever it is you just learned? You still think it's a good idea?"

"Maybe not, but I promised her, Josiah. No matter what it was, no matter how bad. I can't not bring them to her."

Josiah let out a long breath of disappointment or frustration, perhaps both. "Wait a few minutes, and then meet me in the parking lot over on the south side. But after that, I'm done. I mean it." He stood, giving the brim of his hat a curt tug. "You're a good girl who's going through some things, which is the *only* reason I'm in this at all. But it's time to put a stop to this foolishness, Dovie. Time to be done with dead people."

She watched him as he turned and walked away, ducking behind a thick screen of oaks and disappearing from sight. It wasn't too late to change her mind. She could still decide not to go after him, let him do what he wanted with the letters—toss them or burn them—as long as she didn't have to decide. She could look Dora in the eye and tell her the trail was cold, that there was nothing more to know. But she had made a promise. Rising from the bench, she turned down the path and headed for the south parking lot.

twenty-eight

Austin grabbed a pen and a pad of Post-it notes from the desk and began to scribble. After a moment, he peeled off the top sheet, crumpled it, and stuffed it into his pocket before trying again. Another try. Another aborted attempt.

Get a grip, man. It's a note. Not a marriage proposal.

After a third try, he was satisfied. Peeling the sheet off the pad, he pasted it to the phone where Dovie was sure to see it. He was turning to leave when he heard a voice out in the hall—female and vaguely familiar.

"Girl, what are you doing here? I thought you were sick. You sure look sick. In fact, you look like hell. Is it the flu?"

It was the girl he'd spoken to in the lobby, the one who told him Dovie was out sick. And he'd wager the family fortune it was Dovie she was talking to. Things were about to get awkward.

"It's not the flu, Theda. I'm just . . . I'll be in tomorrow. I came to grab a couple of files. Then I'm going home."

"Good. Rest is what you need, honey. Oh, and soup. Hey, before you go in I ought to warn you—you have a visitor."

"A visitor?"

"I was on my way to the cafeteria when Austin Tate showed up. I told him you were out sick, and that I'd be happy to give you a message, but he asked if he could leave it himself."

"So you just let him go back to my office?"

"Of course I did. I didn't think I needed to worry about him stealing your stapler. Besides, he's—"

"A Tate?"

"I was going to say *fine*. But yeah, that works, too."

Austin stifled a groan. *Awkward* was now officially in the rearview mirror, and they were coming up on *just kill me*. There was some unintelligible grumbling, an exchange that fell somewhere between heated and vaguely annoyed, but he couldn't make out the words, and maybe that was just as well.

Finally, he could hear Dovie again, her voice petulant and louder now, mingled with footsteps, as if she were hollering down the hall. "If you were my secretary I'd fire you!"

Theda's reply floated back, crisp and matter-of-fact. "If I was your secretary, I'd quit. Go home and eat some soup."

And just like that he found himself in the crosshairs, still working on something clever to say when Dovie walked in and pinned him with her denim blue eyes.

"What are you doing here?"

Jesus, she did look terrible. She wore sweats and no makeup, and her hair was scraped into something loosely resembling a ponytail. But it was more than just the hair and clothes. Her eyes were red-rimmed and dull, her nose a shiny shade of pink, and she looked completely wrung out, as if she'd been through the kind of storm that had nothing to do with wind and rain. If he had to make a guess, he'd say she'd been to the cemetery again.

"Your friend was right," he said, more gruffly than he intended. "You do look like hell. What's wrong?"

She straightened, lifting her chin. "Nothing's wrong. I had a bad night, that's all. I just came in to pick up some work and then I'm going home."

"You look like you could use some rest. Or a good stiff drink."

The chin came up another notch. "What are you doing here, Austin? I thought we agreed it would be better if we steered clear of each other."

"Actually, I can't remember us ever agreeing on anything, though we did have a few good moments the other night at McCrady's—before I ran you off, that is."

Dovie's eyes slid from his. "I don't suppose you're used to women walking out on you in restaurants."

"No, as a matter of fact. You were the first."

"What are you doing here?"

He reached for something clever to say, then abandoned the idea, pointing to the Post-it instead.

Dovie peeled the yellow sheet from the phone, reading the scribbled words aloud. "Any chance for renewing our truce?" Her head came up sharply. "Are you serious? All we do is bang heads. I think it's better if we maintain a safe distance. Your secretary's been very efficient, and most of the gala stuff is done. There's really no need—"

"I'm not here about the gala. I came to ask a favor."

She eyed him warily as she wadded up the note and tossed it in the trash. "What kind of favor?"

My mother has a birthday coming up—her seventieth—and I want to get her something special. She loves art, but I don't know where to start. I know a good sailboat when I see one, good music when I hear it, but when it comes to telling a good painting from a bad one, I'm clueless. I was hoping you'd help me find something she'd like."

"You want me to pick out your mother's birthday present?"

"I'll make it worth your while."

Dovie stared at him as if he were speaking a foreign language. "Worth my while?"

"You really don't know how to flirt, do you? I meant I'll take you to dinner. Or try to, if you think you can stand my company long enough to stay in your chair. You can do all the talking." He flashed his best smile. "Don't think of it as a date. More like a bribe."

If she found him charming she hid it well. Instead, she closed her eyes, splaying the fingers of one hand out on the desk, as if to steady herself. When she began to sway, he stepped around the desk and laid a hand on her arm.

"I thought you said you weren't sick. You should be home in bed."

She shrugged free of his hand and took a step back. "I'm *not* sick. I just didn't get much sleep last night, and then forgot to eat. I'm fine."

"You don't look fine. You look like . . . How do you *forget* to eat?"

"There was . . ." The words dangled as her gaze slid away, lingering on the bust in the corner. After a moment, she shook her head as if trying to dislodge a thought and brought her eyes back to his. "I'm fine."

"Something's happened," he said, knowing in his gut he was right. "Something to do with William."

"How did you . . ." She blinked heavily, once, twice. "Never mind. I'm going home."

Austin caught her arm as she tried to push past him. "Yes, you are. But first you're going to eat something, or you won't make it home."

He was surprised when she let him steer her out through the office doorway and down the hall. And even more surprised that she didn't protest as he led her through the lobby, down the steps, and out onto the sidewalk. "There's a little café across the street called Sips. They don't have a very large menu, but what they do have is good. They do a great cappuccino, too, though I think we should rule out caffeine for the time being. Can you make it across the street?"

She stared at him, pale and wide-eyed, like one of those people on the Weather Channel who had survived some natural disaster only to learn they'd lost everything they owned. She managed something like a nod, and he took her arm again.

The lunch crowd was already beginning to thin as they entered the café and chose a booth near the back. Dovie was already looking skittish, as if she might bolt at any moment. He flagged down their waitress, a plumpish redhead named Kelly, and asked her to bring a sweet tea and some breadsticks. Kelly took one look at Dovie, dropped two menus on the table, and headed for the kitchen.

"I recommend the she-crab soup," Austin said, pointing to the specials board behind the counter. "Some of the best in town, believe it or not, and it'll help warm you up. In the meantime, nibble on a couple breadsticks."

Kelly dimpled prettily as she set down the requested tea and breadsticks. "Have y'all decided?"

"Dovie?"

"Hmm?"

"Have you decided?"

She blinked heavily. "Oh, um, soup. I'll do the soup."

"That's all? Just soup?"

Dovie nodded mutely, then ducked back behind her menu.

"Two of the she-crab," Austin told Kelly. "And bring us a turkey and Brie on sourdough."

When they were alone again, he peeled back the cloth from the bread basket and pushed it to Dovie's side of the table. "Eat."

He watched as she picked up a breadstick and began to nibble the end. By the time their order arrived she had put a small dent in the basket, though he doubted she'd tasted a bite. When Kelly returned to place the soup and sandwich in front of her, she looked up in confusion. "I didn't order a sandwich."

"I did. *Bon appétit*."

She laid her hands on either side of her bowl, but didn't pick up her spoon. "Why are you doing this?"

"Doing what?"

"Being nice."

He grinned, his own soupspoon halfway to his mouth. "You're insinuating that I'm not usually nice?"

Her eyes fell, hovering on her bowl. "Please don't be clever. I can't deal with clever right now."

"I'm sorry. I didn't mean to make light of . . . whatever's going on." He waited a beat, pressing further when she didn't respond. "What is going on?"

"Nothing is going on. It's nothing."

"If it was nothing you wouldn't look like that."

She looked up, her expression defensive. "Like what?"

"Like you just found out the boat you're rowing is taking on water. And don't deny it. I know that look—and that feeling."

"You?"

"You think because my last name's Tate I'm immune to the things that hurt other people?"

"I just meant you don't seem like someone who'd be . . . vulnerable."

"I'm not—now. But we were talking about you. You're not in a good place."

"And you care because . . . ?"

"Because I'm a person, and you're a person. Does it have to be more than that?"

"I don't need you to feel sorry for me," she shot back.

"I don't feel sorry for you, Dovie. I don't even know what's going on. But I'd like to. You'll feel better after you've talked it out."

He waited then, holding his breath. If she was going to walk out, this was when she'd do it—the moment of choice. The time you decided to either run away or make the truth real by saying it out loud. He'd chosen the former all those years ago, and had been paying ever since. He hoped Dovie would choose differently.

She was studying him now, still clutching her soupspoon as she sized him up, wondering if she could trust him, wondering why she'd even want to. But there was something else in those eyes, something he recognized all too well, the temptation to pour out her pain, to spill her guts to someone whose judgment she didn't give a damn about.

"I know why William killed himself." She said it quickly, like yanking a bandage from an old wound. "Last night, I . . . I was talking to a friend of his, and I finally understand. No, that isn't right. I still don't understand. But I get why he did what he did."

He was quiet for a moment, letting the words settle between them. "Isn't that what you wanted? To know why?"

"I thought I did, but now . . ."

"There was someone else?"

Dovie's mouth hung open a moment. "You knew, didn't you? Somehow you guessed it. That's what you were hinting at the night I walked out of McCrady's. Did you know him?"

"William? No. But there were things you said that tipped me off. Like him traveling so much, but never taking you with him. You both having separate places, and you never going to his. It just felt . . . off."

"Why?"

He weighed the question a moment, perhaps a moment longer than he was comfortable with, before deciding to say what he was thinking. "Because when a man's lucky enough to have someone like you in his life, he'd have to be crazy to go two feet without you, let alone to New York or San Francisco. He'd want you with him all the time. He'd want you there when he fell asleep and when he woke up. Unless there was another woman he wanted more, which is pretty hard to imagine."

Dovie put her spoon down and pushed her bowl away. Her eyes glittered with tears as they met his. She dashed them away. "There was someone he wanted more, but it wasn't another woman."

"Oh." It was all he could think to say, though somehow he wasn't astonished.

"Yes, oh. A friend of his who lived in New York."

"Did you think I'd be scandalized?"

She shrugged. "I don't know. Guys are funny about stuff like that. The macho thing, I guess. I thought you might be one of those."

"No, I'm not one of *those*, as you put it, though my father was, and so are a lot of my friends. Personally, I don't care. Men and women get together for all sorts of reasons, most of them the wrong reasons, if you ask me. So if two people *do* manage to find each other for the right reasons—because they love each other and understand what that means—it shouldn't matter to anyone what their version of happiness looks like. What I do have a problem with is loving one person while pretending to be in love with someone else. That's deception, and it's wrong."

"That's just it. He wasn't pretending. In my heart, I know that. Maybe it wasn't the kind of love most people think about when they think of marriage, but the bond we shared was very real. It just . . . wasn't enough. He never meant to hurt anyone. He just couldn't be honest about who he was."

"And because *he* couldn't, *you* wound up getting hurt."

Dovie toyed with the napkin in her lap. "All this time, I've been trying to figure out what went wrong, how I could have stopped it, or changed it, and all this time it wasn't even about me."

"You were collateral damage, a casualty in someone else's war."

"I wouldn't put it like that. You said it yourself, the last time we talked. Sometimes we help people keep secrets, especially when we're afraid it's something we might not want to know. I think you were right about that—about me turning a blind eye. I didn't want to look too closely at our relationship, didn't want to admit that it was different from the relationships my friends had. I guess you could say I was complicit."

"So you're going to keep blaming yourself?"

"No, but—"

"Dovie, loving one person doesn't give you the right to hurt someone else. What William did was wrong. You're allowed to be angry. Hell, you need to be angry. But you think because someone's dead, it's wrong to be mad at them, no matter what they did to you. So you choke it down, and *keep* choking it down. Meanwhile, it's eating you up inside, until you're so numb you're not sure you'll ever feel anything again."

Her eyes went soft and wide. "How do you know that? How could you possibly know any of that?"

"I'm a good guesser."

But she wasn't letting him off the hook. "I mean it. How did you know?"

Austin reached for his water glass and downed a long sip, stalling while he figured out how to answer without answering. He hadn't meant to go off like that, but he couldn't just sit there and let her beat herself up. Her darling William had been a coward and a cad. The sooner she acknowledged it, the sooner she'd get in touch with her anger. It was the anger that would pull her back. Anger could get you through just about anything.

She was still looking at him, still waiting for some kind of response. Setting down his glass, he leaned back, arms folded. "That's a conversation for another day."

Or never.

twenty-nine

Dovie sat up, blinking against the gathering gloom, gritty eyed and sleep numb, but no longer exhausted. She peered at the clock—almost six. She'd been out for more than three hours, though she suspected her motives for crawling into bed in the middle of the day had as much to do with seeking oblivion as the need for actual sleep.

Her tearful confession to Dora. The fact of Kristopher. An entire bag of letters she still needed to deal with. The events of the last few days had hit her hard, so hard she barely remembered stepping back out onto the sidewalk after her impromptu lunch with Austin. Of all the adjectives she might have used to describe Austin Tate, *empathetic* wouldn't have made the list, and yet he had been just that, knowing what to say and how to say it. But there had been something else, too, something in his eyes and the set of his jaw that said he'd walked in her shoes, that at some point he'd experienced his own emotional storm, and while he might have managed to come out on the other side, he hadn't come out unscathed.

She felt ashamed now as she recalled his words. *"You think because my last name is Tate I'm immune to the things that hurt other people?"* It was *exactly* what she'd been thinking, though she should have known better. If William's suicide had taught her anything, it was that rich parents and a pedigreed last name didn't always pave the way to happiness.

But there was something the Prescotts could do, if not to bring happiness to their son, to at least fulfill what Dovie was sure would have been his final wish. Before there was time to change her mind, she picked up the phone and dialed the Prescotts' number. Amanda answered on the second ring, and for an instant Dovie considered hanging up, but there were things that needed to be said, truths acknowledged—and perhaps wrongs set right.

"It's Dovie," she said flatly. "We need to talk."

There was a moment of silence before Amanda Prescott responded. "I said everything I needed to say the day you brought that man into my home."

"Maybe," Dovie shot back. "But I haven't said everything I need to. For a year now, I've been punishing myself for what happened, wondering how I could have missed the signs. And the other day I sat there and let you blame me for all of it. Now I know what happened—and why. The funny thing is, I think you do, too. In fact, I think you always knew."

She paused, waiting for some kind of response, but was met with only silence. "I deserve the truth, Amanda. And closure. So I can finally move on with my life."

"My son is dead. That isn't closure enough for you?"

Dovie chose to ignore the unspoken accusation, pressing for an answer instead. "We can do this over the phone, or we can do it in person, Amanda. It's your choice. But there are questions I need answered, things I need to hear from your lips."

"I don't know—"

"Yes, you do. And you have from the beginning. You knew William wasn't really in love with me—that I wasn't what he wanted—but you pushed until he asked me to marry him. I always wondered why you were in such a hurry to get us down the aisle. Now I understand. You were afraid he'd back out. Because you knew about Kristopher. You knew William loved him. But you didn't care what William wanted. You pushed and manipulated, until Kristopher finally broke things off. And all you cared about was that you had gotten your way."

"It wasn't like that, Dovie," Amanda whispered hoarsely. "Things would have been better after the wedding. He would have changed. You two would have made a home and started a family. He would have forgotten all about the art dealer."

"Kristopher. His name is Kristopher. And no, he wouldn't have. He would have been miserable. He knew it, too. That's why he did what he did. He couldn't live the lie you wanted him to, so he swallowed a handful of pills to make sure he wouldn't have to."

"You think . . . you're saying it was my fault?" She seemed stunned by the thought, as if her own culpability had never occurred to her. "How dare you!"

Dovie stifled a sighed. "I'm not saying it was your fault, Amanda. It was William's responsibility to tell the truth about who he was and how he wanted to live his life, something he never found the strength to do. What I *am* saying is you and your husband didn't make it any easier for him. He lived with your disappointment every day, about his art and, well, everything, and it eventually wore him down. He *wanted* to please Kristopher, but he *needed* to please you. There was no way to do both, so he found a way to not have to choose at all."

"I'm hanging up," Amanda blurted, her voice sharp now, almost desperate. "I won't listen to this . . . this . . . nonsense. We gave William everything he could have wanted."

"Except the freedom to be who he was."

There was another gap of silence, this one so long Dovie wondered if she'd hung up. Finally, she was there, her voice chilly and flat, as if she'd flipped some switch on her emotions. "Is that all? Do you have your closure now? Now that you've accused me of driving my son to suicide?"

"That's not what I did. Or at least not what I meant to do. I called because I need to hear you say out loud that you knew I wasn't what your son wanted, and that you did everything in your power to hide that truth from me. I also need you to admit that there was nothing I could have done to change what happened."

"I really did think I could . . . fix things. I thought if he married you he'd see that what you had together was right."

"Amanda, what William and I had wasn't what you thought. It wasn't even what I thought. I'm just beginning to see that myself. I've spent the last few days trying to be mad at him for lying to me, and for leaving me wondering what I'd done. But mostly, I think I'm mad at myself."

"I don't understand."

"I barely understand it myself. But it's about pretending things are the way you want them to be rather than how they really are. It never works, and people usually wind up getting hurt."

"You mean William?"

"I mean all of us, Amanda. You and your husband aren't the only ones who got hurt in all this. I've spent the last year blaming myself for something I had no control over, and Kristopher was devastated—is still devastated. Why not let him have the sculpture?"

"That's what this call is about?"

"Partly, yes. Because it's what William would want."

"My husband has already decided that matter." Her voice sounded brittle, and dangerously close to breaking.

"Mrs. Prescott—Amanda—you loved your son. I know you did. And in some warped way, you thought you were doing what was best for him in trying to get him to marry me, but I think we both know that wasn't true. If it was, William would still be here, and we wouldn't be having this conversation."

"I never meant to hurt him. You have to know that, Dovie." She was sobbing now, choking on her words. "I just didn't understand. Maybe I didn't want to. Harold was disgusted by what William . . . by what he was. And he expected me to be, too. I had to choose sides. My husband or my son. And now you're asking me to choose again."

"I'm asking you to do what's right, Amanda. Only that."

There was another long stretch of silence, but something about this one felt different, less hostile somehow. Dovie held her breath, determined not to open her mouth and say something that might darken the mood again.

"Fine."

"Fine, as in Kristopher can have the sculpture?"

"Tell him to take it. I'll deal with my husband."

"Thank you, Amanda."

"I know you think we're terrible people, Dovie. And maybe we are. Maybe we care too much about what other people think. Maybe we're insensitive. And maybe we're selfish. But we never meant to hurt our son."

"Of course you didn't. There was never any question of that, Amanda."

"Thank you for that." Her voice was hushed, still thick with tears. "I think it would be best if we didn't have contact going forward. It would be . . . awkward."

"Yes, I suppose it would. Take care of yourself, Amanda."

Dovie felt numb as she ended the call. She had expected to feel victorious, pleased with herself for seeing justice done. Instead, she felt emptied out, painfully aware of the fact that every word she had said to Amanda was true. She had been lying to herself and, for a very long time, mourning a happily-ever-after that was never meant to be.

William once told her that before her there had been no other women. She had written it off as gallantry. But in all likelihood, he'd been telling the truth. Like Amanda, she had been in denial, consciously or unconsciously ignoring the signs—both those that were there and those that weren't. Things like the sheepish way he would always turn up on her doorstep after one of his prolonged absences, bearing wine and flowers, as if he had something to make up for. Or the way he would sometimes glance at his phone when it went off, and then slip out of the room to answer the call. And perhaps most telling, how, toward the end, he would claim to be too tired for sex, even after they'd been apart for more than a week. Their sex life hadn't been bad—far from it, in fact. William had been a skilled lover, always tender, always slow and thorough. But in retrospect, she had to admit that his attentions had felt a bit deliberate at times, as if he were methodically going down some checklist, making sure to tag each base before moving to the next. Should she have guessed the truth? She still couldn't say. But she knew it now.

And suddenly, she knew there was something else she needed to do. In the hall, she opened the closet and dragged the nylon garment bag from the back, tugging down the zipper. The satin glimmered ghostlike in the dim hall light, a pale reminder of a past that had never truly existed. For a moment her fingers hovered, almost touching but not. Instead of letting her fingers have their way, she tossed the gown over her arm and headed for the front door, stalking toward the green plastic can beside the garage.

She should take it to a consignment shop, she told herself as she lifted the lid and peered down at the can's grimy bottom, or maybe run one of those sad classifieds in the *Post and Courier*. *For sale: Designer bridal gown. Never worn.* But suddenly the urge to get rid of the dress—to get it as far away from her as possible—was more important than the month's salary it had cost her. It was therapy, she reminded herself as she stuffed the dress into the can and slammed down the lid. It was closure.

Back inside, she eyed the dusty bag of letters on the kitchen counter with a mixture of dread and curiosity. She knew Dora was desperate for answers, but there was something else she needed to take care of first. Fishing her cell from her tote, she pulled up Kristopher's number and hit DIAL. She couldn't help smiling when she heard his voice. No matter what awaited Dora in those letters, for now at least, she would be the bearer of *welcome* news. Later, after she had showered and scared up a little dinner, she would sort through the letters and begin the business of putting Alice Tandy behind her, too. Josiah was right; it was time to be done with dead people.

thirty

9 East Battery Street
Charleston, South Carolina
January 13, 1963

Dearest little one,

My heart was coming out of my chest this morning as I boarded the bus for downtown. I lay awake most of the night, rehearsing what I would say when I got to the Tates' house. I would get off on Meeting Street, ask directions to the Battery, which Cathy told me was down near the water, and then walk the rest of the way. I also found myself praying that I hadn't been duped. For all I knew, the address on that paper didn't even exist and Danny was somewhere counting his money and laughing up his sleeve.

The thought left me queasy, but not as queasy as my first glimpse of Charleston Harbor as I rounded the corner onto East Battery Street. The sight of so much water, churning pewter grey as far as the eye could see, reminded me of the long trip over and the seasickness that had plagued me most of the time.

I craned my neck as I continued down the sidewalk, past crisp white balconies, clever little courtyards, iron gates wound through with honeysuckle vines, and more chimneys than all the houses in Sennen Cove put together. I had never seen such grandeur in my life, and I marveled that a child of mine—a child born within the abysmal walls of Blackhurst—could have ever come to live in a place like this.

My heart began to hammer when I spotted the shiny brass plaque engraved with the number 9, and suddenly my legs seemed made of lead. I couldn't move, or remember any of the things I was supposed to say. I just stood there, counting windows and chimneys, trying to ignore the gallop of my heart against my ribs.

And then it was time to walk through that fancy iron gate and do what I had come to do. Somehow I made my way up the brick-paved walk and the front steps, wondering with every step how I had found the cheek to even come to such a place and demand the return of my child. It was preposterous, of course, this notion that they would believe me. And yet I reached for the brass knocker.

My mouth went dry all over again when the door swung open, whatever I'd meant to say shriveling in my throat. A black woman in a starched white uniform stood there eyeing me up and down before eventually pulling back the door and ordering me in.

"The missus been expectin' you," she said, giving me another sharp once-over. "You're early. Agency said you'd be along about ten."

I opened my mouth, but no words came. There was only one reason they'd be expecting me. Danny must have gotten caught. My stomach lurched as I imagined him trying to save his skin, blurting out my plans to Mrs. Jennings. Suddenly, I was glad I had skipped breakfast.

"Landy, has she come?" The voice drifted to the foyer from somewhere deep in the house, high and musical, and I shot a frantic glance over my shoulder, looking for a route of escape. And then she was there, the lady of the house, coiffed and gracious as she stepped into the foyer.

"Welcome," she said, holding out a manicured hand. An enormous diamond winked from her ring finger. "I'm Gemma Tate."

I took her hand, somehow, and might have smiled. "Alice," I mumbled. "Alice Tandy."

"You're English. How lovely! They didn't tell me that. I assumed you'd be . . . well . . . never mind. We'll have some tea, then, shall we? Landy, can you bring a pot of tea into the parlor?"

Landy gave me one last look as she turned away with a sniff that reminded me of Mrs. Jennings. I held my breath as I watched her go, trying to reconcile the woman's open disapproval with Mrs. Tate's warm welcome.

"Why don't we sit and have a little chat? We should get to know each other a little, don't you think?"

I nodded, though I had no idea what she meant. I shuffled behind her, too anxious to take in my surroundings, except to note that I had seen pictures of palaces that weren't half so grand. Everywhere I looked, something seemed to be gleaming: chandeliers, mirrors, mahogany tables, even the foil wallpaper in the enormous front parlor. I did my best not to stare but failed miserably.

Mrs. Tate settled herself on a tufted velvet sofa and patted the cushion beside her. "Now, then," she said, smiling as I eased down beside her. "Tell me all about yourself."

I blinked at her, still trying to grasp what was happening. She obviously knew why I had come, yet she didn't seem the slightest bit put out by my presence in her parlor. But then, a woman rich enough to buy a child probably wasn't put out by much of anything. I studied her out of the corner of my eye, her silk suit and creamy strand of pearls, and hated her just a little. Not for the things she had, or the life she lived, but for the status she enjoyed—a married woman of means, the kind Mrs. Jennings believed deserved to raise other people's children.

Her eyes were still trained on me, I realized. She was waiting for me to say something. Finally, she reached over to pat my hand. "Come, now, Alice. There's no need to be shy. If you're going to be looking after my son, we need to get to know each other."

Looking after her son? There was a loud buzzing in my ears as my brain scrambled for an explanation. Did she think I had come about a job? A job raising . . . her son. Gemma Tate had a son.

I had a son.

A son. The words beat against my temples like a pulse. But how was any of this possible? When Landy mentioned the agency I thought she was referring to Sacred Heart, but it was beginning to look as if I wasn't the only one who'd jumped to a wrong conclusion.

I was relieved when Landy appeared brandishing a tray loaded down with a china tea set. She said nothing as she set down the tray, but threw me another sharp glance as she shuffled out. When she was gone, Mrs. Tate filled two cups and handed one to me.

"Now, then, you were about to tell me your story."

"My story," I repeated numbly, as the events of the last twenty-four hours blurred into this impossible moment. Suddenly, I was tired, so bone weary I wasn't sure I could keep my head up long enough to do what I'd come to do. I had spent the last two hours rehearsing my story—how I'd been sent to Blackhurst against my will, how my child had been taken from me, how I had vowed to find that child at any cost—but the words all evaporated.

"Perhaps you'd be more comfortable if I told you a little about us first. Then we can talk about you. I have to be honest, hiring a nanny wasn't my idea. The truth is, I couldn't bear the idea of sharing that little boy with anyone, but with my husband gone so much of the time it makes sense to hire someone, and so here you are. I want my son to have the best of everything, and that includes the best nanny. His name is Austin, by the way, after my daddy."

"Austin." I repeated the name, out loud at first, and then again in my head. It felt wrong, not like any name I would have chosen. I made up my mind to change it the moment I had you out of the house.

She was still going on between sips of tea. "I still can't believe it. My husband and I waited so long for that child to come along, and what a child he is. You've never seen such a smart little boy in your life. I'm convinced he's going to be walking any day now." She clamped a hand over her mouth, shaking her head. "Will you listen to me ramble? I suppose every mother thinks her baby's an honest-to-God miracle, but my Austin truly is. Sometimes I still can't believe it—a mother, after all those empty years. I feel like Sarah from the Old Testament; the Lord saw fit to bless me just when I'd given up hope. He teaches us faith in some mighty strange ways, I guess, and thank heaven he does. Would you like to see him?"

I think my heart must have stopped in my chest. She had just offered to let me see my baby—my son. You. How long had I waited to hear those words? And yet the question caught me off guard. I was still trying to find the nerve to say what I'd come to say, but the words wouldn't form, because I could see that nothing would ever make her give you up. Her eyes were luminous, lit with pride and the kind of love only a mother can feel, deep, possessive, fierce, and I knew in that moment that she would fight for you, and that she would win. If it was left to the courts and women like Mrs. Jennings to decide, I would lose you all over again.

Still, I couldn't help myself. I got to my feet and followed her up the winding staircase. The floor seemed to tilt as we reached the top, and for a moment I went still, clutching the banister as a terrible idea began to take shape.

What if I were to play along with Mrs. Tate's charade and take the job as nanny? And what if, one day after I'd put a little money aside, I took you to the park to play—and never brought you back? Kidnapping is an ugly word, but is it really kidnapping if the child is your own? Could they put you in prison for something like that? The thought left me so giddy I stumbled over my own feet and had to grip the banister with both hands.

Mrs. Tate reached out to steady me, her kind eyes sweeping over me. "Alice, my goodness, you've gone white as a sheet. Are you ill?"

I let go of the railing and squared my shoulders. "Not at all, Mrs. Tate. I'm fine."

She studied me another moment before continuing down the gallery. Somehow I made my feet move, following her to what I assumed must be the nursery door, wondering all the while how hard it would be to get you back to England.

She was beaming as she opened the door, inviting me to enter ahead of her. My heart throbbed against my ribs, and I wondered that she didn't hear it, too, and guess my monstrous thoughts. Instead, she just stood there, smiling and radiant, as she prepared to introduce me to her little miracle. I recall nothing of the room, nothing of the furnishings or carpet or draperies, only the pair of bright eyes peering at me through the slats of an enormous crib—eyes that felt as unfamiliar to me as Mrs. Tate's had when I entered the parlor downstairs.

But how could that be? I looked at him again, peering out at me through the wooden bars. This was all wrong. He was supposed to look like my Johnny, with dark hair and sea-colored eyes. But there was nothing of my Johnny in his face—or of me, either.

Mrs. Tate's face glowed as she peered down at him in his crib. "He's beautiful, isn't he? I was so nervous the day he came home from the hospital. I was terrified I'd drop him and break him."

"From . . . the hospital?"

"He was running a fever and they wouldn't let me take him until his temperature went down. You can't imagine what it's like having to wait like that. But finally they said he was ready to come home. I swear, I held my breath the whole way. I had no idea what I was doing, and my husband was away at the time. Just look at that face. He's the absolute spitting image of my daddy at that age. He had those exact same dimples. Austin, honey, this is Alice. She's come to see about being your nanny."

The green eyes that were not Johnny's seemed to brighten as they took me in, pleased with what they saw—or at least curious. Crabbing toward the crib railing, he curled chubby fingers around the slats, offering me a gummy smile.

My heart seemed to come apart all at once. For months—long before Mam ever sent me to Blackhurst—I had imagined the moment I would look into your eyes and feel the bond that only exists between mother and child. But there was no bond, no heart-stopping, throat-thickening moment of recognition. This child was a stranger to me.

I mumbled something unintelligible, and I think I may even have managed a smile, but I still can't be sure. I had made a terrible mistake. And in my desperation had been prepared to make an even bigger one, to kidnap a child who didn't belong to me.

He was still gurgling as Mrs. Tate scooped him from the crib and, after planting a kiss in the crook of his neck, deposited him into my arms. He smelled of soap, and milk, and talc, the way I always imagined you would smell. My eyes blurred at the unfairness of this fresh new loss, my throat so tight I could scarcely breathe, let alone speak.

"There, now," Mrs. Tate was cooing. "Let me look at the two of you together. Oh yes, a fine fit, I'd say. Oh my, Alice, are you . . . are you crying, honey?"

I shook my head, handing Austin back to her, then turned away to wipe my eyes. "I'm fine, really."

"Nonsense. People don't cry when they're fine. They cry when something's wrong. And you're still a funny color. When did you last eat?"

Her voice seemed to be coming from a long way off, and I couldn't make out the words. I felt boneless, as if all the fight had gone out of me in one long gush. "I don't . . ."

"Never mind. Come with me." After settling her son back in his crib, she turned back to me, her face the picture of determination. "No protests, and no pretending you're fine, either. We're going to get some food in you, and then you're going to tell me what's wrong."

She had me by the elbow before I could answer, steering me back down the stairs. A good thing, too, since I'm quite sure I would have pitched down headfirst had I tried it on my own.

I wanted to bolt for the door when we reached the bottom, but Mrs. Tate led me to the couch instead and dropped down beside me. I heard her call for Landy to bring some sandwiches to the parlor, along with a glass of milk. Her kindness made it worse. I had come to take her child, to steal him if necessary, and there she was, holding my hand and worrying about when I'd last eaten.

"Now, then," she said, looking me straight in the eye. "Tell me what's happened. You look as if the whole world's come crashing down around your ears."

Perhaps it was the kindness in her wide brown eyes, or the warmth in her tone, but suddenly I was undone, and the whole hideous calamity of the past year began to unravel in a torrent of choked words and crushing sobs. I told her about you, and how your daddy died before he could give you his name, about how Mam was so ashamed that she made me give you away. I left out the bit about Blackhurst and the nuns, and about stealing the watch and the money so I could come to America to get you back. I sounded hysterical enough without adding those bits, and for reasons I couldn't explain, I wanted Gemma Tate to think well of me.

I had been staring down at my lap, working at the pleats of my skirt as I made my confession. Now, as I ran out of words and the room went quiet, I had no choice but to look up. I expected disapproval. Instead, Gemma Tate's eyes were shiny with tears, her chin quivering like a child's.

"Oh, honey, that's the saddest thing I've ever heard. To have to go through something like that at your age, all alone and so far from home. And your baby . . . it's just so tragic."

I said nothing, afraid I would cry again.

"Where is home, exactly?" Mrs. Tate asked, handing me the glass of milk Landy had brought. "England, I'm guessing, but what part?"

I eyed her warily and pressed my lips tight.

"I'm not going to try to contact your mother, honey. I'm just curious."

"Cornwall," I said at last. "A little fishing village called Sennen Cove."

"Does she at least know where you are? Your mother, I mean?"

"No. And I don't want her to know. She's nothing to me now."

"Oh, honey, don't say that. You've been through an awful thing—a truly awful thing—but your mama will always be your mama. You'll forgive her in time."

"No, I won't!" I shot back fiercely. "You have your son. You don't know what it's like to ache for a child, to have a hole in your heart because a part of you is missing."

"But I do know, Alice." The tears that had pooled in her eyes finally spilled, leaving shiny tracks on her cheeks. "I felt exactly like that before Austin came along, like I would never be whole without a child of my own. My heart was just so . . . empty. I know it's not the same as what you went through, but I know that ache, honey, and it hurts me to know you feel it, too, and that it's put a rift between you and your mama. Maybe in time . . ."

"Time won't change the way I feel," I said more harshly than I meant to. I appreciated her words, and even her tears, but they stung a little, too, because she was right—it wasn't the same thing. "I said a lot of terrible things to her before I left, and I meant them all. I'll always mean them."

Mrs. Tate reached for a napkin from the tea tray and dabbed at her eyes. When she spoke again, her voice was slow and measured. "Even mothers make mistakes, Alice. It doesn't mean we don't love our children. There isn't anything in the whole wide world I wouldn't do to protect that little boy up there, because he's mine and that's just the way it works. And maybe that's what your mama thought she was doing when she sent me away and made me give you up—trying to protect you."

"I don't care what she was trying to do. My baby's gone. I'll never forgive her for that."

Mrs. Tate nodded. "What will you do now?"

I shrugged and looked away.

"Would you like to work for me, do you think? As Austin's nanny?"

I stared at her in disbelief. I remembered the look on Mrs. Jennings's face as she assessed me from over the top of her glasses, summing me up in one head-to-foot glance, like I'd just crawled out of a dustbin, and I searched Gemma Tate's face for it now. But there was no judgment, no scowl of disapproval. I didn't understand. "But what I just told you—about the baby and not being married. Doesn't that make me . . . unsuitable?"

Gemma tossed her head back and laughed, a soft tinkling sound that made me think of crystal glasses at a party. "Honey, there are all kinds of reasons you're not suitable, but none of them have to do with you having a baby. It's more about you being white. The women in my circle tend to bring in colored women to look after their babies. It's just how things are done here. One thing's for certain, you'll be the talk of my ladies' club. But I don't care, if you don't. Let them talk. The only thing I care about is hiring someone who will love my son as much as I do, and you've got a whole lot of love in your heart to give. If you're interested, that is. It would mean living here with us, though. Would that be a problem?"

The tears came again, quieter this time. I knew what she was doing. She was taking pity on me—a disgraced woman with no money and no prospects—and I didn't care. I hadn't a shred of pride left. How could I, without a friend in the world or a penny in my pocket? It was an act of Christian kindness, scraps from a rich woman's table, and I jumped for it.

Perhaps I should have told her the truth then and there, that I hadn't been sent by an employment agency, that I had paid a man to tell me who had adopted my child, and that that man had lied to me, but I didn't. I had fallen into this woman's kindness, and would not risk it by telling the truth. And so, my little one, that is how I came to be nanny for one of the richest little boys in Charleston. Looking after someone else's child, day after day, when I've been deprived of my own, will be the cruelest form of torture, but I'll have a job and a place to bide my time while I think how to keep on with my search. For that, and so much more, I will always be grateful to Gemma Tate. Please don't think for a moment that I've stopped yearning for the day we'll be together. I haven't. You're out there, somewhere, and I promise to find you if it takes my last breath.

All my love,
Mam

thirty-one

PALMETTO MOON MOTEL
CHARLESTON, SOUTH CAROLINA
OCTOBER 25, 2005

Dovie stole a glance at Dora, pale and stoic on the bench beside her, seemingly oblivious to the sinking sun and the soft amber rays filtering down through the ancient oaks overhead. It had been an unusually balmy day for November, a last gasp of warmth before fall finally gave way to another chilly Lowcountry winter. Dovie had suggested they go out to the little courtyard near the pool while she read, hoping the fresh air and change of scenery might help Dora's cough and perhaps even lighten her mood.

It was impossible to ignore the precipitous decline in Dora's health. She'd lost an alarming amount of weight since their first meeting nearly three weeks ago, and seemed to be having more bad days than good, despite the array of pill bottles beside her bed. But it was the chronic wheezing Dovie found most worrisome, along with the coughing spells that seemed to come with greater and greater frequency these days.

She had promised to hold nothing back in reading the letters, and technically, she'd kept that promise. But given Dora's deteriorating health and fragile state of mind, she had decided a little restraint might not be a bad thing, which was why they had agreed that Dovie would be sharing the letters in increments of no more than two or three at a time, to give Dora a chance to absorb whatever might be in them. Now, looking at the set of Dora's shoulders, stooped with the weight of new sorrows, she wondered if even that had been too much.

At least they finally knew how Alice had come to work for the Tates, how she'd been duped into believing she was near the end of her quest, only to discover she'd been taken advantage of in the most heinous way by the greedy and opportunistic Danny. To have endured so much, sacrificed so much, for the love of a child she'd never even held in her arms was an admirable thing, though the details had proven hard reading indeed.

"You raised a brave and remarkable young woman," Dovie told Dora quietly. "You should be proud of that. Through everything, she never lost sight of her child. That took courage, and a whole lot of will."

Dora shook her head, a slow, heavy lolling. "She was those things in spite of me, not because of me. It was her father she took after. A will of steel that boy had. You could see it in his eyes, green as the sea in a storm, and hard. When he wanted something he took it. And when he didn't he let it alone. Just like he did me. That's where she gets her backbone. Not from me. I've always been a coward."

"You had a daughter out of wedlock and raised her on your own. That's not something a coward does."

"When she needed me, I turned my back on her. There's a coward for you. When I should have—"

Her voice fell away as the coughing came, rattling and wet, racking her slight frame until Dovie feared she would topple off the bench into a heap in the grass. Instinctively, she reached for her cell, wondering if this time she would need to dial 911, but the cough eventually subsided.

"I'm sorry," Dora said, giving one last wet rattle. "It just comes on like that, all of a sudden, like something's got me around the chest. It's better now. When will you come again?"

Dovie eyed her closely. Her breath was still coming hard, but the bluish tint around her mouth was beginning to fade. "I was going to come tomorrow, but I think we should wait a few days. Today was a lot to absorb. The letters aren't going anywhere."

"No waiting," Dora wheezed. "I'm running out of time." She paused and looked away. When her eyes came back her lashes were spiked with tears. "No waiting. Please."

Dovie had no way of knowing if Dora was referring to her return ticket, or if she had used *running out of time* in a more existential way, and it really didn't matter. She understood. Dora needed to fill in the blank places of her daughter's life, and finally know the truth. All of it—for better or worse.

"All right. But not tomorrow. Saturday. Is there anything else I can do for you before I go? Some tea, maybe? Is it time for your medication?"

"Not for hours yet. And I can make my own tea, if I want any. There is something you can do for me, though, now that I think of it. You could take me to her on Saturday."

"To Magnolia Grove?"

"To the cemetery, yes. And bring the letters. I'd like to be near her when you read them. I was planning to go on my own, but I'd like it if you were with me."

Dovie ran through the potential pitfalls of the request. She had no idea what the next letters contained, whether they would finally answer Dora's questions about her lost grandchild or simply lead to more heartache. But more to the point, she had serious doubts that sitting beside Alice's grave would be beneficial to the poor woman's spirits.

"How about I pick you up Saturday morning and we go to breakfast and then down to the Battery instead? It's supposed to be a pretty day, and the park is lovely. And of course, there's the harbor, which you probably haven't seen."

Dora laid a hand over Dovie's. "I don't care about pretty days, and there's a harbor back in Sennen Cove if I want to look at the water."

Dovie nodded. "All right, then. Saturday. But we do breakfast first, and if I decide you're overdoing it, we're leaving. Now let's get you back to your room."

The sun was all but gone when Dovie left Dora and stepped out into the parking lot. She still wasn't sure about the cemetery on Saturday—Dora's condition was going to require a close eye—but she was glad she had left work early to come tonight. Or maybe she'd just been looking for an excuse not to go home. She had worked late for the last three nights, tweaking and retweaking the details for the new spring exhibits, then laying out the schedule for the summer lecture series, neither of which were due until after the holidays. But it beat going home to an empty house, and another dinner of cold leftovers.

She'd been numb for so long she couldn't remember ever feeling any other way, comfortable in her aloneness, where no one asked too many questions or forced her to look too hard at herself. But now, with her quest for answers at an end, grief had turned to glaring self-awareness. It was time to rejoin the living, as Josiah put it. She knew it—even wanted it—she just wasn't sure how to go about it. And until she figured it out, it felt better, and safer, to stay busy.

The realization was an unsettling one. So unsettling that she was almost grateful when her cell went off. She answered without looking at the caller ID as she started the car, one eye on her mirror as she prepared to back out of the Palmetto Moon's sparsely populated parking lot.

"It's Austin. Is this an okay time?"

"This is fine," she lied, fumbling to put the car back in park. Just the sound of his voice had her flustered. The last time they spoke, she'd been such a mess she had nearly slumped over in her soup. "I was just . . . leaving a friend's. How can I help you?"

"I was calling to see if you'd come up with any ideas for my mother's birthday. It's coming up pretty quick, and I don't want to look like the proverbial bad son. It's okay if you haven't. I know you have a lot on your plate. I just need to have a fallback plan, is all."

"Oh God, the present. I'm sorry. Things have been a little crazy at the museum, and I've been working late all week. I honestly forgot we even talked about it."

"No worries. You weren't exactly in peak form the last time we saw each other."

Dovie smothered a groan. Of course he remembered. "No, I wasn't. And you were very kind. I can't remember if I said thank you. In case I didn't, thank you. For lunch, and for listening. I don't usually dump my sob stories on total strangers."

"I wouldn't call us strangers. And it was no big deal. So, how are you. How are . . . things?"

"They're good," she mumbled. "I'm fine. Everything's fine. So, listen, I do have an idea for your mother. There's an artist whose work I happen to know she likes. His name is Ivey Clark. He's local and I know him a little, through the museum. I could give him a call and see if he's got anything finished that's not commissioned. What does your budget look like?"

There was a brief pause before Austin's smoky laugh filled up the silence. "I knew you were going to ask that."

"It's a perfectly valid question."

"Yes, it is. But it forces me to say I don't have a budget, and that makes me sound a little pretentious. Not exactly the kind of thing that's going to make you like me—and I've decided I want you to like me."

Dovie let the words sink in, the warm, almost honeyed weight of them setting off a little bloom in her belly. She closed her eyes, pushing the feeling down, and steered toward safe ground. "Okay, then. I think I have a pretty good idea what she'd like. I'll touch base with Ivey in the morning and see if he's a possibility, then ring you back."

"Sounds good. And I really do appreciate this, Dovie."

"I'm happy to help."

There was silence then, not the kind that came after the line went dead, but the empty, clumsy kind that yawned awkwardly when neither party knew how to end the call. It was Austin who finally broke it.

"I guess I'll wait to hear from you."

"Right. Hopefully tomorrow. Good night."

Dovie put the car in gear but couldn't seem to press the gas. Instead, she sat staring at the phone, trying to deny the quivery schoolgirl feeling in the pit of her stomach. The last thing she needed while trying to put her life back together was a crush on Austin Tate.

thirty-two

Fridays were always crazy at the museum, but today was shaping up to be one for the books. A busload of eighth-graders on an art-appreciation field trip had descended on them at ten a.m., disrupting a morning that had already gotten off to a rocky start when a visitor knocked over a large handblown vase, shattering it into atom-size fragments and forcing the closing of an entire exhibit room. Next, a bus tour that was scheduled for the weekend had shown up a day early, to find their appointed docent out having a root canal, leaving Dovie to fumble her way through the first half of the presentation until another guide became free.

When the dust settled, she made a beeline for her office, where she planned to close her door, slip off her shoes, and scare up a couple of ibuprofen for the drums beating in her head. She was halfway down the hall when Jack flagged her down.

"Last time I saw juggling like that the guy was wearing floppy shoes and a big red nose. Nice work this morning."

"Thanks," she said with a dramatic roll of her eyes. "Is it too early to start drinking?"

"Not today, it isn't. Seriously, though, way to be on the ball."

Dovie was still smiling as she sank into her desk chair and kicked off her heels. He hadn't said it out loud, but the sentiment had been there, just the same. *Good to have you back, Dovie.* And it felt good to be back, to feel competent and confident again. To feel . . . hopeful, as if the fog she'd been living in was finally beginning to lift and some part of her was whispering that it was time to turn her face to the sun. Now, if she could just shake the nerves she got every time she thought about picking up the phone and calling Austin. It was business, and nothing more. Wasn't it?

". . . And I've decided I want you to like me."

The words had been tumbling in her head all morning. Though maybe not so much the words themselves as the way he'd said them. Even now, replaying them for the hundredth time, she felt an almost visceral impact, as if something that had been sleeping for a very long time had suddenly begun to stir. She didn't like it. She hadn't felt this way since . . .

She couldn't even finish the thought. She'd *never* felt this way. Growing up, and all through school, she'd been immune to the schoolgirl crushes her friends seemed to fall prey to every other week, choosing instead to keep her nose to the academic grindstone. And then, with William, it had all been so comfortable, so safe. No butterflies or lightning bolts, just an easy companionship that never seemed to demand too much from either of them.

And now, inexplicably, there was Austin—handsome playboy and consummate charmer. How had he managed to fly in under her radar? She wasn't sure. But the one thing she was sure of was the sooner she wrapped up her business with him, the safer she would be.

She picked up the phone and dialed his cell. He answered on the second ring.

"I've got good news," she blurted before he even finished saying hello. No need for chitchat. This was business. "Ivey Clark has two pieces that might work. He's getting ready for a show in Miami next month, but when I told him who the painting was for he said no problem. He's heading to Charlotte for the weekend, but said he'll drop them off at the museum on his way out of town. That'll give you a chance to swing by and look them over, then choose the one you think she'll like best."

"Wow. You pick up the phone and just like that, he's dropping off two paintings. I'm impressed. There's only one problem. I can't get there before the museum closes. I've got something scheduled that I can't miss. Is there a way I can see them tomorrow?"

"Tomorrow's Saturday, and I have plans in the morning. All day, really. But I guess I could bring them home with me, and you could stop by and take a look. Would that work?"

"When's a good time?"

"I should be home by noon. I'm out in Heron Marsh—number seven."

"Number seven. Got it. See you then."

Dovie ended the call feeling more rattled than when she had picked up the phone. The idea had been to put a quick end to the business. Instead, she had invited the handsome playboy and consummate charmer to her house.

Saturday had dawned clear and bright. Dovie was glad the warm weather had held for their outing. She had settled on Denny's for breakfast, mostly for its close parking and easy access. Dora had been too fidgety to eat, managing only a slice of toast and half a glass of orange juice, before asking if they could go.

Now, as they wound through Charleston's quiet weekend streets, she realized she should have known better. Dora had one thing on her mind this morning, and it wasn't bacon and eggs. She was wearing the gray wool suit she'd had on the day she first appeared at Magnolia

Grove, along with her hat, and sat looking straight ahead, clutching the familiar black patent leather handbag in her lap.

There were plenty of parking spaces available at this early hour. Dovie chose one as close as she could get to their destination. There would still be a walk, but not a bad one, so long as they took it slow and steady. But Dora wasn't taking anything slow. Her pace quickened as the weathered stone wings came into view.

"It's so lovely," she breathed, staring up at the angel's tearstained face. "Every time I see it, it gets more beautiful. Someone must have loved her, don't you think, to put up something like that?"

Dovie nodded. She had no idea if the Tates or anyone else had loved Alice Tandy, but she liked the sentiment, and saw that Dora did, too. But there was something else in Dora's expression. An eagerness to get on with what they'd come there to do.

"The letters," she prodded.

Dovie led her to her usual bench, then sat down beside her, careful to look everywhere but at William's grave. It felt strange coming empty-handed. Saturday was flower day, after all, and part of her had been dreading the thought of William's grave devoid of flowers, but the time had come to shed old rituals, and perhaps even create new ones. William didn't belong to her now. In truth, he never had.

Finally, she could avoid it no longer. She must have let out a breath or a sound of some kind, because she felt Dora's gaze turn in her direction. She had expected the grave to be barren. Instead, there was a bright burst of orange and yellow mums in the little vase at the foot of William's headstone, as fresh as if they'd just been picked.

Perhaps William's mother had brought them. If so, it would have been a first. As far as she knew, neither of William's parents came to visit their son's grave. But then, maybe their conversation had at least brought Amanda around. She hoped so.

Dora was still watching her. "Is something the matter?"

"No, I . . . No, everything's fine. I just . . . never mind." Dovie reached into her tote, pulled out the letters, and laid them in her lap. "I only brought two. I thought that would be enough for today, and we agreed that if I think you're getting tired, we'll leave. I know you think I'm being bossy, and that these letters belong to you, but someone has to look out for you, and I'm that someone."

Dora nodded, resigned. "Have you . . . read them?"

"Not these, no. I was afraid I'd be tempted to go back on my word if I knew ahead of time what they said. It's hard to see you hurting and know that I'm the one who started all this. I'm still not sure which would be worse—breaking my promise to you or breaking your heart."

"You really are a good girl, you know, to care what happens to an old prat like me."

"Thank you," Dovie said, giving Dora's frail hand a squeeze. Only she didn't feel like a good girl as she opened the first letter and smoothed it out on her knees. She had meddled in something that was none of her business, and because of it, there was a very good chance that before it was all over, Dora Tandy was going to wind up paying the price with a broken heart.

thirty-three

9 East Battery Street
Charleston, South Carolina
March 2, 1963

My dearest little one,

Forgive me for not writing sooner, but I've been busy getting my bearings and learning my new duties. The hardest part, aside from learning which doors went to which rooms, was learning the names of the other people who work here. It took a full month to sort them all out—names like Eulie and Lindy and Elron that still feel strange on my tongue—but I have them now, or at least think I do. However, I do still occasionally blunder into the wrong room, carrying a tea tray into the nursery, or a stack of freshly laundered nappies into Mr. Tate's study.

I'm rather like a carnival attraction in the Tate house, an oddity among the familiar. It's because I'm white, you see. And in places like Charleston, white women don't look after the children, or the laundry, or the silver. That's left to the colored women. It's a tradition in the South, or so I'm told, the way things have always been done, though it feels like something else to me—something puffed up and faintly condescending.

And so I'm not well liked by the rest of the help. They say I have no business taking a job that should have gone to a colored woman, taking food out of her mouth, and out of the mouths of her children. Not any specific woman, mind you, just a colored woman in general. But it isn't only that. I'm an outsider here, an intruder encroaching on their territory with my English manners and funny way of talking. I hear them when they don't know I'm nearby, making fun of the way I speak. It never occurs to them that they might sound just as silly to me. Probably because they were here first. That's usually the way it works. There's a pecking order, and someone's got to be at the bottom.

And it isn't only the help who have an opinion.

I've seen Mrs. Tate's friends give me sideways glances now and then as well. They smile their pointed little smiles, and whisper behind their gloved hands, teasing Mrs. Tate about her little prince being too good to be raised by a colored woman, warning her that if she isn't careful I'll have her child singing "God Save the Queen" and eating crumpets instead of corn bread. They say other things, too, when her back is turned, about how if she doesn't keep a sharp eye out I'll have Harley Tate eating crumpets, too, and not the kind you eat with jam. The man's known to have a taste for sweets, after all, and if they're waved right under his nose, well, what does she expect?

As if they all lead such spotless lives. Sometimes it's hard to hold my tongue when I know whose husband came home at three in the morning reeking of cheap perfume, or who recently toppled headlong down the stairs because she'd been at her husband's bourbon. You learn a lot eating in the kitchen with the help, where the table is always humming with what goes on in Charleston's finest homes.

And yet there are more reasons to be happy than unhappy. Austin said "Mama" today. He didn't say it to me, of course, but to his own mother. Still, it made my heart smile, and perhaps ache a little, too, because it made me miss you even more than I normally do. He's such a clever thing, walking already and getting into everything. I know it's silly, but I've come to think of him almost as your brother. In my mind, his accomplishments are yours. And in sharing those moments with him, I am somehow sharing them with you.

And Mrs. Tate—or Gemma, as she now insists I call her—is only too happy to share her son with me, better I'm sure than I would be about sharing you with someone else. Yesterday, we were out in the gardens, where she spends most of her afternoons, pruning and weeding in an old straw hat. Austin and I were on a blanket in the shade. I was reading aloud from one of his favourite storybooks when he scrambled up onto his chubby legs and tottered across the grass to his mother. By the time I put the book down and went after him, he had traded his teething biscuit for a fistful of dirt and was preparing to make a snack of it.

I was expecting to be scolded for not watching him closely enough. Instead, she looked up at me, her brown eyes shiny with laughter, and said, "What are we going to do with this boy of ours, Alice?"

This boy of ours.

I think they just might be the kindest words anyone has ever spoken to me. But then, Gemma is always kind. She doesn't put on airs, or even dress the part of a fine lady, unless she's off to some tea or luncheon, which she is far more often than she cares to be. In fact, I think she's happier in her garden than just about anywhere else, up to her elbows in the Carolina soil. Except for the time she spends with Austin, of course. That's when her heart is fullest, and it shows—as if every time she picks up that little boy is the first time.

We've grown close, Gemma and I, despite the difference in our ages, as if some unseen connection has always existed between us. The rest of the help see it, too, and dislike me for it. I can't say I blame them. I'm treated more like a sister than an employee, adored, even coddled at times, as if she's trying to make up for the things I've been through, for Blackhurst, and for losing you, my darling.

Things have changed a little, though, since those first early days when I came to work here. Gemma's husband—his name is Harley—is back from Chicago, where he's been working for the last few months on a big real estate project. He's so rarely at home, and then usually shut up in his study, that it's easy to forget he lives here at all, so that when we did come face-to-face one night on the stairs, I was actually startled to see him there. And he was no happier to see me, glaring at me like I was some kind of intruder. In all my life, I've never seen a man with a colder pair of eyes.

I could have excused his coldness if it was only directed toward me, but it isn't. He's insolent to Gemma one moment, then condescending the next, and barely acknowledges poor Austin, unless it's to find fault or shoo him away. I wouldn't have thought it possible for a man to be so impervious to his own flesh and blood, but I've seen it for myself. Gemma makes excuses—he's tired after such a long trip, and has a lot on his mind—but there's no mistaking such obvious disdain, or excusing it, either.

Luckily, I don't have to see him very often. I'm usually in the nursery with Austin, or out in the gardens with Gemma. And when I'm finished with my duties, I have a large bright room just down from the nursery, with a little writing desk where I sit down at least once a week and write another letter, in the hope that someone somewhere will help me. I think sometimes about asking Mrs. Tate for help. Surely she has connections, the kind of people who might be able to make more successful inquiries. But those same people might make other inquiries. They might learn that I ran away and am still underage, and might force me to go back to Mam and Sennen Cove. But that isn't the only reason I'm reluctant to mention my promise to her. I'm afraid to tell her that my real motive—my only motive—for being here is to find you and get you back. If she thinks I might leave my position, she might not want to keep me on. And for now, at least, I'm happy here.

No more iron beds and tasteless porridge. No more sewing, or laundry, or forced prayers to a deaf God. For now, at least, I have resolved to make my way in this new place, and with this new set of people, and to content myself with looking after Gemma Tate's little prince, who has, little by little, begun to melt my heart. I was uncertain at first that I had it in me to care for another woman's child, to be reminded daily of what the Sisters of Mercy took from me, but I find I can bear it almost cheerfully, because he helps me remember you, my angel, and to keep the promise I made to you burning brightly.

Though sometimes I fear it burns a bit too brightly. Everywhere I go—to the park, or the market, or for a stroll along the Battery—I find myself looking for you, searching the face of every child I pass, hoping for a glimpse of your father's eyes. I would know you if I saw you. I'm certain of it. And so I will keep looking, though it scares me at times to think what I might do if I did find you. I haven't forgotten—will never forget—that brief but terrible moment when I contemplated snatching poor Austin away. It was a kind of madness—temporary, but mad just the same. In a very short time, I have come to realize that a mother will do almost anything—lie, cheat, even steal—for the sake of her child.

I wonder sometimes if it's quite normal to miss a child I've never once laid eyes on, because it doesn't always feel normal. Sometimes, when Austin looks up at me with one of his dimply smiles, I think again how easy it would be to simply take him and disappear. Those are the times I wonder if Blackhurst has left me warped in some way, and if I'm fit to be looking after a child at all. Perhaps not, but I'm too fond of him now to leave. Besides, where would I go? This is the only home I have now—until I find you, little one. And I will find you.

All my love,
Mam

thirty-four

MAGNOLIA GROVE CEMETERY
CHARLESTON, SOUTH CAROLINA
OCTOBER 26, 2005

Dovie did her best to study Dora's face without appearing to. This morning's letters hadn't been as hard on her as some of the others. While they had been far from happy, there had at least been a measure of comfort in them. After months of struggle, Alice had landed in a safe place where she was treated well, and perhaps even loved.

But for Dovie, the most intriguing details had to do with the little boy in Alice's care. The letters had provided a grim glimpse into Austin's childhood, stirring memories of their conversation at McCrady's, when he had casually confessed that his father never loved him. At the time, she had just assumed he was being glib. Now, based on Alice's words, it looked as though the remark had been more fact than fiction.

The realization came with a deep pang of sadness. What must it be like to live your whole life knowing you weren't loved by one of your parents? At least Gemma had made up for it. That she had adored him was clear. And she had loved Alice, too, enough to share her most precious possession—her son.

"She had a friend," Dora said, as if reading Dovie's thoughts. "Mrs. Tate. She looked after my girl, took care of her when I couldn't. Would she see me, do you think? So I can thank her?"

Dovie gnawed at her lower lip, not at all certain that was a good idea. That Gemma and Alice once shared a special relationship seemed clear. What was less than clear was whether that relationship had been intact at the time of Alice's death. She thought about the rumors—decades old now—that had been resurrected with Harley Tate's death. Rumors of infidelity with a young woman in his wife's employ. Alice had clearly held no fondness for Austin's father, but that didn't mean he hadn't managed to seduce her—or worse. If he had, it would have certainly severed the friendship between the two women. It would also account for Gemma's rather abrupt retreat when Alice's name had come up in conversation the day Dovie had dropped off the folder.

"Dora," Dovie said gently, determined to sidestep any mention of the rumors. "I'm not sure Mrs. Tate is up to visitors just now. She hasn't been well lately. It seems she's taking her husband's death pretty hard."

At the mention of Harley Tate, Dora's face went stony. "That old tosser? Why should she give a snap about him? Good riddance, I say!"

Dovie reached for her hand, patting it gently. "I know. He doesn't seem like a very nice man, but she's entitled to her grief, the same as us."

Dora nodded grudgingly. "I suppose."

"We need to go soon. Are you ready?"

Dora's gaze strayed to the stone angel several yards away from their bench. "Can I just have a few minutes? I'd like to have a word. I know it's silly, and she can't hear me, but I'd like to just the same."

At Dovie's nod she stepped away, crossing the path to the place where her daughter lay buried. She stood there a moment, staring up into the stony, tearstained face, her expression so rife with grief that

Dovie felt a knot rise in her throat. She was so lost in the moment that she didn't notice the shadow that had fallen across the bench.

"Well, now," Josiah said. "I wasn't sure I'd be seeing you much anymore."

Dovie smiled up at him. "I didn't come for me. I brought a friend." She pointed across the path to where Dora stood. "We've been reading some of Alice's letters."

Josiah shot Dovie a long, sideways look. "I asked you once if you'd lost your mind. Now I know you have. What in the world were you thinking, bringing that poor woman here? Look at her standing there, nothing but skin and bone, blubbering after her dead girl. You can't drag old folk to a place like this and read the kind of stuff that's in those letters. You just can't do it."

"She asked me to, Josiah. I tried to talk her out of it, but she wouldn't listen. She might be skin and bone, but she's stubborn as anything. I knew if I didn't bring her, she'd just come on her own. This way I'm with her if something happens."

Josiah sighed, a long, heavy sound that meant he was going to leave it alone. "I don't know. We all have our own way of dealing with grief. Guess butting into this poor old lady's life was yours. And who knows? Maybe this will help her find some peace." He paused, jerking his chin in the direction of William's grave. "You see the flowers?"

Dovie nodded. "His mother and I had a little chat."

"Wasn't her," he said, in a way that made Dovie turn to look at him. "Was a tall man dressed all in black. Came last night, just before sunset. Stayed a long time, too. Just stood there all by himself. Never seen him before." He paused a moment. "You have, though, I reckon."

Dovie nodded.

Josiah nodded back. "Thought as much. You best go now, and see to Mrs. Tandy."

thirty-five

Dovie did her best, on the drive home, to shake off the image of Kristopher standing vigil over William's grave. He was back, apparently, just as he said he would be, to attend his sister's wedding and presumably crate up *The Agonies* for shipping back to New York. She had expected to feel something like jealousy, tiny echoes of the instinctive possessiveness she had felt the first day she saw him. Instead, it felt right somehow. The torch had been passed. He would take her place now—albeit, from a distance.

It was almost noon by the time she got home. She dropped her tote on the kitchen counter and made a beeline for the remote, flipping to ESPN in hopes of catching the last few minutes of Game Day. If she hurried, she could get the nachos into the oven and still have time to change before kickoff.

She'd just opened the fridge when the phone rang. She made a face when she saw her mother's number pop up on caller ID. She wasn't in the mood for chitchat right now, wasn't interested in which of her friends had had a tummy tuck, or whose daughter had just run off with the gardener's son. Right now she was in the mood for beer, nachos, and a little college football.

"Gamecocks Central," she answered brightly as she picked up the phone, a subtle, or maybe not so subtle, reminder to her mother that kickoff was less than twenty minutes away.

"You sound like you're out of breath, honey. Were you exercising or something?"

"No, I wasn't exercising." Tucking the phone under chin, she moved about the kitchen, pulling salsa, cheese, and sour cream from the fridge. "Kickoff's in a few minutes, and I'm trying to get the nachos in the oven."

"Are we playing Clemson?"

We? Who was we? Her mother didn't know a tight end from a split end. As far as Rowena Larkin was concerned, there were two teams in all of college football—South Carolina and Clemson. And the only reason she knew those was that Dovie's father had played for the Gamecocks—and had hated the Tigers with a white-hot passion.

"No, Mother. Clemson was two weeks ago. We play Florida today, in fifteen minutes, as a matter of fact, so I'm a little rushed."

"All right, then, I won't keep you. I just called about lunch next week. It's been so long since we had a nice long chat. We could hit Magnolia's and then do a little shopping."

"It's not a good time for me right now, Mother. You know I've got that big fund-raiser in a few weeks, and I'm up to my ears getting ready."

It wasn't exactly true; the majority of the details had been finalized last week. But it was as good an excuse as any to avoid what would almost certainly begin with an inquisition into her love life and end with a shopping spree for things neither of them needed and would probably never wear.

"Can we do it another time?"

"I suppose we could, but have you given any thought to what you'll be wearing to this little shindig? And, more important, to who'll be escorting you?"

The platter slipped out of her hands and onto the counter. "Escorting me?"

"Yes, escorting you. You can't show up to something like that without a date on your arm, sweetheart. It isn't done."

"I don't need an escort. I'll be working."

"Working as in pouring drinks and passing out crab puffs? Or working as in schmoozing potential donors? There's a big difference, honey. I learned that the hard way, when I did all those charity dinners for your father. You're definitely going to need a new dress—and a date. You can't show up looking like some wallflower."

Dovie stifled a groan as she shoved the platter of nachos into the oven and set the timer. She wasn't sure which terrified her more, the idea of shopping for a gown or finding someone to drag to this affair. "I don't need to go shopping, Mother. I'm sure I have something in my closet that will work."

This brought a snort from her mother. "I've seen what's in your closet, honey, and no, you really don't."

"I'll borrow something from Robin," she said, heading down the hall now to change. "God knows she's got a closet full of ball gowns, and she isn't likely to need them with a belly full of baby."

"Dovie, since when have you been able to wear anything of your sister's? For one thing, she's a good three inches shorter than you. Not to mention, as you have been pointing out to me since you were eight, you do not do ruffles. Face it, honey. You're going to have to bite the bullet and go shopping. We could all go together. You, me, and Robin. She says she hasn't heard from you in a couple weeks. It would be nice for us to all catch up."

"Fine. The three of us," Dovie agreed. At this point, giving in seemed to be her only hope of getting off the phone and back to the kitchen before the nachos caught fire. "We've got a night game next week. I can do it then. Look, I hate to cut this short, but I've got food in the oven. I'll touch base with you later in the week to firm up a time. I promise."

She had just dragged her T-shirt over her head and flipped to CBS when the doorbell rang. *Fabulous.* If she didn't know better, she'd swear there was a conspiracy afoot. Then she remembered telling Austin she'd be home after noon. And of course, here he was, right on time, just as the Gamecocks were coming out of the tunnel.

He stood there smiling as she opened the door, looking tanned and boyish in faded jeans and a navy blue Windbreaker. It was a new look for him, and definitely a good one.

"You did say noon, didn't you?" His eyes lingered a moment on her bare legs and feet, before sliding up to meet hers. "I'm meeting someone later this afternoon, so I thought I'd come early and get it out of the way."

There was something vaguely annoying about the remark, as if she was something to be checked off a list before he could actually begin enjoying his day. "Well, then, let's—" Before she could finish, the oven timer cut her off. "Sorry. Give me a minute, and I'll be right with you. The paintings are on the desk if you want to start looking them over."

She returned a few minutes later to find him standing in front of the desk, arms folded, head tilted to one side, as if listening to song lyrics he couldn't quite make out.

"His name is Ivey Clark," she said, coming to stand beside him. "There are already several of his pieces hanging in your mother's study, so I think you're safe no matter which you choose. She loves his work, like I do. It's so . . . palpable."

Austin lifted his brows, clearly out of his depth. "Palpable?"

"It means substantial, physical."

"If you say so. Like I said, when it comes to this stuff, I'm hopeless. I do know paintings have names sometimes. Do these?"

Dovie dragged her eyes from the TV, where Florida had just won the toss. "They do, in fact. I've got them in my planner, along with the prices. Let me get them for you."

She felt a moment of panic as she reached into her tote and saw the envelopes from this morning's outing with Dora. Austin would have no way of knowing what they were, of course, but it was a strange reality to be faced with, having the subject of those letters standing in her living room. What would he say if he knew what she'd been up to? Poking around in his family's business, reading letters that didn't belong to her, obsessing over the woman who had been his nanny.

But then, he didn't know, and wouldn't—unless she told him. And maybe she should. Maybe, if she explained that her interest had nothing to do with his family's past, that she was just trying to help an old woman find some peace before she died, he'd understand, and even want to help. But then, that wasn't likely, was it? After he'd made it clear that poking around in his family's business was off-limits. And there was another reason she was reluctant to tell him about the letters and her involvement with Dora. Part of her—a part that scared the hell out of her—wanted him to like her, too. And he wouldn't if he knew what she'd been doing behind his back.

He had been muttering for several minutes, scrubbing his chin and shaking his head. "Okay, I give," he said, swinging his gaze in her direction. "Which one's better?"

Dovie laughed. "It isn't about better, Austin. Good art almost never is. It's about choosing the one your mother will enjoy the most. Which one will *speak* to her. Which one *feels* like her."

"And if I told you I still didn't know?"

Dovie moved to his side. She hadn't planned on giving an art lesson today, but she'd miss the whole game if she didn't step in. "Well, they're very different, aren't they? One's a cityscape, lots of movement and strong contrast. It feels bright and vibrant, like the bustle of downtown. The other is a marsh at sunset. The colors are soft and muted, and the light feels almost watery. It's remarkable, really. There's a stillness to it, but there's life, too, underneath. A warmth you feel rather than see."

Austin had shifted his gaze from the painting and was looking at her now, his eyes searching her face. Dovie felt herself flush. "What?"

"It sounded like you were describing you, just then. *Still, but with a life underneath. Warmth you feel rather than see.* That's you to a tee."

"I was describing the marsh."

"If you say so."

His voice was low and warm as he continued to hold her gaze, as if he'd just discovered some secret and was still trying to digest it.

It was Dovie who looked away. "So, what do you think? About the paintings, I mean."

"Which is *your* favorite?"

"That's the wrong question."

"Why?"

"Because you're not choosing a gift for me. You're choosing a gift for your mother. But I guess, if it were me doing the choosing, I'd go with the cityscape. It's a better fit with the other two she has. Does that help?"

"Enormously. Who do I make the check out to?"

Dovie handed him Ivey Clark's business card. "There you go. It's called Weekend Downtown, by the way. It's right there on the back of the card, if you forget."

"Oh, you can count on that." Austin grinned as he handed her the check. "Seriously, you have no idea how much I appreciate this."

"Like I said, I'm happy to help, and I'm sure your mother's going to love it. Oh, and Ivey said he'd frame whichever you chose at no charge and drop it back by the museum. I can give you a call when it's ready."

"That would be great."

Dovie stole a quick glance at the television, grimacing when she realized she had missed the entire first series. Without meaning to, she inched closer to the set, watching as the Gators lined up to punt the ball away. At least they hadn't scored.

For the first time, Austin seemed to notice the snacks set out on the coffee table. "I'm sorry. I didn't realize . . . Are you expecting company?"

"Company?" Dovie shook her head. "Not unless you count Vern Lundquist from CBS. It's my Saturday afternoon ritual, nachos and beer and college football. And today's a big game. We're playing Florida, which just happens to be our coach's alma mater, so it's this weird love-hate rivalry for them."

Austin eyed her shorts and Gamecocks T-shirt with obvious approval. "That explains the attire. It's a good look for you, by the way."

Dovie looked away, flustered by the undisguised appreciation in his tone. Carolina had the ball, or would as soon as the punt was away. She watched as it sailed high but short, then held her breath during the return. "Yes! Out to the forty-six. Now do something with it!"

"You're a Carolina fan."

"Die-hard. My father played fullback back in the day."

Austin unzipped his jacket, exposing an enormous orange paw print emblazoned across his chest. "I played QB for Clemson."

Dovie let out a sigh. "Bless your little heart, of course you did."

"What's that supposed to mean?"

"Nothing," she said, all wide-eyed innocence. "Someone's got to go there. Not everyone can get into Carolina."

"So it's going to be like that, is it?"

"I'm afraid so." She turned back to the game as Carolina lined up in the shotgun, then aired one out for a twenty-two-yard pickup. "Yes! Did you see that bullet?"

"Your dad get you interested in football?"

Dovie smiled, but with just a touch of the old bitterness. "I was the son he never had."

"No brothers?"

"No. Just my sister, Robin, and she hated football. That left just Daddy and me on Saturday afternoons. We didn't win much back then. That was before Spurrier, though. Now we've got an offense, and recruiting's getting better every year. The four and five stars are actually giving us a look."

Austin's brows notched up. "I'm impressed."

"Why? Because girls don't know football?"

"Because of how intense you are about it. You're like that about everything, though. You take everything so seriously. It's . . . impressive."

Dovie eyed him suspiciously, surprised by the compliment—if that's what it was. "I thought you said once that I was too serious."

"That was before I knew you. I teased you, but now I can't help wondering. Maybe if I'd been a little more serious I could have avoided some of my more spectacular mistakes. I guess we'll never know."

His pensive tone caught Dovie's attention. "What kind of mistakes?"

Austin shrugged. "Not important. By the way, your boy Mitchell just threw a pick, and it looks like Florida's about to take it in for six."

"No!" Dovie dropped to the arm of the couch in time to see Florida's Demetrius Webb high-step into the end zone. "Well, damn. Not a very auspicious start." She stifled a grin as she turned to him. "And don't you dare stand there looking smug, you . . . Clemson fan."

Austin smothered a grin of his own. "It's way too early for smug. But the guy needs to stop telegraphing his throws, or that won't be the last one of those we see."

Dovie cringed as she watched the replay. Austin was right. Number fifteen had read Mitchell's eyes the whole way. Sighing, she pushed to her feet.

Austin cocked an eye at her. "Where are you going?"

"To the kitchen. We're down seven points, and I'm a nervous eater."

In the kitchen, she pulled a Coke and a Bud Light from the fridge, then grabbed the plate of nachos. Austin was perched on the edge of the couch when she returned, cell phone to his ear. It was impossible not to overhear his half of the conversation.

"Hey, Ted, something's come up, and I'm not going to make it. I need to sit with a friend who's going through kind of a rough time. No, it isn't serious. Just a nervous condition." He paused, throwing Dovie a wink. "I'll be keeping the four o'clock with Tyler's father, though. Bet on that. I've been trying to pin the guy down for weeks. Today, he's going to listen to what I have to say." He paused, nodding at whatever was being said in his ear. "Sure thing. I'll call you when it's over."

Dovie set down the nachos and passed Austin the Coke before curling up in the corner of the couch with her beer. "Dig in," she said, pointing to the coffee table spread. "As you can see, there's plenty. I always do enough for an army. Chalk it up to my nervous condition."

"Again, I'm impressed. You're an art expert, a football expert, *and* you cook. Is there anything you *don't* know how to do?"

Dovie made a face as she took a sip of her beer. "Let's leave that list for another day, shall we? Is everything okay? I couldn't help overhearing your conversation, and it sounded intense, like maybe poor Tyler's father's in for an earful."

"Tyler's father deserves an earful."

"Who's Tyler, if you don't mind my asking?"

"A kid I've sort of taken under my wing at the Outlook Club."

"Outlook Club?"

"It's a youth center I started with a friend of mine a few years back. It's for troubled kids from rocky homes—boys mostly. And when I say rocky homes, I don't necessarily mean they come from the wrong side of the tracks. Kids with trust funds can have crappy home lives, too. *At risk* is the term they use now, I think."

"And you started this center on your own?"

"Not on my own, no. I have a friend, Ted Atkinson, who worked with me on the concept and helped me navigate the organizational hurdles. I bought the land, but he did most of the rest. We've got a certified counselor on staff, and a handful of volunteers. It's not a lot of kids, but we try to be hands-on. We won't change the world, but we do what we can."

"This boy, Tyler. He's in trouble?"

"Not legal trouble, no. But there are worse things than getting busted for shoplifting or breaking into cars. His mother died when he was seven. For years, it's just been him and his dad. Then, about six months ago, his father remarried. He's so busy with his new bride that he seems to have forgotten he has a fifteen-year-old son who still needs him. Needless to say, Tyler's been feeling a little displaced. He feels like he's lost his whole family, which is why he's been acting out."

"Acting out, how?"

"That time I had to run out on you at your office—the day we met—I'd just gotten a call from Ted telling me he'd run away. I found him, eventually, out on the dock where I take him sailing. It took some doing, but I got him to agree to go home."

Dovie thought back to that day, and that call. When he mentioned the word *club* she'd just assumed he'd meant country club. Clearly, there was a side of Austin Tate she hadn't seen. One she was starting to think she'd like to see more of.

"What did you say that finally convinced him to go home?"

"I told him things would never get better if he kept taking off, that he needed to stay and learn how to talk to his father. He didn't like that part very much. He's pretty angry. And hurt."

"I'll bet."

"And I told him there are all kinds of families. That family isn't just something that shows up on a blood test, that there are people who care about him."

Dovie swallowed an unexpected lump in her throat. "You keep surprising me. I wouldn't have pegged you as a softie, but here you are, doing this amazing thing. Not just writing a check, but actually touching lives. That *is* how you change the world, by the way."

Austin shrugged. "It's my mother's fault. She's big on strays and charity cases. Always has been. I guess it rubbed off on me."

Dovie nodded, thinking about Alice. She had been one of those strays, an *at risk youth* long before the term became part of the landscape, and Gemma had taken her in. He did come by it honestly. But she couldn't help thinking that there might be more to Austin's involvement with Tyler than just his mother's kind example, that in helping this boy he was trying to rewrite his own history with a cold and unloving father. It made her sad, and a little angry, too.

"Why doesn't anyone know this about you? The papers like to make you out as this hard-partying playboy. Fancy sports cars and a blonde on every arm. They never, ever talk about this."

Austin smiled, but there was no warmth in it. "The other stuff's sexier."

"Maybe it's time you set the record straight."

His smile was a bitter one. "And have the Outlook Club look like some sort of publicity stunt? No, thanks. Ted's the front man, and I'm fine with that. I'll just keep doing what I do—quietly."

"But why? It's not a publicity stunt if it's true. And you can't tell me you enjoy people thinking of you as a male version of Paris Hilton. Famous, for being . . . famous."

Austin's face hardened unexpectedly. "I don't want people to think of me at all, Dovie. That's what no one seems to get. I don't need anyone keeping score. And speaking of keeping score . . ." He paused, pointing to the television. "You might want to pay attention. Your boys are in the red zone."

Dovie let her gaze linger a moment before deciding to let the matter drop. If there was anything she had learned about Austin Tate, it was that when he was done talking about a thing, he was done.

Near the end of the third quarter, Austin stood, announcing that it was time for him to go. “I need to get over to Sullivan’s Island by four, and I don’t want to be late. I’m not giving Tyler’s father any excuse to run out on me.”

Dovie stood, too, feeling a pang of disappointment as she walked him to the door. “Thanks for hanging out and watching the game,” she said, feeling shy all of a sudden. “It was nice to have company for a change. Even if it *was* a Clemson fan.”

“What would you say to a little company later on? Say, dinner?”

Dovie froze, feeling like the proverbial deer in headlights. “You mean, like a date?”

“I mean, like an experiment. A chemistry experiment, to be precise. I’m interested to see if we can share a whole meal without there being an explosion of some kind.”

Dovie managed a grin. “If it’s in the name of science, I don’t see how I can say no.”

“You pick the place. Whatever you’re in the mood for. Just not McCrady’s. I’m not sure my reputation could take it if you walked out on me again.”

“God, I really am sorry about that.”

Austin reached out to tuck a loose strand of hair behind her ear, his fingertips warm where they brushed her cheek. “Then make it up to me.”

Dovie’s breath caught as she met his gaze. “How?”

“Stay for dessert.”

thirty-six

It was Saturday night, and the Porch was packed. But then, Dovie couldn't remember a time when it wasn't. Opened twenty years ago, by Theda's grandmother and two of her aunts, the place had quickly become a local landmark, drawing tourists and locals alike, and well worth the numbing stretch of highway connecting Mount Pleasant and Georgetown.

By anyone's standards, the Porch was a hole-in-the-wall, a weathered clapboard shack with a sagging wraparound porch and a long, listing dock that knifed out over the marsh. Dovie glanced at Austin's face as he pulled into the rutted dirt parking lot. He wasn't frowning, exactly, but he was definitely taking it all in. He might be wary now, but he'd soon change his tune. The place might not look like much at first glance, but when it came to authentic Gullah cuisine, no one offered a more mouthwatering experience than Mama Hettie and her daughters.

Patrons hovered in clumps on the peeling front porch, some making use of weathered rockers while they waited for their names to be called. Austin eyed the crowd, not bothering to hide his surprise. "All these people are waiting to get in there?"

"Yup." She led him up a set of creaky steps and onto the porch.

"Mama Hettie doesn't believe in reservations. She does believe in *haints*, though," she added, pointing to the blue shutters all along the porch.

"In what?"

"*Haints.* It's Geechee for 'ghosts.' That's why the blue paint. It symbolizes water, and since everyone knows haints can't cross water, they use it to confuse the spirits and keep them from crossing over into their homes, or in this case, businesses."

"Like kryptonite," Austin said, craning his neck to study the pale blue ceiling. "But for ghosts."

"Exactly. Let's go put our name on the list."

Inside, the air was warm and thick, heady with the aromas of exotic spices and down-home cooking. Every table was full, and then some, with chairs and high chairs spilling into the aisles, so that servers had to squeeze between diners, trays of food held above their heads.

Dovie paused to point out the walls, rough-hewn boards darkly stained, studded with sweetgrass baskets and colorful Gullah art pieces, many of which bore price tags. "The artwork is Theda's mother's contribution to the family business. She's all about supporting local artists and showcasing Gullah culture to visitors."

Before Austin could reply, Theda's Auntie Jevet had spotted Dovie and was elbowing her way through the throng. She was as regal as ever, tall and sturdy as a tribal totem, though carved of stronger stuff. And beautiful, with wide almond eyes and skin like polished ebony.

"You should've called to let us know you was coming, baby girl!" Her full mouth pursed as she looked Dovie up and down, then subjected Austin to the same scrutiny. "Look at you, always so pretty. Your fella ain't bad, either."

Dovie opened her mouth to protest but thought better of it. It was far too noisy to go into explanations about who Austin was and wasn't. "It was sort of spur-of-the-moment," she said instead. "We don't mind waiting."

"Nonsense. What you think Theda's going to say if she comes out of the back and finds you standing here like some stranger?"

Dovie felt the first niggling of unease. "Theda's here?"

"Sure is. Back in the kitchen. Mama Hettie likes for her to keep a hand in. Not that she's ever goin' die. Eighty-four, and she goin' to her grave with all those recipes in her head. Won't write 'em down to save herself. One day she'll drop over, and the joke goin' be on her. Wait and see. I'll go tell Theda you're here. And Hettie, too."

Before Dovie could protest, Jevet had melted back into the crowd. Dovie watched her disappear with a growing sense of dread. She'd been looking forward to seeing Mama Hettie again, but Theda was a different story. She was guaranteed to make too much of Austin's presence, meaning Monday would be an excruciating marathon of twenty questions, mixed with a little truth or dare.

"Does she mean Theda from the museum?"

Dovie nodded gravely. "I'm afraid so."

"I thought you two were friends."

"We are, but she has very strong opinions about my social life—or rather my lack of a social life—which means she's going to make a big deal out you being here with me. Damn, here she comes."

Theda was smiling as she made her way over, wiping her hands on a smudgy white apron, her face shiny with kitchen sweat. "Well, well, Miss Larkin, as I live and breathe. What brings you out into the real world?"

Dovie was about to reply when she felt Austin's arm snake around her waist. "We spent most of the afternoon on the couch, and thought it was time to get out of the house. Great place your grandmother has here, by the way. Dovie's been raving about it for weeks. I'm glad we finally made it out."

Theda's almond-shaped eyes narrowed. "For weeks, huh? Looks like someone's been holding out on me."

"It's not like that," Dovie corrected hastily. "We're just out for a meal."

"Together. Yes, I see that."

Dovie shot her a pleading look. "I'll talk to you on Monday."

"Oh, sweetie, you can count on it. Right now, though, I've got to get back to the kitchen, or Mama Hettie'll skin me. Lord, here she comes. Enjoy your, eh . . . meal, you two."

Dovie wriggled away from his arm and snapped her head around. "What did you do that for? Do you have any idea how long it's going to take to convince her you were just kidding?"

Austin's lips curled mischievously. "I wasn't kidding. We were on the couch most of the afternoon. Besides, I think people who make up their minds about other people should get exactly what they expect. It's just easier that way."

"Easier for you, maybe," Dovie grumbled as Mama Hettie approached. "Oh, I should warn you. Hettie can be hard to understand, at first. You'll probably be all right, though. She usually reserves the Gullah for tourists. They come to the Porch for an authentic Gullah experience, and that's what they get—Gullah rice and Geechee talk, washed down with lots and lots of sweet tea. It's the damnedest thing. She can turn it off like a switch. So can Theda."

"Guess it's a good thing I brought an interpreter, then."

"Dovie, girl!" Mama Hettie burst out, somehow managing to convey both cheerfulness and severity. "How long since I *shum* you, and huccome you stay gone so long? I been asking after you, and asking after you, telling Theda to 'suade you to come, but she jus' shake her head and say you having a time."

Mama Hettie looked every inch of her eighty-four years, stooped and hollow-boned, with skin like old leather and an infant's gummy smile. Her hair, or what there was of it, was the color of ash and was wrapped in an elaborately knotted turban of bright teal blue. But it was Hettie's eyes that had always fascinated Dovie, jet-black irises surrounded by a thickening blue-white haze. It was a startling combination, and one that gave her a slightly witchy appearance, which Dovie suspected pleased the old woman to no end.

"Mama Hettie, it's good to see you again."

"That's my pretty gal," Mama Hettie said, taking both Dovie's hands in hers. "You done brought a pretty boy, too, I see. And about time. Who you?"

Austin eyes widened, but he quickly recovered. "I'm Austin Tate. And I'm guessing you're Mama Hettie."

"Dat's right," she boomed back at him, before returning her attention to Dovie. "Good to see you got a fella."

Dovie swallowed a sigh. Having to explain Austin's presence over and over was getting old. "Mama Hettie, Austin isn't my fellow. He's . . . a friend. Theda knows him, too, from the museum. William died last year, remember?"

"Course I do. You think I'm tech'd? Jus 'cause you lost one man don't mean you can't go get yo'self another one." She paused, giving Dovie a sharp leer. "Girl don't need a man, if she strong. But she'll want one if she smart." She turned away then, sweeping Austin with her witchy eyes. "You come to eat like the Gullah?" she asked, at last, slipping into her broken patois.

"Yes. Though I'm not sure what that means. I guess I'm in your hands."

Mama Hettie managed to beam and look grave all at the same time. "In my hands is the best place to be. No *buckruhbittle* here, though, so you know ahead."

Austin turned to Dovie, looking for a translation.

"White man's food," Dovie supplied with a grin.

Hettie nodded her turbaned head. "Dat's right. Only good Gullah food. When I'm t'rough feedin' you, I promise you goin' be so sattify you be ruined. My girl Jevet will take you to your table while I go cook your *bittle*. Some *osiituh*, I think, all fried up nice in buttermilk.

Thatta hold you for a little. Attahw'hile, I come with more. Sump'n tase'e'mout I gonna make speshly for you two."

And with that she was gone, leaving Dovie smiling and Austin dumbfounded. A moment later, Jevet was back, gesturing for them to follow her. She led them to a corner table at the back of the restaurant. Taped to the windowsill was a hand-printed sign with the word RESERVED hand-lettered in red Magic Marker.

"Her Highness said no menus, but I brought 'em anyway so's you could look 'em over while you wait. Can I bring y'all something to drink? Tea? Swamp water?"

Austin glanced up from the laminated menu. "Swamp water?"

Dovie couldn't help giggling. "It's not what it sounds like. It's tea mixed with lemonade. It's quite good, actually. But the peach sweet tea is to die for."

"Two peach teas it is, then." He watched as Jevet retreated, waiting until she was out of earshot to speak. "Who is she again?"

"Theda's auntie Jevet. Her auntie Riah works here, too, but I haven't seen her tonight. Maybe she's in the kitchen with Theda."

"So it's the whole family?"

"Just the women. Except for Theda's mom. She broke away when she was young, and got her PhD. She teaches languages at Avery Research now and lectures all over the country on Gullah culture. She even does some storytelling at festivals and things. I swear, I could listen to her talk for hours."

"I never realized it was a thing. I mean, you hear the words *Gullah* and *Geechee* thrown around, but I didn't realize it was such a big deal."

"It's a very big deal to them. And it's not just about the baskets. The Gullahs helped build the rice plantations that made South Carolina what it is today, and now their culture is being eroded by developers, and even the government. Luckily, there's been a move toward preservation in the past few years, of both their lands and their traditions. That's what Theda's mom is all about, making sure the culture isn't lost for future generations. They're an amazing people. Especially the women. Theda's ancestors came from Senegal, but Gullah slaves came from Angola, Sierra Leone, Madagascar—all along the West African coast, really. They were highly prized for their ability to cultivate rice, so we basically went over there and took them."

"I've lived here all my life and didn't know those things. How'd you learn all this?"

Dovie smiled. "Theda. When it comes to the Gullahs, she's like a walking encyclopedia. Plus, there's an exhibit at the museum. You should check it out sometime."

"Do I get a guided tour?"

Dovie felt herself squirm. He was flirting again, and he was good at it. But perhaps even more disturbing was the unexpected temptation to flirt back. Luckily, she was spared having to respond when Jevet reappeared, a tray expertly perched on one shoulder.

She was all business as she set down two glasses of tea, followed by a pair of flat sweetgrass baskets lined with waxed paper and nuggets of crispy brown goodness. "Hettie say this is just to tide you over. Fried oysters and crab puppies. Rest coming tuhreckly. She say she'll bring it herself when it's ready."

"Thank you, Jevet. It looks wonderful."

Dovie lifted her tea to her lips and took a deep sip, the taste of ripe peach exploding on her tongue, so icy-sweet it made her teeth ache. Relieved to have a distraction, she pushed the baskets toward Austin, then reached across with her fork and took an oyster for herself. "Make sure you try them with the sauce. It's to die for."

Austin groaned as he bit into one of the crab puppies. "I don't think I've ever tasted anything better in my life. What's that sauce?"

Dovie shrugged. "Not much chance of finding out, I'm afraid. You heard Jevet. Hettie's bent on taking her recipes to the grave. I'm glad you like this. I wasn't sure you would."

"Why's that?"

"Well, it's not exactly what you're used to, is it?"

Austin gave her a sheepish smile. "I can't argue with you there. I can't think of a single woman I've ever dated who would have chosen a place like this."

"No?"

"The type of women I date prefer champagne to sweet tea—as I'm sure you've noticed."

Dovie toyed with a crab puppy as she digested the remark. His *type* was hardly a secret—the social rags had seen to that—but the disdain in his voice was both glaring and unexpected.

"Sounds to me like you need to find some new women to date," she teased, then reached for her tea as she realized the remark had come dangerously close to sounding like an invitation—which it absolutely was *not*. "I'm sorry. I have no idea why I just said that. Who you date is none of my business."

"Actually, I've been thinking the same thing, lately. Thinking about it a lot, as a matter of fact."

There was something in his voice, a lazy smokiness, that made Dovie's cheeks tingle and go warm. "I prefer to save the champagne for celebrations. I guess that makes me a cheap date."

It was a lame attempt to lighten the moment, one that left Austin studying her far more closely than she was comfortable with. "I don't believe that," he said, after a moment. "Quite the opposite, in fact. Something tells me you could be very costly indeed."

The moment stretched, weighty and awkward amid the collective din of Saturday night diners. Dovie had no idea how to respond to such a statement, or if a response was even expected. In the end, she settled for a clumsy segue. "You haven't said how your meeting with Tyler's father went."

Austin cleared his throat as he reached for his fork, appearing every bit as relieved to change the subject as Dovie. "It went about as well as you'd expect, I guess. He was pretty pissed off at first, that a stranger would have the nerve to lecture him about his own son. I expected that. And maybe he had a point. I don't have kids. Where do I get off giving anyone parenting advice?"

"Did he at least listen?"

Austin speared an oyster and popped it in his mouth. "Eventually. But I think by the time I was done I'd given him a few things to think about. At least, he said I had. I honestly don't think the man had a clue how Tyler was feeling."

"You did a good thing, Austin."

"We'll see. I did what I could, at any rate. And how did your Gamecocks fare?"

"We won—thirty to twenty-two, against a ranked opponent. We've still got a long way to go, but it's a nice win for the program."

Mama Hettie appeared just then, carrying a tray loaded with enough food to feed the Gamecocks' starting lineup. "Here yo *bittles*, all fixed with Mama Hettie magic. Got some okra soup, some shrimp and grits. Poke chop, sweet tettuh, and succotash. Hunnuh eat 'em up now."

Dovie surveyed the spread, overwhelmed. "Mama Hettie, this is too much food. We'll never eat it all."

"Then tote it home. But don't put it in no microwave. Microwave kill da magic."

Austin sat back as Hettie placed a steaming bowl of okra soup in front of him. "Well, now you've got me curious, Hettie. What's the deal with the magic?"

Hettie fixed him with her best tribal elder stare, and just the hint of a smile. "Yes, suh. I cook wid da magic. Say words over the food."

"What kind of words?"

Hettie lowered her voice and leaned in close. "The blessing kind," she said, with a wink of one witchy eye. "Work on all kinda ting, it do. Hunnuh got trouble in da finance—magic. Hunnuh got trouble in da body—magic. Even if hunnuh got trouble in da heart—not the sickness kind, mind, the other kind—the magic work. That's why folk keep comin' here, even if they ain' know it." She grinned then, screwing up her old brown face. "'Cause, who ain' wan sum blessin' pun hunnuh food?"

Austin looked up at her with a smile of his own, and something like wonder. "Mama Hettie, I couldn't have said it better myself. Who indeed ain' want sum blessin'?"

Hettie gave his shoulder a slap, flashing her dark gums. "*Nyam*, now," she said firmly. And with that, she was gone.

Dovie ate slowly, watching with a strange sense of pleasure as Austin spooned up his soup with gusto, then moved on to the shrimp and grits. The food was every bit as amazing as Dovie remembered: fresh local ingredients seasoned with garlic, ginger, celery seed, and mustard, then slow-cooked with care—and if Hettie could be believed, just a pinch of magic.

Austin had just pushed away the plate of pork chops and sweet potatoes, declaring himself ready to burst, when Jevet appeared with a bowl and two spoons.

Dovie groaned, holding up her hands in mock surrender. "Jevet, I think I speak for both of us when I say we couldn't eat another bite."

"Hettie's bread puddin' and praline sauce," she said flatly. "You got to eat it."

Dovie eyed the bowl Jevet had placed between them and sighed. "I'm afraid she's right. Hettie's famous for her bread pudding. And I did promise to stay for dessert. We'll walk it off when we're finished."

Austin frowned, spoon poised over the bowl. "Walk it off, where? We're in the middle of nowhere out here."

"There's a long deck out back. It's beautiful when the moon's up."

"Is the moon up?"

"I don't know. Let's go see."

thirty-seven

Austin held his tongue as he followed Dovie around the side of the building, past the listing back porch and a pair of drunken lampposts, but considered balking as they neared their apparent destination—a narrow ribbon of weathered boards that might once have been called a dock.

"This?" he said incredulously. "This is where you want to walk? A rickety boardwalk in the pitch-dark?"

"Afraid?"

He couldn't see her face but could hear the smile in her voice, softly teasing. "No, I'm not afraid. But I'm not insane, either. Tell me you're not planning a stroll out over the marsh when you can't even see where you're going."

"Just stand there a minute," she told him. "And let your eyes adjust. It's not as dark as you think."

He did as he was told, waiting for his eyes to adjust. Gradually, things began to take shape: narrow estuaries snaking through tall grass, moonlight glinting off sloping banks of tidal mud, a quicksilver flash as a redfish broke the water's inky surface.

Dovie stood with her head thrown back, gazing up at the night sky, her face bathed in watery light, hair swirling like a halo in the darkness. She wore a little half smile as she pulled in a breath, then let it out very slowly, as if the stars had shared some secret with her. And then, without a word, she stepped out onto the boardwalk, leaving him to follow.

He caught up to her in a few strides, falling in beside her. He kept his eyes on his feet at first, careful not to veer too close to the edge and pitch into the swampy darkness. But after a while he found himself relaxing, content to stroll and gaze out over the moonlit stretch of sea grass.

They had almost reached the end of the dock when Dovie stopped, arms hugged to her body. "I love the marsh at night," she said almost reverently. "Some people find it creepy, but I think it's beautiful, alive with things you can hear but not see—like a pulse."

"I can't say I ever thought of it that way. Remarkable . . ."

"What is?"

"You are. This afternoon, you said I keep surprising you. I don't think I understood what you meant until now. But it's you who keeps surprising me. You see things. Underneath things that most people don't. Like the marsh."

"I used to come with my mother, back when she used to paint. We'd bring a picnic lunch and spend all day. I think that's why I fell in love with it, because I spent so much time watching it and listening to it. There's a special kind of peace here, everything moving slow and sure, carrying on whether we notice or not, the tides pushing in and out, the seasons turning right on schedule. Steady. Dependable."

"And those things are important to you."

She met his gaze, as if considering his words. "Yes, I guess they are. Maybe more than they should be."

"How do you mean?"

Her eyes slid away from his. "I mean I settle, rather than take risks. I've been that way most of my life, I guess. Less chance of being disappointed that way. Or of having the rug jerked out from under me."

"And how's that been working for you?"

She ducked her head. "Touché."

"I'm sorry. That wasn't nice."

"Maybe, but it was appropriate. I've been such a mess since William died. Things are better now, though. Or at least they're starting to be. I actually find myself looking ahead, feeling almost . . . optimistic. It's like I'm starting to remember who I used to be. Some of that has to do with you."

It was a response he hadn't expected. "With me?"

"I've been piecing it all together, and you were right. That's why I walked out on you that night at McCrady's— you were right about William, and about me. I was part of the lie, and part of me knew it. I just wasn't ready to see it, or to think about what it said about me."

"And what *did* it say?"

"That I'd been playing it safe. I wasn't in love with William. I was in love with the idea of him, of what I thought we had. I conned myself into believing it was all so perfect. Then, when he died, everything got turned upside down. There was this sense of . . ." Her voice trailed. She closed her eyes, shook her head. "It was almost like relief. Like I'd gotten a reprieve, and I couldn't understand it. And so I kept lying—to myself and everyone else."

In the moonlight, her face was all shadow and contour, lovely angles of hollow and bone. And there were tears in her eyes, silvering her lower lashes like tiny stars. She was a beautiful mess, still trying to figure it all out, not quite ready to let herself off the hook for things she'd had no control over, but reaching toward the future now, too. For her sake, he hoped she found it easier than he had.

"Sometimes lying is the kindest thing we can do," he said quietly. "For ourselves and everyone else."

She made a quick swipe at her eyes. "It still seems unbelievable."

"Of course it does. Losing someone the way you did—without any kind of warning or understanding—is a special kind of hell.

There's no good-bye, no resolution. You're just left behind, twisting in the wind. There's nothing to do but get on with things, whatever that means. And live with the regrets."

"Do you have regrets?"

She was looking up at him, her eyes wide and luminous, vulnerable, and so achingly beautiful. "If I didn't before, I'm probably about to."

It took only a step to close the distance between them, to pull her into the circle of his arms, to cup her face in his hands, to find her mouth with his. She tasted of peaches and pralines, so ripe and sweet he could have swallowed her whole. And there was the smell of her hair, salt air and rainwater and some kind of flower. He ran his hands through the silky warmth, registering an almost visceral shock as he realized just how long he had wanted this. Her touch. Her mouth.

Her.

And she wanted him, too. She had opened to him without a moment's hesitation, her lips soft and pliant. Hungry. Her hands were inside his jacket now, the warmth of her palms bleeding through his shirt like a pair of brands on his chest. There had been no one since William. If he hadn't been certain before, he was now.

He was the first—or would be, if he let this happen. But was she ready for what came next? Come to that, was he? The blood pounding in his ears told him he was, but there was more to what was happening between them than hormones. The sparks had been flying for weeks—on his end at least. So why was his brain trying to put on the brakes?

The kiss deepened, moving from tentative surrender to exploration, from hesitance to assurance, the warm pressure of her hips and breasts searing through his clothes until it was hard to tell who was kissing whom. If he didn't put a stop to this, and soon, one or both of them were going to regret it in the morning.

"Dovie, we shouldn't." But she gave no sign that she'd heard him. It took everything he had to finally push her away. "Dovie, wait."

Finally, her eyes opened, heavy lidded and confused. "We can't. I can't."

"Did I miss something? Didn't *you* just kiss *me*?"

"Yes, but I shouldn't have. I'm not the right guy for you."

She stepped back, folding her arms across her body. "It's a little early for the *it's not you, it's me* bit, don't you think?"

"I'm trying to be honest, because you deserve that. You need someone who knows how to do the whole thing. Popcorn and a movie on the couch. Sunday mornings with coffee and the paper. I'm not that guy. I'm dinner and the sack."

"Is this because I didn't want champagne with dinner?"

Jesus, she wasn't making this easy. "Trust me, you'll thank me in the morning. This seems like a good idea right now, with the moonlight shining down on the marsh, and Mama Hettie's magic in your veins, but tomorrow I'll be Austin Tate again. I have a short attention span, and to be honest, it works for me."

"I see."

"No, you don't. But I do. I can't be your rebound guy, Dovie. I have no idea if you're ready to move on, or what you'll want when you do. I just know I haven't got it to offer."

Her mouth sagged open a moment before she found her voice. "You think that's what I'm looking for? A rebound guy?"

"I think you're trying to get back on the horse, and I think doing it with a man whose name and picture pops up in the newspaper on a weekly basis is a bad idea. I'm a bad idea, Dovie. I hurt people—maybe without meaning to, but the result's the same—and you've been hurt enough."

Dovie took another step back, then turned away, her back to him as she looked out over the moon-bleached marsh. "For months, people have been telling me it's time to get on with my life. I think I even recall you saying it, or something like it. Now, all of a sudden, I'm not ready?"

"That isn't what I'm saying. I'm saying *I'm* not ready. It's absolutely time for you to get on with your life—just not with me. I know it sounds harsh, and I know I'm confusing the hell out of you right now. I'm a little confused myself. It would be so easy to let this happen, because some part of me does want it—the popcorn and the Sunday paper, the happily-ever-after thing—but I know myself. You have to trust me on this, Dovie. I'd wreck you. And probably myself, too. I swore a long time ago that that was never going to happen again, and I haven't changed my mind. I just . . . forgot for a minute. Now let me take you home. It's getting late, and it's freezing out here."

thirty-eight

She had never been one for sleeping in, even on Sundays, but if there was ever a day Dovie longed to pull the covers back over her head, it was today. She didn't want to think about last night, didn't want to relive the kiss, and then the brush-off. Didn't want to ask herself one more time how she had gotten the signals so very, very wrong. Maybe she was rusty. Not that she'd ever been very good at that sort of thing. With William there had been none of that to navigate, no steamy glances or coy remarks, no *does he or doesn't he*. No games. Or none that she'd suspected at the time. At least Austin had been up front.

So much for Mama Hettie's magic. And for sleeping in.

Kicking off the covers, she padded to the bathroom, grabbed her toothbrush, and then headed to the kitchen. She had just pressed the BREW button on the coffeemaker when her cell phone went off.

She knew something was wrong the minute she saw the Palmetto Moon's number pop up on caller ID, and she was right.

"Ms. Larkin, it's Heidi, from the Palmetto Moon. I'm sorry to bother you so early on a Sunday, but I remembered you telling me that if there was anything Mrs. Tandy ever needed, or if something was wrong, I should call you, and I think there might be something wrong. This morning when the maid knocked on her door she didn't answer, and since there was no sign on the door, she used her key to go in, and, well, Mrs. Tandy was still in bed. She didn't look so good. She said she was fine, and not to bother you, but I thought I'd better call. You know . . . in case."

In case she died. Dovie understood. "I'll be there as soon as I can. Please make sure someone stays with her until I get there."

It took less than thirty minutes to throw on some sweats and drive to the outskirts of town. Dora turned her head as Dovie let herself in. She tried to raise a hand, but it fell back to the bed. "I told them . . . not to trouble you," she said, fighting for breath between words. "Just a little . . . setback."

Heidi scrambled up out of her chair with a look of relief, darting toward the door without a word. Dovie moved to the bedside, pressing a hand to Dora's cheek. It was hot and dry, and her skin was the color of wallpaper paste, the blue around her lips more pronounced than Dovie had ever seen it. More alarming, though, was the fact that she was breathing through her mouth, a wet spongy crackling that seemed to come up from her chest.

"Have you been taking your pills like you're supposed to?"

Dora closed her eyes but managed a nod.

"How long have you been like this?"

"Last . . . night."

"Why didn't you call me?"

"Happens . . . sometimes. Gets better."

"Dora, I think you need to go to the hospital."

"No . . . hospital. Let me sleep. Be . . . fine."

"How can you possibly sleep, Dora? You can barely breathe. I'm calling 911."

Dora's head lolled on the pillow. Dovie wasn't sure if it was in agreement or protest, but it didn't matter. Dora Tandy wasn't dying on her watch.

The ambulance arrived in less than fifteen minutes. While the medics strapped Dora to a stretcher, Dovie scooped the pill bottles off the nightstand and into her tote, then followed them out to the parking lot, ignoring the growing gaggle of onlookers as she slid behind the wheel of her car. Her heart was still hammering as she pulled into the emergency room entrance, playing scenarios over in her head and blaming herself for not having seen this coming.

There was nothing to do but watch as the medics unloaded Dora from the ambulance and wheeled her into the ER, her face white as chalk beneath the clear oxygen mask. "I'm here, Dora!" she called as the gurney rushed past. "I'll be right here."

Dovie had no idea if Dora could hear her, or if she was even conscious, as they wheeled her down a long corridor and through a set of swinging doors. The next forty-five minutes were spent at the admissions desk, trying to explain her relationship to Dora and provide what few details she could about the woman's health, which were next to nothing.

Finally, an intern in faded green scrubs and a lab coat that looked as though it had been slept in appeared at the mouth of the corridor and called her name. His name badge identified him as Dr. Bradley Gatlin.

"I'm not sure how much you know about Mrs. Tandy's condition, Ms. Larkin, but she's suffering from advanced COPD."

"The smoker's disease?"

"Not necessarily. COPD stands for chronic obstructive pulmonary disease, which is often caused by smoking, but not always. Mrs. Tandy's condition is likely genetic, since she was never a smoker. At any rate, the COPD makes her more susceptible to chest infections like colds and the flu—or in this case, pneumonia. A pretty nasty case, in fact. She's running a high temp and she's dehydrated. We've started her on fluids, antibiotics, and a course of steroids, as well as treating her for hypertension, which isn't at all uncommon in these cases.

We're also going to change the meds she's been on and see if we can't make it a little easier for her to breathe. There's always portable oxygen, but I don't think we're there yet. For now, she'll go home with an inhaler, a bronchodilator that will help relax the muscles around her airways. Someone will need to make sure she has it with her at all times and that she's using it properly. I'd also recommend a respiratory therapist to help manage her condition long term. We'll write her a referral before she's discharged."

"So she can go home?"

"Not tonight. Like I said, it's a pretty nasty case, and she's already so frail. We'd like to keep her a few days, just to make sure her white count is stabilizing and she's responding to the antibiotics. While she's here we'll do some lung function tests, and keep an eye on her O_2 levels."

Dovie bit her lip, not sure how to broach the thoughts that had been nagging at her for the past hour. "I don't know if she has any kind of insurance. She's from England and I think they do things differently there. Is there going to be a problem with—"

"Right now let's focus on getting her stable, shall we? We'll worry about the bean counters later."

Dovie smiled up at him, relieved and grateful. "Can I see her?"

"Yes, but not for long, and not too much talking on her end. In her condition, talking is like running a marathon, which is why we need her to stay calm and quiet. They should have her in a room in about forty-five minutes. In the meantime, the cafeteria coffee's not bad."

Nearly an hour later, Dovie tiptoed into Dora's semiprivate room, moving past the empty bed near the door to where Dora lay with her face turned toward the window. Her eyes were closed, and her breathing and color had definitely improved since the last time Dovie saw her. Still, she looked so fragile and small in her faded blue hospital gown, a plastic ID bracelet swimming on her stringy wrist.

She was wearing a nasal cannula, and clear IV tubing snaked over the metal railing, connected to an IV pump. Her antibiotics, Dovie supposed, and who knew what else? Somewhere behind her, a cardiac monitor beeped softly. It was a reassuring sound, but a reminder, too, of how close Dora might have come to dying.

"Dovie, girl."

Dovie started at the sound of her name. She hadn't realized Dora was awake, or that she was looking at her with the ghost of a smile on her thin lips.

"Always been a bit of a drama queen. I'm sorry. I didn't mean to scare you."

"Maybe not, but you did. You look better now, though. Do you feel better?"

"I do. They say I have to stay a few days."

"They want to make sure you're responding to the meds."

Dora's lids fluttered closed with a sigh. "More pills."

"Different pills. And an inhaler. Look, I've been thinking. When you get out I don't want you going back to that motel. When they discharge you, you'll come stay with me."

Dora managed another smile, this one tinged with sadness. "Time . . . to go home soon."

"You can't travel until you've recovered, Dora. I'm sure the doctor will tell you that. And if he doesn't, I will. You need to get your strength back before you get on a plane and go flying across the Atlantic. Now, I'm going to go and let you rest, but I'll be back tomorrow. Is there anything I can bring you?"

"Letters. Bring . . . the letters."

"Dora, I'm not sure that's a good idea. You know you get upset when I read them, and you can't afford that right now. The letters can wait."

"No."

"It'll just be a few days, a week at most. Just until you're better."

"You promised. No saving . . . my skin."

Dovie sighed. She'd seen this stubborn streak before, but this time she wasn't winning. "Dora, when I made that promise it was about not sparing your feelings, but this is different. We're talking about your health here, and Dr. Gatlin was very clear about you needing to stay calm, which is why my answer has to be no. No letters until you're out of here and at my place, being properly looked after."

Dora stuck out her chin, as if to protest, but quickly abandoned the effort. Dovie couldn't say if she had given up so easily because she knew she wouldn't win, or because she simply hadn't the breath to argue. Either way, the matter was closed for the time being.

"I know you're upset with me, but it's for your own good. You need to rest. Tomorrow, I'll go to the motel, pack up your things, and settle your bill. As soon as I'm finished I'll be by to visit."

Dora reached for Dovie's hand on the metal bedrail. "You're a good girl," she said so softly Dovie barely caught the words. "A very good . . . girl."

"Well, I don't know about that. I just know you're in no shape to stay by yourself. I have plenty of room, and I'd be a wreck with you halfway across town, and all by yourself. Now promise me you'll rest."

Dora nodded, eyes closed, but breathing easier now.

Dovie lingered a moment, watching the steady rise and fall of her chest beneath the thin hospital blankets. Lord, she was exhausted, and tomorrow wasn't going to be any picnic. She had an early meeting with a new vendor, and then lunch with Theda, which they had set up last week and she had almost forgotten. The subject of Austin was sure to come up, and she knew Theda too well to hope she'd be allowed to sidestep her questions.

Dovie watched as Theda deconstructed her chicken sandwich, extricated the pickles, then put the thing back together. "Why don't you just order it without pickles?"

"Because I like pickles. I just don't want them on my sandwich."

"You could order them on the side."

"Then they forget them altogether and I have to go back up and ask for them. Too much of an ordeal. And speaking of meals . . ."

"Were we?"

"We're about to. But then, you already knew that. So spill. What's the deal with you and Austin Tate, and when were you going to tell me?"

"There's no deal, Theda. And there's nothing to tell. It was a spur-of-the-moment thing. We watched part of the Carolina game together. When he was leaving he asked if I wanted to grab dinner."

"And whose idea was the Porch?"

"Mine. I thought it would be fun. Please don't make more out of it than it was. I promise you there's nothing going on between Austin and me. He's made that abundantly clear."

Dovie regretted the words the minute they were out of her mouth, but by then it was too late. Theda seized the remark with both hands. "And when was this?"

Dovie sighed, still kicking herself. "After dinner the other night. We were talking out on the dock, and all of a sudden he kissed me."

Theda jerked forward in her chair. "He kissed you?"

"That's what I said, yes."

"And how was it?"

"Just like you'd think."

"Dovie, throw a girl a bone. I haven't had a date in three months."

"What do you want me say, Theda? There was a connection. At least I thought there was—until he pushed me away."

"He pushed you away? You?"

Dovie shrugged. "He doesn't want to be my rebound guy. He can't be the guy I deserve. You know, all the stuff a guy says when he's not interested. Only I could swear he was. He'd been sending signals all through dinner. The voice. The eyes. And then he pulls back. I don't get it. It's not that I'm miffed. It was just a kiss, but I can't figure out how I misread the signals."

"Maybe you didn't. Maybe he just doesn't know what he wants. Or doesn't want to want what he wants."

Dovie put down her sandwich and stared across the table. "I have absolutely no idea what you just said."

Theda sighed, that overly patient sigh tutors use with slow students. "Sometimes guys get weird when they start feeling things *above* the waist. Maybe he's just freaking out a little because he realizes he's starting to have feelings for you. Real ones."

Dovie traced a finger through the ring of sweat at the base of her glass. "He said he'd just end up wrecking me, and probably himself, too—whatever that means."

A crease suddenly marred Theda's brow. "Did you say wreck?"

"That's what he said. I'm sure it's just a line he uses when he's ready to make an exit."

"No. There was something . . . I can't remember now . . . something about him in the paper a long time ago. Something to do with a car crash. Do you remember it?"

"No, but I've never gone in for the gossip stuff. I mean who cares who wears what or who's dating whom? Most of us have real lives."

"I'm not talking about the *Wave* or *City News*. I'm talking about the real paper. I think it was even on the news. I just can't remember what it was all about now. It was a big deal for about a week, and then it all just went away. I can't pull it out of my head—I hardly ever watch the news—I just know it had to do with your Mr. Tate."

"Sorry, can't help you. And he's not my Mr. Tate."

"So you say. But don't be surprised if he shows up again, once he gets his head straight."

"He'll be wasting his time if he does."

A sly smile tugged at Theda's mouth. "I thought you said you weren't miffed."

Dovie lifted her tea glass, trying to look nonchalant as she sipped. "I'm not. I'm just taking his advice and steering clear. I can't afford to get *wrecked* again, Theda, and something tells me this time would be worse. Besides, I've got enough on my plate with work and Dora."

"Lord, are you still messing with that woman? I thought she was going back to England, or wherever she came from."

"She's in the hospital with pneumonia. I got a call yesterday from the woman who works at the front desk of her motel. When I got there she was so bad I called the ambulance. They say she's going to be okay, but she's not in good shape at all at the moment."

"That's too bad."

"I'm bringing her home with me when they discharge her."

Theda was about to sample one of her pickles but changed her mind. "Dovie, have you thought this through?"

"Of course I have. I can't let her go back to that motel. She's all alone here. And we're . . . sort of in the middle of something."

Theda rolled her eyes. "Lord, give me strength. It's the letters, isn't it? You're still playing detective, trying to find out what happened to her daughter. Dovie, this has been going on way too long."

"I know, but I promised. She deserves to know what happened."

"Have you told Austin about this? Because I'm pretty sure he'd be pissed if he knew. The last thing he wants is anything surfacing about his father and that girl."

"And it won't, Theda. It's not like we're going to the papers with whatever we find. She just wants to know how Alice died, and if she ever found her child."

"And what if you find out something terrible? Are you going to just keep it to yourself?"

"I promised I wouldn't keep anything from her. And technically those letters belong to her, not me. As for Austin, there's no need for any of this to touch him—or his mother."

Theda checked her watch and pushed away her half-eaten

sandwich. She cast a sideways look at Dovie as she stood. "I hope you're right, 'cause I sure don't want to think about what could happen if this all blows up in your face."

Dovie dragged her tote up onto her shoulder and pushed to her feet. She didn't want to think about it, either.

Dovie checked her watch, closed her planner, and made a beeline for the parking lot. She'd gotten a call from Dora's doctor an hour before. Apparently, she was responding nicely to the new meds but was still refusing to eat, grousing about the atrocities of hospital food and sending her trays back untouched. Could she possibly come by and explain to Dora that she couldn't go home until they knew her appetite had returned? She had promised to come by straight from work.

Dora's impending discharge was definitely good news, but it meant Dovie needed to start thinking about getting the spare room ready for company, which would be no small task, since the bed was currently buried beneath boxes that had been there since she moved in more than a year ago. Also on her mind was how to handle the letters going forward. That Dora would want to get back to them immediately was certain. Dovie just wasn't sure it was a good idea to subject her to that kind of emotional stress. What if one of the letters contained something shocking, something too terrible to bear? She could relapse, or worse. Perhaps if she read ahead, and knew what to expect, she would at least be forewarned. And forewarned was forearmed.

thirty-nine

9 East Battery Street
Charleston, South Carolina
July 5, 1963

My darling little one,

I have written to you before of my dislike for Harley Tate, but I have new reasons for disliking the man. Reasons that have nothing to do with his son, and everything to do with the way his eyes seem to find me whenever his wife steps out of the room, like he's eyeing a table spread with puddings and wondering where to dip his spoon first.

And then last Saturday afternoon, while Gemma was out to one of her charity teas, Mr. Tate came into the nursery. I had just put Austin down for a nap and was startled to see him there. He never comes to the nursery.

"Hello, Alice," he said without warmth.

"Mr. Tate. I just put Austin down, but I'm sure—"

"I didn't come to see Austin." He took a step closer, and then another. "I thought we might have a little talk, you and I. We never have, you know . . . talked."

Something about the way he was looking at me made my throat go dry. "We'll wake Austin," I said, glancing anxiously at the crib.

His eyes never left my face. "You're a lucky girl, Alice. A very lucky girl."

I looked down at my feet. "Yes, sir."

"My wife is very happy with you. She says you're wonderful with Austin."

"He's a wonderful boy, so smart and happy, and he's—"

"She told me about you," he said, cutting me off. "About your little . . . predicament." His tongue clucked in disapproval, but there was something like amusement in his eyes, too, like a cat toying with a mouse. "Not many families in our circle would have hired a girl like you. Damaged goods, they'd say. You know that, don't you?"

I nodded, feeling sick. Where would I go if he dismissed me?

"A smart girl would be grateful for the opportunity to work in one of the finest households in Charleston, and know that she was employed only by the good graces of the head of that household."

I nodded again, because I saw that he expected me to.

"Are you . . . grateful, Alice?"

Something in the tone of his voice, the way it had dropped several notches, made me go cold inside. I stood there, staring at the floor, bracing myself for whatever came next.

"You do understand that if I wanted to, I could turn you out right now, don't you? No matter what my wife says?"

I was startled when I looked up, to find him standing right in front of me, so close I could smell cigarettes and liquor on his breath, mingled with the oily scent of his hair tonic. I took a step back, and then another, until I found myself pinned against Austin's crib.

"You're a pretty thing, aren't you?" he said, brushing my cheek with the backs of his fingers. "And so young." He traced his thumb over my lower lip, then down the side of my throat, sticky where it touched my skin. "I'll bet that mouth of yours is just as sweet as a fresh-picked peach."

I was too stunned to reply, sickened by his touch, and by the realization that for all his fine clothes and lofty reputation, Harley Tate was no different from the greasy little janitor from Sacred Heart, except that instead of shoving me into the backseat of his car, he was prepared to seduce me in his son's nursery.

My thoughts flew to Gemma. Worshipful, dutiful Gemma, always ready with an excuse for her husband. But even she couldn't excuse this kind of behavior. And then I remembered the whispers of her so-called friends, about his taste for sweets, and realized she had probably been excusing it for a very long time now. Suddenly, the thought of her walking in on us, of what would she would think if she saw us at that moment—me staring up at her husband, him with his hands hovering near the opening of my blouse—filled me with a mixture of fury and panic.

I wanted to rail at him, to tell him exactly what I thought of his bullying and his unwanted attentions. And yet I knew saying those things would have me out on the street before I could pack my things. He'd said it himself; he could fire me anytime he wanted. And I could see in his face that he would do it if I didn't give him what he was after.

I was still trying to find something to say, some way to divert his attention, when my throat suddenly constricted and I reached for the crib railing, bracing for the coughing fit I knew was coming. They come like that sometimes, when the air is particularly damp or I've tired myself out, fits like I used to have at Blackhurst. They told me I might suffer with them on and off, but this was a bad one—so bad it nearly bent me in half. When I finally got my breath back, Mr. Tate was staring at me with something like annoyance.

"What in God's name is wrong with you, girl?"

I stared at him, startled by the naked disdain in his eyes, the same disdain I had seen in Ellie Gleason's eyes the day I bumped into her outside the druggist's back in Sennen Cove, and suddenly I thought of a way to ward off Harley Tate's attentions without actually refusing them.

"I'm so sorry, I've . . ." My words trailed off as the coughing resumed—this time on purpose. "I've had this cough . . . for about a year now. A lot of the girls had it where I was. From the damp, the doctors said. Some died, but I came through. Just the cough left over. They said it's almost never catching after this long. I thought your wife might have told you."

It took all I had not to smile when he took a sharp step back and pulled a handkerchief from his back pocket to cover his nose and mouth. I knew full well there was no risk of it being catching, but I saw no reason to volunteer that to Harley Tate. Let him think what he wanted, so long as he kept his distance. I suppose it was rather naïve of me to think the matter was closed.

The next day I was called to Gemma's study. She rose, smiling, as I entered. I was surprised to see that she wasn't alone, that a somber man with a heavy black satchel was seated in the wingback next to hers. His eyes lingered as I stood in the doorway, appraising me in a way that made me uncomfortable, though not in the way Harley Tate's gaze had the day before.

"Alice," Gemma said in a too-bright voice. "This is Dr. Ponder. He's been our family physician for years, and he's come by today to make sure you're well."

I digested the words with a sickening lurch. It was her husband's doing, of course, a way to be rid of me without raising a lot of questions. I had been so clever, warding off his advances without actually rebuffing them. What I hadn't stopped to consider was that the very illness I had used to fend off Harley Tate could also be used against me—as a threat to the health of his son.

"My husband is . . . concerned about your cough," she explained, not quite meeting my eyes. "He wants to be sure it isn't anything . . . serious."

I nodded. She meant contagious but couldn't bring herself to say the word.

"I told him we had discussed it when you first came, and that there was no reason for concern, but he thought it would be a good idea for Dr. Ponder to examine you. It's just a precaution, honey. You understand that, don't you?"

"Yes, of course."

We went to my room then, Dr. Ponder and I, and he performed his examination. He looked down my throat and made me take deep breaths while he listened to my chest, front and back. When he finished, he snapped the latches of his black leather bag closed and with a kind smile began with a list of questions. He asked about the first time I was sick, about how long I had been ill, what kind of pills they had given me, and if I remembered what they said I had. I told him what the sisters told me. That my lungs had been badly scarred by the consumption, and I might always have a cough—that in time it might even worsen—but that I was past the infectious stage, which was why I had been allowed to go home.

And then he scolded me, asking what had possessed me to come all the way to the United States when I had to have known I wasn't fully recovered. That's when I told him about you, little one, how I had come here to find you and wouldn't stop until I did—things I never even told Gemma. Enough time had passed that I no longer felt the need to keep my promise a secret, and it felt strangely good to say it out loud. I only prayed Dr. Ponder was as kind as he looked, and hadn't just come to justify Harley Tate's plans to give me the sack.

Sometime later, Gemma came to the nursery. She closed the door behind her and stood watching me as I tugged a clean shirt over her son's head, then smoothed down his dark curls. I held my breath, waiting.

After a moment, she cleared her throat, once, twice, but her voice still seemed a little rusty when she spoke. "Dr. Ponder says there's nothing to worry about. Based on his examination, and the information you gave him, he agrees with the diagnosis of tuberculosis but says any danger of it being contagious has long since passed."

I bobbed my head, so relieved I couldn't speak. If Harley Tate was going to fire me he'd have to use something other than my health as an excuse. And yet as I looked at Gemma, I sensed there was more.

Until that moment, I hadn't noticed that her eyes were puffy, her cheeks splotched red and white. "He told me . . . about the place you were sent to, Alice, and the terrible things that happen to the girls there. He also told me you came to the U.S. to look for your baby." There were tears in her eyes, now, making them look even larger than usual. "Oh, Alice, why didn't you tell me any of this when you first came? I didn't know. I just . . . I had no idea."

I looked away, not wanting to remember that first day and the wild thoughts that had run through my mind. "I probably should have told you, but I was afraid I might be sent back, and then I'd never find him—or her. It's crazy, I know, like looking for a needle in a haystack. But it's what keeps me going. I have to keep on believing and keep on trying, or I don't think I could get out of bed every morning."

"You're going to keep searching, then?"

"Forever, if I have to."

"And what will you do if you . . . if you find him?"

"Get him back," I said without pausing to think. "Or her. I'll spend my last cent, take out ads in the paper, plead with every adoption agency I can find, hire a private detective—whatever I have to do. Because I made a promise. I just don't have the money to do most of it yet. Lawyers and detectives want money. So for now, it's just letters. I've been writing to different adoption agencies, asking if they'll help. So far, none of them have."

Gemma drew a ragged breath, shaking her head. "I'm sorry, Alice," she whispered, her voice hoarse, and close to breaking. "So very, very sorry."

"Please don't be. It had nothing to do with you, and you've been so kind, taking me in the way you did. I don't know what I would have done. And now you and Austin have become my family."

Gemma brightened as she blinked away her tears. "We have, haven't we? We have become family—the three of us. We'll share him, then, and raise him together." She paused when her voice began to fracture. "My son will be your son, too."

I stood there with an aching throat, stunned by her generosity. She had waited so long to become a mother, had given up hope of ever having a child of her own, and there she stood, offering to share her little boy with me. Even now, as I write this, I cannot fathom her doing such a kindness for a woman she didn't know a year ago. Still, I'll take her up on her offer to share her little boy, because I find I cannot say no, and because it may help to fill the hole in my heart—until I can fill it with you, my angel.

All my love,
Mam

forty

Dovie scanned the guest room with a critical eye. She'd spent the morning clearing out boxes of old junk, putting fresh sheets on the bed, making space in the closet and dresser, and was finally satisfied that she was ready for Dora's arrival tomorrow. Jack had surprised her by agreeing to let her work from home next week, which would allow her to be home with Dora until she felt more comfortable about her condition. She'd be available by phone if she was needed for any last-minute catastrophes, and had promised to run through her checklist to confirm final details with all the vendors.

One thing was certain, it was going to be quite a week. With Dora coming to stay, and the gala just six days away, her plate was full, and then some. And to top it off, she still needed to find a dress. Which reminded her, she was supposed to be picking her mother and sister up in an hour.

Just the thought made her tired. It wasn't that she didn't want to spend time with them. It was that she was exhausted, and the last thing she wanted to do was to spend the day dodging questions about her love life. At least Robin would be there to run interference. If there was one thing her socially adept sister knew how to do—aside from having babies—it was handle their mother. She could do this. She could be pleasant, find a dress, have some lunch. The whole thing would be over in a couple of hours. She hoped.

An hour later, she pulled into her mother's driveway and honked the horn. She felt an unaccustomed pang of nostalgia for her childhood home as she sat there waiting. The porch was decked out for fall, a wreath of sunflowers and autumn leaves hanging on the front door, porch steps brimming with colorful gourds and potted yellow mums—her mother's handiwork.

Suddenly, she was reminded of her mother decorating the house the day after their father left, arranging garlands on the mantel, fussing to get the ribbon just right. Dovie had wanted to slap her. How on earth could she worry about garlands when her husband had just walked out on her? It wasn't until Dovie realized her mother was quietly weeping that she understood. It was about keeping up appearances—for the neighbors, and the children, and perhaps even for herself—because that was what Southern women did. They took their blows, squared their shoulders, and simply got on with life. Not everyone would understand that kind of strength, the kind that bent but never broke. Dovie barely understood it herself. But she admired it.

She was surprised to find herself blinking away tears as Rowena Larkin came down the porch steps and made her way down the drive. She looked lovely in a cranberry-colored pantsuit and matching scarf. On impulse, Dovie leaned over and dropped a kiss on her cheek as she slid into the passenger seat.

"Well, now," Rowena said, surprised. "What was that all about?"

"I'm just glad to see you, that's all. You look wonderful, by the way."

"Thanks. It's last year's, but I've never worn it."

Dovie watched her fumbling to fasten her seat belt, a crease between her neatly penciled brows. "Is everything all right, Mother? You seem a little flustered."

"It's your sister. She isn't going to be able to join us today. Her ankles startled swelling yesterday, and her blood pressure's up. The doctor's put her on bed rest."

"It's nothing serious, though, right? I mean, they'd send her to the hospital if it was."

"She says it's just a precaution, but who knows? I offered to go over and stay with her, but she says she's fine and that we should go shopping."

Dovie smiled. "That sounds like Robin. God forbid we put off shopping. So, where should we start?"

"For an evening gown? Christian Michi, I think. And if we don't have any luck there, we'll hit Evaline's. If all else fails there's Saks."

"I'm going to wear this dress once, Mother. I don't need to drop a month's salary on it. We're talking about a fund-raiser for work, not the Oscars."

"I distinctly remember you telling me this was the most important project you've ever overseen, and that every detail needed to be perfect."

"It is. And they do."

"Well, then, you need to be perfect, too. And since this little hoedown is next week, I suggest we start with the shopping. When we're through, I'll take you to Magnolia's for lunch."

Two hours later, they had settled on a compromise, a simple sheath of lustrous teal taffeta with strappy silver heels and a braided rope of iridescent glass beads. As they locked the car and walked the half block to Magnolia's, Rowena chattered about earrings and updos. Dovie hated to admit it, but it was turning out to be a pretty good day.

Magnolia's was buzzing with lunchtime patrons, but they managed to get a table near the window. They each ordered a glass of chardonnay and the fried green tomatoes to share while they looked over the menu.

After a quick glance at the specials, Rowena set her menu aside and spread her napkin in her lap. "According to the papers, this shindig of yours is going to be a pretty big deal. But then, with Gemma Tate involved, you can count on there being plenty of press coverage. Such a lovely woman, always so elegant and tasteful. But that son of hers, she's going to have her hands full keeping his face out of the papers. Quite a playboy, that one."

Dovie closed her menu and reached for her wineglass. "Austin's not who people think he is. In fact, the money the Tates gave us for the new wing was his idea."

Rowena's brows shot up. "Austin, is it? We're on a first-name basis, then?"

Dovie resisted the urge to roll her eyes. "He's the point person for the gala. We see each other from time to time."

"See each other?"

And . . . here we go.

Dovie smothered a sigh. "In meetings, Mother. Planning meetings. Mrs. Tate hasn't been well, and someone had to approve the details. That someone was Austin."

"How's *that* been going?"

Dovie could hear the skepticism in her mother's voice, and felt an inexplicable need to defend Austin. "It's been going well, actually. The media harps on the playboy angle, but there's a lot more to him once you scratch the surface."

Her mother set down her wineglass, dabbing her lips with her napkin. "And have you . . . scratched the surface?"

"Mother."

"You brought it up, sweetheart. I'm just asking the follow-up."

"It isn't like that."

"What's it like, then? Because the last time I saw your face that color, Brian Marshall had just asked you to the prom."

"Brian Marshall? Good Lord, have you memorized the names of all my boyfriends?"

Her mother's smile faded. "There haven't been that many, Dovie."

"What's your point? As if I don't already know."

"Only that the clock is ticking, and neither of us is getting any younger."

"Robin's about to spit out grandchild number three. You don't need any more."

"I wasn't talking about babies, Dovie. I was talking about years passing and you getting more and more comfortable being alone, about letting life pass you by until it's too late to do anything about it. Honey, I just want you to be happy."

"And you think Austin Tate is the answer to my problems?"

Rowena seemed to consider that but after a moment shook her head. "No, I suppose not. Not with his track record and that mess a few years back."

Dovie's fork stopped short on the way to her mouth. "What mess?"

"You know. The accident."

"No, I don't know, but Theda mentioned something the other day about Austin's name being in all the papers."

"Well, of course. Don't you remember? There was a terrible accident, and his wife was killed. I guess it's been about ten years ago now."

Dovie set her fork down in what felt like slow motion. "Did you say . . . wife?"

"Her name was Monica or Monique, or something. It was pretty big news. How do you not remember?"

"You know I don't pay attention to that stuff. I didn't even know he was married."

"Well, I can see you missing that part. Apparently, they eloped. No one seemed to know much about the girl. Anyway, she was driving out on Highway 17 one night and wrapped her car around a telephone pole.

It was raining like anything, but I think she must have been speeding, too, because from the pictures there wasn't much left of that car."

Dovie felt a strange numbness creeping up her legs, and a pain that started somewhere just south of her breastbone. He'd never mentioned a wife, let alone a fatal accident. But then maybe he assumed, like everyone else, that she'd seen it in the papers. She could understand him not wanting to talk about it. "He must have been devastated. Was he in the car when it happened?"

"From what I understand, she was alone. And I'm sure he was devastated. They'd been married less than two years when it happened. Maybe that's why he's the way he is. With women, I mean. Always dashing around town with a new one on his arm. Maybe he's compensating for a broken heart."

"I have no idea," Dovie said, careful to keep her voice even. "He's never mentioned it."

But maybe he had. *"I hurt people—maybe without meaning to."* Was that what he meant when he said he would wreck her? Had he been thinking of his wife's death and somehow been blaming himself? The thought made her head spin. She had been mystified by his insight about her guilt over William's death. Now, suddenly, she was beginning to understand. It wasn't just psychobabble, or a lucky guess. He had lived it.

She managed to fake her way through the remainder of lunch, nodding at her mother's anecdotes, even managing a few syllables between bites of salad, but all she could think of was getting home to her laptop and finding out more about the accident that had killed Austin's wife.

As it turned out, there wasn't much to find. A brief marriage announcement in the *Post and Courier* gave the bride's name as Monica Lynne Mullins of Indianapolis, Indiana, and reported that the marriage had taken place at an undisclosed location in Palm Beach, on July 12, 1993. News about the accident was equally vague.

> **November 1, 1994. Charleston, S.C.**—Monica Tate, wife of Austin Tate, daughter-in-law of Mr. and Mrs. Harley Tate, died last night when the car she was driving spun out of control and struck a telephone pole. The investigation into the accident is still ongoing, but it is suspected that Mrs. Tate's car was traveling at a high rate of speed when the crash occurred. Weather is also thought to have played a part in the accident. The victim's remains are to be cremated and flown back to Indianapolis, in accordance with the family's wishes. A memorial service is scheduled next week for friends and family at First Congregational Church.

Dovie shut down the laptop and rubbed her eyes. The few articles she had managed to find had been almost identical, but then she supposed the facts were the facts. It did seem strange that she hadn't been able to find much of any follow-up to the initial story. There had been a flurry of coverage in the days following the accident, and then . . . nothing. Nothing more about the investigation, or the coroner's findings, not even a photo taken at Monica Tate's memorial, which felt odd in and of itself, since the Tates could scarcely eat a meal in public without it appearing in print somewhere.

She scanned the article again. *Cremated and flown back to Indianapolis in accordance with the family's wishes.* That explained why there was no grave for Monica in the Tate family plot. What she didn't understand was why, with all the times her grief for William had been a part of their conversation, Austin had never once let on that he'd experienced a tragedy of his own.

In the kitchen, she peered into the refrigerator, trying to decide if she was hungry, or just restless. Probably a little of both, since she'd left most of her lunch on her plate. She was reaching for a container of leftover kung pao when she saw the flashing blue light on the phone. Her mother's voice filled the kitchen as soon as she hit the button.

"It's me, sweetheart. I guess you're not home yet. I just wanted to thank you for a lovely day. Oh, and I forgot to ask if you ever lined up a date for the gala. Anyway, that's it. Have a good night."

Dovie deleted the message but stood staring at the phone. The absolute last thing she needed right now—or wanted—was a date. But what if her mother was right? She knew Jack was bringing his wife. Would she be the only one going stag? A wallflower, as her mother had so succinctly put it?

Abandoning the kung pao, she wandered back to her bedroom. The black vinyl garment bag hung from the closet door, the name *Evaline's* emblazoned across the front in florid gold script. She tugged at the zipper, running her hands along folds of shimmery teal taffeta. She couldn't remember the last time she'd worn anything so feminine—or the last time she'd been out on a date. Did she even know any single men anymore?

Against her will, and certainly against her better judgment, her eyes slid to the cell phone on her dresser. It didn't have to be a big deal or anything. He had to be there. She had to be there. Where was the harm in going together? She'd just pick up the phone and see what he was up to, and if there happened to be an opening in the conversation, she would suggest they attend the gala together. As companions, of course. Business companions. Platonic business companions.

Her fingers felt stiff and clumsy as she pulled up his number and hit DIAL. She closed her eyes when it started to ring, scrambling for something to say. She must be out of her mind. He'd already given her the brush-off once. Why ask for it again?

Hang up! Hang up before it's too—

"Dovie? What's up?"

Damn. Too late.

"Not much," she said, trying to match his tone. He sounded so casual, as if the kiss had never happened, though she supposed he'd had plenty of practice shaking off unwanted females. "I was just . . ." *You were just what? What? Say something!* "I just wanted to know how your mother liked the painting."

"She loved it. In fact, the first thing she asked was if you picked it out. So, if she happens to walk up to you at the gala and thank you, that's what it's all about."

Dovie squeezed her eyes tight, the way she used to when teetering at the edge of the high dive. "So, about the gala . . ."

"You know, I'm actually looking forward to it. Black tie isn't usually my style, but it looks like it's going to be a great night. I think my mother's really going to enjoy herself."

"Well, I was thinking, since we both have to be there, I was wondering if you maybe wanted to go together."

There was a sudden burst of noise, of voices and laughter, and what sounded like glasses clinking in the background. She could hear his hand covering the phone. "I'm sorry, Dovie. I couldn't hear. What did you say?"

God, was he really going to make her say it again? "I said maybe we should go to the gala together, since we're both going anyway."

"Oh, wow. I'm sorry. I'm sort of . . . spoken for."

Dovie froze for a moment, wondering how on earth she hadn't expected this. Of course he was spoken for. "Oh, sure. Hey. No worries. It was just a thought. I really just wanted to know how the painting went over. I'm glad she loved it."

"Dovie, I—"

"Have a good night," she blurted in a too-cheerful voice, before ending the call. She didn't need to hear the rest. She got it. It might have taken her two kicks in the teeth instead of one, but she got it. Flirting might be Austin Tate's favorite pastime, but when it came to anything serious, he wasn't interested.

Of course he'd already lined up a date. And there she'd be in her shimmering teal taffeta—on no one's arm. *God.* Maybe it was time to give Brian Marshall a call and ask if his wife would consider letting him escort her, because at the moment she couldn't think of anything she dreaded more than looking like a wallflower while Austin escorted one of his champagne blondes around under her nose.

On impulse, she picked up the phone again, scrolling through her contacts until she found the number she was looking for. Before she had time to change her mind, she dialed.

"Bloom," came the elegant voice after two rings. "How can I help you?"

"Kristopher, it's Dovie. I was wondering . . . are you still up for that drink?"

forty-one

It had been three days since Dora was discharged from the hospital. Three straight days of blowing rain that already had half of Charleston's downtown streets underwater, which was why Dovie now found herself addicted to the Weather Channel. She stared at the radar, willing the green blob stalled over the South Carolina coast to shift. North, south, she didn't care. It just needed to move out in time for Friday night, or Charleston's wealthiest art patrons might just decide to stay home.

"You do know listening to them say the same thing over and over isn't going to make the rain stop?" Dora pointed out as she spooned up more of her tomato soup. "Why don't you do something to take your mind off it—like eat your lunch?"

Dovie looked down at the tray on her lap, her grilled cheese sandwich barely nibbled, her soup growing cold. "I just keep thinking about how much work I put into this event, and now it might all be for nothing if this silly storm doesn't move out."

"Your boss can't hold you responsible for the weather, Dovie."

"It isn't that," she said, peeling the crust off one side of her sandwich and folding a bit of it into her mouth. "It's about proving he didn't make a mistake when he recommended me for the promotion. I was so proud of how I pulled everything together, and on such short notice, too. And now we might have to cancel if it keeps on like this. We can always reschedule, but everything's already booked through the holidays, so it would have to be after the first of the year. And by then people are tired of parties, so response could be low."

"Maybe you could read something," Dora suggested, peering over the glasses Dovie had finally retrieved from lost and found. "Might take your mind off your troubles."

Dovie eyed Dora shrewdly, knowing exactly what she was hinting at. "And what about your troubles? You know what happened the last time I read you one of those letters. You wound up in the hospital the next day. Maybe we should wait until you're stronger."

Dora's eyes flashed with impatience, a sure sign that she was feeling better. "Ending up in the hospital had to do with my lungs, not what was in those letters. Now, you promised you'd read me some more when I was out of the hospital. Here I am."

Dovie sighed. "One," she said, holding up a single finger. "I'll read you one."

forty-two

9 East Battery Street
Charleston, South Carolina
July 18, 1967

Dearest one,

I almost wrote little one, but caught myself in time. I keep forgetting you're not a baby anymore. It's hard, sometimes, to remember that for you time hasn't stopped, that somewhere in the world you're growing up without me. I can't blame you for that. It's what children do. But I can blame myself—and do.

My search so far has been a futile one. I've written letter after letter, contacted every agency I could find, and I'm still no closer to finding you. Because none of the agencies will help me. There are rules, it seems, put in place to protect adoptive parents. But where are my rights? They say I have none, that I gave them up when I gave you up, that all ties between us have been irrevocably severed. But how can that be? The bond between mother and child—the bond of flesh and blood—cannot be severed with ink.

I'm sorry. I didn't mean for this letter to be a sad one. It's only that Austin has just turned five, and it's made me realize how quickly the time is passing—and how badly I miss you. We had a party for him on Saturday, and what a party it was. The house was full of cake and noise—and far too many overdressed women. Anyone would have thought it was the social event of the season, rather than a child's birthday party.

I was put in charge of the children's games while Gemma mingled with the other mothers, most of them women from her club, all powdered and shellacked in their hats and little white gloves. I know most of them by name, but little more. I'm always careful to remember my place when they're here, to not appear too familiar. It would be awkward for Gemma to have to explain our friendship. The women in her circle would never understand her befriending her son's nanny—black or white.

For the most part, I'm invisible to these women, but there are times when I feel their gazes lingering on me, curious and critical, because in their eyes I'm not what I should be. But there's one in particular whose disapproval I feel most—Mrs. Melanie Sue Bowles, who actually hails from Baltimore, though she hates anyone to remind her of it. It seems there's a bit of confusion here in Charleston about whether Maryland is truly part of the South. It's her eyes that always linger the longest, whose little pug nose always seems to lift just a little when I catch her looking.

She was at the party yesterday, with her baby-doll daughter, huddled in the corner of the dining room with the rest of her snooty little hens, whispering and sending me one of her glares, when I heard her say in her carefully cultivated Charleston drawl that she wondered if Gemma ever worried about Austin getting too close to his nanny.

"I mean, it must be awfully confusing for the boy, her being white and all. She wouldn't have to worry about that if she'd hired a colored woman, like I told her to—or about that little English tart forgetting her place, either." She paused to sip her lemonade, giving me another

long look. "Yes, sir, that one will be trouble before it's over, mark my words. Imagine, sticking something like that under Harley Tate's nose. Poor thing. Half of Charleston's talking about it, for heaven's sake. Either she's blind, or she's a fool."

Hate is an ugly word, one Mam never allowed me to use, but at that moment I hated Melanie Sue Bowles. Yes, and the women who nodded knowingly as she continued to spew her well-meaning venom. I hated them, too. I turned away, my cheeks prickling with anger and shame. Not for my sake, but for Gemma, who had overheard the remark—as she was almost certainly meant to.

Her gaze found mine over the perfectly coiffed head of Joanne Spivey, an apology in her soft brown eyes. I wanted to tell her she had nothing to apologize for, that the slight had been intended for her and not me. For women like that, there is no sport in hurting me, someone who's little more than a maid in their eyes. But Gemma Tate, the beautiful and elegant wife of one of Charleston's most prominent men, must have seemed a worthy target indeed.

Gemma must have read my thoughts, and been afraid I might act on them. She forced a smile and gave her head a little shake before turning to speak with another of her guests. She's rather good at putting on a brave face, but I could see that the words had cut more deeply than she cared to admit, even to me. And as I thought of the day Harley Tate had come into the nursery and put his hands on me, I couldn't help wondering if the remark had cut Gemma so deeply because she didn't believe her husband capable of what they were insinuating, or because in her heart she knew he was.

I've never let on about that day, and I never will. I'd sooner cut out my tongue than hurt my friend. And no matter what she pretends, it would hurt her. She loves him, though I can't fathom why. Yesterday, at breakfast, he announced without blinking that it was time for Austin to go away to school. And not just any school. A school in Virginia where the boys live in dorms and only come home on holidays. Austin pushed out a quivering lip, his face screwed up and splotchy red as he stared down the table at his father. There was a moment of silence as he gathered a deep, shuddering breath, followed by a long plaintive wail that rang like a siren off the papered walls of the dining room. Poor Gemma looked as if she'd just had her heart cut out, her eyes wide as saucers, her cheeks the color of chalk. And yet she said nothing. She was used to holding her tongue when her husband made up his mind. But I couldn't hold my tongue.

I know a little something about the ache of loving a child from a distance, of having the thing you love most torn away from you, and would not wish it on an enemy, let alone a friend. I'd be lying if I said I hadn't been thinking just a little of myself, too, when I told him that sending his son so far away would be barbaric. Not because I would no longer be needed, but because I have come to love Austin almost as my own. He will never be a substitute for you, my angel, but he has been a kind of consolation, a way to fill the empty places the sisters left when they took you. To lose him now would be like losing you all over again, and I don't think I could bear it.

It was a terrible scene. So terrible poor Austin was sent to his room without his breakfast. I believe Harley would have strangled me on the spot if Landy hadn't been close by. Instead, he settled for a look so black I found myself backing away before he finally stormed from the breakfast room and out of the house. I could see the relief on Gemma's face when the door slammed behind him. I was relieved, too, especially when a week passed and I still hadn't been sacked. Gemma says she smoothed it over, but wouldn't tell me what that meant. She says I don't ever need to worry about being let go, that as long as she's alive I'll have a home with her. But part of me is still uneasy. Because I know I've made an enemy of Harley Tate. And because I know if he ever gets the chance to pay me back he will.

I still don't know what I've done to deserve Gemma's kindness, but I'm more grateful than I can say. There's only one place I've called home since leaving England, and that's here, with Austin and Gemma. Where would I go if I were suddenly slung out? Certainly not back to Sennen Cove. Perhaps I'm being hard, even cruel, but there's nothing left for me there. Nothing, and no one.

There, I've done it again, gone and gotten all gloomy. I don't mean to. I just seem to be so tired these days, perhaps because my cough has returned, especially at night when I try to sleep. I've done my best to hide it from Gemma. She has enough to manage without worrying about me. So long as I can keep up with my duties, there's no need to alarm her. I will close for now, and rest a little, if I can, and promise to be sunnier the next time I pick up my pen. Sweet dreams, my darling, wherever you are.

All my love,
Mam

forty-three

PERFORMING ARTS CENTER
CHARLESTON, SOUTH CAROLINA
NOVEMBER 8, 2005

Dovie pirouetted at the foot of the bed, giving Dora the full show, complete with strappy heels and a sleek little silver clutch. She couldn't remember when she'd taken so much time getting dressed. She had barely recognized herself when she looked in the mirror.

"You look like a princess," Dora said, smiling. "All you need is a tiara."

"I feel like I'm playing dress-up. Do you think the rhinestone clips are too much?" She turned to peer in the mirror again, fiddling with the clips holding her updo in place.

"I do not. But that jacket is. You're much too lovely to hide yourself under that frumpy thing."

"It isn't frumpy," Dovie threw over her shoulder. "It practical. This isn't the prom, it's a work thing." On impulse, she undid the black velvet cape, letting it slide off her shoulders.

"Better," Dora pronounced, startling her. "You shouldn't hide your light under a bushel."

"It wasn't my light I was trying to hide," Dovie said dubiously, scowling at the creamy swell of flesh above the neckline of her gown. "Are you sure you're going to be all right by yourself? I hate leaving you. What if you have a relapse while I'm gone?"

"That's hardly likely, is it? You've been hovering for four days and I've been fine. Besides, I'm not planning anything more strenuous than a little telly."

"Promise me you'll call if you need anything. I left my number by the phone."

Dora sighed. "Yes, you did. Along with the number for the doctor, the hospital, the fire department, my pills, my inhaler, a glass of water, a box of tissues, a pot of tea, and a brand-new package of digestives."

Dovie did her best to look menacing. "Promise you'll call."

"All right. If you promise to stop fussing and have a good time. How soon before your young man comes for you?"

"He isn't my young man, Dora. Just a friend. And he should be here any minute."

Dovie pulled back the bedroom curtain, breathing another sigh of relief that the storm had moved out in time. The rain had let up sometime yesterday, leaving a watery sunshine in its wake. A bit later than she would have liked, perhaps, but it would do. As long as they wouldn't need an ark to ferry people back and forth to their cars.

She was about to let go of the curtain when Kristopher's rental appeared in the drive. "Here he is now," she told Dora, making another hasty scan of the room, checking for anything she might have forgotten. "So you're going to call."

"No, because I won't need to. Go have a good time, for heaven's sake. And forget about me. And stop fussing with that silly cloak."

Dovie felt like a princess as she entered the ballroom on Kristopher's arm. She could feel heads turning as they crossed the room, and she couldn't blame a single one of them. In his black-tie attire, Kristopher looked as if he had stepped right out of *GQ*—tall, dark, and handsome, and not a hair or crease out of place. She scanned the room, wondering if any of those heads belonged to Austin. As far as she could see, none of them did.

She felt Kristopher's eyes follow hers and then return to her face. "Is he here?"

"He?"

"Whoever you're looking for. I'm assuming it's a he?"

Dovie felt her cheeks go pink. "Is it that obvious?"

"Don't ever play poker in Vegas."

"God, *please* don't ask questions."

"You have my word. You look stunning, by the way. Whoever he is, he's either remarkably lucky or remarkably stupid."

"Let's go with *stupid*."

He threw her a wink, followed by a devastating smile. "For the record, I think so, too."

They spent the next half hour circulating, sipping champagne, and chatting with guests. Now and then, she posed for photos with prominent guests, and was silently grateful that her mother had insisted she buy a dress for the occasion. She felt herself relax as she looked around the reception area. Turnout was looking good, and Jack was clearly pleased, but she could tell by the way his eyes kept sweeping the room that he'd feel better when the guest of honor finally appeared. As it turned out, they didn't have long to wait.

Dovie followed Jack's gaze to the main doors where a small commotion had arisen, and the crowd had begun to part. She stiffened when Austin's dark head popped into view. He was dressed to perfection, smiling and nodding like a movie star on the red carpet. It was all Dovie could do not to stand on tiptoe to catch a glimpse of whatever lemony confection he had chosen for the night's festivities. Instead, she feigned indifference, continuing to nibble her crab puff and sip her champagne.

There was a flash of red satin as the crowd parted, the cool glint of gold and diamonds on a slender wrist, a heavily jeweled hand tucked into the crook of his arm, and then, finally, a perfectly coiffed brunette head.

Gemma.

Spoken for. Of course.

"I take it that's him," Kristopher said under his breath. "Not bad. Not bad at all. Sadly, something tells me I'm not his cup of tea. Appears to prefer the well-heeled menopausal type."

"His name is Austin Tate," Dovie hissed near his ear. "And she isn't his date. She's his mother—and the guest of honor."

Kristopher's brows shot up. "You're competing with mater?"

Dovie waved the words away. "Stop it. It's nothing like that. Her husband died a few months ago, and she hasn't been well. He could have his pick of half the women in Charleston. Instead, he's escorting his mother."

"I'll tell you something," Kristopher said over the rim of his champagne glass. "He could have his pick of almost as many men were he so inclined."

Dovie shot him a sidelong glance. "He's not."

"Are you sure?"

"Quite sure."

"C'est la vie," he said, feigning a sigh. "Can't blame me for trying."

"Look, I know you find this enormously amusing, but I need to go say hello. Can I trust you to behave yourself?"

With a discreet nod, Kristopher tucked her hand into the crook of his arm. "You wouldn't have called me if you thought otherwise."

"Touché."

Gemma was chatting with a grizzle-haired lawyer type when she spotted Dovie moving in her direction. She smiled as she broke away, taking Dovie's hands as they met at the center of the room. "It's good to see you again, Dovie. Everything looks beautiful. Just lovely."

Dovie pasted on a smile, pretending not to notice Austin staring at her over his mother's shoulder. "Thank you, but none of this would be possible without your generosity. We're so grateful for everything you've done."

"It's my absolute pleasure. You remember my son, Austin. Well, of course you do. And who is this?"

Dovie blinked a moment, then realized she must be talking about Kristopher. "Oh, I'm sorry. This is Kristopher Bloom."

Gemma offered a hand. Kristopher took it, bowing smoothly. "A pleasure to meet you. Dovie tells me you're the guest of honor tonight. And if you aren't, you should be in that gown. You're fabulous."

Dovie watched, fascinated. Any other man attempting a line like that would have come off as smarmy, even groveling, but Kristopher had pulled it off with aplomb. He positively oozed charm, the kind that made women weak at the knees. And unless Dovie's powers of observation were on the fritz, Gemma was far from immune. The woman had just turned seventy, and there she stood, blushing like a schoolgirl.

"Actually, I think it's the museum we should all be honoring tonight. But that's kind of you to say. You don't sound like you're from Charleston, Mr. Bloom. How do you happen to know Dovie?"

Dovie felt a moment of panic. She hadn't thought about what she'd say if anyone asked about their relationship. As it turned out, she needn't have worried.

"Please. Call me Kristopher." His smile was utterly disarming as he dropped an arm about Dovie's waist. "Actually, Dovie and I go way back. We met through a mutual friend and were literally shocked to learn how much we had in common."

The moment was so absurd Dovie nearly laughed out loud, and probably would have if Jack hadn't appeared at her side. "Time to go in to dinner," he announced with a flourish, before leaning close to her ear. "I switched the place cards. You're sitting at the grown-up table tonight."

Dovie felt as if she'd just had a shot of Novocain. "With the Tates? Why?"

"For starters, you deserve it. You've done an amazing job pulling this thing together. And because you seem to have Gemma Tate eating out of the palm of your hand. Enjoy the night. You've earned it."

Dinner was delicious, but tense. Fortunately, Gemma and Kristopher kept the conversation flowing, chatting about places they had traveled, bistros they'd dined in, museums they'd visited. Now and then, Dovie chimed in with anecdotes from her art studies abroad while Austin sat chewing mechanically, eyes glued on Kristopher. It was a heady feeling, seeing him glare across the table, and thinking he might be a little bit jealous. Or maybe it was just the champagne. Perhaps it was time to switch to water.

As dinner wound down the orchestra began to play, a sinuous, jazzy number that conjured thoughts of Dean Martin and Frank Sinatra.

Gemma lit up. "I just love this song. I haven't heard it in years."

Kristopher folded his napkin and set it aside. "Perhaps you'd care to dance?"

Gemma glanced toward the empty expanse of parquet with thinly veiled longing. "No one else is."

"Who better to break the ice than the guest of honor?"

Before he could stand, Austin pushed to his feet. "I couldn't agree more, Mr. Bloom. Mother?"

Gemma gave her son a quizzical look but allowed him to lead her to the dance floor. There were murmurs of approval as they began to move to the music, a smattering of applause as Austin steered his mother through a slow and graceful spin.

"Sorry," Dovie said, eyes trained on the dance floor. "Looks like you're stuck with me."

Kristopher nodded toward the floor. "Care to trip the light fantastic?"

"The only tripping I'm likely to do is over my own feet. I'm afraid I'm a bit rusty."

"Darling, in that getup no one—and I mean no one—is going to be looking at your feet." He stood then and held out a hand. "Shall we?"

Dovie felt almost light-headed as she stepped onto the floor with Kristopher. She was starting to see why William had fallen for this man. He was gorgeous, charming, and had a wicked sense of humor. It was a heady combination.

The song ended and another began, this one slower and more fluid. Kristopher held her close, perhaps a little closer than was necessary, their cheeks touching now and then, his hand pressed to the small of her back as he steered her across the floor. The man seriously deserved an Academy Award for this performance.

"You're amazing," she told him as he spooled her out, then reeled her in, molding her tight to his body.

"Your boyfriend isn't the only one who took dance lessons," he murmured against her ear.

"He isn't my boyfriend. Not even close."

"But you'd like him to be."

"No. Maybe. I don't know."

"Yes, you do."

Before she realized what he was up to, he had steered them through the smattering of couples until they were swaying beside Gemma and Austin. Gemma lit up when she saw them.

Kristopher took his cue. "May I cut in?"

For a moment, Dovie considered kicking him in the shin. She had seen enough old movies to know what was supposed to happen next. The customary thing, the *polite* thing, was to trade partners. She also knew Austin couldn't always be counted on to do the customary thing.

She held her breath, waiting. Finally, he held up his arms and Dovie stepped into them. They said nothing for a time, moving almost mechanically. They were both watching Kristopher and Gemma, who were murmuring and laughing like old friends.

"Your mother looks beautiful," Dovie said, hoping to ease the tension. "Last week, when I called, you said you were spoken for. I didn't realize . . ."

"That I was talking about my mother?"

"Yes. It's . . . nice."

"It's her first public event since my father died. I didn't want her sitting here on her own, smiling and faking her way through the evening."

"I'd say her smile looks pretty genuine at the moment."

"And why not, with Prince Charming on her arm? Where'd you find him anyway?"

"We met through a mutual friend."

"So he said. He also said you have a lot in common. Frankly, I don't see it."

Dovie tipped her head back, eyes wide. "Don't you?"

"No."

"You'd be surprised," she said, laughing. She had begun to enjoy herself enormously. Or maybe it was the wine she'd had with dinner. And before dinner.

Austin was still scowling across the dance floor. "He looks like a male escort with his hair slicked back like that. Kristopher Bloom. What the hell kind of name is that anyway?"

"Dutch," Dovie said pithily. "It's spelled with a *K*."

"Of course it is."

"He happens to be a very nice guy."

"A very nice guy who's currently making a move on my seventy-year-old mother."

Dovie laughed again, her head swimming a little as the orchestra struck up yet another song. "I promise, she's quite safe."

"You're that sure of him, are you?"

"I am, as a matter of fact. He's just being . . . Kristopher."

Austin sniffed as he eyed Kristopher again. "That's what I'm worried about. Come on, let's get some air."

"Are you sure you trust them alone, with just two hundred people to chaperone?"

"Funny. Let's go."

She was still grinning as she trailed Austin out onto the balcony. The night had grown chilly and she'd left her wrap at the table. She shivered as she looked up at the night sky, crystal clear and pocked with stars, the air washed clean after days of rain. The drone of happy guests filtered out onto the terrace, a low pleasant hum. Or maybe the hum was all in her head, the giddy by-product of success and champagne. Closing her eyes, she breathed deep, reveling in the music spilling through the open doors, sweet and oozy, like honey pulled through a straw.

She was surprised when Austin took her hand, but even more surprised when he curled it against his chest and pulled her close, swaying to the music. She tipped her head back, trying to meet his eyes, shadowed now by the moonlight. "I thought we were done dancing."

"We weren't." He ran his fingers along the length of her spine, the touch surprisingly warm through her gown. "I just needed some air. I was feeling . . . confused."

"About what?"

"About why I sat through dinner plotting ways to murder Kristopher with a *K*. It never occurred to me that you might show up with someone, and certainly not someone like him. I just assumed . . ."

"That I'd be sitting at home, pining for you?"

"It just surprised me, that's all. I didn't know you were seeing anyone."

"I'm not. Kristopher and I are just friends."

"What kind of friends?"

"The safe kind."

"He doesn't look all that safe to me."

"Trust me when I tell you he's as safe as it gets. Our mutual friend was William. The thing—the only thing—we have in common is William."

Austin's jaw went slack. "You mean Kristopher with a *K* was—"

"William's lover, yes. And as strange as it seems, we've become friends."

"Well, I'll be damned. I had no idea."

"So, is that what we're doing out here? I showed up with a guy who threatened your masculinity, so you thought you'd better stake your claim?"

Austin took an abrupt step back, chin jutting mutinously. "First, and let me make this perfectly clear, Mr. Wonderful does *not* threaten my masculinity. Second, I've never treated you like a conquest, or whatever you seem to think I'm up to. In fact, it was me who pulled away the other night, because I wanted to be up front with you. You might try remembering that the next time you decide to throw rocks at my head."

"You're right," she said. "I'm sorry. I'm just trying to figure out what's going on. Why *did* you bring me out here?"

"Like I said, I needed some air. And I—"

The sound of approaching footsteps made Dovie turn. It was Kristopher, his smile flashing in the thin moonlight. "I was wondering where you'd gotten to. I'm not interrupting anything, am I?"

Dovie found Austin's eyes in the darkness. "Is he?"

"Not at all. We were just about to go in, as a matter of fact." He reached for Kristopher's shoulder, giving it a hearty slap. "She's all yours, Bloom. I need to go round up my own date."

Dovie said nothing as she watched Austin go.

"Sorry," Kristopher said when he had disappeared. "I didn't mean to break anything up. I just hadn't seen you in a while and was afraid I was being a bad fake date."

"You didn't break anything up, but you can drop the fake date thing. I outed you."

"Why?"

"Because he thought you were putting the moves on his mother."

"On Gemma?" He seemed to consider that a moment. "I could do a lot worse. She's thoroughly charming, and still quite beautiful. And something tells me she could do with a bit of fun in her life. Maybe I'll give up the gallery and become her pool boy."

"I don't think they have a pool."

"Pity. Oh, I almost forgot, your boss was looking for you. Something about the crowd starting to thin."

Dovie glanced back at the doors. "Right. I better get back and make sure everyone's leaving happy. He'll string me up if I let Gemma slip out without saying good night."

Inside, the crowd was indeed thinning, shaking hands and kissing cheeks as they drifted toward the exits. She couldn't say she was sorry to see the night finally drawing to a close. Her wine buzz was wearing off, taking the last of her enthusiasm with it. Wearing her best hostess smile, she began to circulate, thanking guests for coming, and for their very kind generosity. She meant it, too, and in the morning, when she could feel her feet again, she would bask in the glow of a successful event and what it meant for the museum going forward.

"Dovie, honey, there you are."

Dovie turned to find Gemma standing behind her, clutching her wrap and purse. "Kristopher has offered to take me home, and assures me you won't mind, but I want your blessing before I steal your date. We thought we'd stop somewhere for coffee, or maybe a drink downtown, so we can talk a little business. He's been thinking about opening another gallery here in Charleston, and I'd love to help grease the local wheels for him. Austin said he doesn't mind dropping you home."

Behind Gemma, Austin stood stonily, his face unreadable. Kristopher, on the other hand, looked rather pleased with himself, knowing full well there was no way for her to wiggle out of this without looking rude. She shot him a look, though he pretended not to notice. Instead, he nodded almost imperceptibly in Austin's direction, the corners of his mouth turned up in smirk that clearly said, *You're welcome.*

forty-four

Austin watched his mother slip out the door with Bloom at her side. He loved her to death, but there were times when she was about as subtle as a jackhammer. For whatever reason, she had set her sights on Dovie Larkin—a subject he'd be broaching first thing in the morning. He didn't need saving. And sure as hell not by someone who was still navigating her own disasters.

He watched as she stood chatting with her boss and his wife, charming, radiant, and completely unaware of how lovely she was. After a few moments she turned, running her eyes over the guests still milling about. He lifted a hand, feeling an absurd pang of pleasure when she spotted him and began to move in his direction.

"I'm sorry about this, really. Why don't I just call a cab? It's late, and I'm sure you want to get home."

"Don't be silly. You're right on my way."

In the parking lot, Austin opened the passenger door, then went around to slide behind the wheel. "Are you tired?" he asked as the BMW purred to life.

"A little. There's always a kind of letdown after an event. Even when it's gone well. Why?"

Austin hesitated, wondering if it was wise to do this now—or at all, really. He had hoped the night would go differently, less . . . awkward. Then again, after the way things had gone on the balcony, maybe now was the perfect time for a peace offering. "I was wondering if you were up for a little ride. There's something I'd like to show you."

"Now? I don't know. It's getting late. And I—"

"It won't take long, I promise. Then I'll take you straight home."

It took less than twenty minutes to reach the Isle of Palms. Not nearly long enough to figure out how he was going to do this thing—or to explain why he even felt the need. It didn't really matter. They had arrived.

Dovie eyed the three-story beach house through the windshield. "Where are we?"

"My place."

Before she could say anything he was out of the car, coming around to open her door. A parade of emotions clouded her expression as she looked up at him. "I thought you wanted to show me something."

"I do. And this is where it is." He grimaced even as the words were leaving his mouth, like some slick first-date line. "It's okay, really. I'm not being creepy."

She fixed him with a skeptical look but finally took the hand he offered, allowing him to help her out of the car and along the stone path that led to the back of the house. She dropped his hand when the path ran out, and stood staring out over the moon-bleached sand and an endless stretch of silver sea. "You wanted to show me the beach?"

"No. I just like to come out here when the moon is full and everything looks like it does now. It's like you and the marsh, I guess." He paused, filling his lungs with chilly salt air. "I take a walk every night before I go to bed, so I can sleep. Most of the time."

"Most of the time?"

He could feel her looking at him, but didn't turn. "Sometimes your head goes places you don't want it to go, and you just can't shut it off."

"Do you want to walk? Now, I mean?"

"No. You'll ruin your dress. I just wanted a minute after all the noise, and all those people. Honestly, I don't know how my mother did it all those years, smiling and being gracious at all those parties, when my father knew damn well she'd rather be anywhere else. But then, she's always been a trouper."

"Well, I hope tonight was a little more enjoyable. The museum—" Dovie's words fell away as a gust of wind blew up, catching one of the rhinestone clips that held the left side of her hair in place. She laughed, lurching slightly as she pushed the tumbling mess off her face. "I think it's hopeless."

"Leave it," Austin said, catching her around the waist to steady her. "Messy works for you."

Time seemed to stop as she looked up at him, as if even the sea had suddenly gone quiet. He stepped back abruptly, dropping his hands. He should never have touched her. He knew it the minute he felt the warmth of her. And he was still standing too close. Close enough to see the reflection of the moon in her eyes. She seemed an almost otherworldly thing standing there, her hair swirling around her face, her gown billowing in the moonlight—like a mermaid on dry land.

No, he thought, taking another step back. He should never have touched her. Touching wasn't what this was supposed to be about. "Let's go in. You look cold."

He didn't take her hand this time, just turned to make sure she was following as they climbed the deck stairs and opened the sliding glass doors.

She lingered in the doorway, gazing out over the beach. "You must have some view in the morning."

"I have to say, it's rather spectacular." He tugged at the bow tie that had been strangling him all night, then frowned at the gesture, feeling like a lounge singer doing a set at the Copa. When the hell had he become so damn awkward? “Can I get you something to drink? A glass of wine, maybe?”

“No, thanks. I think I’ve had enough wine for one night. For two nights, actually.”

She was wandering now, eyeing the framed prints that lined the wall opposite the fireplace, hovering over the cluster of photos on the bookcase. “What’s this one?” she asked, zeroing in on a shot of him on a sailboat with a gaggle of skinny-legged boys.

“It’s some of the kids from the Outlook Club. The one wearing the ball cap and the frown is Tyler. And that one in the back is me during my Clemson days, all suited up for the game.”

Dovie picked up the photograph, tilting it toward the light for a better look. “Wow, you were pretty good-looking back in the day, even in that ugly orange jersey.”

Austin snatched the picture away and returned it to the shelf. “I did not bring you here to insult me.”

“Then why did you bring me here?”

“Like I said, I wanted to show you something.” He smiled, suddenly feeling like the cat that swallowed the canary as he took her by the shoulders and turned her to face the fireplace. “I wanted to show you that.”

She went still when she saw it, her mouth open as she took in the painting propped up on the mantel. There was a crease between her brows when she looked back at him. “I thought you didn’t like the marsh.”

“I never said that. But I didn’t buy it for me. I bought it for you.”

Her eyes rounded in surprise, confusion, or a mixture of both. “Why?”

He shrugged, scraping a hand through his hair. How could he explain when he didn’t know himself? “As a thank-you, I guess. I don’t know. Does it matter?”

"It matters to me."

"I saw the way you looked at it the day I came by your place. And then the way you talked about the marsh that night on the dock. I couldn't *not* buy it. It's called *Low Tide*."

"You know I can't accept it, Austin."

"Because I make an ass of myself every time I get anywhere near you?"

She smiled at that, but shook her head. "No. Because it's too extravagant. I know how much it cost, remember?"

"What it cost has nothing to do with it. It's a gift—between friends."

"But we're not, are we? Friends, I mean. We're just two people who can't seem to figure out what we want from each other."

"Friends is all I'm capable of right now, Dovie. Probably all I'll ever be capable of. And a few months ago, I wouldn't have cared. But I do now. From the moment I met you, you've been under my skin. You were so broken and fragile, but there's this other side to you, the side where you keep all your strength. And you're finally starting to find it. I'd ruin that."

"You don't know that."

"*I* do," he said, more sharply than he meant to. "I know, because I've done it before."

There was a long pause while she seemed to digest his words, as if weighing what to say next. "This is about Monica, isn't it?" she said quietly. "About the accident?"

He felt himself go cold. "How do you know about Monica?"

"I didn't until last week, but I went back and read the papers."

"Ah yes. It was in all the papers."

"Austin, you can't blame yourself for what happened that night. The weather was terrible, and they say she was driving at a high rate of speed. Short of being behind the wheel, there was nothing you could have done to prevent what happened."

He tugged at his collar. All of a sudden it felt like he was choking. "Oh, there was plenty I *could* have done. I just chose not to do it."

Dovie stood very still, studying him through narrowed eyes. "I don't understand."

"It wasn't like they wrote it, with Monica on her way to a friend's, and me the poor grieving husband. It wasn't anything like that."

"What *was* it like?"

"She was drunk, or well on her way to it, and high as a kite, when she got behind the wheel that night. And she'd just left me."

Her lips parted as understanding dawned. "Oh, Austin . . ."

"Don't," he snapped, eyes flashing. "Don't feel sorry for me."

"I just . . . I had no idea."

"No one did, at first. But eventually my parents picked up on the substance abuse. Hard not to after she passed out one day at my mother's birthday party. I said it was the flu. My mother pretended to believe me, but she had to have known. By then, Monica was using every day. She hid it pretty well in the beginning—even from me. By the time I realized she was in trouble, it was too late. When I cut off her money, she packed a bag and told me I'd be hearing from her attorney. She made quite an exit, screaming and stumbling down the driveway. And I just watched her go. I knew she was in no condition to drive, but I was so relieved that she would finally be out of my life that I just . . . let her go."

Dovie stood staring at him, arms hugged tight to her body. "There was nothing in the paper about alcohol or drugs."

"No. My father made sure the story was . . . sanitized. He didn't do it for me, of course. It was all about him, and the Tate name. And I let him. I went to the memorial and played the grieving husband while he paid off whoever you pay to make things go away. It did, too. Dried up overnight. The drugs, the booze, all of it, gone. It was awful. Everyone was so damn nice, so sympathetic. I couldn't take it. I took the first flight out. Disappeared for almost six months. It seemed easier to just run away. So that's what I did."

"Where were you all that time?"

"Everywhere," he said with a shrug. "And nowhere."

"So, all this time you've been—"

"Living a lie? Yes."

"I was going to say, all this time you've been punishing yourself for choices someone else made."

Austin shook his head, unwilling to accept the premise of her statement. "I knew she had a problem, and I did nothing. I could have made her go to rehab, but I never forced the issue. I knew she was drunk, and I let her drive that night. Those were my choices, Dovie. Mine, and no one else's."

She studied the nails of her right hand for what felt like a long time, smoothing her cuticles one by one. When she reached the last finger, she looked up. "You said once that some people are good at keeping secrets, especially when we look the other way. I thought you meant me when you said it, but you were thinking about Monica, weren't you?"

"You can only ignore what's in the mirror for so long. Sooner or later, you have to see what's there. And I did see it. I just chose to ignore it. And because I did, someone died."

"Monica's death wasn't your fault—any more than William's was mine. They made their choices, Austin, because they were hurting, and didn't know any other way to make that hurting stop. I know all about that kind of guilt. And I know what it can do to you if you let it."

He turned to peer out the glass doors, hoping to catch a glimpse of the sea. Instead, he saw his reflection, hardened and grim in the mirrored surface. He didn't realize she'd crossed the room until he felt her hands on his shoulders, their warmth bleeding through the fabric of his shirt. And then, suddenly, her face was there, too, beside his in the glass, her eyes reflected back to him, soft and full of feeling. It took everything in him to look away, to fight the urge to turn and take her in his arms, to let himself feel all the things he'd been denying. He couldn't, though, for her sake.

"Don't," he said, flinching from her touch. "I shouldn't have brought you here."

"Why?" She was so close now that he could feel her breath on the back of his neck. "Because it isn't safe? I know something about playing it safe, Austin. I know it's the biggest lie of all. We tell ourselves we're okay, that as long as we keep our walls up nothing can touch us. And then someone comes along while we're not looking—someone we never expected."

He did turn, then, locking eyes with this woman whose heart might be his salvation, a way out of the dark place he'd been living in for so long, this woman who was always trying to fix things. And now she was trying to fix him. Did he want to be fixed? Did he deserve it? After so many years, was it even *possible*?

"Our stories aren't the same, Dovie. It's not as simple as just forgiving myself."

"But it is. It *is* that simple. You just say it, and you let her go. You let all of it go. You stop worrying about what you did, or didn't do, and you move on. Because you've done your time."

"You sound so sure of what you're saying."

"Because I am. The man who married Monica doesn't exist anymore. He made mistakes, and he learned from them. And the way I know that is *that* guy would be thinking of ways to get me into bed right now, instead of holding me at arm's length."

She touched her lips to his then, the barest of touches—a gift—and something at his core let go. She wanted him, and he her. But what then? What happened when the passion was spent and the sun came up? Could he do that part? He didn't know. But maybe it was time he found out.

Her body melted into his as he pulled her close, all sinew and flesh and unspoken need, as if some long-quiet thing had suddenly uncoiled itself—for him. And just like that, all thoughts of safety vanished, replaced with a craving that left him hollowed out and shaken, hungry for something he hadn't wanted in a very long time.

She matched him with a hunger of her own, touch for touch, and need for need, heart thundering against his ribs as he tasted the soft underside of her jaw, then the hollow of her throat, grazing the pulse there with lips and teeth. His hand moved slowly, savoring the warm, smooth length of her spine, the rounded curve of her backside. And then, without a word between them, they were moving up the stairs.

He paused when they reached the doorway of his bedroom, searching her face in the dimness. A question or a declaration—he couldn't say which. She answered by pressing two fingers to his lips, stilling whatever it was he might have been about to say, then took his hand and pulled him toward the bed. There was only the moonlight spilling in through the glass doors, but they needed no more than that. Nor did they need words. It was as if everything had already been said, all the questions asked, the answers given. And maybe they had. He prayed they had.

Her skin felt like satin as he pushed the gown from her shoulders, cool to the touch, and so very smooth. He heard the silk sigh to the floor, then felt his breath catch in his throat as she stood there before him, exposed, unashamed, breathtaking.

After a moment—perhaps the longest of his life—she stepped out of the silky puddle and reached for him. Somewhere along the way, he had shucked off his coat, and she set to work on his shirt studs, her fingers moving with a purposeful and maddening slowness, until the last one was free, and her hands went roaming, leaving the brand of her fingertips on his skin.

She peeled away his shirt, letting it fall, then eased herself down onto the edge of the bed, drawing him down beside her. It was a moment he had thought of often over the last few months, but never, ever like this—primal and sweet, raw and warm, as long-denied need found its way in the dark, breaths mingling, limbs straining, wills yielding. Exploration and discovery. A journey's end. And, perhaps, a beginning.

forty-five

Dovie opened her eyes, letting them roam in the predawn gloom. It took a moment to get her bearings, to reconcile her naked body, puddled evening gown, and unfamiliar sheets, but finally the feverish details of the previous night came drifting back. She smiled as a rush of warmth flooded her limbs, along with the sweet soreness that came with thorough lovemaking. It had been a long—long—long time.

After a deep and languorous stretch, she rolled over onto her side, expecting to find Austin still asleep beside her. Instead, she found a tangle of cold sheets and an empty pillow. She peered at the clock on the nightstand—just after six thirty—and felt the first prickle of dread.

Please just let him be an early riser.

Sliding from the bed, she scooped Austin's rumpled tuxedo shirt from the floor and slipped it on, savoring the mingled scents of shaving cream, cologne, and the faint tang of salt air. It was the same mix of scents she'd noticed that first day in her office, the smell she now realized she had come to associate with him. After a bit of fumbling, she managed to fasten enough of the studs to feel covered and headed downstairs. She had nearly reached the bottom when it hit her.

Dora.

After a scan of the living room, she managed to locate her handbag and pull out her cell phone. She held her breath as she counted the rings. Three. Four. Why wasn't she answering? Finally, the ringing stopped and a frail voice said hello.

"Dora. Thank God. Is everything all right?"

"Well, of course it is. Where are you? I woke up around two and your bedroom door was open. Then, this morning, your bed hadn't been slept in. Did you have some sort of trouble?"

"No. No trouble. I just . . . it got so late that I decided to stay at a friend's. I'm so sorry. I didn't mean to leave you alone all night."

"A friend, is it?" Dora cackled, before breaking into a fit of coughing.

"Your cough sounds worse. Did you have a bad night?"

"No. I just took a little spill this morning on my way to the loo. Tripped over my own two feet, and down I went like an ox."

"A spill?" Visions of fractured skulls and broken hips flooded Dovie's head. "My God, are you hurt? You sound like you're having trouble breathing."

"I'm fine. Just a little winded. But I've taken my medicine, and a puff from that thingy the doctor gave me, and now I have the kettle on. I'll be right as rain as soon as I have my tea."

"All right. I'm coming home. In the meantime, turn off the kettle and get yourself to bed."

Dovie ended the call, furious with herself. She'd been so adamant that Dora not be alone after leaving the hospital, and just days after wheeling her out of Bon Secours, she'd gone and left the woman alone all night.

Now all she had to do was find Austin and tell him why she was running out on him at the crack of dawn—and do it without explaining who Dora was. Except he was nowhere to be found. On impulse, she went to the sliding glass doors and stuck her head out, scanning the wide stretch of beach. That's where she found him, about a hundred yards down the shoreline, standing near the water's edge, legs planted wide, eyes fixed on the horizon. She wanted to believe this was part of some morning ritual, jogging or yoga or sunrise meditation, but she knew from his posture, and from how very still he stood, that it was something else. Something bad.

There was a jacket on one of the kitchen stools. She grabbed it and dragged it on as she headed down the back steps, painfully aware of her pants-less state as she turned up the beach and headed into the stiff morning breeze. The sand was chilly on the soles of her feet as she tracked down the shore, clutching the oversize jacket tight to her body. Finally, she came to a halt a few feet from where Austin stood. He turned, as if sensing her there, and ran his eyes down the length of her, lingering on the loose cuffs of his dress shirt hanging limply from the sleeves of his jacket. "Good morning."

"It was either my gown or your shirt," she said sheepishly.

"You must be freezing."

"I'm fine. What's going on?"

"I came out to clear my head."

Dovie felt the knot in her belly tighten. "Why don't I like the sound of that?"

There was a stretch of silence while he seemed to weigh his words, filled with the lazy shush of morning waves, the low whistle of wind over the dunes. Finally, he scrubbed a hand through his hair and released a long breath. "I'm sorry, Dovie. About last night. About all of it. I thought I could do this, have something—someone—that meant something. Then I woke up in the middle of the night, and there you were next to me, and all I could think about was how it was going to end, and I just . . . can't."

"So last night was . . . what? A mistake?"

"Jesus, I hate the way that sounds, but yeah, it was."

Dovie blinked at him, stung by his tone. "I get it," she said, shoving her hair back from her face. "Things got a little too real, so you're pulling the plug before it gets messy."

"I know it sounds cliché, Dovie, but this really is for the best. Nights like last night lead to promises, and I can't make any. Not to you."

She huddled deeper into the jacket, shivering. "So this is it? This is the wrecking part?"

Austin's mouth twisted bitterly. "Trust me when I tell you we're not even close to the wrecking part. And we're never going to be. That's why we're having this conversation. When it comes to relationships, I make mistakes. Big ones. And I'm not making one with you. I don't know how else to say it, or how else to make you understand."

"Well, then," Dovie said. "I guess that's that." She was about to walk away when she turned back. "I'm glad last night happened, Austin, or was. Because I thought we had gotten past some things, that maybe you were ready—that we both were. But I was wrong. This is just your m.o. And that's fine. It's not like you didn't warn me. I just wish it could have been different."

"Me, too."

She looked at him, wishing there was something else to say, anything else to say, but there wasn't. He'd said it all. They both had. "I need to get going anyway. There's something I need to take care of at home."

"Go in and get dressed. I'll be there in a minute to drive you home."

"No, thanks. I'll call a cab."

"Don't be silly. Even I know it's bad form to send your date home in a cab."

Dovie dropped her purse and keys at the front door and headed for the guest room. "Dora? I'm home." Her heart beat faster when she received no answer, and faster still when she reached the doorway and found Dora in bed, eyes closed and absolutely still. "Dora?"

Dora dragged one eye open. "Why all the fuss? I haven't snuffed it, for goodness' sake."

"You said you fell. Are you all right?"

In response, Dora held up her arm, elbow out. "Just gave myself a bit of a knock and skinned my elbow, but I still look better than you. Did you sleep in that dress?"

"Not exactly, no." She bent down to examine the elbow, pink as a strawberry and bleeding a little. "Do you think we should get you x-rayed?"

"Heavens, I only need plaster. You call them Band-Aids over here, I think. Would have done it myself, but I didn't know where to look."

"They're in the kitchen. I'll be right back." Moments later, she returned with cotton balls, peroxide, antibiotic cream, and the box of Band-Aids.

Dora eyed the armload of supplies. "It's a skinned elbow, not a knife wound."

"I'm just going to clean it up," Dovie insisted as she opened the bottle of peroxide. "And then I'll fix you some breakfast." She dabbed a bit at the elbow with peroxide, then blotted it dry, trying to ignore Dora's careful study of her appearance.

"It's to do with a man, isn't it?" she said. "That face of yours?"

Dovie reached for the tube of antibiotic cream, wrenching the top off with her teeth. "Yes, it is," she said, around the plastic cap in the corner of her mouth. "I thought we'd gotten to a place where things could work out."

"But they can't?"

Dovie screwed the cap back onto the tube and set it aside, reaching for a Band-Aid. "No. I've been assured they can't."

"You love this man?"

"It's . . . complicated, Dora. And I'd rather not talk about it just now. I need a shower and some coffee. Will you be okay while I hop in?"

"I won't bleed to death, if that's what you're asking."

Dovie managed a smile. "You are feeling better, aren't you?"

"Yes, I am." Dora's face grew serious. "After you've had your shower and your coffee, do you think you might read me a letter or two?"

"Yes, all right," Dovie said. She could do with a distraction right about now, anything to keep her mind from wandering back to this morning's scene with Austin. "I'll fix us some breakfast when I get out of the shower, and then we'll read a letter or two."

She felt better after the shower and a little breakfast, well enough to start worrying about what Alice's next letter might reveal. Pulling the plastic bag from her desk, she spilled out the contents, sorting the letters into two piles—*read* and *unread.* When she was finished, she was startled to see that there were only three letters left.

She lifted the remaining envelopes one at a time. They were thin, not more than a sheet or two apiece if she was guessing—the last threads of connection Dora would ever have to her daughter—and one last chance to let go of her guilt. Was it possible she could come away empty-handed after hearing them? Or worse, that instead of redemption, they could contain the exact opposite—condemnation? Yes. In fact, it was highly possible. But if there was a chance of finding even the faintest glimmer of forgiveness in Alice's final words, then any amount of tears would be worth the risk.

forty-six

9 East Battery Street
Charleston, South Carolina
October 17, 1968

My dear sweet child,

It breaks my heart to say what I'm about to, and to do it with so little warning, but I fear the time for truth has come at last. I have been reluctant to put the words on paper, as if writing the thing will somehow make it more real. But it's real enough as it is.

I've been told my time is short.

I've been doing my best to hide it—and, I suppose, to deny it—but I've been steadily growing thinner, and my cough finally became so persistent that Gemma insisted on sending for Dr. Ponder. When he left she called me into her sitting room and closed the door. She smiled as she invited me to sit beside her. But it was a sad smile, the kind that didn't quite reach her eyes, and I knew the news was bad. Her chin was quivering, and I saw how hard she was trying not to come apart.

There was a tea tray on the table in front of her. She poured out two cups and handed one to me, then passed me a plate of biscuits, which I declined. She's always trying to fatten me up, but I have no appetite these days. She glanced away as she set the plate down. That's when I saw her eyes go bright with tears. I pretended not to see, pretended not to know what was coming. But I did know. I saw from the way she held her shoulders that she wasn't going to soften the blow, that she was going to tell me the truth, and I wanted to make it easier for her—easier for us both.

Finally, she reached for my hand. "I'm afraid the doctor didn't have very good news, Alice. It's bad, honey. And it's going to get worse. He suspects something called pulmonary fibrosis. It's scarring and inflammation left over from the tuberculosis, which can happen when an infection goes untreated for too long. It's why your cough has never quite gone away, and why it's been getting steadily worse. Apparently, the scars continue to spread even after the disease is gone." She lowered her eyes, letting them slide away from mine. "He says it's not something you're likely to recover from, that eventually . . ." Her words thickened and trailed off.

"I'll die."

"Yes."

She had whispered the word, gulping back tears as she turned her face from mine. It broke my heart to see her weep, and yet I felt a kind of calm, too, as if some part of me that had been holding on too tightly had suddenly let go. Because I realized that somewhere deep down, I had already known. Perhaps it's the dream that's been coming nearly every night now. Something is reaching for me, something I can't see, but can feel, like invisible fingers on the back of my neck. And no matter how fast or far I run, it just keeps coming.

"There was a girl at Blackhurst," I said quietly. "Mary Matthews was her name. She came down with the consumption before any of the

rest of us, back before they knew what it was. We watched her waste away. She grew so thin, so blue and pale that you could see the bones through her skin. She died before she could give birth to her baby."

Gemma was past hiding her grief. Her eyes welled as she reached for my hand. "Oh, honey, it won't be like that. Dr. Ponder has a call in to a specialist in Columbia who's coming up with new treatments all the time. He says with some of the new advances they're making, you might have years."

I smiled and said thank you. I even pretended to believe her. But I knew better. And for all her promises, I saw that she did, too.

Since then, we've been walking on eggshells, afraid to meet each other's eyes for fear one or both of us will burst into tears. I still look after Austin on the days I feel strong enough—the doctor has assured Gemma there's no danger in me being around him—but those days are getting more and more rare. He is my only joy now, though sometimes my heart aches just a little when I look at him. He reminds me of you, and the promise I now know I will never be able to keep.

Perhaps that's why my health is failing so rapidly now, because without my promise there's nothing to cling to, no hope for the reunion I have always dreamed of. The unfairness of it sears me, and yet so much is my fault. I should have stood up to Mam when she wanted to send me away, I should have run away and had you on my own, I should have fought the nuns when they took you. These are the things we think about when our time is ticking down, how many ways we have failed, how we could have done things better.

There's so much to regret, so much I miss. I miss home. I never thought I would, but I do. I miss the emerald sea and sunsets on the pier, the way the air tastes of salt and the hills are always green. But mostly, I miss Johnny, the plans we made, and the life we were going to have—all gone now.

Gemma asked me if I'd like to go home when it's all over, and offered to arrange it if that's what I wanted, but I told her no. I don't want to go home in a box. Besides, Charleston is my home now. I leave nothing behind, no legacy or mark on the world, except you, my angel—the child I never held, but always loved. I pray your life is a good one, that you are loved, and well, and happy. That's all any mother can hope for, my dearest. Know that I hope it for you.

All my love,
Mam

Dora's face was ashen when Dovie looked up from the page, her eyes open but unfocused. "She missed the sea. She missed the air. She missed her Johnny. But not me." Her eyes closed then, a single tear spilling down her cheek. "Not me."

"I'm so sorry, Dora."

Dora shook her grizzled head. "It's what I deserve, isn't it?"

"Don't say that. Please."

"How can I not? When the thing that killed her came from that place? If I hadn't been so proud, hadn't sent her away, she'd be alive today, instead of lying dead in the ground. I wasn't even there with her. I should have been with her."

"And you would have, if you knew, Dora. You would have done anything to get here. Just like you're here now."

"Too late," she whispered as a fresh rush of tears trailed down her cheeks. "And the child . . . I still don't know what happened to the child."

Dovie folded Dora's hands together and placed her own over them. "There are only two letters left. I can read them now, if you want, or you can rest a little, and we can do it another time. They might be . . . hard."

Dora shook her head firmly. "No sparing, remember?"

9 East Battery Street
Charleston, South Carolina
December 5, 1968

My dearest,

The doctor has been again today, likely for the last time. The last X-rays were not good, and the newest round of pills doesn't seem to have made a dent. There's nothing more to be done. No new doctors to visit, no more medicines to try. My disease must and shall run its course. And until now, I haven't minded so very much. I breathe through a tube now, much of the time, and rarely leave my room. The days are long, and the struggle to breathe is scarcely worth the effort, so that the end has begun to seem like a blessing—a good long rest, with my Johnny waiting on the other side.

But Johnny must wait a little. There's a thing I must do, a promise I must extract to set things right after I'm gone. Perhaps I should have waited a little before writing this, until my temper had cooled and I was feeling stronger, but in my case, waiting could turn into dying, and I've already been cheated of far too much to leave the truth unsaid. Please be patient, sweet one, and forgive a sick woman's rantings. I must let out the poison or choke on it.

Where do I begin? There is so much to say, and so little time to say it, so many questions to ask and answer. How does one reconcile kindness with betrayal, joy with heartache? After so much practice, I should be better at such things. Instead, I've been a fool, too blind to see that deception often disguises itself as charity. When I think of how much time I wasted, and what trusting a friend has cost, I'm filled with a despair so raw it makes my bones ache. Such have been my lessons, my angel, though I fear they have come too late.

But fate is not without its kindnesses, if you know where to look. Kindness, you see, is a stealthy thing, coming from places you least expect. A dagger's thrust becomes a mercy. An intended cruelty becomes balm to the soul. A sworn enemy becomes a kind of friend. I will always be grateful for Harley Tate's great kindness that day, though he meant it as no such thing. He meant to be cruel, to wound me mortally, and he has very nearly succeeded. But it's the way a thing ends that counts, and we've not reached the end just yet.

There is more to say—much, much more—but I find I haven't the strength just now to tell it properly. I had hoped to write more, to lay it all out for you, just as it happened, but events have taken their toll. I will sleep a little and begin fresh in the morning. Good night, my sweet one.

All my love,
Mam

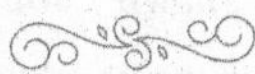

Dovie stared at the single sheet of stationery, feeling strangely hollow. It was all so cryptic and foreboding. Alice's health had clearly deteriorated, but something else had happened, something that had shaken her badly. She had written of betrayal and despair, the cost of trusting a friend, and perhaps strangest of all, a cruelty that had somehow become a kindness.

Dovie stole a glance at Dora, a shade paler now than after the previous letter, but stoic, too, with her hands folded over her chest, braced for whatever the last letter might contain. Taking a deep breath, Dovie pulled opened the envelope and teased out its contents, then did a double take as she spread the sheets on her lap.

She hadn't noticed when putting them in chronological order that the handwriting didn't match, but now the difference was glaring. Alice's writing was open and loopy, even in the last few letters, where the lines tended to sag and slant, likely the result of her failing health. But the words in this final letter were tight and elongated, and with a decidedly elegant slant. She didn't need to scan the bottom of the page to know Gemma had written it—or that Alice was gone.

January 30, 1969

My dearest friend—

Yes, I will call you friend, because that's how I still think of you, the dearest friend I ever knew. But you're gone now—gone from me, and gone from Austin—and my heart is broken as I sit at your little desk, surrounded by things that remind me of you. Your clothes. Your shoes. And your letters.

I found them while I was packing up your things, just where you said I would, tucked away in that little sewing basket I gave you when you first came. You must have known I would read them, and I have—every one, to the last. It struck me as odd, at first, writing letters you never expected to be read, and yet here I sit with my pen. I miss you so terribly. I miss your face, and your voice, and the silly English songs you used to sing to Austin when he was tiny. I miss our time in the garden, and our talks over tea. And so I thought, why not? If pen and paper once brought you comfort, why not me? One last letter to a dear friend, and the sister of my heart, a plea for forgiveness for what I'm about to say.

I find I must return your letters. They sit beside me now, along with the watch you always wore, though it never ran in all the time I knew you. It grieves me to go back on my word, and I did mean every word I said that day. Truly, I did. But is it fair to hold me to a promise exacted at such a moment? With your fingers clutching at my sleeve, your fevered eyes pleading even as the light was leaving them? Surely you know it was not, and understand why I cannot do as you asked with the letters. I simply haven't the strength, though I find I cannot keep them, either. They're too glaring a reminder of how I have failed you. And so I have decided to return them to you in the only way I know how.

I wish I had decided it sooner. It would have been easier to bury them the day we buried you. But nature will see to it soon enough. We have, both of us, lost so much already. Let our parting be the last of it. Fate can be cruel. I know this in my own way, though perhaps not as harshly as you, sweet friend. But some things cannot be undone. A broken promise, least of all. It was out of love for you that I made it, and out of love for another that I now find I cannot keep it. Forgive my selfishness, then and now.

With love, and the profoundest regret,

G—

forty-seven

Dora had wept for nearly an hour, keening softly and rocking back and forth. Dovie had remained at her side, holding her hand, doling out tissues, and wondering how her good intentions had gone so terribly wrong. She'd had such high hopes for a happy ending, a feud mended, a heart unburdened. But there had been no happy ending. Not for Alice, or Dora, or even Gemma, it seemed.

When Dora had finally fallen asleep, Dovie slipped from the room and out onto the back porch. Night was coming on, shadows stretching long dusky fingers over the marsh, turning the spartina a deep shade of blue. The rocker creaked as she eased into it and kicked her feet up onto the railing. Her head felt heavy and dull, crowded with questions that would never be answered. At least the mystery of how Alice's letters had wound up in Magnolia Grove's lost and found had been solved, if not the why.

I have decided to return them to you in the only way I know how. I wish I had thought of it sooner. It would have been easier to simply bury them the day we buried you. But nature will see to it soon enough.

Only nature *hadn't* seen to them. They had resurfaced thirty years later, not to answer questions but to open old wounds. Dovie's thoughts drifted to William, and the secret he had gone to such lengths to hide—a drastic and desperate act taken not to wound, but to avoid consequences he was simply unable to bear. Had Gemma's motives for disposing of the letters been similar? And if so, what consequences had she feared?

Had something happened between Harley and Alice that she felt compelled to hide? Given Harley's dislike for his son's nanny, not to mention Alice's failing health, it seemed unlikely. Nor was it likely that Alice would omit such an occurrence when she'd been so candid about everything else. Gemma had written about a promise not kept, one that had been extracted as Alice lay dying. But what kind of promise? She'd read each letter half a dozen times, studying them line by line, but there was something she'd missed—or something that had fallen through the glaring gaps between Alice's final letters.

The sound of the kitchen phone ringing gradually penetrated, dragging Dovie back to the present. She hurried to catch it, afraid it might wake Dora. Her mother was talking almost before she could say hello.

"Dovie, honey, it's your sister. She's in the hospital. It's the baby."

In the fluorescent glare of the waiting room, Rowena Larkin's face looked like a punching bag, mottled and dark, her eyes so puffy they were little more than slits, her nose swollen and an angry shade of red. She pressed a crumpled tissue to her mouth when she saw Dovie and got to her feet.

"She's in trouble, Dovie. They're both in trouble. They let Roger go in with her, but it isn't good."

Dovie's stomach gave a sickening jolt. "What kind of trouble?"

"It's her blood pressure. They're doing everything they can, but she's not responding, and the baby's heartbeat . . ." Her voice trailed off in a fresh gush of tears.

Dovie took her mother's hands, folding them together as she

pressed them to her lips. "It's going to be all right, Mother. They're both going to be all right."

"They said they'll have to take the baby soon, if she doesn't start responding."

A hundred questions crowded into Dovie's head, none of them the kind of thing her mother was likely to have answers to, and none of them reassuring—the what-if questions. What if they couldn't get Robin's blood pressure under control? What if the baby wasn't strong enough to survive? What if Robin—?

No. She was going to stop right there. Nothing good could come from those kinds of questions, and right now she needed to keep a clear head, to be the strong one in the event that the news wasn't good.

After getting her mother back into her chair, she went in search of the cafeteria, returning a little later with a pair of large coffees. Something told her they were in for a long afternoon, and a cup of coffee would at least give them something to do with their hands.

Rowena took the proffered cup and lifted the plastic lid. "Thank you. Did you bring sugar?"

Dovie reached into her jacket pocket, producing several packets. "Any word?"

"No. I keep asking, but no one will tell me anything. Maybe you'll have better luck than I did at the nurses' station."

A few minutes later, Dovie returned, dropping down beside her mother with a shake of the head.

"Let me guess," Rowena grumbled. "There's been no change. The doctors are doing everything they can. As soon as they have any new information, someone will be out to speak with us."

"Pretty much word for word. I guess all we can do now is wait."

"And pray."

Dovie stole a sidelong glance at her mother, noting the fresh tears clinging to her lashes, and was suddenly filled with anger. "Why is she even doing this?"

Her mother seemed startled by the question. "Doing what?"

"Having another baby, for heaven's sake! She already has two. Isn't that enough, for crying out loud?"

"Dovie . . ."

"I mean, is she trying to prove something? Did some woman from one of her clubs just have a third, and she feels like she has to keep up?"

"How can you say something like that? Your sister has always wanted a big family, and so has Roger. It isn't about what anyone else has or does. This is what's important to Robin—children, a family. Someday you'll understand."

"Understand what?" Dovie grumbled, knowing she was being obtuse.

"The bond that exists between a mother and her children. It's like an invisible cord tying your heart to theirs. And it's a cord that can never be broken, no matter how old they get or how far they roam. Being a mother isn't something you plan, Dovie. It's something you are. Your children are a part of you for as long as you live—sometimes the best part. Which is why, from the moment they leave your body, you'll do anything to keep them safe and happy." She looked away then and blotted her eyes before checking her watch for what must have been the hundredth time.

"Mother, I'm sorry. I didn't mean it the way it sounded. I'm just—"

"Let's just sit quietly, shall we?"

Dovie slouched back in her chair, hiding behind her coffee cup. "Yes, all right."

She had lost all track of time when Dr. Delaney finally appeared in the waiting room in her stork-covered surgical scrubs, the smile on her face confirming what she had come to say. They had performed a C-section, and considering what mother and daughter had been through, both appeared to be doing quite well. Robin would be in recovery for several hours, but as soon as she was settled in a room, she and Baby Grace could have visitors. In the meantime, maybe a bite to eat was a good idea.

It was Roger who finally came out to tell them Robin was in her room, and ready for visitors. Rowena moved on soft feet as she pushed open the hospital room door and peered inside. Dovie trailed behind, certain that visitors were the absolute last thing Robin would want after being cut open and then sewn up like a Thanksgiving turkey. She was probably groggy, sore, and exhausted.

But one look at her sister erased that notion. Dovie felt a lump in her throat as she caught her first glimpse of Robin. She was the color of biscuit dough, her usually perfect hair plastered in crazy ringlets to her head, her eyes puffy and ringed with blue-green shadows. And somehow she had never looked more beautiful as she smiled down at the tiny pink face peering up from the tiny bundle of blankets in her arms. She didn't look exhausted at all. She looked . . . happy. Happy, and glowing, and wildly in love with her new daughter.

The image blurred, morphing into dozens of watery prisms. Dovie blinked to clear her vision, recalling her mother's words about the bond between a mother and her children. *Like an invisible cord tying your heart to theirs.* Not so invisible, she thought, experiencing a bloom of pure joy for her sister that would last long after she returned home from the hospital.

It was well after nine when Dovie finally kicked off her shoes and tiptoed in to check on Dora. The TV was on but turned way down, an old classic with Jimmy Cagney in spats and pinstripes. She clicked off the set and looked down at Dora, sleeping soundly, the sandwich she had made her before leaving for the hospital untouched, the pills she had carefully laid out exactly where she'd placed them on the nightstand. She had given up. And why not, when there was nothing left to hope for, no way to know the rest of the story—no chance for forgiveness from her daughter?

Her mother's words floated into her head. *A cord that can never be broken, no matter how old they get or how far they roam.* But for Dora that cord had been broken, and she'd been the one to break it, the day she sent her daughter away. It was the hope of absolution that had kept her going. Now even that was gone. If only there'd been some hint of forgiveness in Alice's final letters, some small glimmer of feeling that Dora could cling to, proof that her daughter hadn't gone to her grave despising her.

But maybe there had been. An image suddenly flickered to life, like an old movie projector being switched on: Gemma sitting at Alice's desk, surrounded by her belongings. Her clothes. Her letters. Her mother's broken watch.

Alice had kept it all those years, despite the fact that it didn't work and hadn't since the day she left Sennen Cove. And she'd been wearing it the night she met Danny in the parking lot. Why wear a broken watch, if not for sentimental reasons? Until now Dovie hadn't given the watch's fate a second thought, but suddenly the question loomed. Was it possible Gemma still had it? That she had disposed of the letters, but kept the watch as a remembrance of a beloved friend?

Suddenly Dovie was convinced it wasn't only possible, but probable. And if she was right, she might be able to provide Dora with proof that in spite of what she had written, Alice had never stopped loving her mother. Unfortunately, getting her hands on that proof would require another visit to Gemma's home, and almost certainly kill any hope of salvaging her already strained relationship with Austin. But if she was right, and it would bring Dora even some small measure of relief, she had to do it.

Dovie felt a fresh flurry of anxiety as she pulled up Gemma's brick-paved drive and cut the engine. She'd been rehearsing what she planned to say all morning, determined to avoid anything that might trigger painful memories or awkward questions. She would simply ask for the watch and be on her way, volunteering as little as possible about what she knew, and how she knew it. There was always the possibility that

Gemma would refuse her request, or deny even having the watch. She'd have to deal with those possibilities as they arose, but she was counting on Gemma's maternal instincts to persuade her to do the right thing.

She pulled in a deep breath as she mounted the front steps and prepared to ring the bell. Austin would be furious if he ever found out she had come, not that it was likely to make a difference at this point. He'd made it pretty clear that there was no place in his life for her—or anyone.

Her mind was still on Austin when the door swung open. "I didn't expect you back for hours. Did you forget your—Oh, Dovie." Gemma stood blinking at her, a pair of florist's shears in her hand. "I didn't expect to see you so soon. Is there something I can do for you?"

Dovie opened her mouth, but no words came, her mind a complete and disastrous blank. "I've come for Dora Tandy's watch," she finally blurted.

For a moment Dovie thought she was about to have the door slammed in her face. Gemma's smile faltered, then vanished altogether as she took a wary step back.

"Please, I'm not here to pry or dig up old wounds. I just need the watch, and I'll go."

"How do you know Dora Tandy?"

"We met at the cemetery. She was there to visit Alice's grave."

"She's . . . here? In Charleston?"

"For several weeks now."

Gemma stood there, clutching the doorknob, her brown eyes wide and unfocused. Finally, she stepped aside. "I think you'd better come in."

Dovie felt a twinge of remorse as she followed Gemma past the half-arranged vase of roses on the foyer table. It didn't seem fair that in trying to ease one woman's grief, she should rekindle it in another. And yet the two were entwined somehow, inexplicably linked by the young woman they had each tragically lost.

In the parlor, Gemma laid down her shears and took a seat on the sofa. "Please," she said, gesturing to a nearby wingback. "I think we'd better start over. Why are you here?"

Dovie eased into the chair, letting her tote slide to the floor. "I know this is strange, but I really am just here for the watch. Dora is a friend of mine, and she's sick. Very sick. I thought it might make her feel better to have something of Alice's."

"If you're a friend of Dora's you know about the rift between Alice and her mother."

Dovie nodded. "I do. And it's why I'm here. She blames herself for so much. When she found out she was sick she came to Charleston to find her daughter, to beg her forgiveness one last time. She had no idea Alice was dead until she arrived. She's been torturing herself ever since. That's why I want the watch, to prove to Dora that Alice never stopped loving her."

Gemma's face was ashen but unreadable. "And you assume I have this watch?"

"I'm hoping you do, yes." Dovie scrambled for a plausible explanation but decided she was wasting her time. There was only one way she could know about the watch, and they both knew it. "The letters you left in the cemetery," Dovie said quietly. "I have them."

If possible, Gemma went a shade paler. "How? After all these years, how could you possibly . . ."

"I have a friend who works at Magnolia Grove. He's one of the groundskeepers. He found them one day, in the lost and found, and gave them to me."

There was a new wariness in Gemma's eyes as she regarded Dovie. "Why would he—"

"Because I asked him to. It started the day I first saw Dora in the cemetery. She was so desolate, I couldn't take my eyes off her. And then she pulled this letter out of her purse and left it on Alice's grave. When she left, I took it home and read it. It was inexcusable, I know, but I was going through some things. My fiancé committed suicide just before our wedding, and I was trying to figure how I hadn't seen it coming, what I had or hadn't done. And here was this woman, leaving a letter to a dead girl. I thought if I read it I might gain some kind of insight. Instead, I found myself obsessed. I had to know Alice's story. That's why I went to Josiah. The next thing I knew I had a whole bagful of letters that had turned up in the lost and found. I've been reading them to Dora a little at a time. It's been . . . difficult for her."

"I never meant for them to be found."

"Why leave them at the cemetery, then?" Dovie asked. "Why not shred them or burn them?"

Gemma shrugged. When she finally spoke, her voice was thick and weary. "I made a promise to a friend—to Alice—but I couldn't keep it. I meant to, I just . . . couldn't. And every time I looked at those letters I was reminded of it. I wanted them gone. Only I couldn't make myself do it. It seemed wrong to just tear them up, and even worse to burn them, maybe because I knew they weren't *really* mine. So I took them to the cemetery and just . . . left them." She paused, fingers pressed to her lips. "Makes you wonder, doesn't it?"

"What?"

"If this is what was supposed to happen. Fate knew I'd never have the courage to do the right thing, so it took matters into its own hands."

"You think Alice's letters were supposed to end up in the lost and found, so they would eventually find their way into my hands?"

She smiled, a tight smile that quickly faded. "It would be nice, wouldn't it, if life worked like that? If, no matter how badly we botched things, they still ended up working out the way they should. I used to believe it. Maybe some part of me still does." She looked down at her lap, smoothing invisible wrinkles from her skirt. When she looked up her eyes were moist. "Alice's mother—you said before that she was sick. Is it . . . bad?"

"She's recovering from a bad bout with pneumonia, but that isn't the worst part. All this time, while we've been going through the letters, she's been clinging to the hope that there might be some word about the child Alice gave up, but there wasn't. I think it would have helped to know that somewhere out there she had a grandchild who was happy and doing well. She's taking it so hard, I'm afraid she's given up. That's why I came today. Because I thought the watch might help."

Gemma sat very still, eyes closed, a hand to her throat. After a moment, she pushed heavily to her feet, as if carrying some invisible weight on her shoulders. "Wait here," she said. "I'll be right back."

A short time later, she returned, her face pale and set as she crossed the room and handed Dovie a small satin pouch tied with a lavender ribbon. "Open it," she said softly.

Dovie worked the ribbon free, revealing a series of accordioned compartments lined in creamy satin. She'd been expecting the watch, but her breath caught as she teased out the pair of familiar-looking envelopes. She looked at Gemma with a mixture of confusion and wonder. "You kept two."

"When you've read them you'll understand. I'd like you to show them to Dora, if you think she's well enough."

Dovie stared at the envelopes. They felt heavy in her palm, ominous and somehow inevitable. She found herself thinking about Gemma's hypothesis that finding the letters was supposed to happen, a tidy arrangement by the Fates to right a forty-year-old wrong. "You said if she's well enough. Are they . . . ?"

"Difficult to read? Yes. I haven't read them for a long time, but after so many years I know them by heart. Perhaps it would be best if you read them now, before you go. You'll have questions, I'm sure."

forty-eight

9 East Battery Street
Charleston, South Carolina
December 10, 1969

Dearest heart,

I wish there was some easy way to tell you what I'm about to. Heaven knows I've searched my heart long and hard before picking up my pen again, wondering if I'm right in what I'm about to do, or if, for your sake, it would be better to leave things alone. I still don't know. Perhaps it's only selfishness, this need for you to know the truth, but after all that's happened, I believe I have the right to be a little selfish. And so I must begin.

If you have read the letters that came before this, you already know the circumstances of your birth, that I was unmarried, and because I was unmarried you were taken from me. You also know I vowed to find you one day. And now I have, though it has come too late, and in a way I could never have expected. It is of those details that I now write, because I need you to know why I was unable to keep my promise.

I hadn't thought before now about where to begin, or how hard it might be to retell such things, but I suppose I should begin with the moment Harley burst into the nursery, where I was doing my best to tidy up. It's been a week ago now, but I recall every detail like it was yesterday. I thought he had lost his mind. He was sneering as he came toward me, his lips pulled back in something like satisfaction.

"Well, well, here she is, the tragic English waif, come all the way across the pond to play nanny. Imagine her good fortune when she's taken under the wing of one of the wealthiest women in Charleston."

I didn't understand what he was saying, or why he was saying it. I only knew I didn't like the way he was looking at me, with a mixture of malice and glee, like he knew some terrible secret and was savoring the moment before he finally divulged it.

"You and my wife are pretty chummy, aren't you? Almost like sisters."

"Yes," I said, steeling myself for whatever was coming.

"And sisters would never do anything to hurt each other. That's how it works, isn't it?"

I nodded, feeling a prickle of some hidden danger. He has never hidden his dislike for me, but this was different, chilling and almost ominous. He stepped closer then, shoving several rumpled sheets of paper into my hands.

"Tell me, then, why I've just found this in my wife's dresser." His eyes glittered as he shoved the papers under my nose. "My supposed son," he said, sneering. "Not a private adoption like she said, but a mongrel with a whore for a mother, palmed off on her by a bunch of do-gooding Catholics."

My stomach lurched when I saw the words "Sacred Heart Children's Society" printed at the top of one of the pages. For a moment, I thought I might be sick, but my eyes kept moving, the words blurring as I read. "Pleased to inform you . . . application for adoption . . . your preference for a boy." I shuffled through the remaining pages, desperate for some proof that I was wrong, that there'd been some kind of mistake. And then I saw it—the sheet of plain white paper covered with careful English schoolgirl script. The room began to spin as I read the line I had penned more than seven years ago.

"Little one, you don't know me . . ."

How had I not known? Not seen? Not felt you right there? I always thought I would know you the moment I saw you, that there would be some sort of connection, a tugging on the maternal cord. And I suppose there was a connection. Yes, of course there was. I just thought it was something else.

I remember hearing a buzzing sound, like a hive of bees in my head, as I buckled to my knees, and then, from very far away, a sort of keening. It was a terrible sound, the kind a wounded animal might make, shrill and primal, and I suddenly realized it was coming from me, tearing from my throat, echoing off the walls. I didn't hear Gemma coming until she burst into the room. Her eyes went wide when she saw me on the floor, the letter still clutched in my hand. I wanted to be wrong, wanted there to be some logical explanation, but I had only to look at her face to know it was all true.

"How?" I sobbed. "How could you do it? When you knew . . ."

"But I didn't know! Not at first. You have to believe me. That day, when you came about the job . . . I had no idea."

"You had the papers! And the letter they made me write before he was born."

"I never read it, Alice. I never read any of it. After I brought Austin home I put those papers away, and that was that. I suppose I planned to go through them someday, but then time passed and there didn't seem much point."

"How long have you known?"

Her eyes slid from mine, lingering on the carpet. "Almost three years. Just after you got sick that first time and I sent for Dr. Ponder. That's when I finally went back and read the papers, after learning the rest of your story. Until that moment, I had no idea. You have to believe me."

I felt the blood drain from my face but managed to get to my feet, shaking her off when she tried to help me. "Three years . . . You let me go on writing letters to adoption agencies all over the country, torturing myself, and all the time he was right here. My son was right here!"

"Please, honey, I know it was wrong, but I was so afraid. I thought if you knew the truth you'd take him away, that you'd go back to England and I'd never see him again. I couldn't bear the thought of losing him. So I convinced myself that nothing had to change, that because we were all so happy together, I wasn't really keeping him from you."

"You had no right to make that decision. I'm his mother."

"I'm his mother, too."

"Because you have papers that say so?"

Her eyes welled with fresh tears. "Because I love him."

Her tears meant nothing to me. I let the papers fall to the floor, preparing to step past her, but she grabbed my arm.

"Where are you going?"

"To talk to my son."

Her grip tightened on my sleeve. "Please don't do that, Alice. Not like this, when you're angry. You'll only frighten him. He won't understand."

"I'll make him understand."

She must have seen that I meant what I said, because she went very still. "What will you tell him?"

"The truth. That I'm his mother. That you've known all the time. That while you were pretending to be my friend you were lying to me, and purposely keeping us apart."

"It wasn't like that. You know it wasn't. I've never kept you from Austin. And I wasn't pretending to be your friend—I am your friend, Alice. And I'm so very sorry."

"Stop saying that!" I closed my eyes and felt myself sway, my breath tight in my chest. "You're not . . . sorry. And why should you be? You've gotten exactly what you wanted. You have Austin, and you can finally stop being afraid. I'll be . . . out of the way soon. What a nice bit of luck for you."

She let go of my arm then, stepping back as if I had struck her. I was glad. I wanted to hurt her, to rip her heart from her chest, as she had done mine. I managed to shove past her and staggered out into the hall. A moment later there were footsteps behind me, more pleas and muffled weeping. It took all the strength I had to keep her from pushing her way into my room. I managed to turn the key, then crumpled into a heap as the floor gave way beneath me.

I woke some time later, still sprawled on the carpet, my clothes drenched and my body on fire. I have a hazy recollection of wandering barefoot down the hall, my throat parched and aching. And then, with no memory of how I had gotten there, I was standing in the doorway of your room, watching you as you slept.

Your head was turned to one side, your face lit like an angel's in the watery light spilling through the window, and I realized with a catch in my throat that I was trying to memorize your face, pressing your features, one at a time, between the pages of my memory—the angle of your cheek, the little mole just below your ear, the way your bangs fall across your forehead—in case it was the last time I saw you. The thought was almost more than I could bear. Where had the years gone? I still remember what it felt like to carry you beneath my ribs, so small and round—the child of my heart. How had I not seen that you were right here all the time?

I used to fantasize about what it would be like when I first saw you. My heart would leap in my chest, and I would know you in an instant. I didn't, though, and because I didn't I felt I had failed you. I thought you would look like me, or like Johnny. But as I stood there, studying your features and committing them to memory, I saw what I hadn't before. Your eyes were the color of mine, but your lashes were your father's. You have my cheekbones, but your chin is his. You have my long limbs, but your father's sturdiness. You were not me. You were not Johnny. You were both of us—and the best of us.

You stirred then and turned away, your face slipping from view. I felt the loss like a physical pain, and the tears came, breaking me open as I stood there clinging to the doorframe. I didn't know Gemma was behind me until I felt her hand on my arm, insistent and startlingly cool. I tried to pull away but couldn't manage it. My head was fuzzy, as if my mind and body were floating apart from each other.

What happened next is still a blur, a jumble of hot broth and cool hands, soothing words and fevered dreams, and through it all, a fire in my chest that seemed to be consuming me. I have a vague recollection of the doctor being there, a tall shadow leaning over my bed, his tone grave as he told someone—Gemma, I suppose—that beyond making me comfortable, there was nothing more to be done.

I remember being relieved. How sweet it would be to close my eyes and not open them again, to no longer feel sick, and tired, and sad. But it wasn't time. There was still something I needed to do.

I can't say how many days passed, but little by little I drifted up from that dark place. I was exhausted and still struggling to breathe, but cool and strangely lucid. Gemma was nearby, dozing in a chair she had pulled up next to the bed. She looked terrible, thin and ravaged, and so horribly pale. I must have moved, or made a sound, because she sat up and reached out to touch my brow.

"Alice, honey, you're awake." Her voice was dry and rusty from disuse, and I could see that she'd been crying. "How do you feel? Never mind. Don't try to speak yet." Our eyes met and held. She swallowed hard. "You were asleep for so long. I thought . . ."

I dragged my eyes away. I knew what she thought, that I might never wake up. I wondered if she was disappointed that I had.

She patted my hand. "Would you like some broth? Some tea?"

I ran my tongue over my lips, cracked and sore. "Austin."

"Oh, honey, he isn't here. I thought it would be better if he stayed with friends until . . . until you were better."

I looked away, willing myself not to cry. We both knew I wasn't going to get better, and that I would never see my son again. I lay there for a time, waiting for her to leave, wondering why she didn't. Finally, she broke her silence.

"What I did was unforgivable."

"Yes." I looked at her with the full force of my hatred, watching as the word struck home, a blow so clean and unexpected that it rocked her back on her heels.

"Please, Alice. Listen to what I have to say. I know you don't want to hear that I'm sorry, but you have to know I would cut off my arm before hurting you intentionally. You can't know what went through my mind when I read that letter. It was as if someone had torn out my heart. I still can't imagine what it would be like to lose your child like that—but I can imagine what it would be like to lose mine—to lose everything. I was afraid, desperate. I still am."

It was true. She was still afraid. I could see it in her eyes. The realization startled me. What could Gemma Tate have to fear from me? I hadn't a cent to my name, no friends, powerful or otherwise. I couldn't even get out of bed.

"What do you have to be afraid of?" I asked her bitterly. "You've already won."

She blinked at me with red-rimmed eyes, as if she, too, was startled. "What am I afraid of? Oh, honey, how can you not know? I'm afraid of losing you, of you leaving me, and never forgiving me. I don't think I can bear it."

"The time to worry about that was three years ago."

"But I did worry. I've never stopped worrying. And if there was a way—any way—I could undo what I've done, I would gladly do it." She paused to brush a tear from her cheek. "When I read the letter,

and thought about what it might mean—for you, for me, for poor Austin—I just couldn't bring myself to do the right thing—because it wouldn't have been the right thing. All these years, he's been as much yours as mine. You know he has. We were a family. We were happy. What good could come from tearing us apart?"

I closed my eyes, wincing as I struggled to draw a breath. The room was very hot again, and seemed to have grown darker. "It wasn't . . . your choice."

"No. It wasn't."

I turned my face away. I wanted no more of her excuses, but her words had struck a chord in me. Somewhere deep down in a place I wasn't ready to look at, a place of bitterness and confusion, I knew there was at least a thread of truth in what she said. All these years, I have been a mother to you. I held you, fed you, rocked you to sleep, taught you your letters and to tie your shoes. I tended your scrapes, dried your tears. What more could I have had of you than that? What more could you have had of me?

There was something else, too, that I was loath to admit. As a Tate, you had enjoyed a life I would never have been able to give you, and would go on enjoying that life long after I was gone. How could I not be grateful for that, or for any bit of good that has befallen you? Fate hasn't been especially kind to me, and my time is growing short. But knowing you will be cared for, my darling, cherished and given every advantage, makes the leaving easier somehow.

I hated this sudden chink in my armor, the soft, exposed place where forgiveness might enter if I was not careful. But I was so tired, my rage burned to ash. What good was all my hating? Time was short and there were things left to say.

Gemma watched me, slowly leaning forward, as if she could sense my caving in. Her chin quivered, she reached for my hand, a sob rolling up from deep in her chest, and suddenly we were both weeping.

"Please, Alice, we have so little time left. What can I do? Whatever it is, tell me, and I'll do it."

My head lolled against the pillow. I felt like I was floating, as if my soul were trying to slip its skin, tethered to the world by a single tenuous thread—the promise I would not leave without. I forced my eyes to focus and met her gaze squarely.

"Tell my son the truth." I watched her face crumple but felt no remorse. Perhaps I meant it to be her penance, a way to finally even the score between us, and if I did, no one can blame me. "Give him my letters. Not now, but when he's ready. So he'll know I never stopped looking for him, never stopped loving him. Say you'll do it. Swear it."

"But, Alice, those letters . . ."

"Swear it."

She nodded, and at that moment I could almost have forgiven her. Not because I accepted her excuses, but because I knew what that nod had cost her. One day, she'll hand you this, and the rest of my letters, and you'll know what she did. Perhaps none of this will matter to you. Perhaps by then you'll have forgotten all about me. But I will never forget you, the cherished son of my heart, and that is all I ever wanted you to know.

All my love,
Mam

forty-nine

"My God." Dovie sat staring at the pages in her lap.

Across from her, Gemma wept quietly, her face in ruins. "There's nothing else to say, is there, but *my God*? All that time. All those letters. And I never said a word. I wasn't lying when I said I didn't know. I truly didn't. I knew she had given up a child. It happened all the time, back then. It just never occurred to me that that child might be asleep upstairs in my nursery. I was so happy to finally have a child of my own. I never stopped to wonder who his mother might have been. I don't think I really wanted to know. The less I knew, the less there was to lie about."

"Lie about?"

Gemma cleared her throat, looking down at the fragments of tissue in her lap. "My husband never wanted to adopt. When the doctors told me I couldn't have a baby, they suggested adoption, but Harley wouldn't hear of it. He could be rather high-minded about certain things. He said he wasn't giving his name to the brat of some addict or streetwalker. So I found a private agency, one known for discretion, where we could be assured of getting a child worthy of the Tate name. Poor girls from good families who'd gotten themselves in a fix. It took almost a year of pleading, but Harley finally gave in. I was so happy. And then I found out we were twenty-third on the waiting list, and that it could be years before we got a baby . . ." She paused then, blotting her eyes, her pain as fresh and raw as it must have been all those years ago. "I was crushed, and terrified that Harley would change his mind."

"So you went to Sacred Heart," Dovie said quietly.

"I'd heard whispers about babies coming over from England and Ireland, being smuggled in with forged birth certificates. I had an attorney make inquiries, and was told that for the right amount of money I could have one of those babies, and that it would all be handled very quickly and quietly. Six months later, Austin came home. Harley was gone so much back then; he left the details to me. It never occurred to him that I'd lie about where Austin really came from."

"Until he found the adoption papers."

"Yes." Her eyes fluttered closed. "I could have killed him that day, for ambushing her like that. Two weeks later, she was dead. I never forgave him for that—or myself. I had a sort of breakdown that summer. The doctors sent me to the mountains, to a place that was supposed to help me get my legs back under me. I think that's how they put it. I came home to find Harley had sent Austin away to school—my punishment."

"Austin doesn't know, does he? You never gave him the letters."

"No, though I really did mean to. But after Alice died, everything just . . . fell apart. Harley never forgave me for lying about the adoption. He wasn't used to being crossed. I told Sacred Heart I wanted a boy. I thought he'd bond more easily with a son, but I was wrong. He resented Austin from the first day he came home." She was weeping again, tears rolling unchecked down her cheeks. "I've hurt so many people—Alice, Austin, my husband, even poor Dora—because I was selfish and . . ." Her words trailed as her gaze slid to the doorway. "Austin."

He nodded coolly. "Mother."

"How long have you been standing there?"

"Long enough to hear that my father never loved me, and why. Does that answer your question?" He didn't wait for a response before rounding on Dovie. "But I think the real question is, why are you here? I thought we had an understanding."

Gemma reached for her son's hand before Dovie could answer. "She's here because she's a friend of Alice's mother, and I have something that belongs to her, something that might help the poor woman feel better. If you'll just sit down we can talk about it."

"There's been enough talk. Too much, in fact." His eyes were steely as he brought them back to Dovie. "I'd like you to leave now. And not come back."

"Honey, please," Gemma pleaded. "None of this is her fault."

Austin seemed not to hear, his eyes still locked with Dovie's. "You got what you came for—and then some. I hope you're happy."

Dovie stood and stepped past him, finding her way to the front door as quickly as her legs would carry her. She was shaking by the time she reached her car and slid behind the wheel. She had known there would be hell to pay if Austin ever found out she'd come to see his mother, but she never once considered that her visit might trigger such an astonishing and gut-wrenching revelation. If he hadn't been finished with her before, he certainly was now.

She was still gripping the steering wheel, too flustered to start the car let alone steer the thing home, when Austin's voice boomed through the open car door. "Why did you come here? What were you trying to prove?"

Dovie glanced up at him, flustered by the question. "Please, I know you're angry about what just happened in there, and you have a right to be. But I had a reason for coming. One I'm happy to explain to you. We just need to talk."

"We most definitely do *not* need to talk. And there's nothing to explain. I was there, remember? I heard the whole thing."

"You didn't hear all of it, Austin. There's more. A lot more."

"Maybe, but I'm not ready to hear it—from you or her. So I guess we're all done here."

Dovie studied him, baffled by his cool indifference. He was angry; that couldn't be denied. But something wasn't right. He was far too calm for a man who'd just gotten the shock of his life. "I don't understand," she said, finally. "You find out the woman you've been calling Mother all your life isn't your mother at all, and it's like you're made of stone. I have no idea what's going on in your head right now. You must have feelings about all this. Anger, shock . . . something."

He smiled, or maybe it was a grimace. "Trust me when I tell you you're better off not knowing what's going on in my head right now. What do you want me to say, that my world's been shattered and I'm going to spend the next ten years on a therapist's couch working through mommy issues? Sorry to disappoint you, sweetheart. Gemma Tate is my mother. The rest is just . . . biology."

"So you're not angry?"

"Oh, I'm angry. But not for the reasons you think. I'm angry that people can't leave things alone when they're asked to. I'm angry that I had to walk in and find my mother in tears in her own parlor. But mostly, I'm angry that I have to stand here and talk about why I'm angry. Which is why I'm walking away now."

Dovie watched as Austin climbed into the BMW and pulled down the drive without so much as a backward glance. Resigned, she reached for her own keys, only to realize that in her haste to escape Austin's wrath she had left them, and her tote, in Gemma Tate's parlor.

Gemma's face fell as she pulled back the door, the visible sagging of her shoulders making it clear she'd been hoping to find her son instead of Dovie.

"I'm sorry to bother you again," Dovie said tentatively. "I left my tote in your parlor."

Gemma motioned for her to follow before turning away. Dovie

picked up the tote and slid it onto her shoulder. "I can't tell you how sorry I am about all this. I never meant to create a rift between you and your son."

"Of course you didn't."

"Are you going to be all right?" she asked quietly, concerned about the almost eerie calm that seemed to have settled over Gemma.

She nodded, her eyes red-rimmed but dry, as if she had finally cried herself out. "I'm just wondering what happens now."

Dovie stared at her. She honestly didn't know. She'd been hoping for a tearful family reunion. Instead, she had inadvertently triggered a slow-motion train wreck. "I tried to talk to him, just now, but he wouldn't listen. He just kept shutting me down. I'm going to try again, though. I have to. This was all my fault."

Gemma shook her head. "Leave him. Time is what he needs, right now. And lots of space. It's how he deals with things. He blows up, lashes out, then retreats."

Dovie winced, flashing back to yesterday morning's conversation on the beach. "I seem to be learning that the hard way."

Gemma studied her a moment, one dark brow arched. "Are you in love with my son?"

The question caught Dovie off guard. "I don't . . . I mean, we aren't . . ."

"Is he in love with you?"

Dovie shook her head. "No. Of that I *am* sure."

"Maybe you shouldn't be. I've never seen my son look at a woman the way he looked at you when you were dancing with Kristopher. You're what he needs, whether he knows it or not."

Dovie shifted from foot to foot, her eyes on the carpet. In light of recent events, it seemed a strange discussion to be having. "Something tells me Austin wouldn't appreciate us having this conversation. Especially after today."

Gemma managed a smile. "No. You're right about that. But he's all I have in the world—at least, I hope I still have him—and I want him to be happy. He's made mistakes in his life. I don't want him to make any more. And I'm afraid he will."

"I understand that. I do. But I don't see how I can help. Your son and I aren't even on speaking terms at this point, and even if we were, I'm not sure I want to be his next mistake. I've already been that for someone, and it didn't end well for either of us."

"Have you ever stopped to think there might be a reason you were in the cemetery the day Dora left that letter?"

It was the second time she'd hinted at such a thing, but Dovie found it hard to consider such an unlikely possibility, no matter how tempting. "You're saying all this was meant to happen, that Dora's letter was just the first domino in some cosmic chain reaction?"

"That's one way of putting it. But I was thinking it's like a butterfly flapping its wings in Japan and creating a tsunami halfway around the world. Dora's letter was the butterfly."

Dovie's lips thinned grimly. "And . . . I'm the tsunami?"

"Today was the tsunami—the truth coming out the way it did in one big crashing wave."

"That doesn't exactly make me feel better."

"Honey, none of us is going to feel very good for a while. That's just how it is with tidal waves." She paused, stepping away to gather Alice's final letters from the table, then dropped them into Dovie's tote. "Take them to Dora. And this." She reached into her pocket then and produced a wadded bit of hanky, pushing it into Dovie's hand. "It's what you came for."

Dovie carefully peeled back the folds of the hanky until the watch came into view, a thick gold disk about the size of a half dollar. She pressed the button on the stem with her thumb. It sprang easily, revealing a yellowed dial with roman numerals and a pair of gold filigree hands.

"It hadn't worked in years," Gemma said softly. "But she never went anywhere without it. I offered to send it out to my jeweler, but she never would."

Dovie smiled as she closed the watch and rewrapped it. "It wasn't for telling time." Her eyes met Gemma's then, an acknowledgment of what this small act of kindness had cost her. "Thank you."

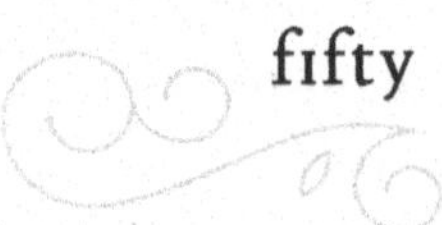

fifty

Dovie's stomach tightened as she turned down the gravel path that curved around to the back of Austin's house. She had rung the bell twice but gotten no answer. Maybe he was around back, out on the beach—or maybe he'd just seen her car and had decided not to answer. Gemma said he needed time, yet here she was, twenty-four hours postdisaster, tracking him down like a bloodhound.

She hadn't been able to bring herself to tell Dora about the letters last night. She needed time to think about how best to broach the subject of Alice's long-lost son. And she still didn't know what she was going to say to Austin, or whether she should say anything at all. Perhaps the best course was to say nothing, to simply do what she had come to do and then leave. After all, there wasn't much they hadn't said.

She drew up short when he came into view, standing at the water's edge, hurling shells one at a time out over the waves. For a moment she watched him, noting the tightly coiled anger that seemed to vibrate through his body with each throw. And then he went still, the remaining shells trickling out of his hand and onto the sand, and she knew he had sensed her behind him.

"Austin."

He pivoted slowly, hands on hips. "Don't you *ever* give up?"

"I just came to give you something," she said, holding out the stack of letters. "These belong to you. I still have the last two. I'll bring them by as soon as Dora's seen them."

He glanced at the letters and looked away. "I don't want them."

"They were written to you, Austin—some before you were even born. You should read them. Once you do, you might even want to talk to Dora."

Austin's face registered a combination of fury and astonishment. "That's what this is about? Me sitting down for a chat with some old woman because she's . . . what?"

"Because she's your grandmother, and she came halfway around the world to find forgiveness—and you. Maybe it's too late for forgiveness, but it isn't too late for—"

"If you're hoping for some teary reunion, there isn't going to be one. That's your obsession, not mine—and it's over, as of now."

He turned then and headed up the dunes, making a beeline for the back stairs. Dovie followed him, taking the steps two at a time to catch up.

"It's not that simple, Austin. You can't put this genie back in the bottle. You need to talk to your mother. And she needs to talk to you."

Austin was breathing hard by the time he stepped through the open sliders and rounded on her. "Did you know?"

Dovie blinked at him. "Know what?"

"When you went to my mother's house yesterday, did you already know what was in that letter?"

"Of course not. How could I? How could anyone?"

"I did."

The words came so quietly Dovie wasn't sure she'd heard them right. "You . . . knew?"

He wandered to the kitchen, grabbed two bottled waters from

the fridge, and handed one to Dovie. "I was ten, and home from school for the holidays. Like any kid worth his salt, I was snooping for presents in my mother's closet." He paused, eyeing the packet of envelopes Dovie had placed on the kitchen counter. "I thought I hit the jackpot when I found that box."

"The letters?"

"Yup. I recognized them the minute I lifted the lid."

"How could you recognize them?"

"I'd seen them once, just before Alice died." He paused to shuck off his jacket, then pulled a long sip from his water. "She was so sick my mother wouldn't let me see her, so one day I snuck down the hall to her room. The door was open, and my mother was there, sitting beside her while she wrote something. Jesus, she looked awful. She was so thin you could almost see through her. I remember starting to cry. I think that's when I realized she wasn't going to get better. After a few minutes she folded whatever she was writing into an envelope and handed it to my mother, who added it to a stack of others just like it. There was something about the way she handled those letters, like she expected them to burst into flames or something. The image stuck with me for days. Longer than that, I guess, because I knew what they were the minute I saw them in the closet."

"What did you do when you found them?"

"What any kid would—I picked the fattest one in the stack and read it. Or most of it. I was too young to understand the nuances, but I got the gist."

"You must have been stunned."

"That's the thing. I wasn't. It was like part of me always knew. Unfortunately, by the time I snuck back to read the rest of the letters, they were gone. I had no idea what happened to them. I figured I'd see them again when my mother thought it was time. Every birthday that rolled around, I wondered if this would be the year she sat me down and told me the truth. But it never was. I thought for sure she'd do it when I turned eighteen, and then when I turned twenty-one. But she didn't. After that, I just stopped thinking about it. I was in school, and then came the business with Monica—her death and the whole hushed-up mess—and all of a sudden I knew what it was like to be so ashamed of something you'd done that you'd do anything to keep the people you loved from knowing. If she wanted to keep the whole thing a secret, who was I to press the issue?"

He was prowling now, stalking from one end of the living room to the other. Dovie settled on the arm of the couch, following him with her eyes. "So that was it? You just went on pretending Gemma was your mother?"

Austin stopped prowling and met her gaze. "I wasn't pretending, Dovie. Gemma *is* my mother. And so was Alice. I meant it before when I said the rest was just biology."

Dovie nodded. She was about to open her water when she spotted the blue nylon duffel near the door. Something clenched in her chest. "Are you going somewhere?"

Austin followed her gaze to the bag. "I've been thinking about it, yeah."

"Because of yesterday?"

"Because of a lot of things. Up until a few months ago, I had a life. Maybe not a great life, but one I built very carefully. I knew what worked and what didn't. I knew what I wanted, and what I couldn't have. Now that life's been hijacked. It's like the ground I'm used to standing on is disappearing out from under me. I don't know how it happened, or why, but I need to figure out how to get it back."

"How long will you be gone?"

"I don't know. As long as it takes. I've got a lot of thinking to do, and I can't do it here, where everything's so . . . close."

Dovie slid off the arm of the couch and moved to the open sliders, determined not to let him see her face. "Your mother says it's how you deal with things—you lash out, then retreat."

"It sounds like me."

"It does," she said, turning back to face him. "But this isn't like Monica. You can't just run away from this one. I don't mean me. You don't owe me anything. I'm talking about your mother. I know it's none of my business, but she's spent the last thirty years terrified you'd find out something you already knew. And now, because she still has no idea you did know, she's terrified you'll never forgive her. At least talk it out before you go."

Austin was silent for a time, his face a parade of unreadable emotions. "You're right," he said. "It isn't your business, and it never was. So you'll excuse me for saying a lecture from you at this point is a bit presumptuous."

"I know."

He hung his head, shaking it from side to side. "Why couldn't you just leave it alone?"

Dovie stepped to the counter, fingering the stack of letters. "Because I made a promise."

"To Dora?"

"Yes."

"I know you think I'm a hard-ass for refusing to see her, but try to see my side. The woman's a stranger to me."

Dovie nodded but said nothing, letting the silence thicken.

Finally, Austin cleared his throat. "What will you tell her?"

"The truth, I guess."

"Yes." Austin's expression was grave. "I suppose it's time for that."

fifty-one

Dovie tiptoed around the kitchen while she waited for the coffee to brew. After a night of no sleep, her head felt heavy and dull, her stomach queasy at the thought of the unpleasant conversation that lay ahead of her. For now, at least, Dora was still asleep, and she preferred to keep it that way until she figured out how to say the things she needed to say. But it wasn't the telling she dreaded most. It was the questions that would come after. Questions about Austin.

Dora's spirits were already at rock bottom. She had no appetite, and getting her to take her medicine had become a battle of wills. She didn't want to think about how the poor woman would take the news that her grandson had been found at last, alive and well, right here in Charleston—and wanted nothing to do with her. The last flicker of hope snuffed out, and a fresh dose of grief, to boot. The thought left Dovie hollowed out. How on earth would she manage the fallout?

The question was still scraping around in her head when the doorbell rang. She hurried to answer, before whoever it was could ring again and wake Dora. She was expecting a salesman of some kind, or a pair of Jehovah's Witnesses. Instead, she found Austin standing on her front porch.

"I thought you were leaving town."

"So did I. Turns out I had some business to take care of. I went to the museum, but you weren't there."

"I'm taking a few days. What are you doing here?"

"There are some things I didn't say yesterday that I need to say now."

Dovie eyed him warily. He'd said a lot of things—none of them pleasant. Which is why she was pretty sure she wasn't in the mood to listen to whatever it was he thought he'd missed. "What things?"

"Are you going to make me say them out here on your front porch?"

"Dora's asleep," she told him coolly. "I'd rather you weren't here when she wakes up. I suppose we could go around to the back porch, if you want."

On the porch, she pointed to one of the rockers. Austin declined, choosing to stand at the railing instead, taking in the broad expanse of tidal marsh, awash in morning sunlight. For a moment there was only the sound of the wind sifting through the spartina, and the high, hollow tinkle of the tiny hummingbird wind chimes hanging from a corner of the porch.

"I should have known your backyard would look like this," he said, not meeting her eyes.

"You said there were things you needed to say."

He nodded, turning away to grip the deck railing with both hands. "The other day at my mother's, and then yesterday, I said some things, bad things, that I need to apologize for. It was just that whole scene, walking in on you reading that letter, hearing my mother talk about how much my father hated me—it brought up a lot of old memories, things I'd worked really hard to forget. And there you were in my mother's parlor, unraveling the whole damn mess. I wanted to strangle you."

"You made that pretty clear."

"I read the letters you left last night. And then I sat down with my mother. She told me how you and Dora met, how you ended up with all of Alice's letters and found yourself pulled into her story. That's why I had to come. You stuck your nose into my family's business, and made a hell of a mess while you were at it, but I should have known better than to question your motives. You were trying to fix things, because that's what you do. And that's why I'm here, to say I'm sorry."

"Thank you for that," Dovie said. "And I'm sorry about . . . all the rest of it."

"Don't be." Austin dropped into one of the rockers, eyes fixed on the expanse of cordgrass beyond the porch. "My mother and I covered a lot of territory last night, stuff neither of us wanted to talk about, but needed to. My father, mostly, and how he screwed us both up. He couldn't stand the sight of me, even as a kid. No matter what I did, or how hard I tried, it was never enough. Now I get that it was never really about me. Unfortunately, my mother blames herself, and I'm afraid she always will."

Dovie eased into the rocker beside his, nearly reaching for his hand before she caught herself. "I don't know what else to say, Austin, but I'm sorry. You both have good reasons to be angry. He wanted to hurt your mother, so he used you as a weapon. He was a coward, like most bullies."

"When I said those things yesterday, I was mad at you, but it wasn't *just* you. Hell, I've been mad for such a long time—at Monica, at myself, at my father—that it almost feels normal. I was too stupid to see that there comes a point where trying to punish someone who doesn't give a damn becomes a complete waste of time. Instead, all I did was hurt a lot of people who didn't deserve it."

They were quiet for a time, rocking in unison, the rhythmic creak of the treads mingling with the quiet thrum of the marsh. It was Austin who finally broke the silence.

"Have you spoken to Dora? About the letters, I mean."

Dovie shook her head. "Not yet. I've been trying to figure out how to break the news. I'm afraid the shock of it all might be too much."

Austin looked away, back out over the marsh, as if weighing something. "I've been thinking," he said, drawing the words out. "I think I'd like to be there, if that's all right."

Dovie was almost afraid to open her mouth, afraid she'd heard him wrong, afraid he'd change his mind. "You want to meet Dora?"

"I think it's time. For her, and for me."

Dora was already awake when Dovie stuck her head through the door. The television was on, tuned to the Weather Channel.

"I've brought you some tea, and it's time to take your pills."

Dora shook her head. "No more pills."

"Please, Dora. You need to take your medicine." She set the tea on the bedside table, then pulled in a deep breath. "And then I have some news—about Alice."

Dora's weary eyes darkened. "What kind of news?"

After careful consideration, Dovie had decided to skip the letters, at least for now. Dora had had enough bad news to last a lifetime. It was time for a little happy news, and even that might prove more of a shock than the poor woman could take.

Easing onto the edge of the bed, Dovie took Dora's hands in hers. "Dora, I need to make sure you're ready for what you're going to hear today. It's a lot to take in, and I'm afraid you might be in for a bit of a shock. Are you up to it, do you think? Because if you aren't, we can wait until you're stronger."

"Now. Tell me now."

"All right, but first your medicine, and a little tea."

Dovie helped Dora sit up, plumping the pillows behind her neck and shoulders, then turned her attention to the display of pills on the bedside table—one white, one yellow, and half a blue. She handed them to Dora, along with a bottle of water, then waited to make sure she swallowed them. "Will you eat some toast if I bring it?"

"Later."

Dovie understood. She wanted the news. Now.

"Fine. But you promised to drink some tea." Dovie gave Dora a stern look as she pressed the mug into her hands. "I'll be back in a few minutes."

She returned a short time later. Austin was with her but hung back in the doorway, looking distinctly uncomfortable. Dora eyed him with a mix of confusion and annoyance, before bringing her watery gaze back to Dovie. "I thought you had some news for me."

Dovie suppressed a smile. There was the Dora she'd come to love, impatient and slightly imperious when she didn't get her way. It was good to see her again. "This is a friend of mine, Dora. He stopped by this morning, and wanted to meet you."

Dora remained mute as Dovie dragged a pair of chairs over to the bed and gestured for Austin to take one. He declined with the barest shake of his head, opting for a less conspicuous position—one more favorable for bolting should he change his mind. She'd better get on with it before he lost his nerve. Or she did.

"I have something for you, Dora," she said, reaching into her pocket to produce a small cotton bundle. "Something I think you might recognize."

Dora stared at the gold watch and chain as Dovie unwrapped it and laid it in her palm, a flurry of emotions passing over her weathered face. Confusion. Disbelief. Recognition. "How . . . where did you get it?"

"From the woman Alice used to work for. She wanted you to have it."

Dora's face crumpled as she pressed the watch to her lips. "She kept it. All those years . . . my girl kept it."

"The woman who gave me the watch is named Gemma Tate. She also gave me two letters—Alice's last letters. There are some things in them—hard things—that I'm afraid you won't like, which is why

I've decided not to read them today. We'll read them later if you want, when you're stronger, but for now I'm just going to tell you some of what's in them."

Dora nodded, sullen but too anxious for news to protest.

"You remember why Alice first went to the Tates—because she was told that's where she would find her baby?"

Dora's eyes glittered like hard gray stones. "The boy—Danny."

"Yes. Danny. And when she got there she realized she'd been lied to."

Another nod.

Dovie reached for Dora's hand, anxiously wadding the bedspread. "She wasn't lied to, Dora. The address Danny gave Alice that night was the right one."

A crease appeared between Dora's silvery brows as she struggled to piece together what Dovie was telling her. She lifted her eyes to Dovie's. "I don't . . . understand."

"I know," Dovie said, giving her hand another squeeze. "It's confusing, but the little boy Alice was helping Gemma raise was actually her own. She didn't know at first. Neither did Gemma. But eventually they realized the truth—that Gemma's son was actually the child Alice had given up at Blackhurst. His name is Austin."

"Is he . . ." Dora's mouth worked mutely as the tears began to well.

"He's here," Dovie said softly. As if on cue, Austin stepped forward, coming to stand beside the bed. "This is Austin, Dora. This is your grandson."

Dora swallowed convulsively as the words gradually penetrated, confusion blooming into understanding, then a broken, bittersweet joy. Finally, a sob tore from her throat, and she reached for Austin's hand, pressing it to her cheek as she rocked and crooned and wept.

Dovie's throat ached as she watched the scene play out, grateful beyond words that Austin had agreed to be part of it. She looked at his face, almost tender as he went down on one knee, taking her hands in his, letting her have her cry.

It was some time before Dora's tears finally quieted, dwindling to moist sniffles and the occasional hiccup. After dabbing her eyes on the edge of the sheet, and sipping from the bottle of water Dovie pressed into her shaking hands, she fixed her eyes on Austin. "Do you remember her?"

Austin nodded, dimpling like a boy. "She taught me to tie my shoes."

"Tell me," Dora pleaded. "Tell me . . . everything you remember . . . about my girl."

Dovie shot Austin a worried glance. "Dora, are you having trouble breathing? You sound a little winded."

Dora was about to protest when Austin patted her hand. "Why don't you rest a little? We'll have plenty of time to talk about Alice, and to get to know each other. Right now I think Dovie would like you to rest."

To Dovie's surprise, Dora sagged back against her pillows, pale and spent. "Thank you," she breathed, with a radiant smile. "Both of you."

Dovie laid a hand on her brow, just to be sure. It was cool, but her breathing was definitely labored. "Dora, do you need your inhaler?"

"Sleep," she slurred thickly, blue-veined lids already drooping. They fluttered open briefly as she groped for Austin's hand, clutching it as if she feared he might vanish. "Don't leave."

The dimples reappeared as he shot her a wink. "Not a chance."

Dovie couldn't say how long she lingered in the doorway, watching Dora sleep, or how long it had been since Austin had slipped out of the room. She only knew she was happy. For the first time in weeks

Dora seemed at peace, her weathered face serene at last, her breathing almost easy. And she had Austin to thank for it.

She smiled as she pulled the door closed, then went looking for him. She found him on the back porch, bent over the railing. He turned when he heard her approach.

"She still asleep?"

Dovie nodded. "Something tells me she's going to be asleep for a while. Thank you, by the way, for what you did . . . and for how you were in there."

"I guess it's been quite a day for her."

"For you, too," Dovie said quietly. "Are you okay?"

"I will be. It's just a lot of reality to deal with all at once. Like waking up in the middle of a Dickens novel—I'm being visited by the ghosts of all my pasts."

"Scrooge was a better man after facing his ghosts."

He shot her a crooked smile. "And as I recall, he went kicking and screaming the whole way, but you might be right. Maybe it's time I faced a few ghosts. God knows hiding from them hasn't worked. I've spent so much of my life pretending nothing mattered that I had just about convinced myself nothing did. Then you came along."

Dovie's pulse skittered. "What do I have to do with anything?"

"You made me see myself, and I hated you for it. It was like you turned this great big spotlight on everything that was wrong with my life, and all of a sudden I didn't want the things I used to want. I wanted something different. And I hated you for that, too. Because I knew I couldn't have those things." He paused, scrubbing a hand through his hair. "Do you understand what I'm trying to say?"

Dovie lifted her chin a notch. "I'm pretty sure I got the part where you hate me."

"That is not what I said. Okay, it's what I said, but it's not what I meant. What I meant was that you made me want things I didn't *deserve*—you made me want you. I knew it the minute I kissed you that night on the dock, and it scared the hell out of me. The happily-ever-after thing? I don't know how to do that, Dovie. All my life I've watched people hurt each other. That's what I know. What my father did to my mother. What I did to Monica. I don't want to do that again—not to you. I don't know what that means. I just know it's true."

"Your mother thinks you're in love with me." The words came out softly, almost breathlessly, catching even Dovie off guard. She held her breath, watching his face, waiting for some kind of response.

Finally, he touched her, the back of a single finger grazing the curve of her cheek, her jaw, her mouth, leaving a tingle of warmth in its wake. "I think she might be right," he said softly. "She usually is."

"Well, then . . ." She paused, kissing him, her lips parted and featherlight as they brushed his. "You should probably know that she thinks I'm in love with you, too."

epilogue

MAGNOLIA GROVE CEMETERY,
CHARLESTON, SOUTH CAROLINA
DECEMBER 6, 2005

Dovie hugged the bouquet of Christmas mums close to her chest as she stared up at the stone angel, its weathered wings spread wide against the chilly gray sky. It felt strange being back, like visiting a friend she'd lost touch with.

As if sensing her thoughts, Austin reached for her hand, his fingers warm and reassuring as they closed over hers. To his right, Dora stood clutching her handbag, thinner and paler than she had been on that first terrible day, but stronger somehow, too, because she was no longer stooped with grief. She had hold of Austin's sleeve, clinging to him like a child to a favorite blanket, as if she still couldn't believe he was quite real. Beside Dora, Gemma stood cradling an armful of peonies, her face somber and very still. After a moment, she stepped forward to lay them at the foot of Alice's grave. She stood there for a time, lips moving soundlessly. When she turned to rejoin them, her eyes were shiny with tears. Austin reached for her hand, giving it a squeeze, then looked expectantly at Dovie.

It was time.

Dovie reached for the envelope she had tucked into her coat pocket before leaving the house. It had been her idea to read Alice's final words here, surrounded by the people who had loved her, but suddenly her mouth was dry, her hands trembling as she slid the single sheet free and began to read.

My dearest Austin,

How bittersweet to write your name—now, when our time is all but run out. Forgive me. I promised myself I would not dwell on such things. Not when there are so many more pressing things to say, things I should have said in my last letter but did not.

Bitterness is a tenacious thing, all bared claws and gnashing teeth. And I was bitter when I wrote that letter, spewing my rage and self-pity out onto the page. And yet it brought me no peace. Because it was done in anger—and was meant to wound a friend. Now my bitterness is spent, and I find there is more to say, wounds to mend, and peace to find.

When you came into the world I was forced to give you up. Now, as I leave the world, I am forced to give you up again. The first time, I railed against fate. But there is no railing now. Because in a way, I have kept my promise. All I ever wanted was for my child—my beautiful, beautiful son—to have a good life and a mother who loved him. And that has come to pass, perhaps not in the way I expected, but maybe in a better way. You have been blessed for a time with two mothers, two women who loved you with their whole hearts. Now you will just have the one. You will feel the loss at first, but not for long. She loves you so much—enough for the both of us—which is why I now relinquish you with a full and free heart. Because the heart holds no grudges, my darling. The heart always lets go.

I have written things, unkind things that I now regret, scribbled in moments of weakness, and the kind of pain that blinds us to any truth but our own. Now, at the end of things, I know that any offense against me was committed out of love for you—and is therefore forgiven. I ask you to do the same.

And now I must ask you to do something else, to take a trip when you can manage it, to the village in Cornwall where I grew up—to Sennen Cove—and ask after a woman named Dora Tandy, who lives in the cottage at the end of Trimble Lane. Bring her back the watch I took the day I ran away, and tell her she has a grandson—and that Alice sends her love.

I must go now, my darling. I'm so very tired, and Johnny has been waiting such a long time. Be a good boy and always mind your mother—and try not to forget your nanny.

Love,
Alice

Love, Alice.

The words seemed to hang in the air as Dovie folded the letter and tucked it out of sight—a gift from mother to child, but also from one mother to another. Dora felt the weight of her daughter's words, too, and reached out to touch the angel's foot, a gesture so poignant it could only be a mother's. Beside her, Gemma's face glistened with tears, and a kind of peace that hadn't been there before. Austin wrapped her in his arms, holding her close. No one spoke, but there seemed no need for words.

They had all heard it. And they all understood. From the very first letter penned at Blackhurst nearly forty years ago, Alice's signature had remained constant—*All my love, Mam.*

Until this one.

The altered signature had been no accident, no mere lapse of memory by a dying woman. Rather, it had been carefully and lovingly penned, a testament to her forgiveness, and her willingness to give her most precious possession—her son—into the care of her dearest friend.

Dovie's throat ached as she backed away from Dora, Gemma, and Austin. They needed a moment, and there was still something she needed to do. A few yards down the path, she stopped in front of William's grave. She smiled when she saw the bloodred poinsettia nearly obscuring the headstone—almost certainly Kristopher's doing. William had loved Christmas.

There was a strange sense of finality as she bent down to place her own flowers at the base of the stone, the feeling that a door had finally closed. They had been friends—through everything, and in spite of everything—but his memories belonged to Kristopher now.

Good-bye, Billy.

She was brushing the moisture from her hands when she spotted Josiah at the opposite end of the path. He tipped his hat as their eyes met, and lifted a hand. Dovie waved back as she watched him turn and disappear. It made her sad to think she wouldn't be seeing him as often as she used to. Theirs had been an unlikely alliance, a strange blend of severity and sympathy. He had offered a shoulder free of judgment, advice when she wanted it, and even when she didn't, and friendship when she had desperately needed a friend. She would always be grateful for that.

Gemma and Dora were already heading back to the car, but Austin was waiting when she stepped back onto the path. He took her hand as they began to walk. "You okay?"

"I am, actually. It's strange. I've spent so much time here feeling sad and miserable, but today was different. It felt good, right. Like an unhappy chapter of my life is finally ending, and I can move forward."

Austin stopped walking and pulled her around to face him. "Speaking of chapters ending, I need to thank you. For what you did for my mother, and Dora, and me. For today. For all of it. Everything feels different now, and it's because of you."

Dovie cocked an eye at him, grinning. "I'm not so sure. Your mother has a theory."

"What kind of theory?"

"It has to do with butterflies and tidal waves, but basically she thinks there was a reason it was me in the cemetery the day Dora left that letter on Alice's grave."

"She's saying it was fate?"

Dovie thought about the word. In fact, she'd been thinking about it for quite some time, but it seemed inadequate somehow in light of the extraordinary events of the past few months. "Fate is one possibility," she said finally. "But I wonder if it wasn't something else, something a little . . . closer to home."

She lifted her gaze to the angel standing guard over Alice Tandy's grave. Austin looked from the angel to Dovie and then back again, his face momentarily blank. Finally, her meaning seemed to dawn.

"You think Alice had something to do with all this? That she was somewhere behind the cosmic curtain, pulling strings?"

Dovie smiled. "I don't know, but I can't think of anyone who'd have a better motive, can you? She waited as long as she could for things to work themselves out, and when they didn't, she stepped in. She needed you to know. Maybe she needed us all to know."

"Know what?"

Dovie reached for his hand, pressing it to her lips. "That the heart holds no grudges. That the heart lets go."

Author's Note

I never set out to tell the story of the Magdalene laundries. In fact, when I began work on *Love, Alice* I wasn't even aware of their existence. I knew only that Alice Tandy was an unwed mother searching for the child she had given up. And then one night I was listening to the news and they announced that the Australian government had issued an apology to thousands of women who had essentially been imprisoned, forced into hard labor, and then made to give up their babies, and I knew Alice was one of those women. And so my research began.

All my life I had thought of the word *asylum* as meaning a place of refuge, but the women forced into the laundries found them to be anything but. Rather, they found places of brutality, degradation, oppression, and psychological abuse. Inmates, some as young as twelve or thirteen, were forcibly detained, often behind a series of locked doors and gates, their names changed, their families as good as dead to them.

They were called *penitents* by the nuns, their unborn babies referred to as *sins* or *mistakes*. Inmates were watched closely and punished vigorously for breaking the rules. Correction included beatings, head shavings, the withholding of food, and being stripped to the skin and made to stand before the other inmates as mortification for the sins of vanity and willfulness. In some establishments, as a final and stunningly heartless act of penance, expectant mothers were made to sew baby clothes and blankets, and even write letters to their unborn children explaining why they were unfit to raise them.

Young women, often heavy with child, were subjected to hours of backbreaking work. The day began at five a.m. and consisted of scrubbing laundry for orphanages, churches, and prisons as well as private businesses such as hotels and schools. The laundries brought large sums of money to convent coffers, with not a cent going to the workers.

Babies were often born without doctors in attendance and without any kind of pain medication. Instead, mothers were reminded by the nuns that their labor pains were the price of sin. In some asylums infants were whisked away the moment they were born. Mothers were not even permitted to hold them before giving them up. The babies were then adopted by wealthy families in exchange for a healthy "donation" to the convent. Adoptive homes were often overseas—frequently in the U.S.—placing the babies forever out of reach of their birth mothers. The luckiest inmates were allowed to return to their families—if their families would have them. Sadly, this was not always the case. The forsaken were put to work in the laundry, where they were dubbed *lifers* and usually worked until they died.

It was disturbing to think such a thing could happen in so-called civilized societies, but it was even more disturbing to learn that Australia wasn't an isolated case. Or that although firsthand accounts often felt like the stuff of Dickens, they did not exist solely in the days of *Oliver Twist*. I was stunned to learn that the last Magdalene asylum closed just twenty years ago in Waterford, Ireland, on September 25, 1996.

In recent years, movies such as *Philomena* and *The Magdalene Sisters* have drawn attention to the plight of women who fell victim to the laundries, triggered in part by the grisly discovery of a mass grave containing 155 bodies on the grounds of a former asylum in Dublin, Ireland. Years later, an even more gruesome discovery was made in County Galway.

The asylum depicted in this novel—the Blackhurst Asylum for Unwed Mothers—is not real but was cobbled together after extensive research and the careful study of firsthand accounts of life in the laundries. In its creation I tried to be as true to these women's stories as possible, though at times it proved uncomfortable. In *Love, Alice*, rumors swirl about a mass grave in an abandoned cistern behind the convent's kitchen. The inspiration for these rumors was a report published in 2014 concerning the bodies of nearly eight hundred babies believed to have been buried in a cistern on convent grounds. The babies are thought to have been secretly buried over a period of thirty-six years—between 1925 and 1961—without headstones or coffins. Reports show many suffered malnutrition and neglect, while others died of birth defects, convulsions, dysentery, tuberculosis, and pneumonia.

In Ireland alone approximately thirty thousand women were imprisoned in laundries during the nineteenth and twentieth centuries, though, to be clear, such institutions were not confined to Ireland. Nor were they exclusively operated by the Catholic Church. Institutions now referred to as Magdalene laundries operated in England, Australia, New Zealand, Canada, and the United States, and while their names may have differed, their missions were the same: to carry out the punishment and subjugation of women for the sin of being sexual.

Over the past two decades, growing exposure coupled with the testimony of brave women who have come forward to tell their stories has led to an outpouring of public outrage as well as demands for both admission of guilt and restitution. On July 10, 2012, a national apology was issued by the Australian government and was followed by similar apologies by the Catholic Church and numerous other governmental agencies involved in the removal of babies from vulnerable young women.

As I said earlier, I did not set out to tell the story of the Magdalene asylums. It's an uncomfortable subject, perhaps even a taboo subject for some. But when a terrible chapter in our history is finally exposed, the only way to guarantee that it won't be repeated is to hold it up to the light and call it what it is, and to acknowledge the pain and damage done to its victims, which is why, in the end, I did tell the story of the Magdalene asylums.

Love, Alice

BARBARA DAVIS

QUESTIONS FOR DISCUSSION

1. Blackhurst Asylum for Unwed Mothers was a fictional institution but depicted conditions prevalent in many so-called "Magdalene laundries" across the U.K., U.S., and Australia. Before reading *Love, Alice*, had you ever heard of Magdalene laundries? If so, what had you heard? What was your reaction to learning the last of the asylums was still operating so recently?

2. A predominant theme in *Love, Alice* is the unbreakable bond between mother and child. It was that bond, and the need to right a forty-year-old wrong, that brought Dora Tandy from Cornwall to Charleston. In what other ways did the mother-child bond play out in the novel to bring about understanding and, ultimately, forgiveness in many of the characters?

3. In times past, suicide has carried a certain stigma or air of taboo. It has been referred to as "the mark of disgrace" or "a sign of the evil eye." Do you think suicide carries as much of a stigma today? What do you think causes these perceptions and how do you think society can better understand the issue?

4. Each of the main characters in *Love, Alice* is dealing with grief in some form or another, and most are having trouble moving past it.

Have you ever known someone, yourself included, who experienced the kind of grief that just couldn't be shaken? Do you feel it's possible to hold on to grief too long, to become so mired in loss that the line is crossed from normal grieving into something less healthy? Or, for you, is grief such a personal thing that there simply are no lines?

5. In the novel, we learn Alice's story through letters written to a child she is unlikely to ever meet. Have you ever considered writing a letter you knew would never be read, and if so, what did you hope to accomplish by writing it? Did you actually write the letter? Was it helpful?

6. Denial is a coping mechanism we've all used from time to time, though it is rarely successful. How does denial play a role in both Dovie's and Austin's past relationships, and how does each of them help the other eventually forgive themselves and move on?

7. The theme of complicity by avoidance is brought up several times throughout the novel, both with Dovie and with Austin. Have there been times in your life when you chose to turn a blind eye rather than face an uncomfortable truth? In retrospect, can you now see how facing that truth head-on might have saved you a lot of heartache?

8. Another issue touched upon in *Love, Alice* is the fallout that occurs when we allow what others think to govern our life choices. Discuss the ways society's rigid roles and mores affected Alice, Dovie, and William. Have you ever been at a place in your life in which you've had to risk a relationship with a parent or partner in order to stand your ground? If so, how did you handle it?

9. The notion of secrets kept, for better or worse, appears throughout the novel. Do you personally believe honesty is always the best choice? Or do you believe there are some secrets that are better kept from a loved one—and if so, under what circumstances?

10. Forgiveness is hard. Sometimes impossible. And yet Alice finds a way to forgive both Gemma and Dora after seemingly unforgivable deeds. What specifically do you feel causes her change of heart by the end of the novel?

11. In times of deep grief nothing is more sustaining than true friendship. As unlikely as the relationship seemed to some, Josiah Ramsey was a friend to Dovie when she badly needed one. How do you feel his life experiences and personal brand of wisdom helped Dovie better understand her grief and eventually move through it?

12. At the end of *Love, Alice*, Dovie hints at the possibility that Alice might have been responsible for orchestrating the events that lead to the novel's happy ending. Do you believe it's possible for a deceased loved one to provide guidance in times of trouble or nudge us in the direction of happiness? Have you ever felt that kind of guidance in your own life?

Mama Hettie's Shrimp and Grits

(Yes, she finally gave up her recipe!)

INGREDIENTS

2 cups uncooked coarse-ground white grits
(Hettie says no quick-cooking grits!)
½ cup freshly grated Parmigiano-Reggiano cheese
¼ cup unsalted butter
1 pound unpeeled medium-size raw shrimp
4 thick slices hickory-smoked bacon, diced
6 tablespoons butter
1 medium-size Vidalia onion, diced
½ poblano pepper, diced
3 garlic cloves, minced
½ teaspoon kosher salt
¼ teaspoon ground white pepper
¼ teaspoon ground red pepper
1 tablespoon all-purpose flour
½ cup chicken broth
¼ cup Madeira
2 tablespoons fresh lemon juice
1 tablespoon fresh parsley, chopped
1 green onion, chopped

DIRECTIONS

Prepare grits per directions on package. Fold in cheese and unsalted butter when tender.

Peel and devein shrimp.

Cook bacon in a large skillet over medium-high heat, 4 to 5 minutes or until crisp; remove bacon from skillet and place on paper towels, reserving 2 tablespoons of drippings in the skillet.

Melt 6 tablespoons butter in hot drippings in skillet. Reduce heat. Add onion, poblano pepper, and garlic. Sauté 2 minutes or until onion is tender.

Add shrimp; cook, stirring often, 1 to 2 minutes. Add salt and white and red pepper. Toss to coat. Sprinkle flour over shrimp mixture. Toss to coat.

Add broth, Madeira, and lemon juice. Cook just until shrimp turn pink, stirring to loosen particles from skillet. Stir in bacon and parsley. Serve over grits. Top with chopped green onion.

Charleston She-Crab Soup

INGREDIENTS

½ cup unsalted butter
1 small onion, finely chopped
8 tablespoons flour
1 can chicken broth
1 cup whole milk
2 cups low-fat milk
¾ teaspoon Worcestershire sauce
1½ teaspoons Old Bay Seasoning
Pinch of nutmeg
Salt and white pepper to taste
1 pound fresh crabmeat
½ cup sherry (do not substitute)
Fresh chopped parsley and paprika for garnish

INSTRUCTIONS

Melt butter over medium-low heat. Add onions and sauté until translucent, about 5 minutes.

Add flour and stir until well blended. Cook about 2 minutes.

Slowly whisk in chicken broth, stirring constantly until smooth.

Slowly whisk in both whole and low-fat milk, stirring constantly.

Add Worcestershire sauce, Old Bay Seasoning, nutmeg, salt, and pepper. Bring to a simmer.

Add crabmeat and sherry; add more milk to thin if necessary. Cook until just heated.

Ladle into soup bowls, then garnish with fresh chopped parsley and a dash of paprika.

Swamp Water

INGREDIENTS

6 tea bags

2 cups boiling water

1 cup sugar

1 (13 oz.) package Kool-Aid unsweetened lemonade mix

Water to fill gallon jug the rest of the way

Fresh lemon slices for garnish

DIRECTIONS

Add tea bags to boiling water.

Boil 3 minutes. Cover and steep 20 minutes.

Pour sugar into gallon jug.

Add 1 package of Kool-Aid to jug, followed by steeped tea.

Run cold water over the tea bags in pan.

Squeeze the tea bags in pan and throw away. Pour liquid into jug.

Fill jug with cold water.

Chill and serve over ice. Garnish with lemon slices.

Makes 1 gallon

NOTE: The adult version, known as "Haint Swamp Water" may be enjoyed by adding a shot of vodka and a splash of Triple Sec to your glass. But be warned: the adult version tends to sneak up on a body when she's not looking (or so I've heard) and haunt well into the next morning.

Photo by Lisa Aube

After spending more than a decade as an executive in the jewelry business, Barbara Davis decided to leave the corporate world to finally pursue her lifelong passion for writing. *Love, Alice* is her fourth novel, following *Summer at Hideaway Key*, *The Wishing Tide*, and *The Secrets She Carried*. She currently lives in Rochester, New Hampshire, with her husband, Tom, and their beloved ginger cat, Simon, and is working on her next book. Visit her at barbaradavis-author.com.